Conquest, Constitutionalism and Democratic Contestations

Two decades since the enactment of South Africa's present constitution, the durability and endurance of 'past' inequalities and injustices illustrate that the 'new South Africa' – lauded as a miracle nation with the best constitution in the world – can no longer be regarded as an unqualified success. The legal and constitutional foundations of post-1994 South Africa are in a process of renegotiation that invites new and alternative perspectives and approaches.

This comprehensive volume explores this process of renegotiation by engaging political and intellectual contestations circulating in South African academic and public discourse relating to continuities and discontinuities between the colonial-apartheid past and the post-1994 constitutional present. The authors analyse the moral, intellectual and political unravelling of post-1994 South African constitutionalism (as legal text and political culture) and enquire whether it has been able to respond adequately to the *fundamental* contradictions generated by colonisation and apartheid. They also consider how centring the historical problem of European domination and conquest in Africa – and South Africa in particular – might provide an alternative frame or lens to theorise and understand contemporary South African realities.

This book marks out a complex field of contestation – involving competing histories, locations, visions and perspectives – that raises multifaceted questions regarding law, history and politics. It was originally published as a special issue of the *South African Journal on Human Rights*.

Joel M. Modiri is a Senior Lecturer in the Department of Jurisprudence at the University of Pretoria, South Africa , and an associate editor of the *South African Journal on Human Rights*. He holds an LLB *cum laude*, and his PhD thesis was entitled *The Jurisprudence of Steve Biko: A Study in Race, Law and Power in the 'Afterlife' of Colonial-apartheid.* He mainly teaches in the fields of Social Theory, Race and Law, and Legal Philosophy.

Conquest, Constitutionalism and Democratic Contestations

South African Perspectives

Edited by
Joel M. Modiri

Routledge
Taylor & Francis Group
LONDON AND NEW YORK

First published 2019
by Routledge
2 Park Square, Milton Park, Abingdon, Oxon, OX14 4RN

and by Routledge
52 Vanderbilt Avenue, New York, NY 10017

Routledge is an imprint of the Taylor & Francis Group, an informa business

British Library Cataloguing in Publication Data
A catalogue record for this book is available from the British Library

ISBN 13: 978-0-367-23684-7

Typeset in Minion Pro
by RefineCatch Limited, Bungay, Suffolk

Publisher's Note
The publisher accepts responsibility for any inconsistencies that may have arisen during the conversion of this book from journal articles to book chapters, namely the inclusion of journal terminology.

Disclaimer
Every effort has been made to contact copyright holders for their permission to reprint material in this book. The publishers would be grateful to hear from any copyright holder who is not here acknowledged and will undertake to rectify any errors or omissions in future editions of this book.

Contents

Citation Information

The chapters in this book were originally published in the *South African Journal on Human Rights*, volume 34, issue 3 (December 2018). When citing this material, please use the original page numbering for each article, as follows:

Chapter 1

Introduction to special issue: conquest, constitutionalism and democratic contestations
Joel M. Modiri
South African Journal on Human Rights, volume 34, issue 3 (December 2018), pp. 295–299

Chapter 2

Conquest and constitutionalism: first thoughts on an alternative jurisprudence
Joel M. Modiri
South African Journal on Human Rights, volume 34, issue 3 (December 2018), pp. 300–325

Chapter 3

Towards a post-conquest South Africa: beyond the constitution of 1996
Mogobe Bernard Ramose
South African Journal on Human Rights, volume 34, issue 3 (December 2018), pp. 326–341

Chapter 4

Decolonising equality: the radical roots of the gender equality clause in the South African constitution
Shireen Hassim
South African Journal on Human Rights, volume 34, issue 3 (December 2018), pp. 342–358

Chapter 5

Is the South African Constitution an obstacle to a democratic post-colonial state?
D. M. Davis
South African Journal on Human Rights, volume 34, issue 3 (December 2018), pp. 359–374

Chapter 6

Democratic constitutionalism in the time of the postcolony: beyond triumph and betrayal
Firoz Cachalia
South African Journal on Human Rights, volume 34, issue 3 (December 2018), pp. 375–397

Chapter 7
On conquest and anthropology in South Africa
Anjuli Webster
South African Journal on Human Rights, volume 34, issue 3 (December 2018), pp. 398–414

Chapter 8
The liberation of history and the end of South Africa: some notes towards an Azanian historiography in Africa, South
Ndumiso Dladla
South African Journal on Human Rights, volume 34, issue 3 (December 2018), pp. 415–440

Chapter 9
Contested substantive equality in the South African Constitution: beyond social inclusion towards systemic justice
Catherine Albertyn
South African Journal on Human Rights, volume 34, issue 3 (December 2018), pp. 441–468

Chapter 10
Decolonisation, compensation and constitutionalism: land, wealth and the sustainability of constitutionalism in post-apartheid South Africa
Heinz Klug
South African Journal on Human Rights, volume 34, issue 3 (December 2018), pp. 469–491

Chapter 11
A decolonial critique of private law and human rights
Emile Zitzke
South African Journal on Human Rights, volume 34, issue 3 (December 2018), pp. 492–516

Chapter 12
South Africa's first black lawyers, amaRespectables *and the birth of evolutionary constitution*
Tshepo Madlingozi
South African Journal on Human Rights, volume 34, issue 3 (December 2018), pp. 517–529

Notes on Contributors

Catherine Albertyn is a Professor and South African Research Chair in Equality, Law and Social Justice in the School of Law at the University of the Witwatersrand, South Africa.

Firoz Cachalia is an Adjunct Professor in the School of Law at the University of the Witwatersrand, South Africa.

D. M. Davis is an Honorary Professor of Law in the Department of Commercial Law at the University of Cape Town, South Africa. He is also a High Court Judge.

Ndumiso Dladla is a Lecturer in the Department of Philosophy, Practical and Systematic Theology at the University of South Africa, and an LLD Candidate in the Department of Jurisprudence in the Faculty of Law at the University of Pretoria, South Africa.

Shireen Hassim is Professor of Politics at Wits Institute for Social and Economic Research at the University of the Witwatersrand, South Africa.

Heinz Klug is Evjue-Bascom Professor of Law at the University of Wisconsin Law School, USA, and Honorary Senior Research Associate in the School of Law at the University of the Witwatersrand, South Africa.

Tshepo Madlingozi is a Senior Lecturer in the Department of Jurisprudence in the Faculty of Law at the University of Pretoria, South Africa.

Joel M. Modiri is a Senior Lecturer in the Department of Jurisprudence at the University of Pretoria, South Africa.

Mogobe Bernard Ramose is a Research Professor in the Department of Clinical Psychology at Sefako Makgatho Health Sciences University, South Africa.

Anjuli Webster is a Graduate Student in the Department of Historical and Heritage Studies at the University of Pretoria, South Africa.

Emile Zitzke is a Senior Lecturer in the School of Law at the University of the Witwatersrand, South Africa.

Notes on contributors

INTRODUCTION

Introduction: conquest, constitutionalism and democratic contestations

Joel M. Modiri

> '[T]he past is not done with us […] it is not past […] it will not leave us in peace until we have reckoned with its claims to justice.'[1]

This special issue of the *South African Journal on Human Rights* comprises a selection of papers that were first presented at a colloquium in May 2017 entitled 'Conquest, Constitutionalism and Democratic Contestations'. Both the colloquium and the articles in this special issue are animated by pressing political and intellectual contestations circulating in South African academic and public discourse relating to continuities and discontinuities between the colonial-apartheid past and the post-1994 constitutional present. Indeed, even the distinction between the 'past' and the 'present' in the South African context is an object of critical interrogation.

Two decades since the enactment of the present constitution, problems of inequality, poverty, violence and social exclusion persist stubbornly along racial lines, and much of the optimism of the early 1990s concerning the promises of new legal and political order has dissipated. On a deeper level, this persistence suggests the continuity and durability of the political ontology, political economy and symbolic order created through colonial conquest and white supremacy. The durability and endurance of 'past' inequalities and injustices illustrate that the 'new South Africa' – lauded as a 'miracle nation' with the 'best constitution in the world' – can no longer be regarded as an unqualified success. A central theme in this special issue is to take seriously the moral, intellectual and political unravelling of post-1994 South African constitutionalism (as legal text and political culture) and to enquire whether it has been able to respond adequately to the *fundamental* contradictions generated by colonisation and apartheid.

Whereas popular scholarly accounts associate the limitations of constitutional transformation with, among other sources, the lack of political will on the part of the ruling party, corruption and maladministration in government, the constraints of global capital and the vagaries of legal interpretation and adjudication, the starting point of this special issue is different. Authors were invited to consider how centring the historical problem of European domination and conquest in Africa – and South

[1] Cameron J in *Daniels v Scribante and Another* 2017 (4) SA 341 (CC) para 154.

Africa in particular – might provide an alternative frame or lens to theorise and understand contemporary South African realities. Thus, each article is premised on an analysis that locates constitutionalism and the ideal of the rule of law within the historical matrix of colonialism and Eurocentrism – not only at the level of political economy, social organisation and law but also at the level of culture and epistemology – and of *resistance* to those formations. The articles are not isolated, however, but speak directly to the theme of the special issue and to each other, albeit in different registers and vocabularies.

Read together, the articles mark out a complex field of contestation – involving competing histories, locations, visions and perspectives – that raises multifaceted questions regarding law, history and politics. While they cannot be reduced to single or fixed propositions, the articles do take unambiguous positions in relation to the South African constitutional order, ranging from optimism about its democratic and transformative potential to scepticism concerning its responsiveness to colonial and imperial histories and extending further to radical and abolitionist critiques of the political imaginary upon which the constitution is premised. Indeed, one angle of reading the special issue may be in terms of a tension between three broad standpoints, namely 'constitutional optimists' (who accept the constitution as the overarching moral, political and jurisprudential lodestar of South African society), 'critical sceptics' (who problematise the grand narratives of post-1994 constitutionalism and expose the limits of law, liberalism, Enlightenment reason, the Truth and Reconciliation Commission and so forth) and 'constitutional abolitionists' (who pose a wholesale challenge to the philosophical, historical and cultural bases of the South African constitution from the perspective of occluded ontologies and epistemologies). If these positions sometimes overlap and may not always be easy to distinguish, a crucial point of contrast between them would be that while constitutional optimists advance a faithful commitment to transformative social change through and within the constitutional framework and critical sceptics are wary of 'faithfulness' as a mode of relating to (the) law, constitutional abolitionists repudiate the social vision underpinning post-1994 constitutionalism on the basis of more far-reaching conceptions of history and justice. The tension along these three positions is developing in the legal academy and beyond, and encompasses many more voices and nuances than could be captured in this special issue. One can only hope that this tension is openly acknowledged and productively engaged in the spirit of intellectual generosity, self-reflexivity, political candour and – most importantly – a striving for deep and meaningful justice.

The special issue comprises an intergenerational and ideologically diverse group of scholars in law, the humanities and social sciences. In this way, it is also a model for future directions in legal scholarship and, in particular, discloses stimulating questions that could inform legal theory and jurisprudence in South Africa. South African law faculties and schools are at this very moment grappling with the process of curriculum transformation instantiated by the national review of the LLB degree together with the demands of institutional and epistemic decolonisation in our universities, so this special issue could not be more timely. Law faculties and law schools in South Africa are having to more openly confront the weight of (their) histories, and while conservative voices defending an unreflective and dated traditional, black-letter legal pedagogy remain in our midst,[2] it is clear there is no turning back. Questions of race, class and gender, poverty and economic inequality, the politics of law, culture and epistemology, as well as the philosophical, historical and sociological contours of law and legal discourse would need to be addressed more explicitly and prominently in legal education and scholarship. This is to say that the legal and constitutional foundations of post-1994 South Africa are in a process of 'renegotiation' that invites new and alternative perspectives and approaches. This special issue represents an attempt at a first opening into such a process of renegotiation.

The scene for the special issue is set with an article by this editor that sets out a critique and interpretation of post-1994 constitutionalism from the perspective of its relationship to the *longue durée* history of colonial conquest, settler-colonialism and white supremacy. In this article, I reflect on this relationship in terms of (dis)-continuity and draw on a variety of critical theoretical perspectives that challenge optimistic and triumphalist accounts of the constitution and expose the fragility of its emancipatory horizon. I describe these accounts as 'constitutional worship' and argue instead for an alternative jurisprudence – a 'jurisprudence from below' or 'jurisprudence of liberation' – grounded in, and attentive to, histories, experiences and knowledges of Black people, both locally and globally.

Following this article are contributions based on the two keynote papers from the colloquium by Mogobe Ramose and Shireen Hassim. In his article, Ramose offers a further development and reflection upon his long-standing work in African philosophy and international law theory. In his article, he deploys the just war doctrine as a basis to critically examine the constitution and to argue that the historical injustice of conquest remains an ethical exigency demanding redress and reparation despite *and against* the present constitutional order. Hassim, drawing on her extensive work as a leading feminist scholar and political theorist, in contrast responds to the decolonisation critique by asserting the radical roots of the equality clause (s 9) of the constitution. Writing from a feminist perspective, her article highlights the agency and contribution of black women in the making of the new constitutional order.

The subsequent articles focus on two broad themes: (1) appraising the emancipatory value of the South African constitution, and (2) evaluating the transformative impact of the constitution on the development of South African law.

In the first theme, Dennis Davis and Firoz Cachalia – in separate but complementary articles – reinterpret the constitution against the binary opposition of constitutional fundamentalists and constitutional critics. For both Davis and Cachalia, the constitution is best seen as a driver of transformative interpretative work and democratic practice, requiring ongoing dialogue and debate. They, therefore, resist arguments that they believe reduce the constitution to a mere obstacle to fundamental change. Their articles diverge sharply from the articles by Ndumiso Dladla and Anjuli

[2] For a recent rehearsal of dated conservative legal ideology defending a narrow and restricted vision of law and legal education and exhibiting poor comprehension not only of critical legal theory but also of the socio-political context of transformation in South Africa, see W Gravett 'Of "destruction" and "deconstruction" – why critical legal theory cannot be the cornerstone of the LLB' (2018) 135 *South African Law Journal* 285–323.

Webster who instead respectively argue that the constitution represents, at the political-ontological as well as cultural-epistemic level, a continuation of the basic organising principles of colonial conquest and white supremacy. Working from the disciplines of philosophy (Dladla) and anthropology (Webster), both articles reconstruct an alternative analytic and historical paradigm informed by the Africanist/ Azanian tradition to illustrate the ways in which the constitutional present silences particular histories and knowledges.

In the second theme, Heinz Klug, Cathi Albertyn, and Emile Zitzke reflect on constitutionalism in the postcolonial legal context. Klug focuses on the burning issue of land and property and argues that part and parcel of South Africa's constitutional property regime is a deep and serious commitment to redistributive justice. Albertyn approaches equality (as both a value and a right) with reference to the contested archive of liberal, egalitarian, socialist and radical conceptions of equality that could shape its interpretation and meaning.

Whereas both Klug and Albertyn develop ambitious analyses to demonstrate the constitution's transformative potential and ability to address the legacies of land and property dispossession on the one hand and systemic inequality and injustice on the other, Zitzke is more cautious. In his article, Zitzke reviews two approaches to the relationship between the South African private law and transformative constitutionalism. The one position he names 'private-law purism' is premised on a traditional vision of the common law, and the other, named 'transformative private law', centres on human rights. While supporting the second approach of transformative private law, he cautions the reader at length to remember the roots of both approaches in Western hegemony. He then introduces a third possibility – of Africanisation through conceptual decolonisation – that could be more responsive to the demand of decolonising the law. We round up the special issue with a critical review, by Tshepo Madlingozi, of Tembeka Ngcukaitobi's recent book *The Land is Ours: South Africa's First Black Lawyers and the Birth of Constitutionalism* (2018).

The summary above does not do justice to the richness and depth of the contributions collected in this special issue. It is for the reader to carefully and robustly engage with the positions taken in the articles. Beyond their specific arguments, however, these pieces are noteworthy for what they signal for the future of critical jurisprudence and legal theory in South Africa, as each one centres South African realities, historical contexts and intellectual traditions in their thinking about law, transformation and constitutionalism. It seems apt, then, to conclude with the words of Costas Douzinas and Adam Gearey that capture the spirit and ambition of this special issue:

> Law's complicity with political oppression, violence and racism has to be faced before it is possible to speak of a new beginning for legal thought, which in turn is the necessary precondition for a theory of justice.[3]

[3] C Douzinas & A Gearey *Critical Jurisprudence: The Political Philosophy of Justice* (2005) 1.

Disclosure statement

No potential conflict of interest was reported by the author.

Conquest and constitutionalism: first thoughts on an alternative jurisprudence

Joel M. Modiri

ABSTRACT
This article examines the meaning and progress of post-1994 constitutional democracy in South Africa from the perspective of its (dis)continuity with the *longue-durée* history of colonial conquest, settler-colonialism and white supremacy. The argument developed in this essay is that the lack of restoration and fundamental change that haunts the present South African legal and political order can be traced to this (dis)continuity. This argument is deepened by a problematisation of the widespread public, political and academic worship of the South African constitution as well as a synthesis of a variety of critical perspectives on post-1994 law, society and constitutionalism into a challenge to the putatively transformative and revolutionary pedigree of the 1996 constitution. This article ultimately defends the emerging critique of the constitutional order as a historical opening for the reimagining of a new social order and, for the purposes of this article, an alternative jurisprudence as well.

The desideratum for democracy and non-racialism cannot replace natural and historical justice.[1]

Mogobe Ramose

The past is no longer imagined as a time that can be overcome. In our liberal and liberalising time, emancipation has given way to accommodation, and reconciliation has displaced revolution as the language of social and political change where the future has been reduced to a mirror image of the present.[2]

David Scott

---

[1] MB Ramose 'The philosophy of the Anglo-Boer War' in I Snyman, I Liebenberg, G van der Westhuizen and M Roos (eds) *A Century is a Short Time: New Perspectives on the Anglo Boer War* (2005) 23.
[2] D Scott *Omens of Adversity: Tragedy, Time, Memory, Justice* (2013) 131.

1. Preface: liberal constitutionalism in the 'Mandela republic'

The prolific literary critic and novelist Lewis Nkosi provides an apposite starting point for this paper in light of the analogy he prompts between certain trends in post-1994 South African literature and culture and the problem of reconstituting a new polity and a new law. The following quote by him sets the tone for these reflections:

> Much has changed in South Africa. Or not much has changed; depending from what perspective you are looking at our ugly past. What has changed is the physiognomy of white power, which allows a white minority to maintain its hegemony under the guise of non-racialism.[3]

In the essay 'The republic of letters after the Mandela republic', Nkosi associates the period that is temporally described as 'post'-apartheid or symbolically as 'the Mandela republic'[4] with 'the failure of South Africa to function as a unitary nation'.[5] This failure, for Nkosi, is linked to the fact that South African literature 'has been held hostage by apartheid', which in his view 'remains a presence, a shadow of unpunished wickedness and inequality ignored'.[6] The unresolved fractures at the heart of the 'new' polity that embody the afterlife of colonialism and apartheid have, according to Nkosi, inhibited the emergence in South African literature of the 'shared assumptions of a national culture'.[7] Nkosi relates this absence of a national culture to South Africa's history *and present* of settler-colonialism – both its denial of ethical and political co-existence between its inhabitants and the unliveable levels of racial stratification and violence it produces.[8]

A number of signifiers mark Nkosi's text and stand in as metaphors of the 'post'-apartheid condition: 'horror', 'anxiety', 'nervous condition', 'malaise', 'shadow', 'double trauma', 'irrecoverable loss'. Nkosi situates his reflections against the background of a critique of the liberal humanist novel that, he argues, represents 'an ideology which, with very good intentions but with very little support, attempts to will into existence the "nation"'. The liberal humanist novel attempts to 'fill the empty category of the "nation" with subjectivities which have yet to come into being'.[9] In addition to a premature triumphalism, Nkosi notes deeper problems embedded in the narrative structure of the liberal humanist novel, namely (1) the pre-eminence of a white literary voice, (2) a liberal conception of race, and (3) an inability or refusal to accommodate an African perspective.[10] The coupling of 'nation' with 'narration' in postcolonial studies led Nkosi, in the early 1990s, to question the very idea of a 'South African national literature' and thus of a 'South African nation' since the very idea of 'South Africa' 'has operated under the sign of a division so profound

---

[3] L Nkosi 'The ideology of reconciliation: its effects on South African culture' in L Stiebel & M Chapman (eds) *Writing Home: Lewis Nkosi on South African Writing* (2016) 149.
[4] L Nkosi 'The republic of letters after the Mandela republic' in L Stiebel & M Chapman (eds) *Writing Home: Lewis Nkosi on South African Writing* (2016) 240.
[5] Ibid 240.
[6] Ibid 240.
[7] Ibid 241.
[8] Ibid 241.
[9] Ibid 244.
[10] Ibid 244.

that only a complete overhaul of the social infrastructure could clear the ground for the emergence of a truly national literature'.[11]

Nkosi continues further to suggest that it is not only that South Africa is not able to sustain a shared conception of the nation that could serve as the grounds for a national literature but also that the idea of 'post'-apartheid is an impossibility[12] – 'a fiction at odds with reality'.[13] Indeed, Nkosi reminds us that, '[I]t is premature to talk about the end of apartheid'[14] since '[M]any social and economic structures remain much the same even after the repeal of apartheid laws.'[15] The negotiated settlement that delivered constitutional democracy in South Africa was 'conclude[d] with a rather banal muted whimper, a finale in which the fundamental economic structures of society would remain largely uncontested'.[16] In the result, Nkosi explains that the post-1994 novel would remain haunted by the 'intractable problems […] bequeathed to us by an *insolite* history of racial division and racial oppression'.[17] In particular, he highlights two burning issues that demand critical attention from writers, cultural workers and intellectuals in post-1994 South Africa: (1) a critique of the 'instant, enforced reconciliation' imposed by the Truth and Reconciliation Commission; and (2) the 'continuing and vexed land question', which remains unresolved by the 'bourgeois nationalist state' under African National Congress (ANC) rule.[18] A focus on these two issues is crucial in Nkosi's estimation for the South African imagination to overcome the false narrative of 'national transcendence' and to resist being pressured into promoting the official and hegemonic narratives of the new dispensation.[19] As he writes: 'At the end of the day, there was a "crime" but no "punishment". The truth of recent South African history can only be told in novels of the abyss […].'[20]

Nkosi thus reads post-1994 South Africa or the 'Mandela republic' as a time and a place in which the past has not only shaped but continues to *exert pressure* on the present.[21] In this way, he has simply rendered as literary a problem that is not only common to all disciplines, including law and jurisprudence, but that characterises the entire social life of the putatively 'new' South Africa, in both its public and private as well as material and symbolic guises. And in this regard, the political question of how we should read the constitutional present in South Africa is intimately tied to the epistemic injustice of the virtually complete silencing of African and black intellectual and political perspectives, voices and realities in legal theory and related disciplines. Through Nkosi's prompting of a connection between the political/historical and the epistemic/literary, the world and the word, we may treat the absence of an experience of historical justice, reparation and meaningful onto-

[11] Ibid 246.
[12] Ibid 248.
[13] Nkosi (note 3 above) 152.
[14] Nkosi (note 4 above) 250.
[15] Ibid 253.
[16] Ibid 248.
[17] Ibid 251.
[18] Ibid 255.
[19] Ibid 255. See also Nkosi (note 3 above) 154–155.
[20] Ibid 255.
[21] Ibid 253.

epistemic transformation in South African lives as a starting point in the search for ways of reading, thinking and imagining, and also living and being, that work outside of state-driven logics, moderate political visions and Western legal paradigms.

2. Introduction

The purpose of this article is to draw the outlines of a historical, political and ethical critique of the South African constitution.[22] It considers South Africa's history of colonial conquest and the persistence of its constituent elements (racism, dispossession, poverty, epistemicide, spatial injustice) into the present period as a critical predicament that unsettles post-1994 constitutionalism and its associated political culture and jurisprudence. The central premise of this article is that South Africa's constitutional democracy has over the years been rendered empty by the absence of concrete historical justice and the non-realisation of an emancipatory experience of freedom and dignity in the lives of the Black majority in South Africa. While a set of external global economic forces and the chronic levels of corruption and maladministration by the ruling ANC government partly accounts for these problems, it is the *longue durée* (long duration) historical unfoldment of European colonial conquest and white supremacy in conjunction with the terms of the constitutional transition and negotiated settlement that will be marked out for critical examination in this article.

Drawing on critical race theory, settler-colonial studies and African jurisprudence, I aim to employ conquest as a framework and basis for a historically grounded analysis of the present legal and political condition in South Africa. As the historical record shows, the mid-17th century European colonial conquest of indigenous peoples in what would only much later be called 'South Africa' and the subsequent installation of a regime of settler-colonial white supremacy constitutes not only a foundational violence[23] but also an ongoing structuring dynamic of social organisation in South Africa and not a mere past historical event.[24] The settler-colonial usurpation of South Africa was marked not only by brutal violence, land dispossession and exploitation of black bodies but also by enduring forms of legal and political governance of indigenous populations; arrangements of socio-economic inequality and extreme poverty; spatial containment and segregation; annihilation of African cultures and onto-epistemes; as well as psychic alienation and imposed symbolic degradation of African personality.[25] Through its racialising

[22] To be consistent with the philosophical spirit and integrity of the text, this article follows Mogobe Ramose (elsewhere in this issue) in subverting the convention that capitalises references to the present South African constitution. The purpose of referring to the constitution in all lowercase is to put into question the hierarchy between the constitution and African law in particular, and to contest the symbolic and ideological elevation of the constitution to the status of human-made deity.

[23] Y Winter 'Conquest' in *Political Concepts: A Critical Lexicon* (2011) <http://www.politicalconcepts.org/issue1/conquest/>; L Veracini *Settler Colonialism: A Theoretical Overview* (2010) 78.

[24] See AT Moleah *South Africa: Colonialism, Apartheid, and African Dispossession* (1993); T Keegan *Colonial South Africa and the Origins of the Racial Order* (1996); N Worden *The Making of Modern South Africa: Conquest, Apartheid, Democracy* (2012); J S Saul & P Bond *South Africa – The Present as History: From Mrs Ples to Mandela & Marikana* (2014).

[25] Worden ibid; GM Fredrickson *White Supremacy: A Comparative Study in American and South African History* (1981) 179–198; Saul & Bond ibid 36.

(or subject-producing) technologies, colonial domination in South Africa both produced and then worked to maintain and institutionalise a political ontology that positioned white people at the zenith of all definitions of humanity (civilisation, reason, morality) while simultaneously placing Black people[26] at the nadir of the social hierarchy and binding them into perpetual inferiority and powerlessness. In this process, centuries of white colonial domination have also generated a protracted antagonism at the heart of the South African society and polity, which is reflected (albeit in different historical stages) by an unceasing irruption of social, political and existential instability and uncertainty felt by all of its inhabitants.

Crucially, the amalgam of powers, systems, relations, identities and logics that comprise colonial conquest and settler-colonial white supremacy stretch beyond the legal and political domains into the socio-economic, cultural, spatial, epistemic/cognitive, psychic and ontological.[27] The racialised social contradictions it engenders leave the entire social landscape with deep, enduring and indelible imprints that are by design resistant to legal and political reforms aimed at formal deracialisation of civil society and integration of historically oppressed peoples into the frame of human rights and citizenship. Since settler-colonialism is, in Patrick Wolfe's famous formulation, 'a structure and not an event',[28] conquest must be understood as an order of constitutive physical, structural and symbolic violence that serves as the *foundation* for the very coherence of South Africa as a territory, polity and community.

It is from the vantage point of this deep and long historical framework that we may examine the progress of two decades of constitutional democracy in South Africa. For such an examination to be possible, however, it is necessary to repudiate the prohibitive intellectual and political conventions in the legal academy and beyond that treat the constitution in South Africa as universal, immutable, faultless and impervious to critique and revision. In this regard, this project shares an affinity with a number of scholars who have opened critical inquiries into the limitations and failures of 'post'-apartheid constitutional democracy, showing in different ways how the origins, spirit and content of the constitution are grounded upon a set of faulty political, conceptual and ideological predicates that not only violate the principle of historical justice but also stand in the way of a radical-democratic, decolonised and liberated future.[29] My own contribution to these

[26] Throughout this article, I shall use the term 'Black' to include groups traditionally labelled as Africans, Indians and Coloureds, unless where context indicates otherwise, in which Black denotes only 'Africans'. Throughout the text, I capitalise references to Black people as a group, not only because, as a specific political and socio-cultural group, they require denotation as a proper noun but also to adhere to the conventions of critical race theory literature and in order to discursively resist the racist diminution and negation of blackness in general, and to challenge the racial hierarchy in which blackness has been historically cast as inferior. It is for this reason that I do not capitalise 'white'. Where I use 'black' in all lowercase, it is in reference to a descriptive category. See KW Crenshaw 'Mapping the margins: intersectionality, identity politics and violence against women of colour' (1991) 43 *Stanford Law Review* 1244.

[27] C Mills 'White supremacy as a socio-political system' in AW Doane & E Bonilla-Silva (eds) *White Out: The Continuing Significance of Racism* (2003) 35.

[28] P Wolfe 'Settler colonialism and the elimination of the native' (2006) 8 *Journal of Genocide Research* 387, 388.

[29] For representative writings, see M Mutua 'Hope and despair for a new South Africa: the limits of rights discourse' (1997) 10 *Harvard Human Rights Journal* 63–114; MB Ramose 'In memoriam: sovereignty and the 'new' South Africa' (2007) 16 *Griffith Law Review* 310, 318–319; M More 'Fanon and the land question in (post)apartheid South Africa' in N Gibson (ed) *Living Fanon: Global Perspectives* (2011) 173–186; S Sibanda 'Not purpose-made! Transformative constitutionalism, post-independence constitutionalism and the struggle to eradicate poverty' (2011) 22 *Stellenbosch Law Review* 482; T Madlingozi 'Social justice in a time of neo-apartheid constitutionalism: critiquing the anti-black economy of recognition, incorporation and distribution' (2017) 28 *Stellenbosch Law Review* 123–147; N Dladla 'Towards an African critical philosophy of race: ubuntu as a philo-praxis of liberation'

lines of critical inquiry will be to reflect on the fundamental (dis)continuity between the historical fact of colonial conquest and settler-colonialism in South Africa and the aims and vision of a constitution made in the image of Western liberal democracy. I propose to argue that the lack of restoration and fundamental change that haunts the legal and political transition of the early 1990s, the seeming intransigence of old and new power structures and vested interests and the ongoing forms of dissent and discontent raging across South African public and political life can all be traced to this (dis)continuity.

In the course of this article, the constitution is figured not only as a supreme law but also a supreme *rationality*. Not only is it a formal law-text but it is also a particularly hegemonic public grammar, political imaginary and a form of historical and social consciousness. It embeds *particular* cultural and ideological values into its fold and as such works to consolidate and preserve *particular* arrangements and relations of power and knowledge. Understood in this way, the constitution must be implicated in the continuation of colonial-apartheid power relations, value systems and subjectivities. How else could we explain why the advent of constitutional democracy in South Africa has left white supremacy and coloniality largely undisturbed? What interests and powers does the constitution secure and leave untouched, and what realities and demands does it silence, minimise or erase?

I shall aim to engage these and other questions in this article, which is structured as follows: in the part that follows, I trace the connection between the excessive and widespread idealisation and worship of the South African constitution to the problem of colonial unknowing (in terms of which the fact of settler-colonialism is erased from theoretical and historical comprehension). Following this, part four considers the possibility that the hallowed status and moral power of the constitution is beginning to wane and puts forward a critical reading of post-1994 constitutionalism in the register of Wendy Brown's *Politics Out of History*, in which she reflects on the political, intellectual and cultural effects of the destabilisation of modernist narratives. Along such lines, I develop an account of the critique of constitutionalism with an emphasis on how such critiques: (1) reconceptualise the traditional historical periodisation upon which the constitution is premised, (2) insert black radical and Africanist imaginaries and vocabularies into legal and political thinking, (3) unearth the ideological presuppositions (and mystifications) of the post-1994 constitutional dispensation, and (4) issue 'uncompromising' demands for concrete justice and fundamental change. Part five concludes the article by briefly revisiting Nkosi's insights and reflecting on jurisprudence, decolonisation and the continuity between the colonial 'past' and the constitutional 'present'.

These reflections are set against the backdrop of the search for an alternative jurisprudence that would work against not only the more conservative positivist/black-letter legal thinking and liberal legalism but also the excessively Eurocentric traditions of critical legal theory. On this score, the invocation of conquest as a historical

(2017) 6 *Filosofia Theoretica* 39–68. See also J Saul 'On taming a revolution: the South African case' (2013) 49 *Socialist Register* 212–240; P Bond 'Constitutionalism as a barrier to the resolution of widespread community rebellions in South Africa' (2014) 41 *Politikon* 461–482; T Delport 'An ethical (anti-)constitutionalism? Transformation for a transfigured public' (2014) 46 *Acta Academica* 104–121; G van Riet 'The limits of political development and constitutionalism in South Africa' (2016) 75 *New Contree* 98–115.

marker for reading the present functions as a counter-narrative to these more dominant traditions of white legal scholarship in South Africa. Yves Winter points to what he calls the 'double narratability' of the concept of conquest: the fact that it contains both the stories, memories and experiences of the conqueror as well as those of the conquered. While conquest mainly denotes a paradigmatic type of violence or technology of acquisition and domination, as a historical trope, it can also be mobilised as the basis for a counter-history and counter-discourse. As Winter explains:

> stories of conquest challenged the official representations of the state and the law to the extent that they rendered society as riven by a binary division between conquerors and conquered. By appropriating this division as an analytical lens, these narratives of conquest demonstrate that the foundational narratology of conquest can be inverted and turned against the dominant class to generate a critique of official history and show the extent to which the hegemonic histories function as forms of ideology. Conquest, in other words, functions also as the paradigmatic form of history from below, a narrative form that justifies rebellion and insubordination and that, beginning in the 17th century, offers an interpretive schema for telling an alternative account.[30]

Following Winter, this article adopts a critical counter-historical and counter-hegemonic standpoint and gathers together a wide variety of thinkers and theoretical approaches in order to contemplate a jurisprudence outside of, and beyond, liberal constitutionalism.

3. Constitutional worship as 'colonial unknowing'

Over a series of publications, the anthropologist couple Jean and John Comaroff have described South Africa as a country in the grip of a pervasive culture of constitutionalism, legality and rights.[31] This culture, they explain, is characterised by an excessive faith in the South African constitution – which they refer to as an '[e]mphatically modernist, Eurocentric, and liberal'[32] text – to solve social problems, a faith they describe as bordering on fetishism. John Comaroff describes this fetishisation of law and constitutionality as being associated with, among other things, the judicialisation of politics; the global hegemony of human rights; the increasing tendency of subjects of class, race, sex, gender, and cultural difference to turn to law and courts as a means of constructing and representing themselves; and excessive litigiousness in society.[33]According to the Comaroffs, this fetishism of law and constitutionalism is a peculiar feature of the postcolonial condition in South Africa[34] and is linked to the governing ANC's aspiration towards a 'Eurocentric ideal of the nation-state'.[35]

Another source of the fetishisation and indeed worship of the constitution is a legal and political theology that views the promulgation of a new national

---

[30] Winter (note 23 above).

[31] J Comaroff & JL Comaroff 'Policing culture, cultural policing: law and social order in postcolonial South Africa' (2004) 29 *Law & Social Inquiry* 513, 521.

[32] Ibid 521.

[33] JL Comaroff 'Reflections on the rise of legal theology: law and religion in the twenty-first century' (2009) 53 *Social Analysis* 193, 195.

[34] JL Comaroff & J Comaroff 'Law and disorder in the postcolony: an introduction' in J Comaroff & JL Comaroff (eds) *Law and Disorder in the Postcolony* (2006) 22.

[35] Comaroff & Comaroff (note 31 above) 522.

constitution after conflict as a substantive and symbolic break with the past. As such, the culture of legality in 'constitution-obsessed South Africa'[36] is central to the production of a particular political culture as well as particular conceptions of nationhood and subjectivity and a particular vision of civil society. But, as Stacy Douglas has pointed out in a paper entitled 'Constitutions are not enough', this centring of constitutions as the central instruments for the production and reconstruction of political community after conflict always comes at the expense of alternative 'imaginations of political community'.[37] It also denies 'the messy realities of subjectivities, and glosses over persistent issues of inequality'.[38]

Because a postconflict constitution signals 'particular kinds of cultural shifts' and 'articulates aspirations for renewal',[39] it often contains a false teleological conceit that casts the social, political and legal order as being on a progressive move from a dark and conflictual past to a democratic future. This fetishistic over-investment and over-reliance on constitutions is problematic given that constitutions and constitutionalism are incapable of providing a reflexive politics[40] and are thus also unable to appreciate how deeply the terrors and conflicts of colonial-apartheid resulted in unstable conceptions of political community – particularly in the context of land, race and culture. Defining the social and political life of a polity mainly through constitutions, constitutionalism and constitutionality represents a closure of politics, rather than its opening – since in binding a political community together through its sovereign devices, a constitution and its devout proponents must also be blind to its own failures and exclusions.[41] The Comaroffs' use of the term *fetish* to describe the prevailing South African fixation and attachment to the constitution goes beyond signalling a law-abiding commitment but highlights the necessarily theological and ideological function of a postconflict constitution. Not only does a 'new' constitution purport to ground a transformed polity and define its values and ideals, it also hopes to hold together the always-already fragile civic bonds of the nation. In so doing, the constitution and the discourses and subjects it produces, *must* repress the difficult issue of the contested foundations and unrealised promises of the new order. It must also monopolise the sphere of public and political engagement unless actively countered by a different, more radical, politics.

The concept of 'colonial unknowing' stands out as an apposite description of the South African legal mind and legal culture in the grip of constitutional worship. Recently introduced to settler-colonial studies by Manu Vimalassery, Juliana Hu Pegues and Alyosha Goldstein, 'colonial unknowing' denotes an epistemological orientation that 'renders unintelligible the entanglements of racialisation and colonisation, occluding the mutable historicity of colonial structures and attributing finality to events of conquest and dispossession'.[42] In other words, colonial unknowing erases

[36] Comaroff & Comaroff (note 34 above) 26.

[37] S Douglas 'Constitutions are not enough: museums as law's counter-archive' in S Motha & H van Rijswyk (eds) *Law, Memory, Violence: Uncovering the Counter-Archive* (2016) 140, 141.

[38] Ibid 142.

[39] Ibid 141.

[40] E Christodoulidis 'Constitutional irresolution: law and the framing of civil society' (2003) 9 *European Law Journal* 401–432.

[41] S Douglas *Curating the Community: Museums, Constitutionalism and the Taming of the Political* (2017) 116.

[42] M Vimalassery, JG Pegues & A Goldstein 'Introduction: on colonial unknowing' (2016) 19 *Theory & Event*.

and overlooks the immoral and unjust historical foundations of settler-colonialism, treating it instead as an immutable, unproblematic and naturalised social fact – as something that happened and can no longer be reversed or challenged.

When 'colonial unknowing' is operative, the possibilities for reversing the colonial order are silenced even before they can be spoken, and the exigency of complete justice is undermined even before it can be demanded. It is through colonial unknowing that the afterlife of colonial-apartheid can at once remain pervasive in the form of inequality, poverty, violence and suffering but not be 'comprehended as an extensive and constitutive living formation'.[43] Colonial unknowing operates centrally through the disavowal, dissociation and normalisation of the history *and horror* of colonialism, land dispossession, white domination and racism. By making settler-colonialism illegible as a historical, political and moral problem, colonial unknowing normalises white hegemony in South Africa, enforces the expiry of colonised people's right to historical justice, and structures the field of sense, knowledge, perception and imagination in such a way as to make substantive decolonisation appear 'unreasonable and unrealistic'.[44]

The centring of the constitution in South Africa's political and legal culture and social discourse has also had the effect of narrowing the space for political contestation and removing from serious analytic view the living memory of South Africa and South African law as artefacts of colonial conquest. In this respect, constitutional worship also contains traces of what Brown has described under the heading of 'moralism as anti-politics'.[45] The moralistic dimension of constitutional worship inheres in its deification of the constitution and its inevitable casting of any criticisms of the constitution as in some way sacrilegious. To be sure, the problem with the pervasive culture of constitutional worship – and the colonial unknowing and moralism it disseminates – is its adherence to a static and undemocratic discursive universe in which it appears as though academics, civil society, political commentators and ordinary citizens cannot live and think outside of, at a distance from or even against the present constitution.

4. Constitutionalism out of history

Brown begins the introduction to her book *Politics Out of History* with the following question: 'What, other than anarchy or free fall is harboured by the destabilisation of constitutive cultural or political narratives?'[46] With this question, she aims to study the reactive political and intellectual formations (anxieties and tensions) that emerge in the wake of the erosion of 'the fundamental premises of an order'.[47] Brown's argument translates productively into the contemporary South African context in which the political-cultural narratives of constitutionalism and rainbowism are no longer as firmly intact as they once were. Brown, though, is writing from the perspective of a world-historical unravelling of Western modernity. In her account, both the universalist precepts of liberalism and its promises of freedom as well as the epistemological

[43] Ibid.
[44] Ibid.
[45] W Brown *Politics Out of History* (2001) 18–44.
[46] Ibid 3.
[47] Ibid 3.

presumptions of the Enlightenment (teleological notion of progress, rationality, objective truth, universalism, sovereignty) have been significantly undermined and disturbed by critical theoretical interventions and political upheavals exposing their falsity and complicities with imperial, racist and patriarchal power.[48] Despite this, however, Brown notes that since alternatives to these narratives have yet to be imagined, we remain bound to them in their 'broken and less-than-legitimate-or-legitimating form'.[49] As this attachment to disintegrating political-cultural narratives tends to generate 'reactionary and melancholic responses',[50] she counsels instead a search for possible alternatives to what has been destabilised.

I am interested in considering what possibilities could emerge from the realisation that the constitution's universal acclaim, transformative pedigree and binding force can no longer be taken for granted and is increasingly being viewed critically. If the constitution has since its enactment functioned as the overarching historical, political and epistemological story of South Africa, what happens when this story begins to fragment in the face of extant material conditions and the (re-)emergence of provocative intellectual currents? I propose that legal scholars, activists and ultimately citizens *give up* the attachment and dependence on the constitution as an instrument for securing consensus and coherence and seek out another futurity for justice that is not grounded in the certainties of Western modernity and its surrounding constellations (liberal democracy, humanism (universalism), capitalism and Eurocentric cosmologies).

For the purposes of this paper, I want to trace some features of the political, intellectual and cultural disintegration of 'post'-apartheid constitutionalism with a view to also providing an overview of scholarly and public criticisms of the constitution.[51] The argument underlying the discussion to follow is that these critiques represent a historical re-opening for the emergence of bold articulations of counter-hegemonic theories and politics.

The general unravelling of the constitutional ideal has been instigated in large part by the social reality of persistent racial and gender stratification and social exclusion. As the hope and euphoria of the Mandela republic waned in the face of the ongoing horror of the black condition and the devastations of global capitalism, the pithy phrase 'you can't eat a constitution' became a popular refrain.[52] In this iteration, the critique of constitutionalism accepts the internal terms of the constitution and is often directed outward to the jurisprudence and reasoning of the courts, to the inaction of government in implementing the provisions of the Bill of Rights, to the conservatism of legal culture and, in more abstract terms, to the limits of law.[53] We might rather call this a critical affirmation of the constitution, as the aim of these interventions was to fortify and ultimately redeem

---

[48] Ibid 3–11.
[49] Ibid 3.
[50] Ibid 4.
[51] Compare H Botha 'Instituting public freedom or extinguishing constituent power? Reflections on South Africa's constitution-making experiment' (2010) 26 *South African Journal on Human Rights* 66.
[52] See M Pieterse 'Eating socio-economic rights: the usefulness of rights talk in alleviating social hardship revisited' (2007) 29 *Human Rights Quarterly* 796–822; and T Thipanyane 'You can't eat the Constitution: is democracy for the poor?' in K Bentley, L Nathan & R Calland (eds) *Falls the Shadow: Between the Promise and the Reality of the South African Constitution* (2013).
[53] See for example KE Klare 'Legal culture and transformative constitutionalism' (1998) 14 *South African Journal on Human Rights* 146–188; K van Marle 'The spectacle of post-apartheid constitutionalism' (2007) 16 *Griffith Law Review* 411–429; C Albertyn 'Substantive equality and transformation in South Africa' (2007) 23 *South African*

the constitution, even as scholars were noting a widening gap between the 'reality and the promise' of the constitutional dispensation.[54]

What emerged from these positions was an ambitious support for 'transformative' law reform and legal development of the colonially imposed common-law rules in select private law fields, such as contract and property, as well as a strong emphasis on socio-economic rights and equality jurisprudence.[55] In this moment of the critique, heavy reliance is placed on a variety of Euro-American schools of legal thought (hermeneutics, Marxist and post-structuralist iterations of critical legal studies (including psychoanalysis, aesthetics, law and literature), legal feminism, civic republicanism, welfare liberalism, Dworkinian interpretivism, international and comparative human rights to name a few) to provide tools to enhance legal theorising, legal interpretation and adjudication with the principal aim of realising, rather than problematising, the aims and vision of the constitution. It is instructive at this point to remember that even if expansive and creative forms of constitutional interpretation could widen the meaning and potential of the constitution, it would be an overstatement to deny that the constitutional project remains constrained by the context of its emergence, the reigning legal and political culture, and by the nature of modern law to draw lines (rationalisation), give effect to a decision (fixity) and perform sovereign acts (closure). In other words, while transformative constitutional discourse can open debate *within* the governing social rules, its ability to contest the actual rules themselves is severely limited.[56]

If the varying approaches described above implicitly discouraged *blind* triumphalist faith in the constitution, they nevertheless remained markedly optimistic about its 'transformative' and 'progressive' possibilities and thus did not occupy themselves with the fashioning of radical alternatives grounded in and sensitive to the specific social, cultural and historical realities of South Africa. Recent studies have furthermore revealed the operation of a hierarchy in terms of which the development and conceptualisation of knowledge on modern constitutionalism is framed through the experiences, institutions and epistemologies of the Global North, with the Global South relegated to a lower, underdeveloped and purely mimetic tier. This attachment to hegemonic North American and European legal traditions and schools of thought reproduces global patterns of legal knowledge that perpetuate the marginality of Southern law and African jurisprudential approaches in knowledge production on South African constitutionalism.[57]

It is of sociological significance that the primary architects and proponents of 'post'-apartheid constitutionalism in the legal academy and in civil society are white leftists and liberal progressives who tend to place much emphasis on litigation and the judiciary as sites of democratic social change. What was famously termed the shift

Journal on Human Rights 253–276; and see generally S Woolman & M Bishop (eds) *Constitutional Conversations* (2008).

54 See for example DM Davis 'Transformation: the constitutional promise and reality' (2010) 26 *South African Journal on Human Rights* 85–101.

55 See for example A van der Walt *Property and Constitution* (2012); S Liebenberg *Socio-Economic Rights Adjudication under a Transformative Constitution* (2010); AJ Barnard-Naudé 'Oh, what a tangled web we weave: hegemony, freedom of contract, good faith and transformation – towards a politics of friendship in the politics of contract' (2008) 1 *Constitutional Court Review* 1–54; P de Vos 'The past is unpredictable: race, redress and remembrance in the South African Constitution' (2012) 129 *South African Law Journal* 73–103.

56 See generally Christodoulidis (note 40 above) and GW Anderson 'Imperialism and constitutionalism' in E Christodoulidis & S Tierney (eds) *Public Law and Politics: The Scope and Limits of Constitutionalism* (2008) 129–140.

57 See D Bonilla Maldonado 'Introduction: toward a constitutionalism of the Global South' in D Bonilla Maldonado (ed) *Constitutionalism of the Global South: The Activist Tribunals of India, South Africa, and Colombia* (2013) 1–39.

from a culture of authority (parliamentary sovereignty) to a culture of justification (constitutional supremacy)[58] meant that the constitution became the overarching frame of social and public discourse and action. And here problems of racial power, voice and representation necessarily loom large. In a social context where white power has insulated itself in the private sphere (as well as in the realms of economics, media, culture and educational institutions) while the public (legal and political) face of the new order is *seen as* black, this vertical gaze (towards organs of the state), as Tshepo Madlingozi explains, means that a largely white 'social justice civil society' community organises its advocacy, litigation and research priorities in a way that juridifies social struggles and appropriates the suffering of marginalised communities.[59] Significantly, this also directs attention away from the economic and cultural power still wielded by the historical beneficiaries of colonialism and apartheid in favour of an ahistorical and 'de-radicalising' programme that contributes to framing the post-1994 black government as the *primary* source of South Africa's failings.[60] Moreover, as courts (rather than the citizenry and communities) became the guardians of the new dispensation, it also happened that predominantly white lawyers, activists and academics emerged as the primary intellectual and moral custodians of constitutional democracy in South Africa.

The anomalous overrepresentation of white lawyers and academics in shaping the practice and theory of South African constitutionalism becomes especially vexed in view of a counter-history of non-racialism that illustrates how white anti-apartheid commitment to democratic reform was never *inherently* antithetical to the perpetuation of white domination and assertions of the superiority of Western culture and civilisation.[61] From missionary education and Christianisation to the proselytisation of black communities into a workerist rather than Africanist politics, and to disproportionate leadership and influence in Congress and trade-union politics, post-1994 public-interest litigation, civil society and non-governmental organisation (NGO) activism as well as constitutional scholarship take their place in a long line of paternalistic impositions by white people of the political and intellectual terms and norms of African resistance to domination and exclusion. What this counter-history further reveals is a genealogy in terms of which, from the late 19th and early 20th century up to the present, white liberal and left participation in black struggles was driven by two interrelated aims, namely: (1) the introduction and normalisation of Africans into a Eurocentric public sphere, and (2) the interception of the development of an autonomous black radical political subjectivity.[62] A third aim might include the universalisation and valorisation of self-identified Western civilisational standards of law, culture and justice.[63] This reflects, to quote Franco Barchiesi, that white progressive

---

[58] E Mureinik 'A bridge to where? Introducing the Interim Bill of Rights' (1994) 10 *South African Journal on Human Rights* 31.

[59] Madlingozi (note 29 above) 144.

[60] Ibid.

[61] J Soske 'The impossible concept: settler liberalism, pan-Africanism and the language of non-racialism' (2015) 47 *African Historical Review* 1–36. This is an insight derived from S Biko *I Write What I Like* (2012) 63: 'The biggest mistake the black world ever made was to assume that whoever opposed apartheid was an ally.'

[62] F Barchiesi 'The problem with "we": affiliation, political economy and the counterhistory of nonracialism' in J Soske & S Walsh (eds) *Ties that Bind: Race and the Politics of Friendship in South Africa* (2016) 125–166.

[63] S Pillay 'Prerogative of civilized peoples: apartheid, law, and politics' (2014) 34 *Comparative Studies of South Asia, Africa and the Middle East* 294–313.

politics – today represented by the humanrights lawyer and the leftist intellectual among others – has been historically punctuated by:

> white claims to possess the ethical and productive norms needed to 'improve' Black functionality in white civil society and political economy, which justifies the positing of Black bodies as objects of white instruction, mediation, concern or coercion.[64]

As much of the litigation taken up in the NGO and civil-society sector involved confrontations with the state's failure to implement and adhere to constitutional and administrative law provisions, this presaged another wave of critiques of the constitution emanating from the ruling party and other proponents of the 'national democratic revolution'.[65] In these critiques, the constitution was conceived as an obstacle to Black majority rule and was seen to subvert the democratic legitimacy of the ruling party by subjecting the decisions of the executive to the scrutiny of the judiciary. Other voices from similar quarters extended this critique to the property clause and its requirement of (*some form of*) compensation for land expropriation, while others highlighted the foreign or Western character of the constitution as out of sync with the cultural worldview of the majority of South Africans.[66] Even if expressions of this critique sometimes took crude forms, such as in the charge that the courts in South Africa are 'counterrevolutionary', it nevertheless represented legitimate frustrations over unresolved political contradictions.

In sum, although there has always been *mild* contestation over the content, implementation and interpretation of the constitution, such contestation never rose to the temperature of probing the epistemological, ideological, cultural and political premises of the constitution itself.[67]

I will now turn to critiques that take far more devastating aim at the fundamental premises and legitimacy of the constitutional order itself, arguing in different ways that the constitution represents a continuation and reproduction of the constituent elements of colonial conquest. Attentiveness to enduring and intractable structures of colonial and apartheid power blurs the distinction between the past and present and, in that way, debunks a constitution's claim to inaugurating a new order and representing a radical break with an unjust 'past'. More to the point, the stark continuity and intensification of racial inequality and unfreedom across South African society disturbs the liberal universalist (non-racialist) premises of the constitution.[68]

---

64 Barchiesi (note 62 above) 129.

65 Another scene of constitutional contestation that will not be discussed in this article also came from conservative and right-wing quarters of Christian and white minority-rights organisations. The Christian lobby critiqued the new secular constitutional order for licensing what they viewed as social vices such as termination of pregnancy, promiscuity, same-sex marriage, alcoholism, disrespectful youths, criminality and so forth. White minority-rights organisations, on the other hand, sought to reframe white South Africans under the new constitutional dispensation as a racial minority vulnerable to crime and discrimination. They accordingly waged campaigns and litigation on a variety of issues tied to protecting the rights and privileges of white people such as challenging affirmative action and race-based redress measures, demanding the retention of apartheid-era street names and of Afrikaans as a medium of instruction in schools and universities, and calling for farm murders to be recognised as a form of racial genocide.

66 See B Ngoepe 'Choosing new custodians of our Constitution' *Sunday Times* (30 August 2009) 11; J Duncan 'The problem with South Africa's Constitution' *South African Civil Society Information Service* (5 September 2011) <http://sacsis.org.za/site/article/631>.

67 A prominent exception in this regard would be the work of Mogobe Ramose.

68 See K Durrheim, X Mtose & L Brown *Race Trouble: Race, Identity and Inequality in Post-apartheid South Africa* (2011).

The unfolding of the afterlife of colonial-apartheid over the past 24 years threatens to slowly erode the constitution's standing as the linchpin of emancipatory and egalitarian progress in South Africa and globally. Consequently, the oxymoronic references to a 'negotiated (or legal) revolution', the description of the constitution as 'the best' in the world', the reference to citizens born after 1994 as 'born-frees' and the designation of the present time as 'post'-apartheid should be viewed with a degree of incredulity. This incredulity is the basis for encasing the phrase 'post'-apartheid in quotation marks or using phrases such as 'neo-apartheid' South Africa to describe the present social and existential reality of the Black majority. On this view, the reliance on law, human rights and an elite-driven process of transitional justice as the primary technologies for political reconstruction and social transformation served only to deny the exigency of historical justice and reparation, insulate beneficiaries and perpetrators of racial atrocities from historical and moral responsibility and assimilate the historically oppressed majority into the 'conqueror's South Africa'.[69]

Less concerned with, though not indifferent to, realising the transformative potential of the constitution, the more fundamental critique of the constitution draws our attention to the anti-decolonisation and non-revolutionary sensibilities embedded in both the constitutional text and the larger political culture and scholarship on 'post'-apartheid constitutionalism. To give a better account of the terms of this critique, I shall highlight a few overlapping themes that underpin its destabilisation of the logic, premises and framework of South Africa's constitutional democracy writ large.

4.1. Redrawing temporal boundaries

The insistence on the endurance and continuation of the underlying social relations and material conditions established through colonialism and apartheid puts into question a number of temporal signifiers that give the present constitutional order its legitimacy and coherence. It contests the putative 'newness' of the 'new South Africa', displaces the privileging of 1994 as a date of liberatory significance and thereby disrupts the linear and teleogical historical casting of the present South Africa as substantively 'post'-apartheid. This contestation, in turn, extends to a problematisation of the official representation and widespread assumption that the constitution marks a transcendence or overcoming of earlier historical periods of oppression and injustice. This posture reflects a mode of reading history in terms of the *longue durée*[70] and has significant implications for our understanding of the post-1994 constitutional present.

First, it undermines the over-emphasis and exceptionalisation of apartheid (a 46-year historical episode) by restoring a focus on the 1652 European colonial conquest of the territories that would later be called South Africa as the proper founding of South Africa's contradictions and antagonism.[71]

[69] See again the sources cited in note 29 above.

[70] See I Wallerstein 'Time and duration: the unexcluded middle, or reflections on Braudel and Prigogine' in I Wallerstein *The Essential Wallerstein* (2000) 160–169.

[71] See L Ntsebeza 'Land redistribution in South Africa: the property clause revisited' in L Ntsebeza & R Hall (eds) *The Land Question in South Africa: The Challenge of Transformation and Redistribution* (2007) 124.

Second, it illustrates with greater clarity how systems of power can outlive the abolition of their more overt legal supports.[72] This means that institutional shifts set in motion through legal transitions are not necessarily coterminous with substantive changes in people's material conditions and social realities. Instead, such systems of power – especially those entrenched through almost four centuries of colonial violence, subjugation and socialisation – tend to undergo reconfiguration over time, permutations in their form but not their force.[73] They do not, in other words, disappear but reinvent themselves in order to adjust to the prevailing conditions. A closely related argument avers that positive gains and advances in racial equality and justice will only occur to the degree that they converge, and thus do not disturb, the material and psychological interests of the dominant social group.[74]

Third, *longue durée* histories concern themselves with that which endures and remains consistent at the level of the deep structures of a society or civilisation. In other words, it pays closer attention to the inertia or static in a socio-political and cultural order rather than the more episodic, inessential, surface-level changes in the body politic. In philosophical terms, this signifies a subversion of Western conceptions of time and history that situate the 'past' in the historical anterior (as *behind* us, but never immediately with us)[75] as well as a certain Hegelian conceit that views historical progress in teleological terms and assumes simply that the conditions of human existence improve progressively with the passage of time.[76] *Longue durée* histories are consistent as well with the African philosophical principle '*molato ga o bole*', which prohibits the automatic cancellation of a historical debt, since neither time nor law can change the truth of what has happened.[77] Similarly, many critical theorists argue that formally 'post'-conflict societies that have undergone liberal legal reform, such as South Africa, can remain oppressive for as long as they are defined by unredressed asymmetries of power and continue to display features of stratification, exploitation, violence, marginalisation, powerlessness and cultural dominance.[78]

Fourth, the rupturing of the division between the colonial past and the democratic present enables the disinterring of forgotten archives and silenced histories. This is evidenced, for example, by scholars revisiting the decades-old debates on the 'National Question' in South African left thought,[79] making the case for a new direction of black studies 'after Mandela' in South African higher education,[80] and showing a renewed interest in non-Charterist political movements and events. Insofar as

---

[72] C Mills *Blackness Visible: Essays on Philosophy and Race* (1998) 119–138.

[73] J Sexton 'The social life of social death: on Afro-pessimism and black optimism' (2011) 5 *InTensions* 1–47.

[74] D Bell 'Brown v Board of Education and the interest-convergence dilemma' (1980) 93 *Harvard Law Review* 518–533.

[75] E Cavanagh 'History, time and indigenist critique' (2012) 37/38 *Arena Journal* 18.

[76] Brown (note 45 above) 6.

[77] MB Ramose 'An African perspective on justice and race' (2001) *Polylog* <http://them.polylog.org/3/frm-en.htm>; MB Ramose 'Reconciliation and reconfiliation in South Africa' (2012) 5 *Journal of African Philosophy* 20, 23.

[78] See for example KW Crenshaw 'Race, reform and retrenchment: transformation and legitimation in antidiscrimination law' (1988) 101 *Harvard Law Review* 1331, 1336; IM Young 'Five faces of oppression' in IM Young *Justice and the Politics of Difference* (1990) 39–65; A Cudd *Analysing Oppression: Studies in Feminist Philosophy* (2006); NM Torres 'On the coloniality of being' (2007) 21 *Cultural Studies* 240–270.

[79] See E Webster & K Pampalis (eds) *The Unresolved National Question in South Africa: Left Thought Under Apartheid* (2017).

[80] See L Modisane, VJ Collis-Buthelezi & C Ouma 'Introduction: black studies, South Africa and the mythology of Mandela' (2017) 47 *The Black Scholar* 1–6.

the struggles they articulate remain unfinished and the freedom dreams they conjure are still unrealised, intellectual traditions such as Black Consciousness, the Non-European Unity Movement, Pan-Africanism, and even the Haitian Revolution, among others, become available for retooling in the contemporary context as sources for alternative theories and praxes.[81] As the time of Anton Lembede, Robert Sobukwe and Steve Biko, among others, becomes temporally entangled with ours, their meditations take on a haunting and prophetic quality in the face of a history that seems to be repeating itself.[82]

To be sure, while the redrawing of temporal boundaries aims to collapse inessential periodisations, it does not amount to the ahistorical claim that *nothing at all* has changed or that no efforts towards change are being attempted. And it is certainly not to deny the immense sacrifices of the women and men who led earlier phases of the anticolonial and anti-apartheid struggle in South Africa. Rather, it shows that the forms and visions of change being employed are not able to successfully dismantle the reigning order at the level of its constitutive or foundational structural elements. Applied to South Africa, this means that the constitutional transformation of South Africa effected change in every area of society *except* where it really matters most. Names of streets and buildings were changed, new faces occupied the seat of government power, official publications were published in a plethora of African languages, a new national flag was designed and a new national anthem composed, a number of old apartheid-era laws were repealed, and the ubiquitous 'whites only' signs were taken down. But consider that in contrast to these spectacular 'changes', actual arrangements of economic power, land and property ownership, spatial segregation, epistemic violence, Western imperialism, psychic trauma and labour exploitation were all left untouched in the new constitutional dispensation.

In sum, the critique of the constitution contests hegemonic temporal framings in order to register the reminder that neither 1994 nor the advent of constitutional democracy signalled the end of white supremacy or Black people's struggle against it.

4.2. Counter-hegemonic political imaginaries

Taking conquest as the historical starting point for framing the South African historical and social reality also redefines the nature of the injustices to be redressed by a process of legal and political reconstitution. The emphasis on apartheid narrowly focuses on disenfranchisement, segregation, discrimination and deprivation of civil rights and hence prescribes democratisation and formal deracialisation as the solutions to these iniquities. An emphasis on conquest would, in addition to racial discrimination, attend to the more comprehensive injustices of genocidal violence, land dispossession, epistemicide, economic deprivation, super-exploitation as well as psychological degradation. This latter understanding would foreground the antagonism between the settler and immigrant white populations and their oppressive relation to the indigenous African and broader Black population and would insist on a more

[81] See for example KM Tafira *Black Nationalist Thought in South Africa: The Persistence of an Idea of Liberation* (2016).

[82] A Veriava & P Naidoo 'Remembering Biko for the here and now' in A Mngxitama, A Alexander & N Gibson (eds) *Biko Lives! Contesting the Legacies of Steve Biko* (2008) 234, and D Hook 'A threatening personification of freedom or: Sobukwe and repression' (2016) 17 *Safundi* 189–212.

thoroughgoing process of material and symbolic decolonisation that would liberate the conquered majority from bondage, dismantle the social and psychic structures that secure the superior status of the white population and thereby dislodge the political ontology of conquest. Whereas freedom from apartheid involves the egalitarian liberal inclusion of the oppressed Black majority into the conqueror's world, liberation from conquest involves dismantling the conqueror's world altogether followed by the collective construction of a new social order.

This analytical, historical and political distinction between apartheid and conquest instantiates a further set of historically grounded category distinctions, primarily between: (1) integrationist, assimilationist and gradualist forms of social change and more far-reaching total or revolutionary transformations of the social order; (2) formal and symbolic forms of change in contrast to concrete and material change; and (3) the legal and institutional reconstruction of state and society versus more comprehensive existential, cultural, epistemological and political-economic re-ordering. Marking these category distinctions is an apprehension of power and injustice in structural terms. Structural conceptions of power proceed from the understanding that socio-political and ideological systems are generated to continually reproduce and normalise deep-rooted hierarchies that disproportionately benefit and affirm the existence of one group while disadvantaging others.[83] These systems operate in the public and private spheres, and proliferate in the domains of the law, economy, media, culture, the environment and educational institutions. They are deeply ingrained in people's mind-sets and subjectivities; they determine and shape life chances and opportunities and, once entrenched, become virtually self-perpetuating – sustained by among other dynamics, 'cultural lag, institutional momentum, accumulated wealth and attitudinal inertia'.[84]

Working from a conception of colonialism and apartheid as systems and structures that produce objective material outcomes rather than casting them as the 'evil' or 'hateful' actions of individuals and institutions exposes the falsity of the presumption that the occupation of government power by a Black majority political party leads to genuine freedom. The term 'neocolonialism' was, after all, coined precisely to capture the dilemma of postcolonial African states that, after gaining national independence, simply replicated the ways of the 'former' colonial power and plunged the formally liberated population into a deepening phase of unfreedom and stagnation.[85] In any instance, the South African case has been said to be a paradigmatic case of white people relinquishing the crown (state power) but keeping the jewels (socio-economic power).[86] The formal abolition of legally sanctioned racial discrimination should therefore not be conflated with the elimination of the structures, practices and relations of coloniality and white supremacy.[87] The failure to redress the *structural*

[83] See IM Young *Responsibility for Justice* (2011).

[84] Mills (note 72 above) 76, 102.

[85] See K Nkrumah *Neocolonialism: The Last Stage of Imperialism* (1974); F Fanon *The Wretched of the Earth* (2004) 97–144.

[86] A Mazrui 'Pro-democracy uprisings in Africa's experience: from Sharpeville to Benghazi' (2011) *Africa Day Lecture* 7.

[87] JM Modiri 'Towards a (post-)apartheid critical race jurisprudence: "divining our racial themes"' (2012) 27 *South African Public Law* 231–258.

continuity of colonial-apartheid renders the constitution's extension of universal suffrage, citizenship and human rights to Black people hollow and abstract.

The shift from racial apartheid to 'non-racial' democracy also relied upon a faulty process of nation building and reconciliation that centred on the experiences of political elites and a narrowly defined set of perpetrators and victims, thus erasing the historical responsibility of beneficiaries of colonial-apartheid.[88] Where perpetrators committed heinous acts of spectacular violence (killings, torture and kidnappings), beneficiaries were socialised to accept their entitlement to a life sustained by the larger structural violence of apartheid that secured for them an infinitely higher quality and standard of living. As the multiple and constant incidents and complaints of racism in white-dominated spaces (shopping malls, restaurants, suburbs, universities, the corporate workplace, farms, holiday resorts and so forth) demonstrate, the failure to attend to the beneficiaries of colonial-apartheid has resulted in a largely untransformed white minority community with a profoundly limited sense of moral and historical awareness. This undisturbed sense of white privilege can be traced directly to the depoliticising modalities of the Truth and Reconciliation Commission (TRC) and its central trope of forgiveness.[89] As the negotiated settlement was driven more by concerns of stability and peace rather than justice, it leaned more towards the protection of white people's unjustly acquired interests, converting them into constitutional rights and shielding them from demands for redistribution and restoration.

In this sense, the South African constitution cannot logically be categorised as 'non-racial', since it actively preserves interests and powers secured through racial oppression.[90] In so doing, it closes off the possibility of substantively abolishing the hierarchically entwined social categories of conqueror and conquered, settler and native, white and black. In the result, notwithstanding the official completion of the TRC's work, a new national anthem and national flag as well as a nominally non-racial constitution, white people would continue to carry the stigmatic markings of 'oppressor' and thus remain unfree as well.

The counter-hegemonic political imaginaries that unsettle the cherished tenets of constitutionalism insist that the questions forgotten, silenced and avoided in the negotiated settlement and constitution-making process be placed once more on the table. In so doing, they renegotiate the hegemonic terms of post-1994 South Africa and insist that freedom, equality, dignity and reconciliation can only materialise in the context of justice, reparations and a reconstruction of the values and institutions that govern society. In simpler terms, they insist on locating and addressing the sources of subordination and suffering at the level of roots rather than symptoms. This is not a question, in the first place, of 'blaming' or 'rejecting' the constitution on account of South Africa's many social ills but of asking to what extent *this particular constitution* and liberal constitutionalism in general is able to provide a framework,

---

88 M Mamdani 'When does reconciliation turn into a denial of justice?' in *Sam Nolutshungu Memorial Lecture Series* (1998) 1.

89 T Lephakga 'Radical reconciliation: the TRC should have allowed Zacchaeus to testify?' (2016) 72 *HTS Theological Studies* 1.

90 See N Dladla 'Contested memory: retrieving the Africanist (liberatory) conception of non-racialism' (2017) 153 *Theoria* 101–127.

vision and language that is 'purpose-made' to address the accumulated social contradictions of colonial conquest, racial capitalism, apartheid and neoliberalism.[91]

4.3. Ideology critique

Even as liberal democracy attempts to universalise its image and to present itself as post-ideological, both its racialised imperial history and its affinity to the social powers of race, class, and gender that produce stratifications along these lines compromise its presumed universalism.[92] The 'excluded others' of liberalism's chequered past and present, together with its deep imbrication in the civilisational assumptions of Western modernity and European colonial expansion, suggests – at best – that there is no natural tension or necessary inconsistency between liberalism (as a philosophy and a political order) and white domination, colonial violence and racial capitalism. From a Marxist perspective, liberalism is seen as bearing the stunning ability to conceal its resubordinating and exclusionary impulses.[93] From a postcolonial feminist perspective, liberalism promulgates a vision of non-Western subjects as inert victims of their own 'backward' cultures in need of saving from Western actors and ideologies.[94] And from a black radical perspective, liberalism is viewed as a less vulgar but nonetheless potent variety of white supremacy that naturalises European definitions of humanity and perpetuates white privilege through its moderate and non-threatening political posture.[95]

Fundamental critiques of constitutionalism emanating from Africanist and socialist traditions take off from this ideological unmasking of liberalism to interrogate other features of the democratic transition and legal architecture of South Africa. One line of critique begins with an exposure of the ruling ANC's own history of elite missionary liberalism – highlighting its acceptance of the colonial sovereignty of the British Crown, its embrace of Western colonial definitions of civilisation, its amenability to white intellectual and political influence, and its surrender of the struggle for land and sovereignty through its agreement to the terms of the Freedom Charter.[96] Consider one historical account of the ANC in the 1950s:

> Sensitivity to racial tensions and white fears had always exerted a restraining influence on the ANC and had caused it throughout much of its history to project African aims in ways that would minimize white backlash. In their anxiety not to be guilty of racism in any form, Congress leaders had many times found themselves constrained by the tendency of whites to label any suggestion of an African takeover of power as 'black racialism' or 'apartheid in reverse'.[97]

---

[91] See Sibanda (note 29 above).

[92] Brown (note 43 above) 7–8. See also R Kapur 'Human rights in the 21st century: take a walk on the dark side' (2006) 28 *Sydney Law Review* 665–687, and C Pateman & C Mills *Contract and Domination* (2007).

[93] See W Brown *States of Injury: Power and Freedom in Late Modernity* (1995).

[94] R Kapur 'The tragedy of victimization rhetoric: resurrecting the native subject in international/postcolonial feminist legal politics' (2002) 15 *Harvard Human Rights Law Journal* 2–37.

[95] b hooks *Killing Rage: Ending Racism* (1995) 184–194.

[96] See GM Gerhart *Black Power in South Africa: The Evolution of Ideology* (1978) 39–44 and CRD Halisi *Black Political Thought in the Making of South African Democracy* (1999) 4–8, 110–131.

[97] TG Karis & G Gerhart *From Protest to Challenge: A Documentary History of African Politics in South Africa, 1882–1990* vol 3 *Challenge and Violence, 1953–1964* (2013) 121.

Further according to this critique, the ANC's largely moderate and liberal non-racial commitments significantly attenuated its ability to mobilise anti-apartheid struggle on the basis of revolutionary nationalist demands. As a result, the ANC entered the 'negotiations' from a position of weakness and ended up agreeing to compromises with the National Party (NP) that resulted in the protection and consolidation of white minority interests, shielding their massive privileges and preventing large-scale redistribution of resources along more egalitarian lines. Each major concession the ANC made in the constitutional negotiations with regard to land, property, the power of the judiciary and the structure of the state ensured the survival of the old order in the new dispensation and legitimised the historical results of colonial-apartheid.[98]

This critique emphasises the ideologically *multivalent* nature of the 'post'-apartheid constitutional project – that it contains *both* its avowed, progressive and transformative elements (rights, institutional stability, rule of law, accountable government; multiculturalism, democracy and so forth) as well as a set of unavowed or hidden ones (a Eurocentric order of power/knowledge; a relatively undisturbed status quo; secret negotiations and elite power-broking; ANC-centric historiography; anti-blackness). Ideological critiques reveal that the South African constitution is not entirely benign or transparent; that it is *not only* what it says it is. Rather, the major signifiers of constitutional democracy in South Africa – Nelson Mandela, the TRC, electoral democracy, the rainbow nation motif as well the constitutional text itself – are seen to have the effect of concealing inconvenient truths about the transition: pacifying critical inquiry and political dissent and euphemising difficult conversations about race, history, and power.[99] On this score, it has been argued that the aesthetic of reconciliation that underpins the constitutional transition should be understood in terms of the verb 'to be reconciled to':[100] to be reconciled to unchanged living conditions, to tolerate racial inequalities and abuses, to forget about the past and move on. The logic of compromise that underlies the constitutional transition could be similarly interrogated in terms of the sacrificial diminution of Black people's historical and moral claims to justice and reparation. As a technique of ideology and as a normative project, the constitution is seen in this critique as aligned to subterranean racial, imperial and economic powers. Understanding the constitution as an ideological device also enables us to see how it imposes a limiting and limited index of what constitutes change, freedom and democracy.

Because it is not restricted to the *realpolitik* of the negotiated settlement, this critique has the value of, among other things, laying to rest the hackneyed claim that the political compromises contained in the negotiated settlement were *singularly and unquestionably necessitated* by the (global and local) balance of forces and the need to avert civil war.[101] While these considerations were certainly factored into the

---

[98] Mutua (note 29 above).

[99] C Teeger & V Vinitzky-Seroussi 'Controlling for consensus: commemorating apartheid in South Africa' (2007) 30 *Symbolic Interaction* 57–78.

[100] S Motha '"Begging to be black": liminality and critique in post-apartheid South Africa' (2010) 27 *Theory, Culture & Society* 297.

[101] Compare H Klug *Constituting Democracy: Law, Globalism and South Africa's Political Reconstruction* (2000); ZP Jordan *Letters to My Comrades: Interventions and Excursions* (2017) and K von Holdt 'South Africa: the transition to violent democracy' (2013) 40 *Review of African Political Economy* 589–640.

constitution-making process, they cannot constitute the whole picture of the transition. Instead the political malaise and incomplete transformation that followed the democratic transition must also be attributed to the lack of a philosophically rigorous and radical humanist ideology to underpin the conception of a new society.[102] This was made worse by the fact that the process of democratisation that gave rise to the new dispensation was driven by interests that were not primarily of the Black majority. A combination of global and local capitalist interests, as well as white people's vested interests in the historical results (socio-economic, cultural, epistemic, psychic and spatial) of settler-colonialism, constrained the imagination of the elite architects of the 'new' South Africa, leaving us with a still unfree and unequal society.[103]

There are, of course, multiple readings of liberalism, the ANC, the transition and the constitution, and certainly not all are aligned with the arguments set out above. The central point, however, is that all of these readings represent *contested ideological assumptions* and, whether intentionally or not, function to secure and protect certain powers, discourses, interests and investments while eclipsing and negating others.

4.4. Radical structure(s) of feeling

The political ethos or structure of feeling that animates the critique of the constitution distinguishes itself from liberal, reformist and accommodationist positions by the ambitious scope, drama and extravagance of its political vision. Where the former positions concern themselves with pragmatic and gradualist responses to social and historical injustice with a strong sensitivity to the fears and anxieties of the dominant group, radical positions traditionally urge a direct confrontation with oppressive power and mobilise and theorise for fundamental and concrete change. What underlies this posture is not simply a set of millenarian and populist political passions or naïve idealism but rather an ethical refusal to accommodate unjust social systems and an analytic hypothesis concerning the intransigence of oppressive power – the fact that it 'concedes nothing without demand'.[104] Although revolutionary violence has been posited as one solution to the colonial situation, other radical policies and calls for constitutional amendment such as reparations and wealth taxes, nationalisation of mines and banks, land expropriation without compensation, criminalisation of colonial apologism, and apartheid denialism and cultural re-ordering ('Africanisation') of state and educational institutions have been proposed. While these latter proposals generally eschew violence, they do entail an embrace of the *catastrophic*, defined not as chaos, suffering and disaster but in terms of its ancient connotations as '*katastrophē*', overturning a governing order.

Radicalism here signifies not only its traditional definition of grasping problems at the root level but also a desire to breach the boundaries that demarcate what is 'realistic' and 'possible' and what is not – especially given that these demarcations themselves are productions of the dominant symbolic order. The emergent contrast

[102] N Gibson 'Upright and free: Fanon in South Africa, from Biko to the Shackdwellers' Movement (Abahlali baseMjondolo)' (2008) 14 *Social Identities* 683, 691.
[103] See S Terreblanche *Lost in Transformation: South Africa's Search for a New Future Since 1986* (2012).
[104] This view was expressed in the South African context by Biko (note 61 above) 100 but originates from the slave abolitionist Frederick Douglass.

between egalitarian formulations of transformation or social justice that seek to *include* the historically oppressed into the existing social order vis-à-vis Africanist formulations of decolonisation and black liberation that seek a fundamental overhaul or annulment of that order is also a difference in feeling and temperament. If an optimistic faith in the promises of a united and equal society living under the rule of law and constitutionalism always involves some measure of seeing past the failures and fragility of the post-1994 political settlement, this sanguine sentiment is mostly the preserve of the privileged and the powerful. The critique of the constitution performs a disruption of this optimism, calling attention, instead, to the dark side and 'hidden cruelties' of the new dispensation.

Another dimension of the radical critique of constitutionalism is the refusal of compromise and negotiation as genuine modes of social reconstruction and reharmonisation. This uncompromising ethics rather than pleading for equality and celebrating incremental gains, opts rather to 'refuse what has been refused'[105] and so is vulnerable to the false charge of nihilism or pessimism. After all, long-standing pressure on Black people to engage 'rationally' with whiteness and white racism, and to adopt moderate and reconciliatory postures in relation to their oppression, reflects not only the imposition of colonial standards of civilisation disguised as humanism but is also a mechanism of preserving white social, economic and cultural power, rationalising quotidian expressions of subordination and affirming the status quo.[106] Similarly, from this view, the constitutional tropes of diversity, tolerance, reconciliation and nation building function as disciplinary technologies, ways of managing and containing the racial Other and thus also as sinister re-inscriptions of the 'Native Question' in a postcolonial guise.

If settler-colonial violence involves transferring the non-belonging of the settler population onto the indigenous people, rendering them foreigners and minorities in the lands of their birth, then it follows that the undoing of settler hegemony would involve reckoning with the fact of South Africa as a Black-majority African country. This socio-historical fact should stand central to any conception of restoration and justice in the South African context and should inform the reconfiguration of a new ethics, politics and way(s) of life.

However, there may be a deeper *aporia* here: both the founding premises of colonial conquest and its unfoldment (as a process of social ordering and subject production) through white supremacy creates an absolute bifurcation of society on the basis of an assumed ontological divide between white and black populations. Through this divide, those racialised as white collectively imagined and institutionalised the idea of themselves as superior and entitled to unlimited social, economic, cultural and psychic dominance over Black people. This resulted in the construction and intergenerational reproduction of arrangements and systems in which equality and freedom for Black people became irreconcilable with the material and existential interests of white people as a group. By normalising the subordination of Black people as a tolerable and even necessary feature of the social order, colonial conquest and its afterlives generated an antagonistic historical situation that is by design not amenable to

---

105 F Moten & S Harney *The Undercommons: Fugitive Planning and Black Study* (2013) 8.

106 See NA Cazenave *Conceptualizing Racism: Breaking the Chains of Racially Accommodative Language* (2016) 13–28.

negotiation, compromise and reform and might only be resolvable through total and complete dismantling.

The view of the South African constitution as the outcome of the choice by the negotiators for a 'new' South Africa to follow a path of democratisation rather than decolonisation becomes significant here.[107] One distinctive feature of settler-colonial formations – in which the European settler comes to stay permanently, supplant and dominate the native population and constitute themselves as a racially distinct community – is their high level of historical resilience. Wolfe speaks of settler-colonialism as 'relatively impervious to regime change'[108] and Lorenzo Veracini explains that since 'settlers carry colonialism "in their bones", settler-colonial forms may ultimately prove unreformable'.[109] Furthermore, the historical record suggests that most settler-colonial polities have followed processes of transition that seek to evade and undermine the exigency of decolonisation:

> [T]he reforming settler polities of the 1980s and 1990s share historiographical debates where a settler colonial past was displaced rather than addressed, and the determinations of a settler colonial present avoided rather than decolonised. In the end, an emphasis on alternative traditions of settler-Indigenous partnership has been easier than insisting on the need to decolonize settler colonial sovereignties, and a widespread disinclination to enact substantive decolonising ruptures resulted in a tendency to avoid disturbing the foundational determinants of settler colonial polities. Foundational settler narratives were ultimately resilient […].[110]

Thus, the turn to reconciliation, liberal constitutionalism, human rights and multiculturalism as the dominant modalities of postcolonial reconstruction has not been primarily about enacting genuine post-settler and post-conquest passages of transition and reharmonisation but rather about expanding the definition of 'who can claim belonging to the settler body politic that leaves the settler-colonial structures unchallenged'.[111] Democratisation preserves what decolonisation aims to destabilise and undo, namely the conqueror's South Africa, and this explains the tendency of constitutional scholarship to emphasise notions of rights, political equality, procedural democracy and good governance while bypassing larger questions of land, political economy, culture, identity and sovereignty tied to settler-colonial histories.

The critiques adumbrated above come from multiple sources and perspectives; they are not unified but, read together, they suggest nothing less than a political and conceptual disorientation of the very organising terms of 'post'-apartheid South African constitutionalism. Constitutionalism, non-racialism, liberal democracy, reconciliation and rule of law have become increasingly troubled narratives, declining in moral power and political legitimacy and crumbling as material formations for organising a society still 'held hostage' by its history. However, ending the argument here may leave other sides of the story untold. I should add that the discussion above relates to the official and hegemonic varieties of constitutionalism. There are also

---

[107] See Ramose (note 77 above).

[108] Wolfe (note 28 above) 402.

[109] L Veracini 'Settler colonialism and decolonisation' (2007) 6 *Borderlands e-journal* <http://www.borderlands.net.au/vol6no2_2007/veracini_settler.htm>.

[110] Ibid.

[111] Ibid.

what we might call 'constitutionalisms from below', enacted by social movements and marginalised communities who engage in legal mobilisation strategies and court litigation to contest state power, issue change-oriented political demands and address immediate legal and socio-economic needs.[112] These movements and communities do not only rely exclusively on rights tactics but also engage in extra-institutional collective political action, consciously eschew constitutional optimism and are cognisant of the limits and limitations of the law in bringing about decommodification of basic necessities, redistribution of resources and participatory democracy.[113] Their own contribution to decentring hegemonic constitutionalisms should also be noted.

5. Closing reflections: 'Tell no lies ... mask no difficulties ... claim no easy victories'[114]

The aim of this article was to challenge the widespread public, political and intellectual hegemony and celebrated status of the South African constitution through the introduction of different political and historical frames, competing theoretical approaches and divergent analyses and visions. In terms of this challenge, I pursued the argument that post-1994 South African constitutional democracy rests on compromised political foundations and has in the final analysis failed to disrupt the historical dynamics and afterlives of colonial conquest. As any empirical and existential account of the present illustrates, the South African socio-political, economic, and cultural landscape remains organised in terms of the political ontology of conquest established almost four centuries ago. The history of colonial conquest in South Africa echoes out into the present as 'unfinished business' as the racial regimes of socio-economic, cultural, psychic and epistemic power that it set in motion appear remarkably persistent and intractable – and not merely as legacies or residual leftovers. In such circumstances, it seems apt to mute or pause the constitutional optimism and national myths that make up the hegemonic story of the 'new' South Africa.

The invocation of conquest as a historical and political analytic with which to read the present South Africa maps a longer history and evokes a deeper injury. In so doing, it may also incite hopes for a radically transformed society. Taking colonial conquest as the basis for a counter-history of the place we call South Africa discloses traces of an alternative jurisprudence – a different thinking of law, politics, history and the social along the lines of a 'jurisprudence of liberation'.[115] The first gesture of such an alternative jurisprudence is not (yet) the provision of a programmatic blueprint or list of solutions but entails an opening of forgotten/erased archives and a disruption of dominant discourses and approaches. My presumption is that a jurisprudence emanating from the imaginations and experiences of the colonised peoples who have been historically racialised as Black and which takes seriously the intellectual heritages of African peoples (African philosophy and black radical thought

[112] T Madlingozi 'Post-apartheid social movements and legal mobilisation' in M Langford, B Cousins, J Dugard & T Madlingozi (eds) *Socio-economic Rights in South Africa: Symbol or Substance?* (2013) 92–130.
[113] Ibid.
[114] A Cabral *Revolution in Guinea* (1974) 72.
[115] See J Modiri 'The jurisprudence of Steve Biko: a study in race, law and power in the 'afterlife' of colonial-apartheid' Unpublished PhD thesis, University of Pretoria (2018).

in particular) would pose very different questions and enact a different orientation towards South African law and constitutionalism than is presently the case in a legal academy dominated by conservative, liberal and even critical traditions shaped by the epistemic standpoint of Western-oriented and white scholars.

In an article entitled 'Decolonisation is not a metaphor', indigenous studies scholars Eve Tuck and K Wayne Yang set out to remind readers 'what is unsettling about decolonisation'.[116] As they argue, decolonisation brings about the 'repatriation of indigenous land and life' and should not be used as a metaphor for 'other things we want to do to improve our societies', such as social justice, human rights and curriculum transformation. They worry that the unsettling and subversive features of the notion of decolonisation have been reduced to a metaphor:

> When metaphor invades decolonization, it kills the very possibility of decolonization; it recenters whiteness, it resettles theory, it extends innocence to the settler, it entertains a settler future. Decolonize (a verb) and decolonization (a noun) cannot easily be grafted onto pre-existing discourses/frameworks, even if they are critical, even if they are anti-racist, even if they are justice frameworks.[117]

Tuck and Yang also caution that the difficult task of reckoning with colonial histories remains impeded by a 'set of evasions', 'settler fantasies of easier paths to reconciliation' and forms of historical amnesia that work to diminish historical justice claims over generations.[118] Drawing on Frantz Fanon, they thus call for a closer attention to an 'ethic of incommensurability', which they explain requires the acknowledgement that ending settler-colonialism 'will require a change in the order of the world'.[119] This change in the order of the world does not entail reversing or replicating the current order of power. The goal is not 'for everyone to merely swap spots on the settler-colonial triad, to take another turn on the merry-go-round'. Rather, it entails breaking with and dismantling colonial and racial power structures. Tuck and Wayne underscore that they are speaking of 'a break and *not a compromise*'.[120] They add further that, '[D]ecolonial struggles here/there are not parallel, not shared equally, nor do they bring neat closure to the concerns of all involved – particularly not for settlers.'[121]

We can situate the present debates on the constitution within the fundamental contrast Tuck and Wayne construct between decolonisation and reconciliation (the latter they argue is ultimately 'about rescuing settler normalcy [and] rescuing a settler future').[122] If the post-1994 constitutional project aspires to the (impossible) construction of a united, non-racial society in which historical antagonisms can be reconciled and formally settled, a critical interruption to this aspiration would seek to highlight what will always remain unsettled, irreconcilable, incommensurate, irreparable, asymmetrical and unfinished in the absence of genuine decolonisation. Wayne and Yang depict decolonisation as a complex and discomforting process and praxis that also

[116] E Tuck & KW Yang 'Decolonization is not a metaphor' (2012) 1 *Decolonization: Indigeneity, Education & Society* 1.
[117] Ibid 3.
[118] Ibid 12.
[119] Ibid 31.
[120] Ibid 31, emphasis added.
[121] Ibid 31.
[122] Ibid 35.

eschews the liberal postcolony's narratives of national consensus, white innocence and historic closure:

> The answers are not fully in view and can't be as long as decolonization remains punctuated by metaphor. The answers will not emerge from friendly understanding, and indeed require a dangerous understanding of uncommonality that un-coalesces coalition politics - moves that may feel very unfriendly […] Decolonization offers a different perspective to human and civil rights based approaches to justice, an unsettling one, rather than a complementary one. Decolonization is not an 'and'. It is an elsewhere.[123]

By following a path of 'friendly understanding' rather than 'dangerous understanding', the constitution-making process in South Africa may have foreclosed a deep (and difficult) reckoning with our colonial and apartheid history, leading us on the trail of an unsustainable future.

This brings us back to Nkosi's lament referred to in the preface of this article concerning the way in which unresolved historical contradictions and unrepaired injustices (land dispossession and systemic racism being his central concerns) have stunted South Africa's ability to imagine a shared national culture that could be the basis for a new sense of belonging and co-existence that could bridge old and new divides and dismantle power asymmetries at all levels of public and private life. Is the constitution not simply the liberal humanist novel in sovereign form? Though Nkosi formulated this problematic in the context of literature and the arts, it does also underscore the need for a jurisprudence that can grapple with this conundrum centrally through contesting and disrupting the moral, epistemic, political, historical and ideological framework of the constitution and constitutionalism. Such a jurisprudence would need to overcome the lure of redemption, transcendence and false optimism in its search for new lines of critique and repair that could confront what Nkosi understood to be South Africa's still abyssal historical condition.

> *'The "freedom dreams" of those who know that what has been institutionalised is not what was imagined have not gone away.'*[124]

Disclosure statement

No potential conflict of interest was reported by the author.

---

[123] Ibid 35.

[124] T Willoughby-Herard 'Fighting for an intervention in history in the face of dreams deferred in the making: twenty years of South African democracy' (2014) 12 *African Identities* 225, 226.

Towards a post-conquest South Africa: beyond the constitution of 1996

Mogobe Bernard Ramose

ABSTRACT

Sebakwa taodisong ye ke gore bao bago tseyelwa naga ka dikgoka ba nale tokelo ya go lwela gore naga ya bona e boele go bona. Ye ke tokelo yeo molaotheo wa 1996 o e gatakileng wa etsa okare sebakwa gase gore naga ye yago bitswa Afrika-Borwa ke bafenyi yona e sa amogilwe bana ba mabu. Taodisong ye re tla fetleka sebakwa se go tswa matlhakoreng a fapafapaneng re lebisitse kudu gore thereso, toka le khutso nageng di kgafetswe thoko bjang le gona ka mabaka afe. Tlhaloso ya rena phetlekong ye e tla bontsha gore botho gabo gona molaotheong. Bothata ke gore botho bo tloga bo tlhokagala phedisanong ya setshaba kamoka. Ka fao, molaotheo o tshwanetse goba mmele le moya wa botho. Re kwisisa gabotse gore go lwela thereso, toka le khutso Afrika-Borwa ke go fega ntwa ye e amang lefatshe ka bophara. Re nganga gore bodidi bja maitirelo bo tshwanetse go fediswa gore toka, khutso le kwano di be gona, di rene mo Afrika-Borwa. Se se tla diragala ge kamoka re ka rerisana mabapi le go thopja ga naga ka dikgoka le ditlamorago tsa ntshe.

The purpose of this essay is to critique the constitution of the Republic of South Africa, 1996 in the light of the just war doctrine. The critique of the constitution involves special attention to the putative acquisition but practical exercise of the ethically questionable 'right of conquest' and its consequences, especially in the epistemological, economic and political spheres. The thesis defended in this essay is that the multi-faced injustice of conquest in an unjust war is still an ethical exigency demanding remedies despite the enactment of the constitution.

1. Introduction

The purpose of the present essay is to reveal and critique the problems arising from the establishment of the 'new' South Africa based on the constitution[1] of the Republic of South Africa, 1996. The interim constitution,[2] being the bridge to the 1996 one, is also the implicit or explicit point of focus in this essay. The specific problems we will focus upon pertain to the spheres of ethics, economics, law and politics. The core thesis to be defended here is that the multi-faced injustice of conquest in an unjust war is still an ethical exigency demanding remedies despite the enactment of the constitution. On this reasoning, colonialism has never ended, despite its successive change of name and face manifesting itself today as the imperial champion of 'democracy', 'human rights' and economic[3] or 'market fundamentalism'[4] benignly referred to as economic globalisation.

In the light of the above, the doctrine of Discovery, being the basis of the international law of colonialism, shall be one of the primary subjects under discussion. It is historically pertinent and ethically imperative to complement our discussion of the doctrine of Discovery with direct and critical focus upon the just war doctrine,[5] which is not a sterile fossil of antiquity in the West.[6] It is neither a relic of the Middle Ages[7] nor the subject of waning philosophical interest in the modern period.[8] The relevance of this doctrine in the conduct of contemporary international politics is attested to, for example, by the collection of essays edited by Brian Wicker,[9] the collection of essays edited by Edward Demenchonok[10] and the collection of essays edited by Craig de Paulo, Patrick Messina and Daniel Tompkins.[11] The ethical dimension of our essay will revolve around the just war doctrine and allow it to permeate our critique of the legal, political and economic bases of the 'new' South Africa. In the course of this critique, special attention will be focussed on epistemic injustice as a theoretical and historical consequence of the ethically questionable 'right of conquest' arising from the unjust wars of the colonisation of the peoples of the territory named South Africa by the conqueror. Ubuntu will be invoked in our discussion of epistemic injustice and the quest for a post-conquest South Africa.

---

1 The term 'constitution' is intentionally rendered in lowercase throughout this article, as there is an epistemic dimension to the exercise of the ethically questionable 'right of conquest' exercised by the colonial conqueror of South Africa. According to Thomas Hobbes, the Leviathan is a 'Mortal God' created by members of the Commonwealth. It is conceptually problematic that the constitution, being a creature of the members of the Commonwealth, should be elevated above its creators and be vested with divine immortality. Historically, constitutions have not always been the product of peaceful human interaction. Therefore, some constitutions may be presumed to be contentious, despite their scientifically precarious appeal to the use of the uppercase 'c'.

2 Constitution of the Republic of South Africa, Act 200 of 1993 (interim constitution). The interim constitution has been repealed.

3 J Kelsey *Economic Fundamentalism* (1995) 2.

4 G Soros *The Crisis of Global Capitalism* (1998) 75.

5 FH Russell *The Just War in the Middle Ages* (1975).

6 Cicero *Cicero De Officiis* (44 BC) (trans W Miller, 1913).

7 T Aquinas *Summa Theologiae* (1485).

8 FC Spits 'Hobbes' views on war and peace' in RJ Akkerman, PJ van Krieken & CO Pannenborg (eds) *Declarations on Principles: A Quest for Universal Peace* (1977) 101.

9 B Wicker (ed) *Studying War-No More? From Just War to Just Peace* (1993).

10 E Demenchonok (ed) *Between Global Violence and the Ethics of Peace: Philosophical Perspectives* (2009).

11 CJN de Paulo, PA Messina & DP Tompkins (eds) *Augustinian Just War Theory and the Wars in Afghanistan and Iraq: Confessions, Contentions and the Lust for Power* (2011).

An integral part of the purpose of this essay is that justice and peace demand a post-conquest South Africa: a South Africa that has responded concretely and effectively to the exigencies of justice with particular reference to disseizin or forcible expropriation of territory without compensation and, as a necessary consequence, the loss of sovereignty over it by its original indigenous owners from time immemorial. In pursuit of this purpose a critical reading of the historiography of South Africa, resulting in his-story, scientifically called history,[12] is imperative. We recognise the historical and epistemic links of conqueror South Africa, as it is at present with her especially Western parentage and allies. This recognition means that the struggle for justice and peace in South Africa is inextricably linked to the dynamics of international politics. 'The bottom billion'[13] is not an historical accident having some of its members in South Africa.

2. Background

2.1. Africa is the mother of all human beings

(1) The national museum of Ethiopia in Addis Ababa confirms this with the inscription: 'and the world became African'. The exodus[14] from Africa precedes the biblical Exodus from Egypt by millennia. Yet, 'the Word was made flesh' is comparatively much better known and exceedingly more powerful than the 'world became African'. Why is this so?

(2) The national museum of Hungary in Budapest, by reference to the geo-historical clock, corroborates the inscription in Ethiopia thus: 'Approximately one-one and a half million years ago, the first humans, already producing simple tools began a journey from Africa fated to populate the World.'

2.2. Language is an ethical appeal to our oneness as human beings

If we really are – as we so evidently appear to be – locked up irredeemably in the prison of cultural incompatibility and incommensurability and deadly ideological dogmatism, why is the suffix '-ia' and its variants – such as '-ya' in Lib-ya or Ken-ya, including the elliptical rendition '-a' as in Argentin-a instead of Argentin-ia – so widespread globally that it can readily assume the role of the tantalising, nay, the seductive saviour leading us out of the self-imposed but deadly captivity of cultural incompatibility and incommensurability – and deadly ideological dogmatism?

Consider the geographic distance in space and time with regard to Ethiop-ia, Ind-ia, Colomb-ia, Tasman-ia, Mongol-ia, Boliv-ia, Zamb-ia, Lithuan-ia, Sardin-ia, Austral-ia, Russ-ia, Moral-ia, Messopotam-ia, Georg-ia, Pennsylvan-ia, Namib-ia, Pers-ia, Monrov-ia, Nicaragu-a, Tanzan-ia, British Kaffrar-ia, Rhodes-ia and Oran-ia.

The list is not exhaustive. It is, however, sufficient to make the point that despite our real and distant geographical separation and multiple variety within cultural boundaries, language – as illustrated by the suffix '-ia' – seems to suggest that at some distant point in the past we spoke a common language when we were the inhabitants of Mother

[12] RG Collingwood *The Idea of History* (1961).
[13] P Collier *The Bottom Billion: Why the Poorest Countries are Failing and What Can Be Done About It* (2008).
[14] C Stringer & R McKie *African Exodus: The Origins of Modern Humanity* (1998).

Africa. Was it perhaps the Proto-Afroasiatic language? According to Ephraim Isaac, the Proto-Afroasiatic language is the root of multiple languages including, 'Semitic and Cushite as well as Omotic' languages.[15]

If Isaac's submission is correct, then the suffix '-ia' is a living reminder of our common linguistic origin. But more fundamentally, it is an ethical appeal that we give only the answer yes in word, and especially by just deeds, to the question: 'Am I my brother's keeper?'[16]

2.3. In the blood, we are a oneness, a living testimony of our sorority and fraternity

Science has classified and categorised human blood. Every human being is a potential donor or receiver of its blood group. Thus blood is there to be shared in safeguarding the lives of one another as human beings. We are yet to find human beings with literally and empirically proven 'black' or 'blue' blood flowing through their veins and arteries. It is so, however, that a certain Dr Town 'and others have maintained, that the blood of the Negroes is black'.[17] Presumably, the claim to 'blue blood' need not have been tested by this learned medical doctor 'and others' because it signified goodness, the living nobility. Perhaps the learned medical doctor 'and others' were so fixated on 'facts' that they failed to discern the fallacy of the social construct called blue-blooded human beings.

Experiments for purposes of medical science are such that willing human beings - not forgetting our sisters and brothers in the animal queendom to which we all belong - serve as guinea pigs. The success of the experiment means that the medicine - be it Panado or some other - is just as good to treat the queen's fever or headache as it is for treating a ragged, dry-skinned, rustic old lady living for many days on an empty stomach and suffering from headache or fever. Thus the assumption of medical science is that whatever is medically proper for a patient with a specific illness is medically appropriate for all other human beings suffering from the same particular disease. If this were not so, then medical science would have no legitimate claim to science because it would go against the hallowed though questionable criterion of 'objectivity'. It is crucial to remember that the 'objectivity' of science exempted medical science from prejudice against Africans, Negroes or Black human beings. In the case of this group of human beings, medical science denied them agency and rather opted for willful ignorance as well as prejudicial rationalisations. For example, 'Relentless in his belief that Blacks were *agent-less*, a white Louisiana doctor, Samuel Cartwright, claimed that some work habits of Negroes were the direct result of what he termed *Dysaethesia Aethiopica*,'[18] a figment of his imagination accepted - just like spermatorrhea[19] - as a valid scientific claim.

[15] E Isaac 'An open letter to an inquisitive Ethiopian sister' (28 December 2013) <https://debirhan.com/2013/12/an-open-letter-to-an-inquisitive-young-ethiopian-sister-by-prof-ephrem-isaac/>

[16] R Burggraeve *Each Other's Keeper? Essays on Ethics and the Biblical Wisdom of Love* (2009) 18–49.

[17] G Leclerc Buffon 'Biological and cultural distribution of mankind' in EC Eze (ed) *Race and the Enlightenment: A Reader* (1997) 24.

[18] G Yancy *Black Bodies, White Gazes: The Continuing Significance of Race* (2008) 120.

[19] EB Rosenman *Unauthorised Pleasures: Accounts of Victorian Erotic Experiences* (2003) 16.

Human sexuality is the leveller, insisting upon equality as human beings regardless of skin colour, race, ethnicity, creed, political persuasion, religion or social rank. Sex unites and delivers all human beings to the level of equality as human beings, because it is available to the insane and the sane, the poor and the rich, the foolish and the intelligent, the liar and the truthful, the religious believer and the atheist, including the beautiful and the ugly. Unsurprisingly, then, Basil Davidson makes the pertinent observation – with regard to South Africa – that its population became 'the fruit of unions between male colonists and female Khoi'[20] He emphasises this point thus: 'However little they might be prepared to admit the fact in public, the Afrikaners knew that a significantly large fraction of their nation were the fruit of unions between Boer farmers and their female slaves'.[21] It was Phillip Tobias who made a similar observation earlier than Davidson.[22] The situation in Australia was no better in this regard as the legal definition of a 'Quadroon' testifies. According to the Western Australia Native Administration Act of 1905 – as amended by acts of 1911, 1931 and 1936 – a Quadroon is 'a person who is descended from the full blood original inhabitants of Australia or their full blood descendants but who is only one-fourth of the original full blood'. This is echoed by the 'one-drop' doctrine in the United States of America.[23] According to George Yancy, Thomas Jefferson was:

> respected as a learned man and scientific in his outlook. Despite his famous five words, 'All men are created equal', Jefferson perpetuated myths regarding the Negro *type*. In addition to reducing Blacks' capacity to express genuine love to some form of base animal desire, Jefferson argued that the black body is more predisposed to sensation than reflection.[24]

Despite his indictment of slavery, Jefferson himself was a slave-owner with racist ideas. Writing in *Notes on the State of Virginia*, Jefferson argued that what he saw as the ugly colour, offensive odour and ugly hair of African American slaves indicated their physical inferiority, and that their alleged inability to create was a sign of mental inferiority. Given Jefferson's alleged relationship with Sally Hemings, one of his slaves, who is said to have given birth to seven of his children, the hypocrisy cries out.[25]

2.4. *'All men are equal'*

Ontologically, no single human being has ever had a conscious and active prior decision about whether or not it should ex-ist at a particular time, in a specific place and as male, female or hermaphrodite. Ex-istence is for every human being contingent. This underlines the ontological equality of human beings in the sense that the only ontologically unique and different human being should be the one able to prove a prior conscious and active decision about their being thrown into the world. No such human being exists. To be is to-be-with, through and among others. This dimension of being demands ethics; the basis for determining and practising what ought to be good for

---

[20] B Davidson *The People's Cause. A History of Guerrillas in Africa* (1981) 23.
[21] Ibid 28.
[22] PV Tobias *The Meaning of Race* (1972).
[23] PC Taylor *Race: A Philosophical Introduction* (2013) 139, 146.
[24] Yancy (note 18 above) 155.
[25] Ibid.

everyone. Ethics feeds on ontology, especially the principle of equality, to make the determination of rules and practices that ought to be good for everyone. Thus the principle that all human beings are equal in their humanness is by character ontological-ethical. As Leslie Lipson argues, 'Equality, even more than liberty, is the most revolutionary of political symbols. Whoever harnesses its power can shake and change the world.'[26]

Tracing the history of 'all men are equal' with particular reference to the United States of America, Lipson notes, appositely, that: 'The concept of humanity does not admit of degree. As men, all are equal'.[27] Applying this to the spheres of economic and social relations, he argues that: 'Equality is [...] indivisible. You cannot have it anywhere unless you achieve it everywhere. Juridical equality of rights [...] will have little practical effect if incomes are distributed unequally, since money is the key which unlocks many doors.'[28] The structural, systemic and systematic sustenance of the unequal distribution of incomes is the basis for agitation and tension between those with ethically questionable, disproportionately larger wealth and incomes than the majority. Unless this condition is addressed at its root, stability and peace shall be maintained only by resorting to coercive force.

2.5. All human beings belong to one family

Contemporary science, especially in the sphere of genetics, tends to reaffirm the view that all human beings are a oneness belonging to one family, a family together with other living organisms or entities.

2.6. Africa is the cradle of humanity

To recognise that Africa is the cradle of humanity ought to encourage and nurture our oneness as human beings. It is a matter of science that language has the potential to bring us closer as sisters and brothers born of Mother Africa, but this potential ought to be welcome as an ethical appeal to embrace one another as brothers and sisters. That we are one in the blood is proven daily by medical science and sex, 'the sting of desire' that humbles even the high and mighty and exposes hypocrites who preach the ontological defectiveness of one segment of humanity. DNA research reaffirms the oneness of human beings as members of one family. Philosophically, humanness is a oneness in which each and every human being has the contingent but equal right to exist and to reason and to live the life worthy of only any other human being.[29] Our failure to take these verities seriously speaks to our very weak claim to wisdom and civilisation.[30] Such a failure turns us into patients suffering from megalomania, the virtually incurable disease of the blind ambitious dogmatist. Is this failure perhaps based on Pascal's observation – cited by Alan Sheridan – that, 'Men are so necessarily mad, that not to be mad would amount to another form of madness'?[31]

---

[26] L Lipson *The Great Issue of Politics* (1970) 121.
[27] Ibid 123.
[28] Ibid 143.
[29] G Gutierrez *The Power of the Poor in History* (1983) (trans RR Barr, 1992) 101.
[30] N Maxwell 'Can humanity learn to become civilized? The crisis of science without civilization' (2000) 17 *Journal of Applied Philosophy* 31.
[31] A Sheridan *Michel Foucault: The Will to Truth* (1980) 13.

We will proceed by way of drawing from this background in two directions. First we will appear to argue against it. This is because culturally entrenched ideas and fixation to specific religions and political ideologies have to a very large extent substituted the elements enumerated in the background. The substitution is such a powerful superimposition that it has acquired the status of virtually the only reality. It is certainly the dominant reality. Our argument against the background provided is intended to challenge this dominant reality in order to reawaken it to the basic elements of the background. Proceeding in this way is for us a method of submitting that the basic elements of the background ought to be restored as the foundation of discourses about the truth of being a human being and of building upon that truth a just and peaceful society.

3. History and colonisation

Leo Marquard submits that, '[T]he process of colonisation is as old as recorded history.'[32] He then proceeds to give examples in history going back even as far as the Roman Empire. It is interesting that he does not bring to bear an ethical critique – specifically in terms of the Discovery doctrine and the just war doctrine – on the various experiences of colonisation. This is rather odd, because his solid claim that, 'Modern colonisation reproduced many of the features of earlier colonisation'[33] brings him very close to posing ethical questions. For example, he identifies the following as some of the features of colonisation: 'the conquest, by superior skill and weapons, of the original inhabitants; the annexation and alienation of their land; and the exploitation of their labour, either as slave or as low-paid native labour'.[34]

Three ethical questions arise with regard to each of the three features of colonisation Marquard identifies. The first question is: what was the reason or reasons for waging war resulting in the 'conquest […] of the original inhabitants'? Since, according to Carl von Clausewitz, war is the continuation of politics in the form of a violent 'duel',[35] it is indeed plain that Marquard distinguishes implicitly between the conqueror and the conquered. In the case of South Africa, it is the alien conqueror that conquered the 'original inhabitants'. The second question is: by what right did the conqueror annexe and alienate the land from the 'original inhabitants', thereby acquiring sovereign title to it and the conquered? According to the legal philosophy of the conqueror, the basis for the acquisition is the so-called right of conquest. It is claimed that by virtue of this ethically questionable right, the conqueror may even interfere with the religion and culture of the conquered by determining what may or may not be retained.[36] This is the specific dimension of epistemic injustice. The third question is: by what right did the conqueror enrich themselves through the acquisition and accumulation of wealth by exploiting the labour of the conquered turned into 'slaves or […] low-paid native labour'? This is the case against unjust enrichment. According to the legal philosophy of the conqueror, unjust enrichment is not permitted, and there must be a remedy for it. However, the ethically untenable 'right of conquest', deeply embedded in the Discovery doctrine, permits unjust enrichment and precludes the

[32] L Marquard *South Africa's Colonial Policy* (1957) 1.
[33] Ibid 2.
[34] Ibid 2–3.
[35] C von Clausewitz *On War* (1832) (trans ME Howard & P Paret, 1976) 75.
[36] JP Verloren van Themaat & M Wiechers *Staatsreg* (1967) 49.

provision of any remedy only in the case of the conquered peoples. These observations on the just war doctrine must be placed within the context of the doctrine of Discovery before we deal with them in detail. It is to this doctrine that we now turn.

4. The doctrine of Discovery or the international law of colonialism

The doctrine of Discovery belongs to the historical period of papal government. It was held in the Middle Ages that the Petrine Commission, found in the christian[37] Bible, Matt: XVI, 18-19, conferred upon Peter-pope the authority to rule the world. The authority is derived from the divine authority of Christ, the second Person of a triune godhead. The words, 'I will give you the keys of heaven' had the effect that that which Peter-pope laid down as the binding law on earth shall also be bound in heaven and, that which he allowed on earth shall also be allowed in heaven. Accordingly, Peter-pope had the divine authority to rule both in heaven and on earth.[38] On the basis of the belief that the 'God' of Jesus Christ is the 'God' of all human beings on earth, Peter-pope or his successors in title would be vested with the same divine authority having the mandate to convert all human beings to christianity. The papal claim to earthly authority did not go unchallenged at the time.[39] It was strengthened by the teaching that the Pope may not be judged by any earthly ruler, since no such ruler has placed him in the position of Pope (*Papa a nemine judicatur*). Only Christ could judge the Pope, since it was Christ who installed the papacy. This licence to tyranny by appeal to divinity intensified the struggle for power between the papacy and earthly rulers (*sacerdotium* and *regnum*). It culminated[40] in the emergence of the modern state in Western Europe under the 1648 Treaty of Westphalia.[41]

It was believed, but not without controversy in the past,[42] that Peter-pope as the vicar of Christ on earth could not err – was infallible – with regard to his teaching on faith and morals. The doctrine of the infallibility of the Pope continues to be questioned even in our time.[43] The understanding that the Pope held the keys of heaven was strengthened by the teaching that 'there was no salvation outside of the church of Christ'. The practical effect of this was that everyone either belonged or would be compelled to belong to the *Res Publica Romanorum.*[44] Hence earthly kings could be kings proper only through the sanction of the Pope – 'the divine right of kings'. The Popes exercised this right in granting the kings of Spain, Portugal, France and England[45] mandate to undertake the voyages of Discovery in countries other than their own. Holland also laid claim to the doctrine of Discovery in its conquest of peoples outside the sphere of Europe.[46] Miller provides ten interrelated elements

---

[37] We take the view, following Wole Soyinka, that to privilege some 'gods' or 'religions' with the use of the capital letter but deny the same to other gods and religions is an injustice based upon a questionable claim to superiority. Accordingly, we write christianity or any other religion with the small letter. W Soyinka *The Burden of Memory, the Muse of Forgiveness* (1999) 32.

[38] W Ullman *The Papacy and Political Ideas in the Middle Ages* (1976).

[39] W Ullman *The Church and the Law in the Middle Ages* (1975).

[40] W Ullman *Juristic Obstacles to the Concept of State in the Middle Ages* (1969).

[41] F Parkinson *The Philosophy of International Relations: A Study in the History of Thought* (1977).

[42] E Gilson *History of christian Philosophy in the Middle Ages* (1955).

[43] H Kung *Infallible? An Inquiry* (1983).

[44] W Ullman *The Growth of Papal Government in the Middle Ages* (1955); RW Carlyle & AJ Carlyle *A History of Medieval Political Theory in the West* vol 1 (1962); CH McIlwain *The Growth of Political Thought in the West* (1932).

[45] RJ Miller 'The international law of colonialism: a comparative analysis' (2011) 15 *Lewis & Clark Law Review* 847, 862.

of the doctrine of Discovery, namely (1) first discovery, (2) actual occupation and current possession, (3) pre-emption/European title, (4) native title, (5) indigenous limited sovereign and commercial rights, (6) contiguity, (7) *terra nullius*, (8) christianity, (9) civilisation and (10) conquest. We will focus upon most of these elements in our discussion of the ethical-political and juridical problem of conqueror South Africa to date. Miller submits correctly that, '[T]he Doctrine provided that Europeans automatically acquired property rights in native lands and gained governmental, political, and commercial rights over the Indigenous inhabitants without their knowledge or consent.'[47] This is a succinct statement on the ethically untenable and politically and legally questionable 'right of conquest' claimed by the European conqueror.

Conquest, in the context of our discussion, happens in war. For this reason we turn to a discussion of the meaning of war.

5. The meaning of war

Clausewitz does not consider 'a theory' of war as a doctrine but rather as a study, because actual war might render rigid adherence to theory useless during the actual conduct of war.[48] He also distinguishes between 'real' and 'absolute' war. The former is the pursuit of war, somewhat contrary to its logic, by having regard to its political aim,[49] whereas the latter is 'an ideal in the philosophical sense, as a regulative idea which gives unity and objectivity to very varied phenomena; an idea like that of perfect beauty in art which may never be attained but constantly approximated'.[50] It is pertinent to observe that in our time, the strategic nuclear weapons that are a present and living threat of omnicide – 'a suicide pact'[51] between Russia and the United States of America – contradict and abolish Clausewitz' concept of 'absolute war'. Paradoxically, these weapons do, at the same time, reaffirm Clausewitz' exposition of the logic and method of war.

According to Clausewitz, there is an inextricable connection between war and 'politics'.[52] This opens the way for the understanding of war as the continuation of politics by resorting to armed force. It is precisely this resorting to armed force that Clausewitz clarifies in order to identify the logic and method of war. Understanding the connection between war and politics, Clausewitz defines war as:

> nothing but a duel on a larger scale [...] War is thus an act of force to compel our enemy to do our will. Force, to counter opposing force, equips itself with the inventions of art and science. Attached to force are certain self-imposed, imperceptible limitations [...] known as international law and custom, but they scarcely weaken it. Force – that is, physical force, for moral force has no existence save as expressed in the state and law – is thus the means of war; to impose our will on the enemy is its object [...] war is an act of force and there is no logical limit to the application of that force. Each side,

[46] Ibid 861.

---

[47] Ibid 849.
[48] Clausewitz (note 35 above) 141, 147.
[49] WB Gallie *Philosophers of War and Peace* (1978) 56–57.
[50] EM Earle (ed) *Makers of Modern Strategy: Military Thought from Machiavelli to Hitler* (1971) 102.
[51] J Schell *The Gift of Time: The Case for Abolishing Nuclear Weapons Now* (1998) 11
[52] Clausewitz (note 35 above) 605.

therefore, compels its opponent to follow suit; a reciprocal action is started which must lead, in theory, to extremes.[53]

The pursuit of the 'extreme' is the logic of war, and its method is the application of physical force with the aim of compelling the opponent to submit to the will of the belligerents.

Although war is the continuation of politics by violent means, it does not follow that every war is just. What then is a just war? The next section is a short answer to this question.

6. The just war doctrine

Perhaps Thomas Aquinas' exposition of the just war doctrine is a good link[54] between what went before him on this subject and what has come after him to date.[55] The doctrine consists of two interrelated divisions, namely *jus ad bellum* (the grounds permitting the waging of war) and *jus in bello* (the rules of conduct during war). The major premise of the first-mentioned category is that all peaceful means to resolve a political conflict ought to have been exhausted before the decision to wage war is taken. Also, the decision ought to be taken with the right intention (*intentio recta*). This means that the purpose of the war must be related to its cause. Following from these premises then, '[O]nly the sovereign may declare war,' according to Aquinas. Subsequent history has called this rule into question.[56] The sovereign may declare war in order to: (1) gain vindication against an offence, for example, injury to honour; (2) repel an injury, either already inflicted or as an imminent and real threat; and, (3) recover that which was taken away (*ad repetendas res*): this is also known as the principle of recoverability. War that does not meet any one of these criteria is unjust; it is ethically impermissible.

Our reflection will focus on both the principle of the repulsion of an injury and that of recoverability with particular reference to the fundamental ethical, political and legal problem in South Africa since colonisation. The *jus in bello* aspects, such as the principle of non-combatant immunity, will emerge as part of our discussion of the fundamental problem: *ad repetendas res* the land question or title to territory in South Africa.

7. Colonisation and the ethical problem of *ad repetendas res* in South Africa

Under the doctrine of Discovery, the papacy emphasised, in particular, the need to pursue the mandate 'to go and teach all the world', converting everyone to christianity. However, the papacy did not totally exclude the economic motive.[57] The kings and queens of Europe, including England, emphasised the pursuit of the economic motive for the sake of making profit. Both these motives were inextricably connected

---

[53] Ibid 75, 77.
[54] MB Ramose 'Only the sovereign may declare war and NATO as well' (2000) 38 *Studia Moralia* 197, 200.
[55] Aquinas (note 7 above).
[56] Ramose (note 54 above) 203–207.
[57] L Bethell (ed) *The Independence of Latin America* (1987).

to the entire colonial undertaking. Thus colonisation may be seen as the ethically unjustified waging of war in the name of 'God' for the sake of making economic profit. In this frame of mind, the colonised, being the peoples conquered in the unjust wars of colonisation, had only one right, namely, to submit or die.[58]

In light of the foregoing paragraph, the doctrine of Discovery:

> was specifically developed to control European actions and conflicts regarding exploration, trade, and colonization of non-European countries, and it was used to justify domination of non-Christian, non-European peoples […] Europeans rationalized that the Discovery Doctrine was permitted under the authority of the Christian God, and the ethnocentric idea that Europeans had the right to claim the lands-as well as the sovereign and commercial rights-of the Indigenous peoples around the world.[59]

With particular reference to Africa, it is pertinent to remember that the papal bull *Romanus Pontifex* was issued 'several times […] In 1455, Pope Nicholas V granted Portugal title to the lands of Indigenous peoples in Africa that Portugal had "acquired and that shall hereafter be acquired" and authorised Portugal "to invade, search out, capture, vanquish, and subdue all Saracens and pagans" and place them into perpetual slavery and to seise all their property.'[60] Valentin-Yves Mudimbe corroborates this.[61] The preceding is the unethical-historical context within which South Africa was colonised. We turn now specifically to the Dutch, the founders of the ethically questionable 'right of conquest' in South Africa.

8. The Dutch colonisation of South Africa

It is important to remember that, '[I]n 1621, the Dutch West India Company was created with the specific goal of occupying and exploiting Brazil.'[62] There is no reason to surmise that the Dutch East India Company had a dissimilar motive. It was the vehicle that landed Jan van Riebeeck on the shores of a land named arbitrarily – in a veritable disregard for the original indigenous peoples, owners of the land living in it from time immemorial – South Africa. It is necessary to make the obvious point that the Dutch did not download from their ship a cargo of land the size of South Africa when they landed in the Cape of Good Hope in 1652. They carried no land in their ship from Holland to South Africa. Yet, Van Riebeeck, a member of the crew, had the courage to have the following conversation with the indigenous peoples of the land:

> The Khoikhoi sued for peace, and tried to regain rights to their pastures, 'standing upon it that we [the Dutch] had gradually been taking more and more of their land, which had been theirs since the beginning of time […] Asking also, whether, if they came to Holland, they would be permitted to do the like.' The Commander argued that if their lands were restored there would not be enough grazing for both nations. The Khoikhoi replied 'Have we then no cause to prevent you from getting more cattle? The more you

58 RA Williams *The American Indian in Western Legal Thought: The Discourses of Conquest* (1990).
59 Miller (note 45 above) 854.
60 Ibid 857–858.
61 V-Y Mudimbe 'African gnosis, philosophy and the order of knowledge: an introduction' (1985) 28 *African Studies Review* 151–153.
62 Miller (note 45 above) 864.

> have the more lands you occupy. And to say the land is not big enough for both, who should give way, the rightful owner or the foreign invader?' Van Riebeeck made it clear 'that they had now lost the land in war and therefore could only expect to be henceforth deprived of it […] The country had thus fallen to out lot, being justly won in defensive warfare and […] it was our intention to retain it.[63]

It is ethically significant that it is the Khoikhoi people and not the Dutch who 'sued for peace'. The Dutch appear not to have made any effort to exhaust all peaceful means to resolve their conflict with the Khoikhoi before deciding to wage war against them. This is contrary to the just-war principle stated above. The Khoikhoi put it to Van Riebeeck that he had injured their right to the ownership of the land from time immemorial. Without having known the doctrine of Discovery, the Khoikhoi were challenging its element of *terra nullius*. 'This element stated that lands that were possessed by no one, or which were occupied but not being used in a manner European legal systems recognised, were empty and available for European Discovery claims. England, Holland, France, and the United States relied on this element at different times to claim that lands actually occupied and used by Indigenous nations were legally vacant or *terra nullius*, and open for appropriation.'[64]

The injustice, as well as the absurdity of the terra nullius element, is illustrated thus: 'Cook made *terra nullius* claims in Australia and Alaska even though he encountered native peoples in both places. In fact, even though Aboriginals were hostile to his presence, he claimed the land as if it were empty.'[65] In the light of this, the Khoikhoi were entitled to repel the injury Van Riebeeck inflicted upon them. The core ethical argument of the Khoikhoi is that a right does not arise out of an injury – *ex injuria jus non oritur*. They went further to make the point that it is Van Riebeeck, 'the foreign invader', who ought to 'give way' and by so doing concede the return of the land to its 'rightful owner'. This is a submission that is consistent with the just-war principle of recoverability – *ad repetendas res*.

In reply to the Khoikhoi submissions contained in the preceding paragraph, Van Riebeeck claimed that the Khoikhoi lost their land and sovereignty over it as a result of their defeat at 'war': a war he waged even though he seems to have been least concerned about whether or not the war was declared by his sovereign. To the extent that this is the case, it goes against principle (1) as stated above. Furthermore, apart from the fact that Van Riebeeck grounds his reason for war on the need for the land of another, he does not argue on the basis of a manifest and solid right to the land that he claims to own by virtue of conquest. Since the conquest is devoid of both the *intentio recta* (the right intention) and the *justa causa* (the right or justified cause), Van Riebeeck's claim to ownership of the land is ethically untenable, politically vacuous and legally empty. His claim is undoubtedly consistent with the element of conquest in the doctrine of Discovery. Accordingly, it is justified for the Khoikhoi and all the other peoples of South Africa conquered in the unjust wars of colonisation to invoke the just-war principle of *ad repetendas res* as the fundamental ethical reason for the continuing struggle for freedom in the enduring conqueror South Africa.

63 F Troup *South Africa: An Historical Introduction* (1975) 53.
64 Miller (note 45 above) 864, 900.
65 Ibid 902.

Contrary to Van Riebeeck, the country was unjustly 'won' in invasive, indeed aggressive, and not 'defensive warfare'.

Just like the English, the Spanish, the Portuguese and the French, the Dutch also appealed either implicitly or explicitly to the element of 'civilisation' under the doctrine of Discovery. The presumption underlying this element is the claim to superiority by these countries with regard to the conquered or yet-to-be conquered. According to the presumption, '[T]heir governments, cultures, and civilisations were superior to those of Indigenous peoples and justified their conquest and domination. These colonising countries and their settler societies shared similar ethnocentric and racial viewpoints and viewed native peoples as lower-class humans who needed the paternalistic care and direction of European societies.'[66] This is a statement on the putative right to epistemicide by the colonial conqueror. It is such because the aim of 'civilisation' was, and continues to be, 'the eradication of native civilisations and cultures'[67] through, for example, the imposition of the language of the conqueror as the 'official language'. The statement also identifies racism as the foundation of conquest and domination by the colonising Europeans. We submit that all the conqueror constitutions of South Africa, including the 1996 constitution, are based firmly on the epistemological paradigm of the conqueror. On this basis, the 'customary law', otherwise the law of the peoples of the land, is subordinated to the constitution. The dominance of this paradigm, exemplified by the total exclusion of ubuntu from the constitution,[68] speaks to continuing epistemicide feeding on delusory racial superiority. It is ethically imperative to recognise by deeds that epistemic justice is an indispensable complement of social justice. There cannot be social justice without epistemic justice.

Davidson compares violent conquest under the Songhai empire with violent conquest under colonisation thus:

> When the Songhay empire fell it was seen that all its constituent peoples had conserved their cultural identity, their command of their local economies, their sense of community and the subjectivities of self-confidence which these gave. They were able to continue with the development of their own history. The violence of the colonial system was of a different nature, not only for its scale and ruthlessness, but also, and still more tellingly, in its demand that constituent peoples should lose their own history. Communities should be severed from their roots and die, not because their cattle or other goods were seized by raiding neighbours, but because their land and even themselves were to pass into permanent possession of the colonising power and its settlers.[69]

Van Riebeeck's vow that it was the intention of the Dutch to retain the country is more than echoed, indeed reaffirmed, 309 years later in the preamble to the 1961 constitution.[70] The preamble is the assertion of the divine gift of land, a way of thinking consistent with the doctrine of Discovery. As such, it is a complement to the 'divine right of kings', a fossil buried in the arid soil of the history in which it was

---

[66] Ibid 908.
[67] Ibid 909.
[68] MB Ramose 'I conquer, therefore I am the sovereign: reflections upon sovereignty, constitutionalism and democracy in Zimbabwe and South Africa' in PH Coetzee & APJ Roux (eds) *The African Philosophy Reader* (2003) 571.
[69] Davidson (note 20 above) 41
[70] Constitution of the Republic of South Africa, Act 32 of 1961 (1961 constitution).

originally born. Article 4 of Act 32 provides that *Die Stem van Suid-Afrika* shall be the national anthem. The refrain of the national anthem, '[...] *ons sal sterwe - ons vir jou Suid-Afrika*' ('[...] we shall die - we for you South Africa') is the reaffirmation of the vow of Van Riebeeck: a claim to territory acquired against the principles of the just-war doctrine. It is the vow of *pro patria mori*, dying for the fatherland. It is a fitting complement - in terms of the element of christianisation in the doctrine of Discovery - to a much earlier christian war song, namely the *Laudes Regiae* with its text: *Christus vincit, Christus regnat, Christus, Christus imperat; ab omni malo plenem suam defendat* (Christ conquers, Christ reigns, Christ, Christ commands; may he defend his people from evil). Do the other conqueror ethnic groups in South Africa, like the English, also sing *Die Stem*?[71]

It is significant that the verbs in *Laudes Regiae* are in the present tense. They are unlike the verbs in the past tense in Caesar's famous '*veni, vidi, vici*' ('I came, I saw, I conquered'). These describe Caesar's act as done and completed. But the present tense in *Laudes Regiae* underlines the point that the action is ongoing, even in our time. The war for the christianisation of souls is on, and thus the doctrine of Discovery is kept alive in our time. Even before the ones who choose to live against the Ten Commandments are doomed to eternal perdition, others are already being doomed with insecticides in liturgical celebration of the 'God' of Jesus Christ. In the Catholic hymnal *Lifela tsa Bakriste, Laudes Regiae* is known as *Ahe! Ahe! Kriste Morena* (Ahe! Ahe! Christ King).

9. The significance of the colonisation of South Africa

The Anglo-Boer war[72] is testimony that different conquerors fought between themselves in pursuit of contending elements of the doctrine of Discovery. Their wars raged as if the indigenous peoples, conquered in the unjust wars of colonisation, simply did not exist, except as the means to attain wealth in a country that was never their own. Their common purpose to christianise and to civilise remained unshaken by the wars between them. Their shared epistemological paradigm in the name of the doctrine of Discovery continues to be their weapon against the indigenous peoples conquered in the unjust wars of colonisation. Understanding the preceding section from this perspective means that our core argument is against unethical constitution making.

The his-story of constitutionalism in conqueror South Africa reinforces our argument. We are not against constitution making. Rather, we are against the surreptitious imposition of a constitution being the reaffirmation of the elements of the doctrine of Discovery. Yilma Makonnen shows that the his-story of the political independence of Africa is a reaffirmation of the elements of the doctrine of Discovery,

---

[71] MB Ramose 'The philosophy of the Anglo-Boer War' in I Snyman, I Liebenberg, G van der Westhuizen & M Roos (eds) *A Century is a Short Time: New Perspectives on the Anglo-Boer War* (2005).

[72] One of the main features of the wars of the colonial conquerors, such as the Anglo-Boer war, is that the conquerors contravened the democratic principle that 'what touches everyone must be approved by all' by compelling the voiceless indigenous peoples to be part of wars that were deliberated in total disregard of their voice. I use the lowercase 'w' for Anglo-Boer war in order to contest the unethical contravention of the democratic principle of *Quod omnes tangit ab omnibus approbetur*.

especially the protection of unjustly acquired economic power and its associated wealth.[73] The inherent injustice of this doctrine renders the constitution as its outcome ethically unacceptable. For us, genuine and ethical constitution-making predicated on the principle of justice for all or for none – *fiat justiam ruart coelum* – is an indispensable starting point in entering into a transformative dialogue[74] for a new constitution arising from 'our story', a story reflective of the experiences of both the conquered and the conqueror synthesised into the constitution as the mirror reflecting the images of all: '*quod tangit omnes ab omnibus approbetur*' ('Let all approve what touches all').[75] Such will be the constitution of a post-conquest[76] country not necessarily to be named in the precise geographical term South Africa. The name is a geographic designation that is ethically hollow.

On the basis of the above reflections, it is preposterous blindness to history to claim that the 'secret talks' held before the 'negotiations' for the 'new' South Africa were not 'between 'conqueror' and 'conquered' but between parties who accepted that no solution was possible unless it was reached between equals;[77] yet, Niël Barnard, who headed up the South African National Intelligence Service in the 1980s, affirms the his-story of conqueror South Africa thus: 'Perhaps my mother's remark to me in my childhood years that English was the "language of the conqueror" had something to do with my refusal to speak it […] At Kakamas, where my mother grew up, the people harboured bitter memories of the Anglo-Boer War. Their teachers taught, "You do not speak English. It is the language of the conqueror."'[78] Barnard also refers to a letter from PW Botha, then South African state president, for the attention of Margaret Thatcher, the British prime minister at the time, in which Botha objects in the strongest possible way to the undermining of Afrikaners by 'our former conquerors'.[79] Barnard evidently accepts the categories of 'conqueror' and 'conquer' only if they are applied to the his-story of conqueror South Africa. He denies the validity and relevance of these categories when it comes to the relations between the indigenous peoples conquered in the unjust wars of colonisation and the conquerors who based their right to conquest on the doctrine of Discovery.

He states the following, 'Like all scientists, researchers in the world of espionage must have an open and honourable intellectual disposition. He or she must be open enough to be convinced by new facts […] and must allow himself or herself to be led by sober truth and not by hot-blooded arguments.'[80] It is not sure how much of this can be found in the author's refusal to concede that the categories of conquered and conqueror do apply to the indigenous peoples of South Africa conquered in the unjust wars of colonisation.

[73] Y Makonnen *International Law and the New States of Africa* (1983).
[74] P Healy 'Rethinking deliberative democracy: from deliberative discourse to transformative dialogue' (2011) 37 *Philosophy & Social Criticism* 295.
[75] Lipson (note 26 above) 121.
[76] MB Ramose 'In memoriam: sovereignty and the "new" South Africa' (2007) 16 *Griffith Law Review* 310, 323.
[77] N Barnard (as told to K Wiese) *Secret Revolution: Memoirs of a Spy Boss* (2015).
[78] Ibid 22–24.
[79] Ibid 95.
[80] Ibid 62.

10. Conclusions

We are aware that the ethical imperative to pursue the birth of a post-conquest constitution for the country will have repercussions in the sphere of international politics. The journey to the 1996 constitution testifies to this. According to Sampie Terreblanche:

> The 'great prize' for the ANC political elite at the secret negotiations was that they, and they alone, would be declared previously disadvantaged individuals […] who would qualify to become political representatives with lucrative salaries or would become beneficiaries of BEE and AA contracts […] While the ANC operated on the moral high ground during the struggle, since 1994 they have slipped into a sleazy underworld where corruption, nepotism and money squandering are the order of the day […] The 'great prize' to which the American pressure groups that participated at the secret negotiations aspired was to convince the ANC to accept the ideologies of neoliberal globalism and market fundamentalism, so that South Africa could become a neocolonial satellite of the American-led neoliberal empire.[81]

Prescription is unknown in African legal philosophy. For us, '*molato ga o bole*' (seSotho), '*Ondjo kai uoro*' (Herero), '*Mhosva haiori*' (Shona) and '*Ityala ali boli*' (isiNguni). Accordingly, a post-conquest constitution is an ethical imperative to be pursued until it is realised. On this reasoning, the contemporary discourse on 'expropriation without compensation'[82] is reminiscent of the doctrine of Discovery, but it is certainly a far cry from the fundamental ethical problem, namely, the unresolved question of the land question, that is, sovereign title to territory. Captivity to a constitution that is not one's own is no substitute to the ethical imperative to invoke the just war principle of *ad repetendas res.*

Disclosure statement

No potential conflict of interest was reported by the author.

---

[81] S Terreblanche *Lost in Transformation: South Africa's Search for a New Future since 1986* (2012) 73.
[82] Parliament of the Republic of South Africa: National Assembly Order Paper No 3 (2018) Fifth Session.

Decolonising equality: the radical roots of the gender equality clause in the South African constitution

Shireen Hassim

ABSTRACT

South Africa has taken centre stage in most accounts of the synergistic potential of law and politics: it is seen to be a case which demonstrates that human rights can be made real, with the favourable combination of institutional and political conditions. Among these conditions, from a feminist perspective, are the inclusion of equality and socio-economic rights in the Constitution, high levels of representation of women in parliament and the bureaucracy, and a strong and free civil society. The country is often invoked, in comparative social science, as an example of a democratic and relatively peaceful transition from authoritarianism, in which the breakdown of institutions was avoided; rather, it is seen as an example of successful institutional redirection from supporting an authoritarian state to advancing a democratic project. However, the Constitution is coming under increasing attack. It is not only conservative forces that seek to undermine rights in the name of culture, or wealthy elites concerned about defending their rights to property through rule of law and opposing high taxation, that are critical. It is also challenged by radical voices that aim at creating a society free of oppression. For the latter actors, the Constitution is less a tool of change and more an example of coloniality, or the imposition of a Western discourse on Africa. These arguments about decolonising political projects require more careful engagement, as the project of decoloniality is one that is in many respects allied to the project of feminism, whose own history required the disabling of the invisibilised male norm on which much legal and political theory was founded. This paper addresses the decolonial critique by showing the radical roots of the equality clause in a century-long history of struggles by black women.

[1] PJ Williams *The Alchemy of Rights and Law* (1991) 159.

Rights are to law what conscious commitments are to the psyche. This country's worst historical moments have not been attributable to rights assertion but to a failure of rights commitment. From this perspective, the problem with rights discourse is not that the discourse is itself constricting but that it exists in a constricted referential universe.

Patricia Williams[1]

1. Introduction

It is a curious fact that a country that is considered an international landmark for its entrenchment of far-reaching human rights is also one in which rights discourses come under the fiercest critiques. The much-lauded Constitution of the Republic of South Africa, 1996 is increasingly attacked from the obvious as well as unexpected sources. The critical voices are not only conservative forces that seek to undermine rights in the name of preserving culture, or wealthy elites concerned about defending their rights to property through rule of law, or to privatisation of their wealth by opposing high taxation. The Constitution is also challenged by radical voices that aim at creating a society free of oppression based on wealth and status. To be sure, the scepticism about the constitutional route to democracy was present throughout the debates in the early 1990s. The Marxist left, for example, was wary of the ideological effects of rights discourses, seeing these as a chimaera that distracted popular forces from the class interests that shaped relations in society.[2] They are joined, more recently, by a new left turn to decoloniality as the conceptual frame in which to located relations of power. For these actors, the Constitution is less a tool of change and more an example of coloniality, or the imposition of a Western discourse on Africa. These arguments about decolonising political projects require careful engagement, as they impact on the legitimacy of the Constitution. Furthermore, the project of decoloniality is one that is allied in key aspects to the project of feminism, whose own history required the disabling of the invisibilised Western male norm on which much legal and political theory was founded.[3]

This article addresses the decolonial critique directly. I argue that it is ahistorical to claim that rights were imposed on to South Africans, or crafted only in a Western idiom and therefore inextricable from the condition of coloniality. Rather, rights discourses have been present in South African political mobilisation for most of the twentieth century, and the equality clause in the Constitution is a product, albeit imperfect, of a century-long history of struggles by black women, sometimes in concert with other oppressed social groupings, and sometimes in tension with them.[4]

1 PJ Williams *The Alchemy of Rights and Law* (1991) 159.

2 Some segments of this old left nevertheless used the socio-economic rights embodied in the Constitution as a strategic lever to push for the redistribution of resources to healthcare and education. Their work is evident in non-governmental organisations (NGOs) and social movements including the Treatment Action Campaign, Equal Education, SERI and Section 27.

3 Feminism, as it is articulated in some places and some periods, has been dominated by the centring of the lives of white women as the normative basis of theorising. See GC Spivak 'Can the subaltern speak?' in P Williams & L Chrisman (eds) *Colonial Discourse and Post-Colonial Theory: A Reader* (1993) 66; CT Mohanty 'Under western eyes' (1984) 12 Boundary 2 338.

4 It is a product of other struggles of black people too, but this article is concerned specifically with the aspect of the clauses regarding equality between genders and to sexual rights.

I argue that the Constitution is the product of a locally defined struggle rather than one that was imposed from outside, or above. I draw very extensively on the history of women's organisations to suggest there are documentary precursors to the Constitution that are products of the everyday struggles of people. The radical past, I argue, offers a way to think about a radical future, and the Constitution could be the ally to that process rather than an obstacle. My starting point is not legal theory, or philosophical exegesis about the concept of equality, but the history of women's struggles for equality. I take lives, and collective struggles, seriously as the basis of theorising. By this I mean that in their messy and complicated attempts to make lives of worth, people also articulate visions for the future. These imaginings are no less important for constitutional framers than those of philosophers, legal theoreticians, or political leaders. The political struggles outlined below were processes of collective making of meaning as well as of identities, both constituted in processes of mobilisation. From this starting point, it follows that the definitions and content of equality are shaped in the processes of struggle between contesting forces under particular, always-constrained circumstances – an agonistic struggle, between unequal combatants, incomplete and certainly unresolved but nevertheless responded to in the Constitution.

2. Background

There are good reasons to treat law, the Constitution and human rights discourses with a large dose of healthy theoretical scepticism. First, the colonial and apartheid state in South Africa was constructed *through* the law. The effect, as Martin Chanock points out, is that 'law was a weapon in the hands of the state rather than a defence against it'.[5] Legalism was central to the ways in which white rule defined itself as superior to indigenous systems of governance: 'The image of legalism, its justice, discernment and restraint, is a counterpoint of the opposing image of savagery, impulse and transgression'.[6] As Heinz Klug[7] has shown, to redeem law from this history of racist and masculinist social control, law had to be legitimised as part of the larger political project of transformation. That is an ongoing political project, in which the terms of legitimacy have to be carefully spelt out, so as not to fall into the reification of law. There are affinities with the formulation of Ricardo Sanin-Restrepo[8] that constitutions are encrypted documents: they can conceal the foundations and workings of power in the language of liberal neutrality and in depoliticised techno-legal language. The effect is to render the actual processes, subjects and agents of democracy invisible. In this context, however, careful historical research has considerable value in rendering processes, agents and subjects visible.

Second, African feminists, perhaps more than any other group of public intellectuals on the continent, have had to grapple with the question of whether the law can express the desires of vulnerable groups, and not just those of the most powerful. Returning to Chanock's work again, it is apparent that the elaboration of colonial law

[5] M Chanock *The Making of South African Legal Culture 1902–1936: Fear, Favour and Prejudice* (2001) 23.
[6] Ibid 127–8.
[7] H Klug *The Constitution of South Africa: A Contextual Analysis* (2010).
[8] R Sanin-Restrepo *Decolonizing Democracy: Power in a Solid State* (2016).

was based on a selective understanding of custom by male colonial officials, at times with the support of male traditional leaders.[9] Belinda Bozzoli[10] described this as process of patriarchal collusion, the effect of which was to create a 'patchwork quilt of patriarchies'. In formal terms, the result was a plural legal system in which black women and black men – not just black people and white people – were differently located in relation to state and legal power, and some categories of people such as those who did not conform to the binary terms of heterosexual norms, were completely excluded. As Farida Banda has argued, plural legal systems had the potential to 'disadvantage women who may be caught in a pincer movement when two or more legal systems collide'.[11] This reality shaped black women's political responses to the manner in which legal controls on their fertility, mobility and rights in families were elaborated. This was true across the African continent, and it produced popular campaigns ranging from struggles for land rights[12] to protections in customary marriages in Zimbabwe,[13] to rights over children.[14] The political campaigns drew increasingly on feminist legal scholarship, which developed apace in the latter decades of the twentieth century. It also relied on a variety of NGOs that produced research and educational materials as well as litigation strategies for women's groups. These included regional organisations such as Women and Law in Southern Africa (WLSA), formed in 1989 and with affiliates in six southern African countries.[15] In South Africa, we may cite several university-based groups such as the Gender Rights Project in the Centre for Applied Legal Studies and the Women's Legal Centre, as well as independent centres such as Tshwaranang Legal Advocacy Centre.

This thickly populated field of political struggle created the basis for forms of feminism that are particular to the conditions of postcolonial African societies. The types of questions that were raised and the methodologies used to address those questions were specific to the historical constraints and possibilities, and far from utilising Western formulaic rubrics for making legal claims, meanings were elaborated in struggle.[16] This should not be read to suggest that there was a hyper-localised approach to rights; there were women's political networks across Africa as well as globally that shared conceptual frameworks and strategies. These were invaluable to South African gender activists from the 1970s, as the impact of postcolonial independence began to be felt. Many states adopted commitments to gender for expedient reasons as Amina Mama[17] has pointed out, in order to tick the boxes for donor and aid monies. There was a wariness among women's organisations that rights discourses received lip service from the state while

---

[9] Chanock (note 5 above) 72.

[10] B Bozzoli 'Marxism, feminism and South African studies' (1983) 9 *Journal of Southern African Studies* 139.

[11] F Banda 'Women, law and human rights in Southern Africa' (2006) 32 *Journal of Southern African Studies* 15.

[12] See <http://wwwjusticeforthepoor.or.id/>; and World Bank, Annual Report. 40; A Whitehead & D Tsikata, 'Policy discourses on women's land rights in sub-Saharan Africa: the implications of the re-turn to the customary' (2003) 3 *Journal of Agrarian Change* 67.

[13] R Gaidzanwa 'Citizenship, nationality, gender, and class in southern Africa' (1993) 18 *Alternatives: Global, Local, Political* 39.

[14] LM Thomas '"The politics of the womb": Kenyan debates over the Affiliation Act' (2000) 47 *Africa Today* 151.

[15] A Armstrong 'Rethinking culture and tradition in Southern Africa: research from WLSA' in A Stewart (ed) *Gender, Law and Social Justice* (2000) 151–176.

[16] R Meena (ed) *Gender in Southern Africa: Conceptual and Theoretical Issues* (1992).

[17] A Mama 'Feminism or femocracy? State feminism and democratisation in Nigeria' (1995) 20 *Africa Development* 37.

resources to implement policies that would address the content of rights, and reduce the underlying socio-economic inequalities, were not provided. These experiences across the continent shaped South African women's organisations' responses to the debates about the nature of society after apartheid.

The extent to which feminism itself is an indigenous political discourse is the political ghost that haunts these debates. Although women and queer activists mobilised against hierarchies of gender in many colonial and postcolonial contexts, the term feminism itself was considered taboo in many African women's organisations. There were two sources of discontent with the word. The first was a simple concern about political currency. Using the word feminism was seen as unstrategic in an environment that was actively hostile to the issues being raised by women, in particular within national liberation movements.[18] As will become evident, in South Africa this was a constant internal battle between women and political organisations on the left.

The second, and arguably more profound reluctance to use the term feminism was uneasiness about being allied to a project that was seen to be rooted in Western women's movements. Some critics continue to argue that the notion of equality itself can be considered to be irredeemably colonial – that is, to be reproducing Western modes of analysis about the sources of women's oppression.[19] Some variants of decoloniality similarly dismiss the importance of rights, and by extension those feminist movements that used rights discourses, as simply not radical enough.[20] In the area of human rights, feminism has been dogged by the spectre of Western liberalism, which has appropriated women's rights as part of the rationale. As Gayatri Spivak[21] has argued, some variants of feminism that were transported by international organisations to postcolonial societies reproduced racialised hierarchies of power, operating with a notion of 'white men saving brown women from brown men'. By the 1980s, however, such hesitation began to diminish as more confidence developed about the ways in which feminist language could capture indigenous struggles against hierarchies of power across Africa and in places where there were anticolonial allies, such as Vietnam, India and Eastern Europe. Feminism's capacity to name the sources and manifestations of gender power, including when that power worked in concert with or was modified by other social stratifications, has proved enormous. As gender activists became strengthened through collective action, including in opposition to postcolonial governments, so they began to use, expand and challenge the theoretical tools of feminism.[22]

Strands of human rights discourses themselves changed, as advocates began to grapple with the limits of simple universalism.[23] The hypocritical aspects of international conventions such as the Universal Declaration of Human Rights, enacted by

[18] A Kemp, N Madlala, A Moodley & E Salo 'The dawn of a new day: redefining South African feminisms' in A Basu (ed) *The Challenge of Local Feminisms: Women's Movements in Comparative* (1995) 131–162.

[19] P Holomisa *A Double-Edged Sword: A Quest for a Place in the African Sun* (2010).

[20] N Maldonado-Torres 'On the coloniality of human rights' (2017) *Revista Critica de Ciencias Sociais* <http://journals.openedition.org/rccs/6793> 117–36; W Mignolo 'Who speaks for the "human" in human rights?' (2009) 5 *Human Rights in Latin American and Iberian Cultures* 7.

[21] Spivak (note 3 above) 93.

[22] P McFadden 'Becoming postcolonial: African women changing the meaning of citizenship' (2005) 6 *Meridians* 1.

[23] See U Baxi *The Future of Human Rights* 2 ed (1996); ME Keck & K Sikkink *Activists Beyond Borders: Advocacy Networks in International Politics* (1998); S Khagram, JW Riker & K Sikkink (eds) *Restructuring World Politics: Transnational Social Movements, Networks, and Norms* (2002); J Nedelsky *Law's Relations: A Relational Theory of Self, Autonomy, and Law* (2011).

governments that actively denied such rights to swathes of populations across the globe, no longer needs pointing out. The idea that rights could be easily imposed in a top-down fashion by international agencies or by national elites is mostly discredited. There is instead more attention to what Sally Engel Merry calls 'vernacularisation', or processes of appropriation and local adoption. As Peggy Levitt and Sally Merry[24] explain it, 'as women's human rights ideas connect with a locality, they take on some of the ideological and social attributes of the place, but also retain some of their original formulation'. However, the problem with thinking about the challenge of the South African Constitution from this perspective – that is, that what is needed to create legitimacy is to vernacularise the rights it embodies – is that it implies a post-hoc process. In this approach, rights continue to hold a universal core as defined in the Western genealogy, and vernacularisation is the political process of making rights acceptable in non-Western contexts. Levitt and Merry define vernacularisers as those people who move between contexts, translating rights in such a way that they resonate with different communities. They 'are people in between, conversant with both sides of the exchange but able to move across borders of ideas and approaches'.[25] Taking a historical approach to rights struggles, this article shows a very different process. It argues that in South Africa, rights were elaborated in a local, vernacular fashion throughout the twentieth century. Activists using rights discourses were rooted in a common struggle, and facilitated the articulation of voice and agency; this was a process of co-production of meaning, not one of translation per se.

Critical race scholar Patricia Williams has argued powerfully that the blanket critique of rights discourses is not only ahistorical, but may reflect a form of white left privilege. White scholars in the critical legal studies tradition, she suggests, have taken for granted that society recognises their humanity. She argues that this has never been the case for black people in the United States, and that rights were a powerful resource for political movements. 'The argument that rights are disutile, even harmful, trivialises this aspect of black experience specifically, as well as that of any person or group whose vulnerability has been truly protected by rights'.[26] Rather than seeing rights as an ideological fig leaf that shifts attention from structural inequalities, Williams makes a case for seeing rights as part of the very process of claiming humanity. 'For blacks […] the attainment of rights signifies the respectful behaviour, the collective responsibility, properly owed by a society to one of its own'.[27] Williams' theoretical framing shapes the article's analysis of how rights struggles have unfolded in South Africa, illuminating the radical roots of rights and challenging the notion of complicity with coloniality.

One final worry remains to which there is no clear answer: to what extent was the domain of possibilities, as imagined by collective movements, itself constrained by a language of modernity that was refracted through Western, male-dominated ideologies? This is a rather more difficult concern to counter. There is little doubt that nationalism

---

24 P Levitt & S Merry 'Vernacularization on the ground: local uses of global women's rights in Peru, China, India and the United States' (2009) 9 *Global Networks* 445.
25 Ibid 449.
26 Williams (note 1 above) 152.
27 Ibid 153.

and socialism were the two major ideologies that formed the crucible of feminist thinking in South Africa. Other radical traditions, such as black consciousness, were delegitimised, and radical Africanist-feminist activists were either marginalised or found ways to work within the dominant left discourses.[28] While the ways in which equality was elaborated in the twentieth century owed some debt to nationalism and socialism, it was not imaginatively constrained by them. This article draws on an alternative archive of the struggle for rights that is not centred on the lives and acts of men. Women's organisations addressed themselves to various cultural notions of women's place, and sought to navigate carefully the borders between all these systems of thought. In the process, they crafted meanings of equality that cannot be dismissed as reflections of Western thought, or simplistically applied conceptions of modernity as Western imago. Neither of the two large framings remained intact: they were engaged, challenged, and transformed. Nor did people live their lives in a binary fashion: urban did not automatically map on to modern, and rural was not static and traditional.

In sum, the article aims to demonstrate that the struggle for equality is deeply rooted in the complex lives of (particularly black) women, and that processes of claiming rights also entailed theorising the content of those rights. Thinking about the history of political claims-making is important if we are to conceive of South Africa, as Jean Comaroff and John Comaroff urge, 'not as simulacrum of the western rational state but in its own right'.[29] Indeed, looking at the political history of the women's movement in South Africa suggests that human rights was a language that enabled collective action and one in which the future of a better society was imagined. Rights discourses, however imperfect, were a mode of political articulation, a means of projecting a moral utopia and of asserting worth in a society in which they were rendered less than human. In this struggle, human rights were not disembodied from the actual bearers of rights, nor were rights conceived *ab initio* in the terms of Western philosophy's particular trajectories. Demands for rights can be read as rooted in the project of decolonisation, not against it. The equality clause in the Constitution, I argue, is the imperfect, partial and incomplete product of a century of struggle (at least) by ordinary people in the very real conditions of the dehumanising and exploitative conditions in racial-capitalist South Africa.

3. Whose rights archive is important?

The idea that women were equal citizens, with all the attendant rights of personhood, dignity and status, was not self-evident to the political organisations that purported to represent women. The African National Congress (ANC) had little to say on the question of the rights of women until women members began to impose their demands on the organisation. There is scant archival material on which to base specific conclusions about the idea of equality. John Tengo Jabavu, one of the founding members of the body, is recognised by the ANC as a champion of women, primarily because he supported the right of women to be educated. The world of politics was

[28] Elsewhere, I have argued that some of this repressed tradition is re-emerging productively since 2015, within the queer and feminist student community. See S Hassim *The ANC Women's League: Sex, Gender, Politics* (2014).

[29] J Comaroff & J Comaroff *Theory from the South: Or, how Euro-America is Evolving Toward Africa* (2012) 33.

male, a 'congregation of chiefs and gentleman',[30] as Cherryl Walker puts it, for whom the exclusion of black men from power was self-evidently wrong but the exclusion of women was unremarkable.

As Julia Wells[31] has shown, it was pass laws that created the spark for a new politics of gender. Passes were a form of legislative control over labour mobility, and an instrument to maintain cheap labour. Although various forms of passes had been used in the nineteenth century, the system was revived in the early twentieth century as a specific form of control of the African presence in the urban areas and mining towns. To be an African without a pass in such an area was to be a criminal. The pass forced Africans into paid labour and then trapped them in relations of employment at the behest of their employers. African women were not subject to pass laws before the 1890s, and early migrancy was largely a male phenomenon. It was assumed that the primary place of residence of African women was in the rural reserves, subsidising the reproduction of cheap labour. It was indeed a patriarchal bargain between chiefs and white capitalists in which male African labour would be provided and female productive and reproductive labour confined to the rural sphere. The economic growth precipitated by the discovery of gold and diamonds presented a conundrum to white rule. In the Free State in particular, where African women had moved to urban areas and sought paid labour, the relations between urbanisation, social reproduction and survival were thrown into tension.

The lives of the educated and aspirant African middle-class woman and the working-class woman were thrown together in the urban milieu, and it was in the alliance between these two classes of women that the kernel of the twentieth-century demand for the right to equality is to be found. As Wells argues, no matter what her class, in the cities the life of an African woman was circumscribed by the restrictions of pass laws. It was a lever used to ensure that women took ill-paid and strenuous jobs as domestic workers, to control choice in the forms of employment, and to expose women to the full force of a racist and sexist police force.

With male leaders of the newly formed South African Native National Congress (SANNC), which renamed itself the ANC in 1923, seemingly unwilling to take up the issue of passes for women, women took up the cause on their own behalf. In 1912, they petitioned the various provincial governments (of the Cape and the Free State) to repeal existing laws. On their own initiative, they met with the supposedly liberal Henry Burton, Minister of Finance of the Union, to present a 5,000 signature petition against passes.

Their arguments against passes referenced equality, but also articulated a demand to end sexual abuse by police. Women joined the branches of the SANNC, and sent women representatives along with the men delegates from the small towns to attend meetings of the organisation in Bloemfontein. By the next year, their appeals to the national and Free State provincial governments had fallen on deaf ears; indeed the women of Bloemfontein found themselves targeted for police action to a much greater extent. In May 1913, a passive resistance campaign was launched in Waaihoek

[30] C Walker *Women and Resistance in South Africa* (1982) 43.
[31] JC Wells *We Now Demand! The History of Women's Resistance to Pass Laws in South Africa* (1993).

location in Bloemfontein; by June it had escalated into a full-out clash between women and the police, with sticks being flourished by the demonstrators.[32]

During World War II, the labour needs of an expanding secondary industry and the decline of the rural reserve economy accelerated women's urbanisation, and, as members of deprived urban communities, women 'formed a significant part of the groundswell of discontent and resistance that rumbled through the townships' in the 1940s, according to Walker.[33] Protests against the incursions of township authorities on the activities of African people, demands for affordable housing or transport, and food riots were frequently led by women, and escalated into much larger community mobilisation.[34] Although these political activities were formulated and pursued independently of the Women's League, the militancy among women had an impact on the league. As the women's wing of the national liberation movement, the league increasingly adopted the role of representative, and the foment among women helped it to build up a mass membership for the ANC. In the process, women (and their rights) became central to defining the modernity of the ANC.[35]

Trade unions were the space in which women's militancy was most marked, and in which a growing sense of class solidarity developed in ways that transcended racial differences. Although initially driven by white women, trade unions – as Iris Berger[36] demonstrates – began militantly taking up shop-floor issues by the end of the 1930s, with radical demands for working women of all races. Among these demands, for example, were equal pay for equal work, prohibition of abuse in the workplace, housing and maternity leave. Black women, too, began to organise workers in sectors such as domestic service.

These struggles form the crucial backbone of the textual archive that was created to imprint women's rights demands firmly into the political landscape. Two documents in particular can be read as a kind of palimpsest to the Constitution: 'What Women Demand' colloquially known as the Women's Charter, adopted by the Federation of South African Women in 1954, and the Women's Charter for Effective Equality, adopted by the Women's National Coalition 50 years later.[37] These are rare documents because they articulate common interests and a political agenda for change in a collective fashion, and from organisations that represented women in a variety of social, economic and racial positions in the country. In these documents, South African women activists articulate a vision of the good society, a set of normative virtues that ought to guide relationships between people, and between citizens and the state. However, they are an invisible palimpsest, with very few analysts referring to these as roots of the Constitution – more frequently, reference is made to the

---

32 Ibid.

33 Walker (note 30 above) 62.

34 G Fester 'Women's organisations in the Western Cape: vehicles for gender struggle or instruments of subordination?' (1997) 34 *Agenda* 45; L Patel 'South African women's struggles in the 1980s' (1988) 2 *Agenda* 28; G Seidman '"No freedom without the women": mobilization and gender in South Africa, 1970–1992' (1993) 18 *Signs: Journal of Women in Culture and Society* 210.

35 Hassim (note 28 above).

36 I Berger *Threads of Solidarity: Women in South African Industry, 1900–1980* (1992).

37 In this discussion I have drawn on the archived versions of the 1954 Charter <http://www.sahistory.org.za/topic/womens-charter> and the 1994 Charter <http://www.anc.org.za/content/womens-charter-effective-equality>. Neither of the charters is properly paginated. The 1954 Charter has no numbering system for the various demands.

Freedom Charter. These Charters extended the concept of equality in three crucial respects: they established the rights of women to full participation and representation in political institutions, they expanded the domain of rights to include the private sphere, and they included notions of sexual and reproductive autonomy in the scope of human rights. All these dimensions of rights stemmed from the ways in which women sought to change the actual conditions of their lives.

3.1. Political community

The two Women's Charters articulate the idea of political community differently from the Freedom Charter, or any other political document prior to the Constitution, in that they include women as full members of the nation. This demand exposed the false universalism of both nationalism and Marxism, the idea that women would automatically be accommodated under the banners of nation and class, or that both those communities could incorporate women and still retain intact their theoretical and policy implications. This idea is firmly located in the Constitution, but without these struggles, there is little doubt that 'we, the people' would not be a formulation that addressed the particular tensions between citizens of different gender, or the hierarchies of power that sustained a multiplicity of patriarchies.

In 1954, a rising nationalist movement was demanding a set of rights and fundamental change in political structures - equal rights regardless of race. Although race and racism were front and centre, there were other political demands that were being forcefully articulated through the first part of the twentieth century. By the 1950s, black women had been involved in a range of organisations from trade unions, the Communist Party and the ANC to stokvels and women's solidarity networks.[38] They had led marches, resisted economic exclusion and put their bodies in the frontline against the police. While they were, then, *political actors* they had limited political *status*. The 1954 Charter was drafted at the inauguration of a new women's organisation, the Federation of South African Women, independent of male control and led by black women but open to women of all races. It was intended to lay out a manifesto for action for that movement. It went against the prevailing assumption that different races were better organised separately, and strove to create one organisation for all women while not obscuring the fact that white women had some rights deriving not just from their status as whites but also from a specific political project of white supremacy. Nevertheless, it envisioned an alternative universalism that was distinct from the ideas of community offered by other political movements of the time, which were centred on race and nation as the dominant, if not the only, framing for political mobilisation.

The first sentence of the preamble of the 1954 Charter demanded 'the removal of all laws, regulations, conventions and customs that discriminate against us as women, and that deprive us in any way of our inherent right to the advantages, responsibilities and opportunities that society offers to any one section of the population'. It is important to dwell on the transcendent notion of gender and the commonalities of

[38] See Walker (note 30 above); Wells (note 31 above); Berger (note 36 above).

patriarchal experiences across races and cultures that the 1954 Charter identified. Whereas the Congress Alliance foregrounded the exploitation and oppression of African people as the central concern, and understood white, coloured and Indian people to be in a position of support for the primary struggle of Africans, the 1954 Charter identified the common forms by which women were subordinated across race: in the family, in the community and in the workplace. Although there were differences in the specific manifestations of subordination, both social and legal, seeking out the underlying gendered relationships in society was a deliberate act of naming and including gender as a form of power. The 1954 Charter went on to note: 'We women do not form a society separate from the men. There is only one society, and it is made up of both women and men.'

The 1954 Charter hints at the difficult terrain on which feminists were working, between claiming forms of political autonomy on the one hand and locating themselves within community on the other. All the reigning political movements regarded women as rooted in family in the first instance, rather than in the public sphere. Women's role in public politics was legitimised within a language of working for the nation, or the race, rather than in the interests of women's liberation per se, independently of struggles against capitalism, colonialism and apartheid. Working with this idea that women's rights were good for the nation, the 1954 Charter appealed on the grounds of 'women's lot':

> We women share with our menfolk the cares and anxieties imposed by poverty and its evils. As wives and mothers, it falls on us to make small wages stretch a long way. It is we who feel the cries of our children when they are hungry and sick. It is our lot to keep and care for the homes that are too small, broken and dirty to be kept clean. We know the burden of looking after children and land when our husbands are away in the mines, on farms, and in the towns earning our daily bread.

We could read this statement in diametrically opposed ways, and indeed those different readings have been the basis of rich feminist debate about the ways in which women's struggles might be theorised.[39] On the one hand, women's right to exist as political collective is justified on the grounds that women bear specific gendered roles as the carers of society, and as the shock absorbers for failures of institutions such as labour markets, families and households. It notes and names the undervalued work entailed in social reproduction, quintessentially 'women's work' while not directly refusing to undertake it. Note, too, how African women's burdens are centred by the naming the effects of farm labour and migrancy, archiving referents for feminism that are outside of the Western models. On the other hand, the very fact of claiming the distinctiveness of gender experiences in itself can be radicalising. Once the proposition was accepted that women had the right to organise themselves, the ends to which they organise were unpredictable. Thus what looked, on the surface, to be an evocation of women's conventional roles contained the kernel of subversion. By the time of the drafting of the 1994 Charter, there was no need for extraneous arguments for full recognition of women's status as persons. Women's agency no longer had to

[39] See C Albertyn 'Women and the transition to democracy in South Africa' in F Kaganas & C Murray (eds) *Gender and the New South African Legal Order* (1995); D Driver 'The ANC constitutional guidelines in process: a feminist reading' in S Bazilli (ed) *Putting Women on the Agenda* (1991).

be defensively hedged by acknowledgements to their relationships to others and their capacities, indeed duties, to act on behalf or for the improvement of others. In 1994, women's claims were made in straightforward fashion on the basis of their citizenship rights, rather than as members of a nationalist movement. 'We are here to claim our rights' it said.

In explaining this shift, we have to turn to the character of women's political formations in the 50 intervening years. Globally, women's movements were growing in scale and impacting on conceptions of democracy in new ways. The overthrow of colonialism, and transitions to new forms of state – not all democratic, and few that included women as full rights-bearing citizens – in what was then called the 'third world' catapulted feminists into renewed attention to the limits of dependence on nationalist movements.

In South Africa, from the late 1970s, in the context of economic crisis and an implacable apartheid state, black women – African, Indian and coloured – began organising at community level. The issues that animated this organisation related to the gendered burdens women bore in households and families: rising food prices and rents, inadequate housing, lack of public transport, access to water and electricity. The so-called 'bread and butter' issues (that is, issues that were in the first instance about the socio-economic condition of people rather than their political rights) inspired a vast network of community organisations with women as foot soldiers, and indeed separate organisations of women.[40] Among the women's organisations that emerged in this period and grew in the early 1980s were the Natal Organisation of Women, the United Women's Organisation, and the United Women's Congress, and the Port Alfred Women's Organisation. These organisations became the bedrock of resistance to apartheid, and as has been documented elsewhere,[41] their demands for women's rights shaped the policies of the United Democratic Front (UDF) and the ANC, leading to the insertion of 'non-sexist' in all the language of those movements as one of the core values of democracy.

Despite the many successes of organised women in developing a robust politics of gender within the anti-apartheid movements, it was also evident throughout the 1980s that the language of equality could be superficially appropriated without women being allowed any real agency and leadership in crafting political strategies. These tensions over the role of women played out in the ANC in exile, where the increasing numbers of women in the ranks of Umkhonto we Sizwe as well as in the political organs in exile were not matched by women's access to the party's National Executive Committee (NEC). They also found expression in the UDF, where women's organisations were incensed that their own programmes of action were frequently pushed aside so that they could take on strategies defined as important by men.[42]

Women's participation in political mobilisation against apartheid and capitalism was dealt a major blow when political parties announced their negotiating teams for the multiparty negotiations in 1992. Not a single party included a woman in their

[40] See S Hassim *Women's Organisations and Democracy in South Africa: Contesting Authority*; Kemp et al (note 18 above).

[41] Hassim ibid.

[42] Ibid.

team. That exclusion symbolised the deeply sexist assumptions of political elites and the astounding failure to even consider obvious forms of male dominance. It galvanised women across political organisations, and across race, leading to a groundswell of anger and a determination to ensure that women would have a place at the negotiations. The Women's National Coalition (WNC) was formed in April 1992, an organisation that strategically used the Federation of South African Women's approach of crafting a form of political alliance that transcended the terms of male-led movements. The WNC was not only a coalition of women across race and class; it was also a coalition across ideological and party differences.[43] It re-instantiated the idea of a political collective on the simplest of grounds: their inclusion in the processes of determining a post-apartheid South Africa. It identified the most common denominator of interest among women who were politically active and in one stroke of brilliance captured the idea that a democracy in which women are not represented is not a democracy at all.

The immediate effect of this was that a small number of women were included in the multiparty negotiating teams, and were able to leverage representation on the specialist committees. Feminist lawyers participated in discussions of constitutional principles and the Bill of Rights, and importantly, they did so with the support of and in consultation with the WNC and with the Emancipation Commission of the ANC led by Frene Ginwala. In other words, they acted as representatives of those organisations and not as politically disembedded technical experts.[44] The outcome was a strong clause on equality.

3.2. The private as the sphere of rights

Both charters framed equality in ways that were substantively more far-reaching than the Freedom Charter, by addressing the rights of women in the private sphere. The women's charters both agree that the economy and the family are deeply gendered, and moreover depend on racialised, patriarchal hierarchies.

In substance, these demands prefigured constitutional debates on socio-economic rights and the idea of gender equality was understood by women's organisations to work in tandem with those rights. It was not only unions that carried this agenda; ordinary women locked out of the possibilities of finding work, or who had to make homes for their families in the bare veld with few resources, well understood the economic underpinnings of exclusion. This shift from the public sphere to address the intimacies of power goes considerably beyond other discourses of the time. The intuition about the limits of formal rights also prefigured debates about human rights later in the twentieth century, which critiqued the inadequacy of law on its own to translate rights into tangible equality outcomes. In later human rights literature, the argument was made that if the right to representation is a core right in any version of democracy, so too is the right to participation in government as well as in civic life. Yet participation is in the public sphere is shaped and at times constrained by

---

[43] S Meintjes 'The women's struggle for equality during South Africa's transition to democracy' (1996) 30 *Transformation* 47.

[44] See Albertyn (note 39 above); F Kaganas & C Murray (eds) *Gender and the New South African Legal Order* (1995).

a set of conditions that reside in the cultural and economic spheres of society. This poses a particular challenge for advocates of decoloniality who place emphasis on racial solidarity above other forms of intersecting relationships. It also challenges their tendency to dismiss law as always on the side of the powerful. True, law displaces horizontal relationships of reciprocity and interdependence and replaces these with the vertical relationships of power. However, horizontal relationships are also embedded in power. It is a romanticisation to portray an ideal egalitarian society that existed prior to capitalism and colonialism; if indeed such existed there is no easy return to it. The framers of the 1954 Charter were very clearly mistrustful of horizontal relationships as necessarily reciprocal. This is evident in the preamble of the 1954 Charter, which calls for the removal of 'conventions and customs that discriminate against us as women, and that deprive us in any way of our inherent right to the advantages, responsibilities and opportunities that society offers to any one section of the population'.

Elaborating the constraints on participation, the 1954 Charter draws attention to property rights, marriage and childcare, and the restrictions on women's mobility. As pointed out above, in the 1950s the articulation of equality had to navigate a difficult political terrain in which women were treated in the first instance as wives and mothers. But even within those constraints, the framers offer an expansive vision of equality in 1954, under the banner of maternalism. The members of the federation demanded the social provision of childcare, free education for all children and state provision of welfare services.

Even in the 1950s, custom and tradition were seen to be obstacles to the equality of women and the private power of men was a matter of concern. Although they worked alongside men in the creation of a better society, their alliance with men was not unqualified. Nor can we say, dismissively, that this was merely a reflection of an adherence to Western modernity; when you read the accounts of women who were active in this period, you see clearly that the concern with male power legitimated by culture arose out of their daily experiences.[45] What they demanded was unqualified personhood – recognition of their humanity, and an end to practices that naturalised unpaid labour, sexual violence and forced reproduction.

In 1994, the WNC was more forthright in naming these practices as patriarchal:

> At the heart of women's marginalization is the patriarchal order that confines women to the domestic arena and reserves for men the arena where political power and authority reside […] Women want to control their lives. We bear important responsibilities but lack the authority to make decisions in the home and in society.

It also proposed a stronger protection for women in the Constitution, demanding in art 9 that 'custom, culture and religion shall be subject to the equality clause in the Constitution'. Article 7 calls for restructuring of traditional institutions in accordance with principles of equality, and demands women's right to participate in traditional institutions of decision-making, equal representation on traditional courts. They were to prevail in this framing, as we know.

[45] For example, E Kuzwayo *Call Me Woman* (1985); A Benjamin (ed) *Winnie Mandela: Part of my Soul Went with Him* (1985); M Tlali *Muriel at the Metropolitan* (1975).

There are some significant shifts over the half-century in the ways in which social equality was understood. The 1954 Charter was clearly heteronormative in its framing of equality; it was assumed that the task was to be equal to men, and that women should have equal status within families as well as the public sphere. But underpinning this demand was a conception of families as the product of conventional heterosexual relationships. Ambivalence and tension stalk the document. Heteronormativity was taken for granted, and modernisation was considered to be a problem for social reproduction even as modernity itself was celebrated. Family failures were understood to be the root of women's loss of status and security: 'there was a time in the African society when every women reaching marriageable age was assured of a husband, home, land and security'. The 1954 Charter paid attention to the destruction of tribal and kinship bonds as a result of the migrant labour system and urbanisation. It recognised that women had become wage earners in their own right, and wanted the reform of laws that rested on older conceptions of women's status. The drafters were clear that while the traditional social structure of families had been disrupted, the solidaristic protections that were offered to women in that system needed to be provided in other ways. Yet they do not offer any inkling as to their thinking about what alternative family and household systems might look like.

By 1994, these kinds of issues had been more widely debated within women's organisations and in women's caucuses within unions, no doubt influenced by the intensification of urbanisation and the greater independence of women from traditional marriage and family systems. Article 8 of the 1994 Charter recognised the diversity of families, and included a capacious demand that 'all family types have to be recognised and treated equally' as well as the right of all people to choose their partners. This article echoes the 1954 Charter in calling for women to have equal rights in marriage, especially with regard to inheritance and property and the right to credit.

In the Women's Charter for Effective Equality, the demand for social justice is more strongly articulated than in 1954. Article 6 on social services demands these 'as a right and not a privilege' and puts the burden of provision explicitly on the state. It lists four principles that should underpin the provision of public services: social justice, equality, appropriateness, and accessibility. The word 'effective' in the title of the 1994 Charter was specifically chosen to describe the kind of equality envisioned: limited not just to political and legal equality but also to women's social and economic power. This equality was to be achieved by the use of affirmative action, with a focus on the equality of outcomes rather than the same treatment for all people.

Both documents see economic inequalities as substantially limiting any formal rights women may be granted. In 1954, the Women's Charter argued for women's right to work and equal pay for equal work, radical demands in the context of apartheid policies that sought to exclude women from the cities. By 1994, women's organisations were much more specific about the importance of attending to the economy. The 1994 Charter recognised for the first time the impact of women's unpaid labour on their access to labour markets and on their gendered burdens in the household. It also noted the predominance of women in the precarious informal economy. The 1994 Charter has a most obvious solution: not only should women have access to household finances, but art 8 calls for housework to be equally shared among all members of the household.

3.3. Embodied rights: sexual and reproductive rights

The women's charters reflect a conception of rights as having to address not only status inequalities but also inequalities that are rooted in bodily differences. They understood that law ascribed different meanings to bodily differences and that it is important when framing and interpreting rights to ask: whose bodies matter, when do bodies matter and which bodies are vulnerable? Bodies, they well understood, are gendered as well as raced in ways that affected life and death – that made and continued to make some bodies vulnerable to rape, to assault and to extreme labour exploitation. There is a faint but important trace between the developing language in the charters and contemporary feminist queer movements as represented in organisations such as One in Nine and the Forum for the Empowerment of Women.

In the Western, liberal framework of rights, law is understood as quintessentially disembodied, as rooted in reason and transcendent of bodily particularity. The result has been to reproduce the binary of male/female, mind/body, reason/nature and culture/rights.[46] In the discussions of equality in both the charters under consideration, the challenges to these binaries were both explicit and implicit. Most explicitly, although women in all the political organisations discussed above sought to create a sense of a political category 'women', they were well aware that racial difference significantly undermined the universalism of the category. In 1954, for example, white women already had some of the rights demanded in the Federation's Charter and the extension of these rights to black women was clearly not a simple matter. For example, white women depended heavily on the low-paid domestic work of black women, and exercised power over black men. Rights could not be articulated without the recognition of the ways in which race differences cut against the group solidarities of gender.

Neither could the group solidarities of race be taken as automatically empowering. It is striking that in both documents women's right to control their bodies is defended, although it is only in the 1994 Charter that sexual and reproductive rights are introduced into the language of equality; these included the right to choose a partner and the 'right to decide in the nature and frequency of sexual contact within marriage and intimate relationships'.[47]

There can be little doubt that the frontier of contestation regarding rights today is the battle for women and queer people to be seen as full members of society, no less than a battle for life.

4. Conclusion: contestation and mobilisation

Equality is a tricky conceptual framework on which to hang the feminist project. Using the idea of equality requires that feminists order and simplify in the process of making claims on the state and society, that some of the nuances of intersectional

[46] D Cornell *At the Heart of Freedom: Feminism, Sex, & Equality* (1998).

[47] Women's National Coalition *Women's Charter for Effective Equality* (1994) art 8.

discrimination are smoothed out in privileging women as a category, no matter how careful we may be in plotting these complexities in theory. As the legal challenge of intersex people such as Sally Gross demonstrates, it may not be capacious enough to contain all the imaginings of a world in which gender does not determine life chances.

The larger questions that were posed by women in the twentieth century – what kinds of futures do we want to create, how can we displace current models of accumulation and patterns of distribution, and how will we deal with the anxieties of those who hold on to hierarchies of power whether of class, race, sexuality or gender, and in all combinations – remain key political and social questions. The answers lie only partially in what happens in the state and the Constitutional Court. As this historical account of women's rights shows, it is in the capacity for organisation and mobilisation of ordinary people that truly meaningful outcomes can be shaped. These contestations are at the heart of democracy, as Chantal Mouffe[48] has argued, and far from lamenting them she makes a powerful argument for articulating democratic norms in radical ways. Part of what could constitute a radical alternative in the Mouffeian, agonistic form of democracy is to recognise that subjects have the power of meaning-making.

The decoloniality moment has forced a rethinking of the democratic project in South Africa. That should not mean, however, that the long and arduous struggles for recognition and rights should be abandoned or delegitimised. Patricia Williams' account of the history of black people's struggles for rights in the US stands as a cautionary for South Africa as well:

> To say that blacks never fully believed in rights is true. Yet it is also true that blacks believed in them so much and so hard that we gave them life where there was none before; we held onto them, put the hope of them into our wombs, mothered them and not the notion of them. And this was not the dry process of reification, from which life is drained and reality fades as the cement of conceptual determinism hardens round – but its opposite. This was the resurrection of life from ashes four hundred years old. The milling of something out of nothing took immense alchemical fire – the fusion of a whole nation and the kindling of several generations. The illusion became real for only a few of us; it is still elusive for most. But if it took this long to breathe life into a form whose shape had already been forged by society, and which is therefore idealistically if not ideologically accessible, imagine how long the struggle would be without even that sense of definition, without the power of that familiar vision. What hope would there be if the assignment were to pour hope into a timeless, formless futurism? [49]

Disclosure statement

No potential conflict of interest was reported by the author.

---

[48] C Mouffe 'Deliberative democracy or agonistic pluralism?' (1999) 66 *Social Research* 745.

[49] Williams (note 1 above) 163.

Is the South African Constitution an obstacle to a democratic post-colonial state?[1]

D. M. Davis

ABSTRACT
This article reviews recent criticisms levelled against the South African Constitution, particularly those focussed on the idea that the Constitution is a Eurocentric document that perpetuates forms of colonial discourse/political and economic structure in South Africa. Written for the *South African Journal on Human Rights* conference on decolonisation and the law, it focuses on two different schools of thought, described as constitutional promoters and denigrators, and then seeks to respond to both approaches.

1. Introduction

It is perhaps now trite to observe that the Constitution of the Republic of South Africa, 1996 no longer receives universal acclaim. From a range of quarters, it is now argued that the Constitution is an obstacle to the radical transformation of South African society. By constituting a shield against fundamental structural change, it is suggested that the Constitution represents a 'perfection' of colonial conquest and the incompleteness of the transition to democracy. It has contributed to an increase of racial inequality, caused in significant part by the failure of the new constitutional dispensation to address the pressing question of historical injustice, the restoration of sovereignty, land and thus accordingly dignity to the indigenous black people of

[1] The concept 'post-colonial' has frequently been used in recent South African literature without much clarity, as is evident from a number of the articles cited in this contribution. Ali Mazrui and Alamin Mazrui, however, provide a useful perspective for the purposes of this article in AA Mazrui & AM Mazrui *Swahili State and Society: The Political Economy of an African Language* (1995) 228: 'We used to think that decolonization consisted of the nationalist struggle against colonialism, the granting of independence and the replacing of colonial symbols of authority with national flags and national anthems. Decolonization was complete [...] when colonially educated members of the African elite came to the fore [...] The question that has arisen lately, however is whether real decolonization is not the winning of formal independence, not the changing of the guard on independence day [...] but the collapse of the colonial state itself, the cruel and bloody disintegration of colonial structures.' The question posed in this article concerns the possible development of a South African society that is not governed by an elite that exploits governance and economic institutions created by apartheid for these own ends but rather empowers 55 million South Africans to share in the shaping of political and economic institutions that promote the self actualisation of all.

South Africa. In this way, the Constitution inhibits the decolonisation of the country and the realisation of social justice.[2]

This article is designed to probe the fundamental question that flows from this counter-narrative: must and does the constitutional project, as it was established in 1994, inevitably produce the consequences that have powered this attack? In turn, this raises the further question about the nature of the core claim of the Constitution – the construction of a society based upon freedom, equality and dignity for all who live in South African society. Does the Constitution promote or retard the development of a South Africa based on the humanity of all 'who live' in the country? Has it substantively addressed the identities inherited from the past, which reflect a profound inhumanity and a refusal by a minority to share the common with all?

Expressed differently this question can be posed as it was by Steve Biko more than 40 years ago.

For the liberals the thesis is apartheid, the anti-thesis is non-racialism but the synthesis is very feebly defined. They want to tell the blacks that they see integration as the ideal solution. Black consciousness defines the situation differently. The thesis is, in fact, a strong white racism and therefore the antithesis to this must, ipso facto be a strong solidarity amongst the blacks on whom this white racism seeks to prey. Out of these two situations, we can, therefore, hope to reach some kind of balance – a true humanity where power politics will have no place.[3]

In short, does the Constitution work, either exclusively or predominantly, as an obstacle to the attainment of a true humanity where the power of a few to disempower and degrade the many is finally dismantled and replaced by a South African identity that has addressed the legacy of class, race and gender? In this regard, Biko said:

> We have set out on a quest for true humanity, and somewhere on the distant horizon we can see the glittering prize. Let us march forth with courage and determination, drawing strength from our common plight and our brotherhood. In time we shall be in a position to bestow upon South Africa the greatest gift possible – a more human face.[4]

Does the constitutional line of march inevitably create obstacles to a human society, where the common is fairly shared and a new South African identity emerges?

This article accepts that, to date, South African constitutional jurisprudence and scholarship has failed to craft a new South African identity and that many of the key

---

[2] See for example, Mzwanele Manyi claiming that constitutional democracy is at the centre of producing spiralling poverty in L Mkentane 'Forum calls for SA to ditch constitution' IOL <https://www.iol.co.za/news/politics/forum-calls-for-sa-to-ditch-constitution-7498118>. In J Modiri 'Law's poverty' (2015) 18 *Potchefstroom Electronic Law Journal* 224, 248-249, a nuanced critique drawing on a range of critical and post-colonial literature, Joel Modiri argues that to the extent that constitutional-rights litigation and rights-based reform involves an acceptance of the key terms of a faulty negotiated settlement, the lack of attention to redistribution and reparations in the public discourse is replaced with a discourse of socio-economic rights and service delivery.

[3] S Biko *I Write What I Like* (1996) 99.

[4] Ibid 100. These passages from Biko's writings reveal a clear distinction between nativism and black consciousness. While nativism recreates a divide of 'we' and 'them' – and thus and intellectual division in which an ideological ghetto is created – black consciousness, of which Biko was a major figure, links to a long tradition of black nationalism, responding to a society in which black equals inferior and black people sought social justice where they could shape their own lives. See A Mbembe in 'Biko's testament of hope' in C van Wyk (ed) *Celebrating Steve Biko: We Write What We Like* (2007) 135.

challenges of restitution, redistribution and the creation of a set of values that may produce substance democracy for the country have not been met. In particular, a substantial change to the profound inequality and levels of poverty fashioned over 365 years of racist and sexist rule has not taken place.[5] Given these monumental failures, this article seeks to determine whether we need to eschew this chosen constitutional framework in order to engage in a politics of retrieval, the nature of which lay at the centre of the hopes of more than a century of political struggle.

To this end, this article engages with two questions: firstly, the nature of law and the inherent dialectic quality thereof and, secondly, the question of race, its meaning and implications. The answer to the first question draws on the body of critical legal realism that has been canvassed previously and thus needs less introductory explication.[6]

The second question relies on the work of philosopher Sally Haslanger.[7] By way of introduction she argues that the analytical task of developing an account of race that will be an effective tool in the fight against substantive injustice must be guided by four concerns, namely:

1. The need to identify and explain persistent inequalities between people of different 'colours', including the concern of how to identify social forces often under the guise of biological forces that work to perpetuate these inequalities.
2. The need for a framework that will be sensitive to both the similarities and differences among individuals and groups demarcated by 'colour', including a concern to identify the effect of interlocking oppression; that is the intersectionality of race, class and gender.
3. The need for an account that will track how race is implicated in a broad range of social phenomena extending beyond those that obviously concern racial differences; that is how art, religion, philosophy, science or law are 'racialised'.
4. The need for an account of race that takes seriously the agency of people of colour of both genders and, within which account, an understanding of agency can be developed that will aid anti-racial and anti-sexist efforts to empower critical social agents.

It will be the submission of this article that the binary approach to the Constitution that dominates present South African legal discourse, namely 'the best constitution in the world' to which we all must pay obeisance versus 'the Constitution is part of a perpetuation of a colonial project', is neither inevitable nor

---

[5] As an illustration, a 2017 Statistics South Africa report ('Poverty trends in South Africa: an examination of absolute poverty 2006 & 2015' <http://www.statssa.gov.za/?p=10341>) has revealed that in 2015, 30.4 million of 55 million South African citizens lived below the upper poverty line of R992 per person per month. One out of three South Africans lived on less than R797 per month, and one in seven South Africans confronted extreme food poverty (R441 or less per month). Forty-seven per cent of the black population lived on less than R672 per month. Poverty affected but 1 per cent of the white population. A March 2018 Davis Tax Committee report ('Report on feasibility of a wealth tax in South Africa' <www.taxcom.org.za/docs/20180329 Final DTC Wealth Tax Report - To Minister.pdf>) shows that the Gini coefficient, which measures wealth, is at 0.93, representing an almost perfectly unequal society. In a 5 April 2018 article in *Business Day* ('Wealth gap a throwback'), Ben Turok writes that the income Gini coefficient of 0.63 is the highest in the world.

[6] See DM Davis & KE Klare 'Transformative constitutionalism and the common and customary law' (2010) 26 *South African Journal on Human Rights* 403.

[7] S Haslanger *Resisting Reality: Social Construction and Social Critique* (2012).

should its diametrically opposing claims be immune from vigorous political contestation in favour of a different political project. If, as Haslanger contends, racial oppression is linked inextricably to the consequences of social forces and hence the power imbalances in society, it will be argued that the Constitution can contribute to the change of the social-economic conditions from which these power imbalances are sourced. Thus, the Constitution may provide an important, albeit not sufficient basis by which to ensure that radical transformation takes place, both within the political and economic structures of the society inherited in 1994, the existence of which, all too sadly, continues to dominate our existing political and economic landscape.

In summary, if a text as constitutive of a society as a constitution can be the subject of earnest contest about its core meaning and race is less about ontology and more about social forces and ideological construct, there may well be more than two approaches to the Constitution.

2. The best constitution

Arguably, the most influential advocate of this view is retired Constitutional Court justice, Albie Sachs. He writes:

> [I]f government hasn't done as much as it could have done, that's a valid point. But we can't put the blame on the Constitution and we should be very weary of tinkering with it […] The Constitution is South Africa's greatest tribute to the people who died in the struggle for liberation. It's a beautifully crafted document, referred to with enormous admiration throughout the world. And it's ours, we made it; we wrote it; and we are applying it today.[8]

Referring to the Bill of Rights, Sachs has claimed that it is not simply another legal document, for '[I]t is life and death, it is who we are, it is the foundation of our transformation as South Africa. It certainly acknowledges and embraces multiculturalism […] but it does so without allowing group rights to become the foundation of the governing structures of our new constitutional order.'[9] Dealing with the question of multiculturalism, Sachs argues that the Constitution's emphasis upon three Ds – dignity, diversity and difference – is central to a new country. Viewed in this context, '[W]e are united in our right to be same, to have the same fundamental rights, yet we are diverse with regard to our right to be different, in terms of how we express ourselves and expressly exercise our rights. The right to be the same and the right to be different are not contradictory. In our constitutional dispensation they presuppose and support each other.'[10]

Sachs has also contended that the Constitution's 'well-honed text gave us the instrument to deal with some of the most difficult problems of our era.'[11] In short, Sachs is clear as to the meaning of the Constitution, which, in his view, is explicitly

8 A Sachs 'Don't expect a beautiful leader, South Africa – protect the Constitution' Biznews 17 November 2016 <https://www.biznews.com/thought-leaders/2016/11/17/albie-sachs-dont-expect-a-beautiful-leader-south-africa-protect-the-constitution>

9 A Sachs address to conference of the FW de Klerk Foundation 2 February 2016; also see A Sachs *We, the People: Insights of an Activist Judge* (2016).

10 Ibid.

11 D Cornell & K van Marle (eds) *Albie Sachs and Transformation In South Africa* (2014) 94-95.

transformative made clear in its express language about the establishment of social justice and the achievement of a non-racial and non-sexist society. Significantly, Sachs concedes in the same contribution that the court eschewed a jurisprudence aimed at achieving greater material equality for, '[N]o particular economic system is either required nor endorsed by the Constitution.'[12] As the constitutional drafters were careful not to prescribe any clear economic framework, Sachs contends that the Constitution does not seek to provide a clear mechanism with which to reduce income and wealth inequality.

I shall return later to the question of the Constitution and its relationship to economy. But, unlike the admission that the text does not support a particular form of economy, Sachs is clear that the Constitution and particularly the Bill of Rights 'has become the cornerstone of […] nation building […] foundational to the achievement of the nation of unity in diversity which in turn is central to the growth of shared loyalty and identity with the nation.'[13]

3. The constitution as an obstacle to transformation

By contrast, Joel Modiri[14] contends that the key ideological and practical functions of the Constitution are to 'inhibit the decolonisation of the country and the realisation of social justice.'[15] For him the entire constitution-making process that led up to the Constitution represented the uncritical adoption of a Western legal paradigm that 'alienates indigenous African epistemologies.'[16] By diluting the power of parliamentary sovereignty and replacing it with constitutional supremacy, the Constitution privileged Eurocentric law, the colonial heritage, culture and institutions, thereby securing the ill-gotten privileges of whites and the consequent debasement of black citizenship, which began in 1652 through colonisation, land disposition and cultural decimation. For Modiri, the Constitution thus represents the 'prolonging of an anti-black colonial project'.[17]

He points to the uncritical construction of the Constitution as advocated by a range of scholars.[18] By this, he means a fetishised belief in constitutionalism, liberal democracy and the rule of law. This line of argument has replaced one metanarrative, being the primacy of the common law with another, the Constitution, the adoption of which raises a warning of totalitarianism by virtue of a 'pathological' attachment to a reigning legal and political order.[19] Constitutional priests develop a universal, unproblematic legal narrative that represents an uncontroversial road map towards an ideal democratic society. In an uncritical rush to create a fresh hegemonic legal basis

---

[12] Ibid.

[13] Ibid 113.

[14] J Modiri 'The time and space of critical legal pedagogy' 2016 (27) *Stellenbosch Law Review* 507.

[15] Ibid 516.

[16] Ibid.

[17] Ibid.

[18] In this group he includes A van der Walt 'Legal research and legal education 20 years after the advent of a democracy' in J de Ville (ed) *Memory and Meaning: Lourens du Plessis and the Haunting of Justice* (2015) 203; DM Davis 'Legal transformation and legal education: congruence or conflict' in A Price & M Bishop (eds) *A Transformative Justice: Essays in honour of Pius Langa* (2015) 172; and G Quinot 'Transformative legal education' (2012) 29 *South African Law Journal* 411.

[19] Modiri (note 14 above) 514.

for society, the same enthusiasm that used to be employed in favour of the common law, being a set of rules and principles of universal validity, now shifts to the constitutional project.[20]

An even blunter critique of the South African constitutional project comes from Terblanche Delport.[21] Delport sees the Constitution as nothing more than an attempt to rearrange an unjust order rather than as addressing questions of historical justice from the perspective of those who were materially oppressed and formally excluded.[22] He goes on to say:

> The fact that the majority of people in the country still lives [sic] in conditions that devoid them from material ability and formal participation speaks to the fact that the Constitution does not ensure the production, reproduction and development of human life in the community. The Constitution does proclaim to grant access to those that have been excluded but time and again ensures that those that have been excluded continue to be excluded. We want to argue that this in-ability of the Constitution to effect a fundamental change in the material conditions of the majority of the people of South Africa is proof that it does not and cannot address these material conditions on a substantive level. This is a direct result of its misdiagnosis of the question of justice as reconciliation instead of reconstruction.[23]

Delport contends that the negotiations for a new constitution were fundamentally flawed, in that there was no equality of power in these talks because the National Party held state power while the ANC were not representative of the majority of the materially oppressed. Unsurprisingly, in his view, the Constitution represents the culmination of these negotiations and thus is unable to address the question of liberation for the victims of colonial conquest.

For their critiques, Modiri and Delport draw heavily on the work of Mogobe Ramose.[24] Ramose observes that customary law, being the indigenous law of the land, is made subject to 'the law of the land', which, in the case of South Africa, is the Constitution. However, '[T]he Constitution of South Africa like that of Namibia and the rest of post-colonial Africa, is arguably neither indigenous nor autochthonous yet it exists to regulate and govern relations between the successors entitle to the questionable "right of conquest" and the indigenous people conquered in the unjust wars of colonisation.'[25] He further suggests that the current reality of South Africa as 'a unitary State' can be considered to represent a serious concern for democratic practice. In his view, this project is impossible because contemporary South Africa has not addressed the challenge of the restoration of titled territory to the indigenous peoples conquered in unjust wars of colonisation. A genuine and truly

[20] For an influential example of the claim that the common law represents universal truth, see JC de Wet 'Gemene reg of wetgewing?' (1948) *Journal of Contemporary Roman-Dutch Law* 1.

[21] T Delport 'An ethical (anti-)constitutionalism? Transformation for a transfigured public' (2014) 46 *Acta Academica* 104.

[22] Ibid 114.

[23] Delport (note 21 above) 114.

[24] See for example MB Ramose 'Sovereignty in the new South Africa' 2007 *Griffiths Law Review* 310 and MB Ramose *African philosophy through Ubuntu* (2002). I should add that, in addition to Ramose, Modiri draws heavily on the work of American scholar Wendy Brown, while Delport relies on Enrique Dussel, the Argentinian-Mexican theorist who has sought to rework Marx in relation to a critique of Western conceptions of modernity. See, for example E Dussel *Towards an Unknown Marx* (2001).

[25] Ramose 2007 (ibid) 324-325

South African constitution would have to recognise how the indigenous peoples were conquered in unjust wars of colonisation and thus ensure parity to the legal paradigms that were swept asunder by colonisation and subsequently by the Constitution negotiated between the National Party and the ANC in the early 1990s.[26]

In particular, Ramose criticises s 25 of the Constitution, the property clause. Its detailed provisions, in his view, are a fatal obstacle to the process of achieving justice for the indigenous people of the country.[27] Significantly, Ramose has devoted a careful analysis to the concept of ubuntu, a 'verbal noun' that denotes a particular state of being and becoming at the same time. To be human, according to this doctrine, is to affirm one's humanity by recognising the humanity of others and on that basis establish humane, respectful relations with them.[28] But for Ramose, without a sustained reconstruction of the indigenous, this attempt to establish humanity is doomed to failure. Indeed by attempting to create a metanarrative of the Constitution, redress and reconstruction through the prism of the indigenous is futile at best, counterproductive at worst.

4. The way out of this binary impasse

Stripped to the essential contention, both the constitutional promoters and the denigrators have the following in common: they adhere to a single interpretation of the Constitution. In the case of the promoters, the Constitution inevitably promotes the construction of 'a rainbow nation', bestows dignity, equality and freedom on all who live within this country, and constitutes the core foundation for the attainment of a non-racial and non-sexist society.

The denigrators contend that the current constitutional dispensation invariably subordinates African customary law to the Constitution,[29] promotes a Western legal paradigm and discourse that alienates indigenous law and culture, 'prolongs an anti-black colonial project'[30] and represents a clear obstacle to the substantive transformation of the economic structure of South African society.[31]

Little acknowledgement of a possible contest about meaning is recognised on either side. However, without appearing to grasp the importance of this observation, Modiri illustrates the poverty of the interpretative approaches adopted by both sides when he concedes that his attack on South African constitutionalism as prolonging an anti-black colonial project is 'an obviously contested argument […] A strong account of democracy, sound pedagogical practice and a serious commitment to justice and freedom requires acknowledgement that both the content and spirit of the Constitution is in serious contest and this contest must be placed at the heart of legal education'[32]

---

[26] Ibid.
[27] MB Ramose & D Hook 'To whom does the land belong?' (2016) 50 *Psychology in Society* <http://www.scielo.org.za/scielo.php?script=sci_arttext&pid=S1015-60462016000100005>.
[28] MB Ramose (ed) *Liber Amicorum Discipulorumque Pro Heinz Kimmerle* (2013) 53.
[29] Ibid 327.
[30] Modiri (note 14 above) 516
[31] Delport (note 21 above) 115-116
[32] Modiri (note 14 above) 516

Correctly, Modiri acknowledges that the very nature of the Constitution and what it represents is contested terrain, inevitably so because the interpretation of the Constitution is itself an engagement in disputed territory. A brief recourse to the work of Paul Grice[33] is illustrative of why this interpretative contest is inevitable. Grice develops a distinction between sentence meaning and speaker meaning. Sentence meaning is understood in terms of what speakers generally intend to get across when uttering the sentence on different occasions. Speaker meaning stands to be analysed in terms of the communicative intention that the speaker conveys when making an utterance; that is the intention to induce a certain belief in the hearer or the reader. To grasp the communicative intentions of a speaker, the hearer or reader would have to exploit a range of clues that include the standard meaning of words as employed in a particular context and the terminological intentions of the speaker. Expressed differently, sentences can be understood by way of a connection shared by members of the linguistic community. Speaker meaning entails an understanding of communicative intention.

This distinction holds clear implications for both the purposivist and textualist approaches to interpretation. The purposivist invokes the intention of the legislature, that is interpretation that takes place in terms of what the legislature intended. By contrast, a textualist claims that these intentions should not be considered in the interpretation of a legal instrument: the focus must be upon the words employed. Both of these approaches have been criticised: the purposivist in that it runs the danger that any or every intention may be ascribed to the words; the textualist because it eschews any influence of context and its role upon meaning.

A legal instrument, including a constitution, is an active form of communication. True, a judgment that interprets a particular provision seeks to achieve closure thereby, but the process leading to this result is all too often the subject of intense conflict between different interpretative offerings. In this context, it is not sufficient to simply argue that all that is required is to find some objectified intention; that is the intention that a reasonable person would garner from the text. To use Grice, this would mean that the sentence meaning is the alpha and omega of the interpretive exercise, because the sentence meaning would be constituted by the regularity of intentions that people seek to convey when using particular words, a sentence or a whole text. Nothing guarantees that words must be understood in terms of a conventional meaning.

Speaker meaning and sentence meaning may be different; hence a conventional meaning does not always determine the communicative intent that is essential to speaker meaning. In short, an earnest engagement with both speaker and sentence meaning is required in a coherent interpretative process.

This article is not the place to develop a fully fledged application of Grice. But the reference to Grice is designed for a particular purpose: to show that unqualified claims about the meaning of the constitutional text by both the denigrators and the promoters of the Constitution suffer from the same problem. This is a claim that eschews any recourse to a rigorous interpretation of a text, certainly a sustained

[33] P Grice *Studies In the Way of Words* (1989).

engagement with communicative intention, which involves context, terminological intentions and the legislative expectations at the very least.

While the Constitutional Court may not have gone so far as to employ Grice, consider the following dictum, namely that when interpreting legislation, a court:

> must understand the provision within the context of the grid, if any, of related provisions and of the statute as a whole including its underlying values. Although the text is often the starting point of any statutory construction, the meaning it bears must pay due regard to context. This is so even when the ordinary meaning of the provision to be construed is clear and unambiguous.[34]

By virtue of the necessity of engaging with context and the need to peer at the text through a historical lens, the exercise of interpretation is invariably contested. A constitutional text is invariably open to significant contestation. It does not automatically or inexorably lead to one meaning, whether it be a roadmap to a substantive, egalitarian democracy or a bulwark against the transformation of the material and political conditions of a society as unjust as that which was inherited from apartheid rule. But both the priests and the rejectionists do no more than asserting that there is one uncontested meaning. For this reason, contrary to Sachs, Modiri, Delport or Ramose, it is contended that an interpretative claim cannot be made without interpretive work. Sachs may consider that the Constitution is a beautifully crafted document, but without the development of some normative framework upon which such an interpretation of the text can be based and that leads to this conclusion, his claim is no more than a romantic assertion. Similarly, Modiri and others, without any concrete historical analysis or engagement with the balance of political forces that existed in 1994 at the time of the negotiations leading to the Constitution and with no attempt to engage in any interpretative work upon the text, write off the exercise as a monument to the past.[35]

5. Towards a different interpretation

Without contending that an alternative approach to the Constitution is the only one or that it can trump the difficulties of a significant interpretive contest, it is possible to present a different understanding of the Constitution: one that more fully embraces a complete break from a racist, sexist and colonial past and certainly one that, contrary to Sachs' eschewing of any form of economic model or Modiri's silence thereon, sustains an economic vision that is congruent with dignity, equality and freedom. Indeed, this approach insists that only a particular range of economic models could support the vision of the Constitution as so articulated, that is one that seeks to promote a substantive conception of equality, freedom and dignity for all.

---

[34] *Department of Land Affairs v Goedgelegen Tropical Fruits (Pty) Ltd* 2007 (6) SA 199 (CC) para 53.

[35] Ramose certainly speaks of humanity but then reverts to a metanarrative that is clearly at war with the former claim, because, in my view, his is at core a nativist view of the world. Modiri and Delport could have, at the very least, undertaken some political analysis to support their bald assertion about the 'sell out' that the constitutional negotiations produced, particularly to understand the balance of political forces in the early 1990s. By contrast see, for example, Padraig O'Malley *Shades of Difference* (2007).

A summary of this different idea of the Constitution can be set out thus:

> The Constitution embodies a dramatically expanded conception of human self-realisation and therefore of democracy. In this vision, the values and aspirations we associate with and because of which we treasure and fight for democracy have implications across many more facets of political and daily life than are traditionally reckoned in theories of democracy. Surely democracy – and ultimately judicial review – must take on a new look in a constitutional regime that aspires to re-structure the private sphere, inter alia, by eliminating patriarchal domination and mandating fair labour practices.[36]

This reading of the Constitution, contrary to both those of Sachs and Modiri and others, seeks to develop a normative premise upon which the necessary interpretative work can be based. Any normative framework, including the one proposed here, will lead to debate and contest. The Constitution is read in terms of this normative claim. In turn, any such claim must be tested by its capacity to provide a coherent reading of the text as a whole. Viewed from the vantage point of the normative framework suggested in this article, institutions and practices are required to provide opportunities for every person who lives in South Africa to realise his or her potential and thereby make meaningful self-expressive choices about is or her life path based on his or her own sense of purpose and promise of living.[37] Human self-realisation lies at the heart of this vision of the democratic enterprise, where politics, rather more so than the work of judges, determine the scope of the Constitution and its possible implementation. Out of a vibrant politics emerges the possibility of a different, progressive discourse that helps frame the kind of normative framework that, in turn, influences the engagement between speaker and sentence meaning. No one meaning is pre-ordained; hence the focus on contest, which invariably must be located in politics and its influence upon discourse.

It is now possible to return to the work of Haslanger. It must follow that a reading of the Constitution that promotes a model of democracy that imagines an engaged self-governing and self-transformed citizen[38] is required to respond to the legacy of colonial rule, the role that race played and continues to play within the fabric of South African society and the need to address past patterns of distribution of income, wealth and thus power. In the approach to interpretation indicated in this article, this set of considerations form part of the context and terminological intentions as divined from this context, together with the expectations of those who passed the Constitution into law.

Haslanger contends that there are both natural and social differences that flow from race. Thus, there are skin-colour differences and, arguably, hair-texture differences. But these differences alone are insufficient to explain the pernicious role that racism has played in South African history. As Haslanger writes, '[R]ace is the social meaning of the geographically marked body, familiar markers being skin colour, hair type, eye shape, physique.'[39] In short, ontology is an insufficient explanation for 350 years of racist rule and practice. For this reason, Haslanger argues that both race

---

[36] KE Klare 'Self-realisation, human rights and separation of power: a democracy-seeking approach' 2015 *Stellenbosch Law Review* 445, 466.

[37] Ibid 467.

[38] Ibid 467.

[39] S Haslanger 'Gender and race: (What) are they? (What) do we want them to be?' 2000 (34) *NOÛS* 31, 44.

and gender are social positions that individuals occupy by virtue of their body being interpreted in a certain way. It follows that physical differences that are assumed to be natural are not fixed. Hence, racism is constituted by an interconnected web of social practices to justify the disadvantage of certain groups, including residential segregation, police brutality, biased hiring, wage inequity, cultural inferiority and educational disadvantage, to name but a few.

For Haslanger, racial inequality is a systematic phenomenon, best understood in terms of dynamic homeostasis:

> There are multiple determinations of social stratification in a society eg wealth, status/prestige, power/authority, autonomy/opportunity. In a stratified society, there are mechanisms that position groups stably and hierarchically along these dimensions. Homeostasis explains the persistence of hierarchy: changes in part of the system are adjusted for elsewhere so that the status quo is maintained. But the system is dynamic: although relatively stable, there is a historical development: the adjustments don't always return the system exactly to the original state but can allow a shift to a different sort of hierarchical structure.[40]

The manner in which legal reform under pressure from political struggle takes place without addressing the core of the societal hierarchy is an example of the Haslanger argument.

This analysis of race points clearly towards a reconstruction of society in which the multiple dimensions of social stratification that are, in significant part, shaped by race,[41] are addressed at core. A reframed discourse that emerges out of a reconstruction of the economic system is vital. The fight for social justice rather than a recourse to identity politics is what follows from this argument.

By identity politics, I mean recourse to categories that, ironically, in light of the cited criticisms of the Constitution, allow 'the body' to be interpreted in a way that spawned the colonial and apartheid projects and in which human agency was replaced with the overdetermination of identity of the body. Social justice, as envisaged by Biko, for example, is an essential ingredient for the construction of a new humanity, by way of political struggle and the exercise of human agency.

To an extent, it is conceded that some of the denigrators mentioned in this article[42] argue in favour of a movement for social justice. However, instead of seeing the fight for social justice as that of humanity and thus a basis for a reimagination of a universal community, the argument leads to secession from the world and the embrace of an exceptionalism. By exceptionalism, I mean the insistence that 'we are different' as opposed to embracing a plurality of voices while at the same time recognising the struggle of millions of disempowered people for rights to secure justice for their own communities. This exceptionalism allows the denigrators to see rights as Western creations that 'we in the developing world' should reject for what they are – Western creations.[43]

---

40 S Haslanger 'Racism, ideology and social movements' (2017) 94 *Res Philosophica* 1, 17.

41 Class and gender being the other two crucial determinations.

42 I have Modiri and, to a far lesser extent, Delport in mind.

43 As an example, see T Madlingozi 'Social justice in a time of neo-apartheid constitutionalism: critiquing the anti-black economy of recognition, incorporation and distribution' 2017 (28) *Stellenbosch Law Review* 123, 146: 'I argued that in historically white supremacist countries, firstly, the human in "human rights" is the conception of

The argument of this article is that 'rights' cannot inevitably be construed as a Western concept that perpetuates oppression. No matter the contest that invariably takes place concerning the content of rights, political struggles of the disempowered – particularly in countries that were once colonies but also in the developed world – reveal the possibility of rights shifting power balances to enable a community to be rebuilt on the basis of freedom, equality and dignity for all.

To be fair to the denigrators, the kind of social justice contemplated here cannot be achieved by the essential body of jurisprudence built up by the Constitutional Court over the past twenty years, particularly as heralded by the promoters such as Sachs. For example, in 2014, reflecting on twenty years of the Court, Sachs defended the Court's equality jurisprudence, based as it was upon a Kantian notion of individual dignity as opposed to 'a concentration on achieving greater material equality'.[44] This defence wrongly creates a binary between dignity and addressing material inequality, as if the former could be promoted in the absence of the latter.[45] Small wonder that the denialists have a basis for critique.

It has been the argument in this article that a reading based upon a Kantian vision of individual dignity or, alternatively, on self actualisation as the key to the normative framework for the Constitution is not inevitable, nor do these readings flow inexorably from the language used in the text.

To achieve a jurisprudence that takes seriously the way law has shaped identity and the pattern of an endemically racist distribution of resources, a critical-realist lens allows for an exposure of the distributional effects of the existing legal system. The work of Haslanger, as I have summarised the key idea, points to widespread racism being constituted by social practices that must be replaced by their very antithesis. For this reason, it is argued that the normative framework advocated in this contribution must replace the existing one, saturated as it is by 350 years of racist rule.

Of course, Haslanger is only one theorist who can be employed. This alternative reading finds further intellectual support, for example, in the work of Achille Mbembe.[46] He contends that the focus of struggle must be directed to belonging fully in this world, which is common to all humanity while altering the status of those excluded to the status of rights-holders who participate equally in the construction and the distribution of the world. For Mbembe, the project of a world in common is to be founded on the principles of 'equal shares' and of the fundamental unity of human beings. These struggles remain a universal project. Until racism is eliminated, the struggle for the creation of a world beyond race will continue. This form of politics inevitably entails a sustained political and ethical critique of racism and of the

---

humanity imposed during colonisation, and that in the absence of the revolutionary approaches that decolonise and reconceptualise "the human", as historically proposed by the PAC and the BCM, the extension of human rights to those historically deemed sub-human is an endeavour to enact transition from the status of sub-humanity to that of being human like the white man.' This set of sweeping generalisations stands in stark contrast to a sustained tradition of a rights discourse sourced in black voices for over a century in this country and that were (and still are) silenced by a white hegemony. This history reminds us of the importance of nuance when we engage with rights and social justice. See the important contribution by T Ngcukaitobi *The Land is Ours: Black Lawyers and the Birth of Constitutionalism in South Africa* (2018).

[44] Cornell & Van Marle (see note 11 above) 95.

[45] Ibid.

[46] A Mbembe *Critique of Black Reason* (2017).

ideologies of difference, or, to put it in Haslanger's terms, a fundamental deconstruction of social practices that have sustained racism with all its manifestations throughout the vicissitudes of South African history. In doing so, the aim is directed at the restoration of a humanity stolen from the majority of South Africans as a result of colonialism and apartheid. It is, in the words of Mbembe, 'not only an economic project but also a process of reassembling amputated parts, repairing broken links, rebalancing the forms of reciprocity without which there can be no progress for humanity'.[47]

Here we find the balance of the answer to the denigrators; that is to the idea that the Constitution in general and the Bill of Rights, in particular, are Western creations that are alien to South African indigenous roots. On this line of argument, the indigenous is counterposed to the rights contained in the Constitution. But other than a vote for a better yesterday, this view, while paying nominal obesience to the idea of humanity, as does Ramose, retreats speedily to a nativism that is bereft of any normative framework by which to judge either social practices or rights.[48] By contrast, Mbembe's conception of a common struggle by the oppressed against racism and class oppression finds itself aligned with the work of key postcolonial theorists Frantz Fanon, Marcus Garvey and Aime Cesaire.[49] In this struggle, the aim is to reclaim humanity for the majority by destroying the foundations that gave rise to racism and its doppelgänger, capitalism. Instead of a retreat to the kind of identity politics of the latter colonial period – in which the East is divided from the West by a colonial discourse in terms of science, rational thought and democracy that are of the West as opposed to magic, mystique and a different view of humanity in the East – this project lifts our political gaze to the roots of oppression and the claim by all humanity to the destruction thereof.[50]

It is important to emphasise that this vision does not eschew the local. Far from it, but it refuses to see a world in which the developing world cannot lay claim to the

---

47 Ibid 182. See also Haslanger (note 40 above).

48 Were it otherwise, Ramose (note 24 above) would be more cautious before so enthusiastically and uncritically endorsing the institution of the Zulu King with all the patriarchy and culture of authority attached thereto. Compare this enthusiasm for a narrow past to the following comment in V Chibber *Postcolonial Theory and the Specter of Capital* (2013) 294: 'It is hard to imagine a more dramatic confirmation of the two universalisms than the demands that came from the streets of Tunisia, Egypt, or the other canters of revolt. These were demands for bread, rights, jobs, and democracy. In fact, without exception, commentators were taken aback by the centrality of secular, universalistic, and materialist demands in the movements. This is not the first time such demands have been seen in the Middle East; secular nationalism was the main political ideology of the region in the middle decades of the twentieth century. But since the 1970s, it was Islamists of varying stripes that had gained traction within civil society. The growth of religious political organizations, and the steady enervation of secular Left forces, had been one of the conditions that lent credibility to the new Orientalism espoused by postcolonial theory. Yet when the Spring's mass movements exploded onto the scene, the Islamists were largely marginal to them. Their banners were hard to find. What the masses of young revolutionaries called for was liberty, justice, and dignity–demands one should expect, if postcolonial theory is to be believed, only in the streets of Paris or New York.' This observation is not intended to mean that indigenous law and culture have no role to play. To the contrary, it has a vital role in a future South African legal system, as long as the rules, application and development thereof is coupled with a normative framework that allows for a critical assessment of all such laws and practices. See, in this connection, C Himonga 'The Constitutional Court of Justice Moseneke and the decolonisation of law in South Africa' 2017 *Acta Juridica* 101.

49 See the exposition of all these writers in Mbembe (note 46 above).

50 See V Chibber 'Eurocentrism, the academy and social emancipation' University of Cape Town vice-chancellor open lecture (14 August 2017) <https://www.youtube.com/watch?v=ioJNQjDylLc> <https://www.youtube.com/watch?v=3rxeCXnbVLU>

same share of the common or of rights as insisted upon and demanded by the developed world, or by millions of black people, women and marginalised groups in the developed world who seek to resist the destructive effects of global capital.

6. Conclusion

We should accept that an engagement with a reconstructed South African identity should be designed to restore humanity as stolen from the majority of the population. Sadly, this has hardly been at the centre of the present constitutional project. The Constitutional Court dabbled early in its tenure with a normative framework borrowed directly from German jurisprudence[51] but then backed off from any further engagement. True, the most blatant racist encrustations of apartheid have been demolished through the jurisprudence of the Constitutional Court over the past two decades,[52] but when dealing with the distribution of resources that are determined by race and class, the Court reverted to a narrow conception of social and economic rights.[53]

Too little has been done to deconstruct the core of the South African legal system so as to embrace the challenges of a reconstitution of humanity and embrace the reassembling of the amputated parts of the South African body and thus also of the laws that have sustained dispossession and patterns of economic inequality that continue to run so markedly along race lines.[54]

This statement now needs a qualification. As I have been at pains to argue, the constitutional text itself is not responsible for this lack of development. Thus, in a recent decision in *Daniels v Scribante*,[55] Froneman J spoke of the opportunity afforded by the Constitution to develop a society where the injustice of the past can be addressed without a denial of dignity, freedom or equal treatment for all the inhabitants of this country. To do so, he noted that three things were required, at the very least: (1) an honest and deep recognition of past injustice, (2) a reappraisal of our conception of the nature of ownership and property, and (3) an acceptance rather than avoidance of obfuscation of the consequences of constitutional change.[56] For the first time, in clear and unequivocal terms, a judge of the Constitutional Court has called for a comprehensive recognition of historical injustice, its causes and its nature and flowing therefrom a deconstruction of the legal system that has underpinned these injustices. On this basis, it may now be possible to commence with the

[51] *Carmichelle v Minister of Safety and Security* 2001 (10) BCLR 995 (CC) paras 54-55, where copious references are made to German constitutional law.

[52] See, for example, S Liebenberg *Socio-Economic Rights: Adjudication under a Transformative Constitution* (2010); D Moseneke 'Striking a balance between the will of the people and the supremacy of the Constitution' (2012) 129 *South African Law Journal* 9; and Klare (note 36 above).

[53] *Mazibuko v City of Johannesburg* 2010 (4) SA 1 (CC); see the criticism of the judgment by L Williams 'The justiciability of water rights: *Mazibuko v City of Johannesburg*' 2010 (18) *Willamette Journal of International Law and Dispute Resolution* 211.

[54] See the criticism of the Court's approach to private law by Davis & Klare (note 6 above).

[55] *Daniels v Scribante* 2017 (8) BCLR 949 (CC).

[56] Ibid para 115. Compare the judgments of Madlanga and Froneman JJ to that of Jafta J in *Daniels*, where the latter vigorously opposes the application of the Constitution to promote owners of property: a reminder of the problem of adjudication rather than the inexorable consequences of the constitutional text.

reconstruction in order to produce a society in which dignity, equality and freedom are honoured.[57]

Mbembe captures the importance of this methodology thus:

> We are condemned to live not only with what we have produced but also with what we have inherited. Given that we have not completely escaped the spirit of a time dominated by the hierarchization of human types, we will need to work with and against the past to open up a future that can be shared in full and equal dignity. The path is clear: on the basis of a critique of the past we must create a future that is inseparable from the notions of justice, dignity and the in-common.[58]

It is now possible to address the denigrator's critique at its core. The Constitution does not preclude a rigorous examination of the nature and implications of our colonial past. To the contrary, only by a painfully sustained consideration of history will it be possible to understand the role of law in the reproduction of the society inherited from the past. And only after this exercise of deconstruction has been undertaken will we be in a position to reimagine a legal system that can contribute to make the country whole.

This model refuses to fetishise a contested reconstruction of the past or the contents of the new (old) metanarrative advocated by the denigrators, namely that their conception of the indigenous assumes the status of unqualified authority.

It has been the argument of this article that the advocated model can be sustained by a reading of the Constitution, one that admittedly has not emerged coherently from the text. Nor is it free from contest or controversy. Its justification must be found less in claims sourced in the literal words of the text or of what one or other contributor to the initial drafting process might have thought. Its reading stands or falls less on this process and more upon the traction of a normative framework that underpins it. But this reading, as shown in the judgments in *Daniels*, must not be incongruent with an engagement between speaker and sentence meaning where the speaker meaning is taken to envisage a society that ultimately may be common to all who live in it.[59] And, while emphasising the importance of the domestic and its influence upon the ideologies that have, to date, constricted our identity, it insists that there can be no sharing of the common until we take seriously the material conditions that have sustained our fractured identities over centuries.

---

[57] The one section of the constitutional text that is invariably the subject of critique is s 25, the property clause. While I would have preferred that there not be such a clause (the Canadian Charter of Rights and Freedoms of 1982, for example, does not contain a property clause, which shows that there is not universal adherence thereto, not even in the developed world), the failure to date to deal adequately with restoration of land after 1994 is a result of a manifest failure of politics and governance far more than it can be that attributable to s 25. See, for example, A Claassens & B Cousins *Land, Power & Custom: Controversies Generated by South Africa's Communal Land Rights Act* (2014).

[58] Mbembe (note 45 above) 177

[59] To emphasise an earlier argument, this should be contrasted with the Ramose approach, which seeks to rediscover a past that itself is deeply contested. To take but one example, the homage that is paid to the Zulu king can certainly be contested on the basis of patriarchy as well as a reproduction of forms of privilege that would continue to reproduce the process of control and privilege in rural South Africa, which are incongruent with dignity, equality and freedom for all.

Disclosure statement

No potential conflict of interest was reported by the author.

Democratic constitutionalism in the time of the postcolony: beyond triumph and betrayal

Firoz Cachalia

ABSTRACT
This paper situates the South African constitutional project in a wider temporal and ideological frame of reference as an anticolonial project and asks what the postcolonial critique of the constitutional project and the postcolonial state can offer to deepen our understanding of contemporary forms of cruelty and injustice in the form of inequality and misrecognition. It identifies the limits of 'Constitutional legalism' and is critical of the 'triumphalist' mode of appreciating the Constitution. Constitutional legalism postulates a text that contains a comprehensive conception of justice that awaits implementation and has settled all relevant questions arising from our colonial past. Instead, the Constitution should be conceived as an 'incompletely theorised agreement' which deferred many questions and which conceals many ongoing disagreements. But this paper also recognises the Constitution and its central propositions - human rights, the rule of law and popular self-government as genuine anticolonial achievements, which provide framework concepts and institutions for collective action and democratic politics. So the paper is also critical of the 'culturalist' critique that denounces the Constitution as a 'betrayal' that inscribes Eurocentric forms of reason as a permanent obstacle to the attainment of a genuinely postcolonial society. It proposes, as an alternative to both the 'legalist' defence and 'culturalist' critique that the idea of the 'demos' should be restored to its central place in the imaginary of South African constitutionalism. The Constitution can then be reconceived not as the perfect product of a singular moment in South African history but as an ongoing activity requiring dialogue, including inter-generational dialogue, and a democratic framework within which to strive for social change.

Take paper and ink
For that is your shield
Your rights are going!
So pick up your pen
Load it, load it with ink
Isaac Wauchope[1]

[1] A Odendaal *The Founders: The Origins of the ANC and the Struggle for Democracy in South Africa* (2012) 44.

When I search for Man
In the technique and style of Europe
I see only a succession of negations of man
And an avalanche of murders
Frantz Fanon[2]

1. Introduction

At the close of the 20th century, South Africa had its 'Accra moment'.[3] The new democratic Constitution of South Africa, 1996 – establishing a political community based on equal citizenship, ending legal discrimination, providing for representative institutions, and enshrining the judicial protection of individual rights – was triumphantly adopted. The birth of a new nation and the adoption of a supreme law were boldly proclaimed in the preamble of the text as a moment of rupture and decisive departure from the injustices of our past.

Two decades later, many continue to assess the 'constitutional project'[4] positively, to value the contribution that the judiciary has made in controlling the exercise of public power[5] and to alleviate some forms of suffering by enforcing the rights of vulnerable groups.[6] In the legal academy, a substantial group of scholars has emerged who are committed to contributing 'constructively' to South Africa's developing constitutional jurisprudence by engaging critically with the decisions of the Constitutional Court. The main preoccupation of these scholars, whether their reading of the Constitution is 'liberal' or 'postliberal', has been to examine the interpretive practices of judges with a view to proposing the 'best reading' or that reading which contributes best to outcomes considered just. This kind of scholarship has made an indispensable contribution to the establishment and legitimation of the post-apartheid constitutional order.

Karl Klare's's[7] seminal contribution to this genre of legal scholarship, for instance, draws on the critical legal theory of Duncan Kennedy[8] and the idea of textual indeterminacy to make the case for 'post-formalist' and 'transformative adjudication' that would result in more just outcomes. His work has been enormously important in making the case for an active state and an active judiciary in a joint project of social change. This has at the least prevented the emergence in 'post-apartheid' South Africa of a newly empowered, ideologically conservative constitutional court acting in defence of the status quo, a real risk that had to be circumvented in the transition to a constitutional democracy.[9] The constitutional project is also supported by the

---

[2] M Hollingworth *St Augustine of Hippo* (2013) 1.
[3] Ghana was the first African country to achieve independence from colonial rule in 1957.
[4] A broader idea than the text of the Constitution.
[5] All exercises of public power are subject to constitutional control – *AAA Investments (Proprietary) Limited v Micro Finance Regulatory Council* 2007 (1) SA 343 (CC).
[6] *Minister of Home Affairs v Fourie* 2006 (1) SA 524 (CC).
[7] KE Klare 'Legal culture and transformative constitutionalism' (1998) 14 *South African Journal of Human Rights* 146, 188.
[8] D Kennedy *A Critique of Adjudication* (1997).
[9] The supine response of the old Appellate Division to repressive and discriminatory legislation passed by a racially exclusive and legally sovereign parliament formed part of the background of experience that informed the drafting

growing tendency of political actors, of all persuasions, to seek the intervention of the courts to resolve their political conflicts.[10] Judicial intervention has also become increasingly necessary to remedy cases of bureaucratic failure[11] and official malfeasance.[12] Such judicial intervention, moreover, even in highly charged political cases, seems to have occurred with broad public support. Such criticism as there might have been about 'over constitutionalisation' and 'judicialisation' seems, for the time being at least, to have become distinctly muted.

However, faith in the constitutional project coexists in the current period with a mood of disappointment and criticism drawing on critical race theory,[13] postmodernism and poststructuralism,[14] Africanist and Black Consciousness political traditions,[15] and postcolonial theory. The elements of this emerging critique are neither easy to delineate nor is there sufficient thematic unity to discern a distinctive school of thought. However, there are some common preoccupations: a concern with racial injustice, cultural erasure and a continuation of the colonial past after the adoption of the Constitution. The critique is not limited to the formalistic interpretive practices of judges.[16] Such criticism, therefore, invites a broader debate about the constitutional project itself, and for this reason is to be welcomed.

In Part A, I attempt to frame a debate about the Constitution by distinguishing between two genres of engagement with the constitutional project: 'constitutional legalism' and 'postcolonial criticism'. I engage critically with both these apparently polarised responses to the constitutional project and also identify points of convergence, since both are preoccupied with the normative content of the *constitutional text*, and both I suggest gloss over the democratic and political content of the constitutional project.

In this debate, I take a sympathetic stance to the constitutional project but place the emphasis on its democratic and popular content. I am, however, critical of the

---

of South Africa's first 'post-apartheid' constitution. See J Dugard *Human Rights and the South African Legal Order* (1978). In this important work, Dugard shows how, for the most part, the old judiciary failed to uphold important rights when an outcome in favour of individual liberty was possible. Klare built on these insights in developing his argument that a change was required in the conservative culture of the legal profession and entrenched patterns of formalistic judicial reasoning if the Constitutional Court was to take its place as the primary interpreter of South Africa's aspirational, 'postliberal' constitution.

10 This has been particularly evident in relation to disputes arising between political parties in parliament. For example, see *Mazibuko* v *Sisulu* 2013(6) SA 249 (CC).

11 *Allpay Consolidated Investment Holdings (Pty) Ltd* v *Chief Executive Officer of the South African Social Security Agency* 2014 (4) SA 179 (CC).

12 The judiciary has had to review improper exercises of the prosecutorial discretion to institute or withdraw charges in cases involving the National Commissioner of Police and the President; *Freedom Under Law* v *National Director of Public Prosecutions* 2014 (1) SACR 111 (GNP), and *National Director of Public Prosecutions* v *Zuma* 2009 1 SACR 361 (SCA). See also the South African Public Protector's 'State of capture' report no. 6 of 2016/17 <https://www.sahistory.org.za/archive/state-capture-report-public-protector-14-october-2016>

13 JM Modiri 'The colour of law, power and knowledge: introducing critical race theory in (post-)apartheid South Africa' (2012) 28 *South African Journal of Human Rights* 405.

14 T Reddy *South Africa, Settler Colonialism and the Failures of Liberal Democracy* (2016).

15 T Madlingozi 'Social justice in the time of neo-apartheid: critiquing the anti-black economy of recognition, incorporation and distribution' (2017) 28 *Stellenbosch Law Review* 123.

16 This kind of critique of the Constitution sometimes includes criticism of extra-constitutional agreements alleged to have been part of the negotiated settlement as well as of policy decisions, such as deficit reduction, limits on public borrowing and trade liberalisation, which were adopted under the Mbeki presidency. These conflations contribute to the 'betrayal narrative' but add little to the issues implicated in the debate on the Constitution itself. See S Terreblanche *Lost In Transformation: South Africa's Search for a New Future Since 1986* (2012).

'legalist' reading of the Constitution, which finds within it a comprehensive conception of justice or what in one judgment was referred to as 'an objective normative value system'.[17] This conception of the project of constitutional democracy leaves nothing for the democratic communities and generations that come after the founding generation to accomplish, except to complete the tasks set for them by their constitutional ancestors. It also overestimates what can be accomplished through adjudication, or what Roberto Unger has called the rationalising legal discourse of 'ameliorative interpretation'.[18]

Social change is a much more complex process, and the requirements of achieving justice in a country with a long history of colonialism and apartheid can hardly be said to have been finally and comprehensively resolved in the drafting of the constitutional text two decades ago, or even in the court's 'post-apartheid' transformative jurisprudence. We must, therefore, revisit some fundamental questions about *injustice* today in the time of the postcolony and to ask what remains unresolved by the Constitution and why.

In engaging critically with 'postcolonial' criticism of the constitutional project, particularly the 'culturalist' critique, I ask whether the object of the critique is to contribute to the project of transformative constitutionalism and social change by showing how law and legal institutions, properly understood in terms of their form and content, can contribute to a project of social change and postcolonial justice, or whether the object is simply to unmask the Constitution as a cloak for continuing violence, oppression and cultural erasure. One should surely expect, given the depth and ambition of the constitutional project's culturalist critics, that alternative conceptions of normative, institutional and political ordering would be advanced. Respectfully, I suggest this task has not yet been persuasively undertaken.

In Part B, I situate the 'constitutional project' in a wider historical and ideological frame of reference than either the 'legalist' or the 'culturalist' paradigms, both of which tend to focus on the conjuncture of the 1990s, the period of 'negotiations', to explain the emergence of the Constitution, which was then either a miraculous triumph, or an abject betrayal. I explore the anticolonial origins of some of the key ideas that made their way into the constitutional text, such as the 'rights idea' and, crucially, the idea of 'democratic self-determination'. Anticolonial nationalist intellectuals consistently proposed democracy as a response to colonial oppression and apartheid for generations before 'negotiations' for a 'constitutional settlement' began. In this process of 'people formation', generations of 'organic intellectuals' in the loosely Gramscian sense – who first emerged through 'print capitalism', and who were linked with resistance movements – produced ideas that shaped politics, law and legal institutions. The project of 'people formation', which is at the core of the 'constitutional project' was therefore also a 'cultural' project. By contrast, therefore, with both the 'legalist' defence and the 'culturalist critique', I argue that the idea of the *demos* is the

---

[17] *Carmichele v Minister of Safety and Security* 2001(4)SA 938(CC) para 54–5. What I question is not the idea of constitutional norms, but only that their 'objectivity' exists independently of the attribution of meaning to the constitution through an ongoing democratic dialogue and contestation in which the constitutional court has the final word exercising its 'settlement function.'

[18] RM Unger *The Critical Legal Studies Movement: Another Time, A Greater Task* (2015) 15.

core idea of the constitutional text, which leaves many questions of postcolonial justice unresolved because anticolonial movements had broader ambitions than the adoption of an aspirational constitution, which includes a bill of rights. The adoption of the Constitution in 1996 should nevertheless be understood as an historical achievement, since it establishes a legal framework for a self-governing community of equal, rights-bearing citizens. It does not itself establish a just society[19] but contains within it an implicit critique of the status quo.

2. Part A

2.1. Constitutional legalism and its limits

The transition to constitutional democracies in former colonies such as Namibia and in Eastern Europe (after the demise of the Soviet Union in the latter part of the 20th century) has its origins in the 'rights revolution'[20] that occurred after World War II. Although this powerful idea of universal human rights can be said to have an ancient lineage in Greek antiquity, monotheistic religion, the French and American revolutions in the 18th century, the experience of the Holocaust in Europe and indeed, as I suggest in this paper, in the universalistic ideologies adopted by anticolonial liberation movements, it is also important to understand their novelty in the way this idea has come to be inscribed in constitutional texts and understood as establishing fundamental norms of political, legal and even socio-economic ordering. The South African Constitution is also the product of this recent global history.

In his book *The Last Utopia*,[21] Samuel Moyn emphasises that while it is 'true that rights have long existed',[22] more contemporary understandings are the result of the 'collapse of prior universalistic schemes',[23] such as socialism and anticolonial nationalism. In consequence, this ubiquitous idea has now apparently come to do all the work of expressing our emancipatory hopes, a burden, I will argue, in agreement with Makua Wa Mutua,[24] *it cannot fully shoulder*. As Moyn comments: 'Though they were born as an alternative to grand political missions—or even as moral criticism of politics—human rights are forced to take on the grand political mission of providing a global framework for the achievement of freedom, identity and prosperity. They were forced slowly, but surely, to assume the very maximalism they triumphed by avoiding'.[25]

This maximalist conception of the rights idea is linked with a method of legal reasoning - which Martin Loughlin has styled as 'liberal normativism'.[26] This rationalistic discourse has become an influential mode of reasoning in public law and

[19] In one of his early essays, *On the Jewish Question*, Karl Marx emphasises both the achievement and limits of political emancipation.
[20] CR Epp *The Rights Revolution: Lawyers, Activists, and Supreme Courts in Comparative Perspective* (1998).
[21] S Moyn *The Last Utopia: Human Rights in History* (2011).
[22] Ibid 7.
[23] Ibid.
[24] MW Mutua 'Hope and despair for a new South Africa: the limits of rights discourse' (1997) 10 *Harvard Human Rights Journal* 63.
[25] Moyn (note 21 above) 9.
[26] M Loughlin *Public Law and Political Theory* (1992).

constitutional discourse in many jurisdictions.[27] It emphasises the autonomy of law, its adjudicative and control functions,[28] the protection of individual rights, and aims to elaborate a comprehensive substantive conception of a political morality that is said to be instantiated in the constitutional texts of liberal constitutional democracies.

This rationalising discourse has also been influential in shaping conceptions of constitutional ordering in South Africa. The supreme Constitution is assumed under its influence to be something settled once and for all and to provide the transcendental substance – what one commentator on the German Constitution has disapprovingly called the 'juridical genome […] from which everything derives'[29] – to resolve all legal disputes, moral disagreements and political conflicts. On this reading of the South African constitutional project, all that is required to achieve justice in a country with a history of colonialism and apartheid is to faithfully implement the precepts and norms imminent within the text triumphantly adopted in 1996. Failure to fulfil the promise of the Constitution is then necessarily attributed too simplistically to political and bureaucratic failure, not the economic, social and cultural legacy of colonialism, racism and capitalism. The idea that justice is the result of the reasoned elaboration of the law also accentuates the tension between the idea of constitutionalism and the idea of democracy, which requires that the terms of social life be subjected to collective self-determination.

What this conception fails to appreciate about constitutions is that 'despite their textuality [they] are replete with gaps, silences and abeyances',[30] as a result of ineradicable political conflict and disagreement about the idea of justice itself, which comes before and after the Constitution. They may, therefore, better be thought of as a genre of what Cass Sunstein calls incompletely theorised agreements[31] – which, while aspiring to endure, are always open to interpretation, completion and revision through democratic politics.[32]

Since constitutions are the contingent outcome of political conflicts, the constituent power of the people – a question which is suppressed in the discourse of constitutional legalism – 'closed off as quickly as possible […] constrained inside vague abstractions […] or in sanitised juridical categories'[33] is never exhausted. Thus, as Loughlin has so trenchantly observed, '[C]onstituent power cannot be absorbed into

27 The jurisprudential foundations for normativism were developed by Ronald Dworkin in various books including *Taking Rights Seriously* (1977); *Freedom's Law: The Moral Reading of the American Constitution* (1996); and, most recently, *Justice for Hedgehogs* (2011).

28 M Loughlin (note 26 above) 60.

29 E Forsthoff *Der Staat der Industriegesellschaft: Dargestellt am Beispiel der Bundesrepublik Deutschland* 2 ed (1971) 144.

30 M Loughlin *The Idea Of Public Law* (2003) 50.

31 CR Sunstein *Legal Reasoning and political Conflict* (1996) 6.

32 A constitution, understood as a framework for democratic politics, and not simply as a text to be interpreted, is therefore constantly evolving through a process of *constitutional construction* involving multiple actors, including the 'political branches', political parties and even 'nonstate' actors. See JM Balkin 'The framework model and constitutional interpretation' in D Dyzenhaus & M Thorburn (eds) *Philosophical Foundations of Constitutional Law* (2016) 241. A constitution, however, also constrains this process by specifically setting out special procedures for its amendment. This is appropriate since any complex political community (including one emerging from the history of colonialism) may want to identify some 'fundamental' questions to place outside the immediate purview of 'ordinary' democratic politics to manage the risk of unmanageable conflict. Even as we pursue justice, questions of political ordering cannot and should not be avoided. Constitutions are, after all, also matters of statecraft.

33 Loughlin (note 30 above) 111.

some basic norm, for this would be to deny the continuity of the political dynamic that provides the state with its most basic energy. This is the normativist fallacy – the conflation of constituent and constituted power'.[34] Constitutions in democratic societies are therefore in principle always provisional, and their meaning always open to contestation. Their legitimacy and efficacy have to be established in each generation through democratic politics. It is only in this way that they can come to endure. This is the paradox at the heart of the constitutional project.

So today, two decades after its adoption, it is not surprising that there is an emerging political debate about *decolonisation* that is also a debate about the normative content of the Constitution. The 'liberal normativist' reading of the Constitution as a rights instrument that provides a new comprehensive normative framework for government does not provide an adequate conceptual grid for engagement with this debate – a debate that raises fundamental questions about the political identity of 'the people' whose existence is announced in its preamble. The Constitution also, 'constitutes the people in certain ways',[35] which is why it 'continues to generate controversy'.[36] But the constitutional text does not fully answer this question and was not designed to do so, and so we have to ask what the Constitution is for and what it leaves unsaid and undone, and what is to be accomplished by generations that come after the *founding* generation?

2.2. Cultural criticism and its limits

Criticism of the Constitution today takes different forms. Some criticism relates to design flaws that are remediable through constitutional amendment. The debate that periodically emerges over the electoral system is a good example. Although it may be difficult to reach political agreement on changes that may be required, such criticism is easily accommodated to the raison d'être of the constitutional project that it aims at improving.

This kind of 'positive critique' should be distinguished from a more thoroughgoing emerging critique of the constitutional project, which includes the constitutional text, its normative content *and* the negotiated settlement[37] that are not always clearly distinguished. Three themes predominate in this critique: continuing racial injustice, land dispossession through colonial conquest and cultural domination, all part of the legacy of colonialism, which it is argued the constitutional project has failed to address.

---

[34] Ibid 112.

[35] Ibid 108.

[36] Ibid.

[37] Terreblanche (note 16 above) attributes the limits that he believes the constitutional settlement placed on the redistribution of wealth to the influence of corporate capital. He was one of the first in South Africa to warn about growing economic inequalities. In this respect, he has been vindicated. His 'left wing' views on economic issues are, however, difficult to reconcile with his 'conservative' views on the Constitution, which he says gives too much power to the dominant African group (on page 79). This is a simple argument against the application of democratic principle of political equality under South African conditions and for the entrenchment of consociational-type ethnic-group rights. How this constitutional arrangement would have produced more socially just outcomes is not clear and not explained.

The focus of this paper is on the latter. The overriding idea is that the constitutional text inscribes *Western* forms of reasoning and knowledge[38] and therefore perpetuates the subordination of indigenous cultural forms by colonialism in the time of the postcolony. This kind of critique can also take the form of a broader questioning of the idea of universal values in the form of human rights and the 'grand narratives of the Enlightenment'. The constitution appears to rest its legitimacy on precisely such claims. One might think of this line of critique as the polarised opposite of the claim made within the legalist paradigm that the Constitution embodies an objective normative order.

One example of *epistemic erasure* is said to be the Constitution's subordination of customary law as a source of law to the litmus test of the supreme Constitution's overriding normative structure.[39] This subordination of African customary law to the law of the land, argues Mogobe Ramose,[40] perpetuates the colonial erasure of African culture and knowledge resulting from conquest. For the South African Constitution to be legitimate, he says, echoing Friedrich Carl von Savigny,[41] it must be the autochthonous product of the culture of indigenous Africans: 'The current constitution is therefore not the mirror of the institutions of the indigenous and conquered peoples of South Africa. It follows that a truly South African constitution is yet to be born.'[42] I would ask, *how*? Through a culturally informed interpretation of the constitutional text and through democratic dialogue or its rejection as a false start to be condemned as a betrayal?

An important theme in the period of anticolonial resistance also concerned the proper cultural content of such resistance, since colonialism suppressed 'non-Western' cultural forms. This debate remains unresolved, as Ramose's observations above illustrate, after the introduction of a 'nonracial constitution'. It occurs after the legal death of colonialism and apartheid in the form of this 'culturalist' challenge to the legitimacy of the constitutional project. As Edward Said has commented: '[A] profoundly important ideological debate at the heart of the cultural effort to decolonise, an effort at the restoration of community and repossession of culture […] goes on long after […] successful nationalism has come to a stop.'[43] So the 'culturalist' critique raises issues not confronted by the 'triumphalist' and 'legalist' appraisal of the constitutionalist project.

But the 'culturalist' lens, and in particular its critique of the rights idea as Eurocentric, is in its own way incomplete and inadequate for several reasons. Firstly, because its rejection of the rights idea as entirely derivative is not supported by the historical evidence. Mahmood Mamdani[44] has shown how the legal categories and institutions of the colonial state simultaneously instrumentalised tribe, ethnicity and customary law in the service of the colonial project, while constituting 'whites' as

---

[38] JM Modiri 'The crises in legal education' (2014) 46 *Acta Academica* 1.

[39] The Constitution, s 211.

[40] MB Ramose 'In memoriam: sovereignty and the 'New' South Africa' (2007) 16 *Griffith Law Review* 318.

[41] Of the school of German Romantics, who conceived of the law not as a codification of universal principles but rather as an expression of the *volksgeist* or culture of a particular people. This was his answer to the French Declaration of the Rights of Man and of the Citizen.

[42] Ramose (note 40 above) 366.

[43] E Said *Culture and Imperialism* (1994) 213.

[44] M Mamdani *Citizen and Subject: Contemporary Africa and the Legacy of Late Colonialism* (1996).

rights-bearing subjects. This bifurcated form of state-generated two forms of anticolonial resistance, one 'modernist', *which invoked the language of rights and constitutionalism* and sought to transcend colonial legal categories, and a 'communitarian' response, which invoked the *language of culture and authenticity,*[45] to challenge the symbolic and ideological content on the colonial project.

The idea of a bill of rights, for instance, was incorporated into the African Claims document in 1943,[46] demanding freedom for Africans after the World War II. Admittedly, the more inflated - and more progressive - version of the rights idea that found its way into the South African constitution was also the product of a global 'rights revolution' and a negotiated settlement.[47] But such 'borrowings' and creative reframings by local political forces can hardly be presented as a continuation of a 'colonial project'.

The rights idea is also not a fixed, determinate concept of invariable normative content. Rights are typically framed in broad language and are therefore open to multiple readings.[48] For this reason, the incorporation of rights in a constitutional text does not signal the end of normative disagreement[49] in any complex society. Indeed, it is precisely in such complex societies, including those with colonial histories, that rights may be required to regulate some endemic and pervasive disagreements. One might, therefore, think about rights in Foucauldian terms as a discourse that provides a field of contestation. Such contestation will, of course, be shaped by the power dynamics in a society. It might also well be that constitutional texts are not endlessly porous in terms of allowing through normative content. Justiciable individual rights always limit the extent to which individual interests can be overridden by collective goals and communitarian values such as Ubuntu. They also function to remove some questions from the field of political contestation, and some might question whether the institution of judicial review is consistent with democracy.[50] But it is not judicial review that is the object of the culturalist critique. It is the rights idea itself that, once condemned as culturally alien, can never be understood as an instrument of anticolonial resistance and postcolonial empowerment.

The theme of cultural domination and cultural resistance in colonial and postcolonial contexts can usefully be considered within the framework proposed by Nancy Fraser for considering questions of justice and injustice[51] in the context of the postcolony. She distinguishes between a recognition paradigm, based on the Hegelian dialectic of master and slave, which targets forms of cultural domination 'rooted in social patterns of representation, interpretation and communication';[52] and a

[45] Ibid 26.

[46] GM Gerhart & CL Glaser *From Protest to Challenge: A Documentary History of African Politics in South Africa 1882–1990* (1997) 209; T Ngcukaitobi *The Land Is Ours: South Africa's First Black Lawyers and the Birth of Constitutionalism* (2018) 257–273.

[47] A Sachs 'Perfectibility and Corruptibility: Preparing Ourselves for Power' inaugural lecture, University of Cape Town (1992); H Klug *The Constitution of South Africa: A Contextual Analysis* (2010) 45–58.

[48] See GCN Webber *The Negotiable Constitution: On the Limitation of Rights* (2009) and CR Sunstein *A Constitution of Many Minds: Why the Founding Document Doesn't Mean What it Meant Before* (2009).

[49] Webber (note 48 above) 2.

[50] M Tushnet *Taking the Constitution Away from the Courts* (1999).

[51] N Fraser & A Honneth *Redistribution and Recognition: A Political-Philosophical Exchange* (2003).

[52] Ibid 13.

redistribution paradigm, which is concerned with identifying patterns of distribution that are unjust from the perspective of liberal political theory.

The latter can be criticised from a Marxist point of view for failing to capture the full depth of capitalist injustice. From a 'political economy' perspective, the rights idea, even when stretched to cast socio-economic claims as legal entitlements, provides an inadequate framing for questions of economic justice, because it does not reach questions of exploitation and commodification rooted in processes of surplus extraction and appropriation.[53] However, Fraser's framework, as she points out, can accommodate such questions being asked about the fundamental economic structure of society.[54]

The recognition idea, at least in the form proposed by the Canadian philosopher Charles Taylor, has also been criticised as being inadequate in colonial contexts,[55] because his proposal for wider accommodation of 'diversity' is, in essence, a proposal for inclusion of subordinated indigenous communities into the institutions of a majoritarian political order, which does not, therefore, address the question of the political sovereignty of such communities. This analysis does not easily apply in the South African context in which indigenous Africans constitute a majority, and are therefore constitutionally self-determining, unless the view is taken that the formal institutions of democracy makes no difference even in this context.

What is most useful about Fraser's framework is that it does not reintroduce the 'false antithesis'[56] associated with the 'base superstructure metaphor' between these two forms of injustice, and therefore invites consideration of them separately, as well as the forms of interpenetration between them in the postcolonial context.

I argue that the constitutional framework and its rights provisions provide the 'scaffolding'[57] but does not fully 'resolve' problems of misrecognition that originated with the colonial project and remains at least partially unresolved today. The imperative to create a postcolonial citizenship 'adequate to building an inclusive political community'[58] is a matter for democratic politics. An essentialist and ahistorical conception of culture, is an obstacle to this project of postcolonial justice because it fixes identities that are produced by colonialism and conflates cultural and political identities.

The culturalist critique, insofar as it presents itself as a critique of both liberalism and Marxism as inscribing 'Western' forms of rationality, also tends to displace concerns with class-based inequalities,[59] and therefore fails to adequately address the

---

53 I Shivji *The Concept of Human Rights in Africa* (1989).

54 Fraser & Honneth (note 51 above) 11.

55 GS Coulthard *Red Skin White Masks: Rejecting the Colonial Politics of Recognition* (2014).

56 Ibid 11.

57 S Woolman 'South Africa's aspirational constitution and our problems of collective action' (2016) 32 *South African Journal of Human Rights* 156.

58 M Mamdani *Define and Rule: Native as Political Identity* (2012) 106.

59 This results in a failure to provide a persuasive account of economic inequality, not only under colonial capitalism but also contemporary globalized capitalism. Furthermore, both the 'legalist' defence and the 'culturalist' critique of the 'constitutional project' suppress consideration of the possibly constitutive relationship between the juridical forms of liberal democracies and the 'logic of capital'. See DS Grewal 'The legal constitution of capital' in H Boushey, JB Delong & M Steinbaum (eds) *After Piketty: The Agenda For Economics and Inequality* (2017).
Grewal's argument, in brief, is that legally guaranteed economic rights, which enable private economic agents to accumulate assets, at least partly accounts for the long-term trend in capitalist economies, identified by Thomas Piketty, for returns to capital to exceed average growth rates (as expressed in the formula $r > g$). This may

material and structural dimensions of the colonial legacy.[60] As Terry Eagleton has observed, cultural struggle is important: 'Some anti-colonial leaders, however, had learned the lesson well: colonialist culture had to be ditched along with colonialist rule. There was no point in simply replacing wigged and robed white judges with wigged and robed black ones.'[61] But he cautions against the tendency of cultural politics to displace politics based on the material concerns of poverty and inequality: '[C]ulture should not be a substitute for social transformation. Irish Nationalists were not just fighting for green mailboxes rather than red ones. Black South Africans are not just fighting for the right to be Black South Africans.'[62]

South Africa's Constitution and our 'postcolonial' condition should, therefore, be evaluated in the light of these two continuing forms of injustice identified by Fraser: cultural misrecognition and material deprivation. The Constitution provides an agonistic framework[63] for dealing with these unresolved questions through democratic practices of dialogue and contestation. But this framework neither fully prescribes nor guarantees desired outcomes. Nor does the Constitution present an insurmountable obstacle to efforts at cultural retrieval, decolonisation and economic justice.

2.3. Constitutional criticism and the political Constitution

'Constitutional legalism', as pointed out above, is centrally concerned with adjudication of 'justiciable disputes' and not primarily with how the political branches function or with the stakes in democratic politics, although such questions are increasingly coming within the purview of judicial determination in South Africa. 'Constitutional legalism' does however, have an abstract theory of the 'political constitution', which includes legally enforceable concepts – such as the separation of powers, checks and balances, representative government and the rule of law – that justify the kind of political institutions that are envisaged in the text of the South African Constitution. Constitutional criticism, inspired by this framework, generally seeks to reconfigure institutions with a limited 'toolkit' to improve their functioning without challenging their normative content.

The 'culturalist' critique concentrates on epistemic questions and has thus far avoided *questions of political ordering and institutional design* as well as questions about how political transitions occur in countries with a history of colonialism and apartheid. This is an omission that significantly weakens the thrust of this kind of criticism of the Constitution, which is then simply dismissed as a 'betrayal'. Ramose is an exception to this generalisation, since he combines a radical critique of the normative content of the Constitution with a conservative critique of its political institutions.

---

explain why the guarantee of socio-economic rights does not necessarily generate egalitarian outcomes. See also S Moyn *Not Enough: Human Rights in an Unequal World* (2018). Moyn's point is that human rights should be defended as part of a larger political programme, which includes a commitment to material equality.

[60] See V Chibber *Postcolonial Theory and the Specter of Capital* (2013).

[61] T Eagleton *After Theory* (2003) 47.

[62] Ibid. See also Chibber (note 60 above).

[63] C Mouffe *The Democratic Paradox* (2000). Such a framework facilitates democratic contestation among adversaries, which includes disagreement about what the framework requires.

Ramose does not object in principle to constitutional supremacy but only to the adoption of the principle in the context of a negotiated settlement that protects the private property rights of 'white colonists'.[64] I argue that the adoption of the principle of constitutional supremacy was important in facilitating a negotiated transition to a democracy in South Africa. No principled, negotiated compromise was possible between the anti-colonial demand, on the hand, for democratic majority rule and the insistence, on the other hand by the incumbent regime, on a system of consociational power-sharing, ethnic-group rights and minority vetoes. The principle of constitutionalism made it possible to mediate these polarised positions, since it constrains all electoral majorities but not the right of the African people to self-determination and democratic majority rule based on the principle of equal political rights, the central demand of anticolonial and anti-apartheid resistance movements.

The principal has also demonstrated its importance in the 'postcolony' by affording some legal protection to vulnerable postcolonial minorities, such as sexual minorities, and by providing an important check on the abuse of power by postcolonial elites. Much of our 'postcolonial' experience in South Africa, our continent and elsewhere has reminded us how important it is to institutionalise a system of constitutional limits on the exercise of state power. Frantz Fanon's critique of postcolonial elites in the *Wretched of the Earth*[65] and particularly in the third chapter on the trials and tribulations of national consciousness was, I suggest, well headed by the drafters of the Constitution,[66] who devoted a whole chapter to the establishment of independent bodies in order to subject the exercise of state power but not the project of social change to legal constraints.[67]

Nor is the idea of 'constitutional checks and balances' foreign to precolonial thought in Africa about political and constitutional ordering. Basil Davidson's observations about the 17th century Asante kingdom on the West African seaboard are most illuminating: 'Power was exercised by powerful persons, but with constitutional checks and balances tending to prevent abuse of power [...] executive power derived from the degree to which its founding principles were observed: in the rule of law, in the diffusion of executive power, and in the encasing of that power within political and legal checks on its use, just as the Asante's blunders and disasters came from failure to maintain those principles.'[68]

Ramose advocates consociationalism[69] and ethnic federation proposed by the Buthelezi Commission[70] as alternatives to constitutionalism.[71] These were the perspectives advanced respectively by the National Party, which implemented the apartheid system, and the Inkatha Freedom Party, which held power over the KwaZulu

---

[64] Ramose 'To whom does the land belong?' (2016) 50 *Psychology in Society* 86, 96.

[65] HK Bhabha 'Foreword: Framing Fanon' in F Fanon *The Wretched of the Earth* (2004) (trans R Philcox, 2004).

[66] Sachs (note 47 above). Sachs's observations in this lecture have proved to be extraordinarily prescient.

[67] Chapter 9 of the Constitution.

[68] B Davidson *The Black Man's Burden: Africa and the Curse of the Nation-State* (1992) 61–62.

[69] The Belgian political scientist Arend Lijphart's ideas were influential in South Africa among constitutional reformers who recognised that reform of the political order was necessary but wanted to avoid majority rule. Lijphart argues that in societies 'deeply divided by ethnicity' a system of concurrent majorities, ethnic power-sharing and mutual vetoes should be adopted as an alternative to majoritarian democracy. In much of the literature applying consociational theory to the South African situation, 'ethnicity', or 'culture' , is used as a proxy for race. See A Lijphart *Patterns of Democracy: Government Forms and Performance in Thirty-Six Countries* (1999).

[70] The Inkatha Freedom Party, governing in the homeland KwaZulu, established the commission in 1982.

[71] Ramose (note 40 above).

homeland, in the constitutional negotiations. The political actors whose constitutional perspectives were shaped by the ideological perspectives of anticolonial African nationalism opposed these ideas as an illegitimate attempt to subvert the logic of the democratic principles of political equality and majority rule, which were at the heart of anticolonial resistance.[72]

The culturalist critique also does not engage with the democratic content of the constitutional project, a blind spot it shares with its legalist adversary. The South African constitutional project, is based on two principles of legitimacy. The first is constitutionalism, which emphasises the binding legal constraints of the rule of law and human rights on collective decision-making in the political association envisaged in the Constitution. The second principle of legitimacy is the *principle of self-government* or popular sovereignty, which provides that constitutionalist constraints are only legitimate to the extent that they can be said to be imposed by the people on themselves.[73] They are therefore always open to revision by the democratic processes envisaged in the Constitution itself. Neither Ramose nor the Constitution's other culturalist critics engage, as far as I am aware, with the question of the extent to which the *legitimacy* of the constitutional project is dependent on the *process of its adoption*, and in this light what the implications are of the fact that the South African Constitution was adopted by an elected body, albeit one that was constrained by a set of negotiated principles.[74]

The critique does also not engage with the implications of the fact that the Constitution establishes a framework *for a demos* where the ultimate *constitutive power* lies. Ramose rests sovereignty on primordial, precolonial, collective ownership of land. The result is a static, essentialist reading of the Constitution. My alternative political conception of sovereignty is based on the idea of collective popular agency by a democratically organised community. It emphasises democracy as the main principle of constitutional ordering. The question of sovereignty is avoided altogether within the legalist framework, or located in the text of the Constitution itself as supreme law and its judicial enforcement.

2.4. Text and context: the Constitution and social change

Constitutional legalists who engage positively with the constitutional project and the critics of the Constitution share a common preoccupation with the *text* and normative content of the Constitution. Constitutional legalists are concerned with interpreting the constitutional text in its best possible light, and to show that so interpreted, the constitution envisages a just society. The critics engage in a critique of the normative content of the constitutional text, while for the most part avoiding direct engagement with the debate about the judiciary's interpretive practices, since it is the ideological content of Constitution itself that is the object of criticism as the source of postcolonial injustice and misrecognition. It is important, in this exercise of critical

---

72 Klug (note 47 above) 45–58.

73 J Tully 'The unfreedom of the moderns in comparison to their ideals of constitutional democracy' (2002) 65 *Modern Law Review* 204.

74 Klug (note 47 above) Chapter 3.

engagement with the constitutional project in the aftermath of its founding, to step outside of the text, and into its context as it were, and to ask what the explanation is and what the implications are of the apparent gap between the normative framework of the Constitution and the facts of continuing injustice in our 'postcolonial' society. This points in the direction of an examination of the relationship between legal and institutional structures of constitutional democracies on the one hand and social and economic structures on the other.[75] It bears repeating that this is an enquiry that is avoided by both constitutional legalists who appraise the Constitution positively as embodying a fully adequate and comprehensive conception of justice, and by its culturalist critics, since the Constitution is considered by the latter to inscribe specifically 'Western' forms of rationality.

The consequence is that neither the reasons for deepening inequalities[76] nor the question how social change[77] occurs and can occur in any given society is addressed. In my view, Stuart Woolman[78] is correct that the gap between constitutional norms and social facts is to be explained as a 'collective action problem' – I would add however, that the possibilities of collective action are shaped by the continuing structural conditions of 'postcoloniality'[79] and the 'logic of capital' *outside the text itself.* The Constitution *as a text* is neither the cause nor the remedy for such 'deep inequalities',[80]which cannot be reached through judicial determinations of its socio-economic rights provisions, no matter how bold. Questions of fundamental structural change present additional questions of political choice as well as of constraint on policy-making under conditions of global capitalism and democratic politics. Such questions cannot be treated simply as ones about the constitutional text and its interpretation.

This problem of the gap between the facts and norms of constitutional democracies is by no means confined to societies with a colonial history. It is a problem that was present from the inception of bourgeois democracies in the *Western world* – when, as Anatole France observed after the revolution in France, the law in its majesty forbad both rich and poor to live under the bridge of the River Seine – and it is a problem that persists in Liberal democracies today. This has implications for the way democratic institutions actually work or fail to function in accordance with constitutionally prescribed norms. Western states, as Deborah Cook writes, are still failing for the most part, to operate in accordance with the constitutionally prescribed

[75] See G Sitaraman *The Crisis of the Middle-Class Constitution: Why Economic Inequality Threatens our Republic* (2017).

[76] T Piketty *Capital in the Twenty-First Century* (2014).

[77] See GN Rosenberg *The Hollow Hope: Can Courts Bring About Social Change?* (2008). The question to what degree and in what ways courts can contribute to social change is important. This includes consideration of the difference the court's interpretive practices can make. To this extent I am broadly sympathetic to the idea of transformative adjudication. I don't think it is correct that it does not ever matter at all, because whatever the court's interpretive practices, a court in South Africa will always arrive at the right transformative outcome. But transformative adjudication has been made to carry the responsibility for a project of social change that it cannot sustain. Two decades after the adoption of the Constitution, we need to revisit the debate on the role of the Judiciary in promoting social change, as well as what the normative and institutional constraints faced by judiciaries positively disposed to a project of social change might be.

[78] Woolman (note 57 above).

[79] S Zondi 'The Africanist turn in South African National Question discourses' in E Webster & K Pampallis (eds) *The Unresolved National Question in South Africa: Left Thought Under Apartheid and Beyond* (2017) 96.

[80] Piketty (note 77 above).

circulation of power based on the 'will of the people'.[81]This is also true of constitutional democracies in the postcolonial south.

The question has to be posed whether the preconditions for the development of a genuinely deliberative democracy envisaged by Jürgen Habermas can develop under the social conditions generated by *capital* in the *West and non-West.*[82] However, unless it can be shown that there is a constitutive 'fit' between the institutional and legal structures envisaged by the Constitution and capital, the identification of this gap between norms and facts of the postcolony cannot provide a convincing basis for a rejection of the Constitution itself and its normative and institutional frameworks as a betrayal.

I argue that the project of social transformation in South Africa requires that we should continue to work critically and strategically (both 'deconstructively' and 'constructively') 'from the inside' the constitutional text and its suppositions, in order to *continue* a project of 'decolonization' and 'transformation' that has its origins in the late 19th century. From that time, anticolonial movements and intellectuals in South Africa and elsewhere, worked creatively and interstitially, and not merely imitatively with a set of propositions associated with the Enlightenment. These principles of political justice have many points of origin, were egregiously violated by colonialism, and defended and elaborated through anticolonial resistance. To the extent that the Constitution can be said to be based on these principles of political justice, it can only be characterised as imposed and alien by re-inscribing Eurocentrism and the dualist cartography of colonialism, according to which the 'orient' and the 'occident' can never meet.[83] Below I show that the 'constitutional project' and its central propositions have their origins in at least a century of anticolonial resistance.

3. Part B

3.1. Anticolonial cultural resistance and the 'National Question'

Debate on the Constitution (whether in the mood of triumph or betrayal) tends to focus exclusively on the 'conjuncture' of the last decade of the 20th century. Here I want to situate the constitutional text – its preambular phrase, 'We the People'[84] – in a broader temporal dimension, which begins not at the moment of constitutional enactment but in the closing decades of the 19th century with the emergence of an African intelligentsia of traditional leaders, lawyers, newspaper editors and journalists, writers and poets, some of whom, like Sol Plaatje, became political leaders.

---

[81] D Cook 'The Talking Cure in Habermas's Republic' (2001) 12 *New Left Review* 135, 138.

[82] J Habermas *Between Facts and Norms: Contributions to a Discourse Theory of Law and Democracy* (1996) (trans W Rehg, 1996).

[83] In his poem 'The Ballad of East and West', the Indian-born English novelist and poet Rudyard Kipling wrote this about the supposed incompatibility between 'East' and 'West':

> *'OH, East is East and West is West, and never the twain shall meet,*
> *Till Earth and Sky stand presently at God's great judgement seat'*
>
> He also authored The *White Man's Burden,* recommending imperialism to the North American Republic.

[84] The Constitution. See also J Klaaren *From Prohibited Immigrants to Citizens: The Origins of Citizenship and Nationality in South Africa* (2017). Klaaren provides an interesting historical account of legal notions such as citizenship and the politics of 'peoplehood' in the period 1837 to 1937.

I want to explore their ideas as expressed in various texts 'as intellectual constructions in their own right',[85] and the intertextual connections between their ideas and the ones that found their way into the constitutional text (or did not).[86] One might think of this group so admirably brought to life in Andre Odendaal's *The Founders*,[87] and their successors, as 'organic intellectuals'[88] in the sense that their ideas were linked over time, with the political and 'civilizational' project of decolonisation.

Who are the people? This is a question – the 'National Question' – that always has to be asked and answered before the question how the people should govern themselves can even be reached. There is, as Ronald Dworkin says, 'no non-historically right answer to this question'.[89] How did we, in a cauldron of Western imperialism and colonial racism, begin to see ourselves as a *people* within the territorial boundaries[90] of modern South Africa?

3.2. Anticolonial nationalism: a project of peoplehood

Anticolonial resistance among colonised Africans in South Africa had an external and an internal dimension. It was concerned not only with independence from the metropolitan colonial power but also with questions of justice and injustice posed by 'internalised' colonial relations of domination and subordination. The central preoccupation was with the 'National Question': who belongs in the political community of equals? What arguments are right and must be made as a matter of political morality against the justifications made to support colonialism and against equality? Is it *true* that human beings are divided into *racial or culturally distinct* groups, or are we not all fundamentally the same by virtue of our common humanity, as Plaatje suggests in his book *Native Life In South Africa*,[91] citing the case of the disparaged Jew Shylock in Shakespeare's *The Merchant Of Venice*.[92]

And what do we make of our obvious bodily, cultural and linguistic and other differences – of colour, for instance? When is it relevant to acknowledge these differences? Is it ever justified to draw distinctions – on the basis of race, culture or some other analogous basis – in allocating political and other rights? The Act of Union, which denied political rights to indigenous Africans on the basis of such irrelevant differences among human beings, unmasked the moralising coloniser as a hypocrite whose only argument is superior force, not superior morality.

The colonised were compelled by their life worlds in the colonial order to ask: what do we believe is just? To seek to answer such questions always involves a process of intellectual and cultural creation. Therefore, '[A]fter a period of "primary resistance," literally fighting against outside intrusion, there comes the period of secondary, that is, ideological resistance, when efforts are made to reconstitute

[85] A du Toit & H Giliomee *Afrikaner Political Thought: Analysis and Documents Volume One 1780–1850* (1983) 15.
[86] Ibid.
[87] Odendaal (note 1 above).
[88] A Gramsci *Selections from the Prison Notebooks* (1995).
[89] R Dworkin *Justice for Hedgehogs* (2011) 380.
[90] The Africanist tradition in anticolonial thought included a challenge to colonial boundaries. See Davidson (note 68 above) & Zondi (note 80 above).
[91] ST Plaatje *Native Life in South Africa, Before and Since the European War and the Boer Rebellion* (2004).
[92] Ibid 116.

a shattered community.'[93] This takes place through efforts to imaginatively enter and reshape the travelling world of discourses and cultural ideals, including the modular forms of nationalism.[94] As Said says: 'To achieve recognition is to chart and then occupy the place in Imperial cultural forms reserved for subordination, to occupy it self-consciously, fighting for it on the same territory once ruled by a consciousness that assumed the subordination of a designated inferior other. Hence, *re-inscription*.'[95]

This process of cultural and ideological resistance was creative, not merely imitative,[96] since it produced new emancipatory ideals in opposition to the ones invoked to justify colonial domination. In opposition to 'the excesses of Eurocentric self-consciousness, anticolonial movements challenged the notion of a racial hierarchy historically steeped in the ethos of the European Enlightenment and dared to seek to re-imagine the very idea of being human'.[97]

The first great ideal to emerge as a response to colonialism in South Africa – in the process of resisting the establishment of a racist unitary state in 1910 and subsequent attempts, beginning in the 1930s, to erode what remained of the 'Cape franchise' – was the universalist idea that since we are all fundamentally the same as human beings, we should all have the same political rights. 'The desire for unity,' wrote Isaac Tabata,[98] came from 'realisation that physical differences, our colour differences, our cultural differences have nothing to do with our economic situation.'[99] He would certainly have extended this universalist argument to include critique of the ideological basis of the colonial political order.

There were many important tactical, strategic, organisational and ideological differences among the movements that emerged to challenge the colonial order. But on the fundamental question that is the subject of this paper – the thematics of anticolonial resistance – there was convergence on the idea that the colonial question could only be resolved through the establishment of a self-governing community of equals or a demos in South Africa. In his speech to the inaugural conference of the Pan Africanist Congress,[100] after splitting from the African National Congress (ANC) because of disagreements about aspects of the Freedom Charter and what he considered to be an inadequate treatment of the colonial land question, Robert Sobukwe made it clear that the new party was committed to the establishment of a 'political

---

93 Said (note 43 above) 210.

94 See B Anderson *Imagined Communities: Reflections on the Origins and Spread of Nationalism* (2006) 4, 48. The South African experience provides striking support for his thesis that nation-ness is a cultural artefact created toward the end of the 18th century, with the emergence of 'print capitalism', and once having been created, 'became modular and capable of being transplanted, with varying degrees of self-consciousness, to a variety of social terrains, to be merged with a correspondingly wide variety of political and ideological constellations'.

95 Said (note 43 above) 210 (original emphasis retained).

96 P Chatterjee *Nationalist Thought and the Colonial World: A Derivative Discourse* (1986).

97 K Motlanthe 'Eulogy during Ahmed Kathrada's funeral in full' *Huffington Post* South Africa (29 March 2017) <https://www.huffingtonpost.co.za/2017/03/29/kgalema-motlanthes-eulogy-during-ahmed-kathradas-funeral-in-fu_a_22016805/>

98 IB Tabata 'Birth of a nation' Address to the Society of Young Africa (December 1951).

99 Ibid.

100 RM Sobukwe Opening address at the Africanist (Pan Africanist Convention) inaugural convention (April 1959). Dikgang Moseneke comments that he made the unanswerable case against the bankruptcy of racism and for non-racialism as well as African humanism. D Moseneke *My Own Liberator: A Memoir* (2016) 271.

democracy as understood in the *West*'.[101] He said that he wished 'to emphasise that freedom of the African means the freedom of all in South Africa, the *European included*', and called for the 'establishment of a genuine democracy in which all men will be citizens and will live and be governed as individuals and not as distinctive national groups'.[102]

This process by which the idea of democracy emerged as the leitmotif of the anti-colonial struggle against settler colonialism has its origins in the closing decades of the 19th century – when an African intelligentsia emerged from educational institutions such as Lovedale and Healdtown college, published newspapers such as *Indaba*[103] and *Ikwezi*,[104] translated books such as *The Pilgrim's Progress*[105] and *King Lear* into African languages, and became involved in shaping the politics of African nationalism.[106]

In an article entitled 'The regeneration of Africa' published in 1906, Pixley ka Isaka Seme,[107] who was to become one of the first leaders of the Congress, *argued* that while the 'African people were not a strictly homogeneous race'[108] and were 'composed like other races of mankind of free and unique individuals',[109] they possess 'a common fundamental sentiment'[110] and an 'ancestral greatness'.[111]

An article also by him published in 1911, in black-owned newspaper *Imvo Zabantsundu*,[112] illustrates some of the preoccupations of the ANC that was formed in 1912 to oppose the exclusion of Africans from the political process. He wrote: '[T]here is today among all races and men a general desire for progress. The demon of racialism, the aberrations of the Xhoza-Fingo feud […] must be buried and forgotten […] *we are one people*'.[113] In this article, written at the beginning of the 20th century, Seme understood *Africans as a people*,[114] and in so doing laid the ideological basis both for a modern South African democracy and continental identity to evolve in response to colonialism.

It would not be long before this idea of peoplehood was extended to include all South Africans. In 1928, the South African Communist Party adopted the Black Republic slogan, committing the Communist Party to fight for 'an independent native South African Republic as a stage towards workers and peasants Republic with full

---

101 Sobukwe (Ibid).
102 Ibid.
103 Odendaal (note 1 above) 28.
104 Ibid 29.
105 Ibid.
106 Ibid.
107 PkI Seme 'The Regeneration of Africa' (1906) *South African Affairs* 404.
108 Ibid.
109 Ibid.
110 Ibid.
111 Ibid.
112 PkI Seme 'Native union' in T Karis & G Carter (eds) *From Protest to Challenge: A Documentary History of African Politics in South Africa 1882–1964 Volume 1: 1882–1939* (1972) 72.
113 Ibid (emphasis added).
114 Here the concept 'African people' is constructed as an anticolonial concept aimed at overcoming imposed tribal political identities. The concept has multiple and contested meanings. When President Thabo Mbeki used the concept in his address to parliament a century later, on the occasion of the adoption of the Constitution, he invoked a more inclusive, nonracial concept of *African peoplehood*.

equal rights for all races, black, coloured and white'.[115] In 1930, the Anglican Church called for full citizenship for all.[116] In 1943, at its annual conference in Bloemfontein, the ANC, in response to the adoption of the Atlantic Charter, adopted the African Claims document,[117] which contained a 'bill of rights' and a demand for universal recognition of the right to self-determination and self-government. In the same year, the Non-European Unity Movement adopted the 'Ten-point Programme', which explained its strategy of non-collaboration with the institutions of the colonial state and included the demand for 'full democratic rights'.[118] And in 1955, the Freedom Charter was adopted, which declared that South Africa '[be]longs to all who live in it, Black and White'.[119] The democratic content of the Charter was uncontroversial. It was on the implications of this phrasing on the land question that led to the Africanist split, as Sobukwe's speech at the inaugural conference of the Pan Africanist conference in 1961 makes clear.

The spirit of anticolonial nationalism in South Africa was also the one Benedict Anderson says was embodied in the heart-rending constitution of Maario Sakay's short-lived Republic of Katagalugan (1902), which said, among other things: 'No Tagalog, born in this Tagalog archipelago, shall exalt any person above the rest because of his race or the colour of his skin; fair, dark, rich, poor, educated and ignorant – all are completely equal [...] There may be differences in education, wealth or appearance, but never in essential nature (*pagkatao*) or ability to serve a cause.'[120]

Alongside this universalist, 'anti-difference' theme, the National Question raised another, emphasising the distinctiveness and identity of the oppressed other. In 1861, Tiyo Soga, a Glasgow University graduate and ordained Presbyterian minister who has been described as 'a figure of crucial importance for the intellectual and political history of South Africa, as a precursor to African nationalism',[121] wrote this: 'Africa was of God-given to the race of Ham. I find the Negro from the days of the old Assyrians downwards, keeping his "individuality" and "distinctiveness" amid the wreck of empires, and the revolution of ages.'[122]

This second theme should be understood as representing a critique of the false universalism of the 'democrat' who 'has no eyes for the concrete syntheses with which history confronts him [...] he resolves all collectivities into individual elements'.[123] In his essay 'Black Orpheus', Jean-Paul Sartre specifically confronts the colonial situation with this insight: 'But although oppression is oppression, it comes in different forms depending on history and geographical conditions: the black man is a victim as a *black man*, as colonised native [...] and since he is thus, where oppression takes

---

115 A Lerumo *Fifty Fighting Years: The Communist Party of South Africa 1921–1971* (1987) 113.
116 Du Toit & Giliomee (note 85 above) 412.
117 Gerhart & Karis (note 46 above) 209.
118 See Tabata (note 98 above). Tabata was an intellectual luminary and president of the Non-European Unity Movement; he stressed the importance of ideas in the struggle against colonial domination for democratic rights: 'the rulers have had their system of education, their myths and superstitions, all of which are calculated to prop up their particular system of society.'
119 Clause 1, *The Freedom Charter*, adopted at the Congress of the People at Kliptown, Johannesburg (1955).
120 Anderson (note 94 above) 153–154.
121 Odendaal (note 1 above) 26.
122 Ibid 27.
123 JP Sartre *Anti-Semite and Jew: An Exploration of the Etiology of Hate* (1948) (trans GJ Becker, 1995) 39.

the form of racial oppression claims for recognition, demand valorisation of identities that have been denigrated.'[124]

Anticolonial resistance produced a rich and complex debate about identity that anticipated many of the questions of recognition and misrecognition that we confront today. When Seme used the concept 'African', he aimed to construct a political identity that transcended colonial constructions of tribal identity. As Mamdani writes: 'Nationalism was a struggle of natives to be recognised as a transethnic identity, as a race, as 'Africans', and thus as a race – to gain admission into the world of rights'.[125]

The idea of 'Africanness' also did not have a fixed meaning. Sobukwe used the concept more broadly than Seme did to include all those who subjectively and sincerely embraced the aspirations of the African people. Similarly, Steve Biko used the concept of 'blackness' as a political construct and strategic concept. When he was asked at his trial why he used the concept 'black' to describe the oppressed, he replied: '[H]istorically we have been defined as black people, and when we reject the term 'non-white' and take upon ourselves to call ourselves what we think we are, we've got in front of us a whole number of alternatives.'[126] This suggests that 'blackness' is a matter of social construction and political choice, not a permanent condition.

This non-essentialist conception coexisted with conceptions of identity, which accepted given identities, even if based on apartheid's legal classifications. So when editorials in the ANC journal *Sechaba* started to refer to coloured people as 'so-called', Alex La Guma wrote to *Sechaba* strenuously objecting to this appellation: 'When we worked for the Congress of the People, we sang, "We the coloured people must struggle to exist".'[127] A certain PG responded: 'We reject the racist framework. We reject their *terminology*.'[128]

This emphasis on identity and difference is not opposed to the universalist principle of inclusive peoplehood, although they appear to be in tension when they are grasped simplistically.[129] Justice requires that we respect individuals as such, as citizens and in their life worlds. Such questions were at the heart of debates and contestation in anticolonial politics for more than a century, along with pressing questions of organisational strategy and tactics. They have re-emerged in the form of the decolonisation debate two decades after the adoption of the Constitution and the revival of interest in the ideas of Fanon and Biko. How should the constitutional project be understood in the light of demands for recognition and in response to unjust misrecognition?

In addition to these two recognition themes, the National Question was preoccupied with the questions of social and economic justice. The political kingdom, to recall Kwame Nkrumah's formulation, was always only the starting point of the process of decolonisation. As Davidson writes: 'Only by thus reforming the social structures of colonialism could there be a transfer of power to colonised majorities, rather

124 JP Sartre 'Black Orpheus' (1948) (trans Chris Turner) in *The Aftermath of War* (2008) 259, 267–8 (original emphasis retained).
125 Mamdani (note 58 above) 6.
126 South African Students Organisation/Black People's Convention Trial (2 May 1976).
127 *Sechaba* (June 1984) 31.
128 *Sechaba* (September 1984) 28 (emphasis added).
129 M Walzer 'Preface' in Sartre (note 123 above) 5.

than the mere adjustment of Imperial attitudes to educated minorities and to the personal or political ambitions of these elites.'[130] The important – and still unresolved – question of the decolonisation of the social structures of our postcolonial society is today sublimated in the form of a postcolonial critique of the cultural content of the constitutional text.

3.3. The Constitution as an anticolonial project

How does the Constitution address the two questions of misrecognition and of social justice after liberation that also preoccupied intellectuals associated with anticolonial resistance movements as they were framed by the 'National Question'? First, it recognises all South African citizens as members of a national political community with equal rights of participation,[131] remedying a form of misrecognition that was the central feature of the political order established through colonialism. As Fraser and Honneth remark: 'In cases where misrecognition involved denying the common humanity of some participants, the remedy is universalist recognition; thus, the first and most fundamental redress for South African Apartheid was universal "non-racial citizenship".'[132] In this context, the principle of abstract citizenship – *which is blind to racial, cultural and other differences* – is progressive. In treating the fact of group differences as irrelevant for the purpose of allocating political rights, it repudiates the ideological bases of the colonial and apartheid political order that constructed group differences as an instrument of political domination and exclusion.

On the other hand, the system of individual rights created by the Constitution empowers individuals to voluntarily recognise themselves as members of groups, or not to do so. This is important because, in conscripting individuals to groups organised in a hierarchy of racial ordering, the apartheid system misrecognised dimensions both of individual selves and the possible forms of human connection, thus restricting human flourishing. At the same time, the system of rights creates the scaffolding for subordinated groups to challenge forms of cultural domination rooted in 'patterns of representation, interpretation and communication'[133] and to *invent new postcolonial subjectivities that uncouple race, hierarchy and inequality.* As we have already seen, this project of cultural affirmation and social transformation has its origins in the century preceding the adoption of the Constitution, when colonial conceptions of political ordering were challenged, imposed identities rejected and alternatives proposed.

4. Conclusion: democratic constitutionalism and postcolonialism

I have stated that the democratic, popular dimension of the Constitution has not received adequate attention in either the 'legalist' or 'culturalist' paradigms. I posited an alternative conception of the Constitution as a framework only (not the 'juridical

130 Davidson (note 68 above) 167–168.
131 Preamble and s 19 of the Constitution.
132 Fraser & Honneth (note 51 above) 45–46.
133 Said (note 43 above) 13.

genome') for addressing the unresolved questions of postcolonial justice posed by the 'National Question'. It does not itself set out a settled comprehensive conception of justice, which depends on certain irreducibly 'European' and prescriptive conceptions of the individual and human nature. It sets out instead a political, not metaphysical conception of justice,[134] which recognises that 'We the People' are normatively plural and politically self determining.

This non-foundationalist understanding of the constitutional project means that we are free to develop our own understanding of ourselves as a people and the meaning of postcolonial constitutional justice in the light of our history, experience and political traditions. This requires ongoing democratic dialogue,[135] including intergenerational and intercultural dialogue. The constitutional project should be conceived as James Tulley suggests, as, 'an activity, an inter-cultural dialogue in which the culturally diverse sovereign citizens negotiate agreements on their ways of association over time in accord with the conventions of mutual recognition, consent and continuity'.[136]

The judiciary exercises an important settlement function of questions that can be treated as legal ones as part of this much broader process of ongoing dialogue, which includes conflict and contestation. However, not all questions of recognition can be treated as requiring resolution through adjudication. A good example is the question of our national identity as a people raised by Thabo Mbeki in his 'I am an African' speech in parliament when the Constitution was adopted.[137] Biko proposed that this identity should be based on a syncretic 'joint culture',[138] which suggests he envisaged that questions of cultural identity and recognition would remain important to address after a formal change in the structures of political representation. Loyalty based on abstract concepts such as constitutionalism, citizenship and rights may be inadequate for a postapartheid 'political community' to cohere as a national community. Something more than a constitutional framework is required.

The constitutional text also does not finally resolve the question of social and economic justice. The incorporation of socio-economic rights in the Constitution institutionalises a system of distributive justice through the fiscal system (the efficacy of which is dependent on efficient bureaucracies, functioning legislatures and a growing economy) and is, therefore, a good start. Most important, it precludes 'Lockean' anti-public-action[139] readings of the Constitution and encourages transformative readings of adjudication. But social justice should not be conceived in this limited way as

134 J Rawls *Political Liberalism* (1993) and R Rorty 'The priority of democracy to philosophy' in R Rorty (ed) *Objectivity, Relativism, and Truth: Philosophical Papers* (1990) 175.

135 Fraser & Honneth (note 51 above) propose the principle of participatory parity as the proper standard for democratic dialogue. This requires relatively egalitarian material and intersubjective conditions that express respect for all participants and provide equal opportunity for achieving social esteem. I have no way out of the dilemma that such conditions do not yet exist. But we do not have to wait for this utopian endpoint before we can begin the conversation with an awareness of the impact of these unjust conditions on the conversation.

136 J Tulley *Strange Multiplicity: Constitutionalism in an Age of Diversity* (1995) 184.

137 TM Mbeki 'I am an African' Speech delivered at the Constitutional Assembly's adoption of the South African Constitution Bill (8 May, 1996).

138 X Mangcu 'Black consciousness as nationalism of a special type' in E Webster & K Pampallis (eds) *The Unresolved National Question in South Africa: Left Thought under Apartheid* (2017) 209.

139 *Lochner v New York* 198 US 45 (1905) invalidated minimum hours in labour legislation. The United States (US) Supreme Court interpreted the US Constitution as precluding regulation that interfered with contractual rights. The South African Constitution was specifically drafted to preclude a reading that constitutionalised laissez-faire liberalism and rendered state regulation constitutionally suspect.

a system of 'tax and transfer'. This welfarist conception of distributive justice does not reach questions such as commodification and exploitation rooted in the economic structure of society. Therefore, it is arguable that economic justice should encompass 'the sort of deep structural economic changes that have historically been associated with Socialism'.[140] Thus it encompasses both affirmative approaches that seek to alter economic outcomes without changing the underlying mechanisms that generate them and transformative approaches that seek to alter underlying mechanisms.[141] The Constitution should therefore not be understood as inscribing welfare liberalism and market capitalism as an *end state*. Democratic constitutionalism leaves such questions open-ended as a matter of principle to be resolved through democratic politics.[142]

The concept of 'democratic constitutionalism' points lawyers and other scholars in directions that neither paradigm explored here allows, to be pursued in further work. At the very least an 'empowered democracy'[143] requires that law extend its critical vocation to questions of institutional design, the arrangements of democratic politics, the institutions of the economy and even the 'regime of rights'[144] in an ongoing exploration of approximations of postcolonial justice. The judiciary can contribute to this project of democratic empowerment by protecting the institutions of popular self-determination from plutocratic capture, thus keeping open the possibility of social change through democratic politics.

Acknowledgements

I would like to thank Justice Sachs, Professor Eddie Webster, and my colleagues in the Wits School of Law, Professors Klaaren, Woolman, Albertyn, Pieterse, Dugard and Mr Sibanda who read earlier versions of this paper and made comments.

Disclosure statement

No potential conflict of interest was reported by the author.

140 Fraser & Honneth (note 51 above) 95–96.
141 Ibid 95–96.
142 I leave aside the question here whether a system of private property rights precludes the kind of structural changes that a postcapitalist economy might require. I do not think there is an a priori right answer. The idea of property has proved to be a malleable concept that can be stretched to expand access to economic assets. But on the other hand, growing inequalities seem clearly to be causally related to private ownership of 'the means of production'. On this point, Marx may have been right.
143 Unger (note 18 above) 15.
144 Ibid.

On conquest and anthropology in South Africa

Anjuli Webster

ABSTRACT
Despite Archie Mafeje's insistence in 1998 that anthropology is incompatible with the intellectual and political project of independent Africans,[1] anthropology remains a robust discipline in South Africa. Mafeje's critique did not simply examine the historical political and pragmatic complicity of anthropology in colonial administration, but identified and interrogated anthropology's epistemological collaboration in conquest and colonialism in Africa. In this paper, I take up Mafeje's critique of anthropology, reading it into a history of the discipline at the University of the Witwatersrand in South Africa. I argue that despite apparent paradigm shifts in anthropological praxis over the last century, the underlying settler colonial schema and internal tropes of the discipline endure largely intact in the present. To support this contention, I trace continuities in anthropological praxis from the 'colonial past' into the 'constitutional present', delineating the silencing of conquest and settler colonialism by anthropology.

1. Introduction

This article emerges from a master's project I completed on the intellectual history of and in the Department of Social Anthropology at the University of the Witwatersrand (Wits) in 2016. The previous year I had completed a research project on gendered reproductive labour on the platinum belt of South Africa. At the time, I believed that anthropology had equipped me with the analytical tools with which to best make sense of the world around me. However, I was plagued with historical-ethical concerns throughout the project. What did it mean to be working with poor black research participants as a white student researcher who did not speak an indigenous language? I had hoped to temper the problem of positionality through feminist ethnography. However, feminist hope turned into feminist failure when I realised that my approach could not make sense of the machinations of racial capitalism that informed black life around the platinum mines, let alone recognise that I was an

[1] A Mafeje 'Anthropology and independent Africans: suicide or end of an era?' (1998) 2 *African Sociological Review* 1.

essential part of those machinations. As a graduate student cohort, we were also trying to read and think against curricula that were in the process of changing through the work of younger progressive staff members at Wits, as well as through the intellectual and political rupture of the emergent Fees Must Fall student movement. I decided to face the problem of anthropology more squarely through an historical study, framing my inquiry using some of the debates taking place within the department in the present (then 2016). At the same time, the article emerges from an engagement with a critical Africanist tradition that understands the conquest of the indigenous peoples of South Africa in the unjust wars of colonisation as the foundational, unresolved, and ongoing historical antagonism that informs the present.[2] Recent iterations of this tradition include current intellectual and political contentions within the Azanian school of thought around what one scholar has termed 'racism and the marginality of African philosophy in South Africa',[3] and is evident in, for example, the recent establishment of the Azanian Philosophical Society.[4] I also engage with some of the critical reflections on the relationship between conquest, settler colonialism, and social science in the settler colonial and indigenous studies fields, and with what it might mean to 'refuse' research in the settler colonial present, to borrow from Tuck and Yang.[5]

I am less concerned with an empirical account of anthropology, than with thinking through anthropology's historical and contemporary epistemological interpolation with conquest and settler colonialism in South Africa. Following Lisa Lowe, I hope 'to open an investigation, and to contribute a manner of reading and interpretation, and not to identify an empirical foundation or establish a new historical object'.[6] I do not conduct an exhaustive survey of anthropology teaching and research in South Africa or at the University of the Witwatersrand (Wits). Rather, I offer some reflections on moments and convergences in the intellectual genealogy of anthropology at Wits from the early twentieth century to the present. Wits is an excellent site for this inquiry, as it is likely the most progressive anthropology department in the country currently.[7] It is particularly important to consider the resilience and continuity of anthropology over the *longue durée* in a department that is making the most significant movements towards change.

[2] In South Africa, this tradition reaches back to the work of Anton Lembede, Robert Sobukwe, Steve Biko, and in the more recent past and present, in the work of Mogobe Ramose. See MB Ramose 'An African perspective on justice and race' (2001) 3 *Polylog*; and MB Ramose 'I conquer, therefore I am the sovereign: reflections upon sovereignty, constitutionalism, and democracy in Zimbabwe and South Africa' in PH Coetzee & APH Roux (eds) *Philosophy from Africa: A Text With Readings* (2002) 463.

[3] N Dladla, 'Racism and the marginality of African philosophy in South Africa' (2017) 18 *Phronimon* 204. See also J Modiri 'Towards a "(post-)apartheid" critical race jurisprudence: "divining our racial themes"' (2012) 27 *South African Public Law* 229 and N Dladla *Here Is a Table: A Philosophical Essay on the History of Race in South Africa* (2017).

[4] See N Dladla 'Post-script to "racism and the marginal(isation) of African philosophy"' (2017) 18 *Phronimon* 249. See also J Modiri and N Dladla, elsewhere in this issue.

[5] For example, P Wolfe *Settler Colonialism and the Transformation of Anthropology: The Politics and Poetics of an Ethnographic Event* (1999); L Veracini *The Settler Colonial Present* (2015); E Tuck & KW Yang 'R-words: refusing research' in D Paris & MT Winn (eds) *Humanizing Research: Decolonizing Qualitative Inquiry with Youth and Communities* (2014) 223.

[6] L Lowe *The Intimacies of Four Continents* (2015) 21.

[7] By progressive I refer to the responsiveness of the curriculum to radical critiques of anthropology.

2. Tracing conquest in the present

The continuity I trace in this paper is a silenced one – the continuity of conquest. Michel-Rolph Trouillot argues that silence is 'an active and transitive process: one "silences" a fact or an individual as a silencer silences a gun. One engages in the practice of silencing.'[8] History is thus the dialectical outcome of mentions and silences. My contention is that conquest has been epistemologically silenced by the discipline of anthropology in South Africa,[9] rendering it an 'unthinkable' fact in the anthropological canon.[10] In 'I conquer, therefore I am the sovereign', Mogobe Ramose explores the history and epistemological significance of conquest in southern Africa. Through conquest, the European conqueror drew the line between reason and unreason, denying the humanity of human beings other than himself and laid claim to possession of a superior civilisation than the African:[11]

> The line between civilization and barbarism thus established the relationship of superior and inferior. Accordingly, the conqueror had competences and rights against the African without any obligations to the African. This was a one-way relationship which precluded the possibility of reciprocity. The African has only obligations towards the conqueror but no rights.[12]

The conqueror also drew the line between fidels and infidels, just and unjust wars, and the geographical rayas and amity lines. The meridian line determined truth and justice and established exclusive power in the conqueror, 'arbitrarily defin[ing] justice as that which was due only to the conqueror'. It followed 'that fraud, forgery, and the use of brute force as a means of conquest were the recognised method of acquisition of title to the territory of the indigenous conquered peoples. By virtue of this conquest the sovereignty of the indigenous conquered peoples was supplanted and their title to territory extinguished.'[13] Conquest remains the outstanding and fundamental historical antagonism that structures and informs political, economic, cultural, and epistemic landscapes in South Africa today. It was the possibility condition for the establishment of settler colonies in the Cape, the movement of various settler populations inland, the progressive dispossession of land and resources from the indigenous peoples of South Africa conquered in the unjust wars of colonisation, the establishment of anthropology as a formal discipline in South African universities in the early twentieth century, and the continuation of white supremacy in the present.

As disciplines are sociologically and epistemologically rooted in historical, geo-political, and juridical contexts, they are sites through which we can trace the continuities between the 'colonial past' and the 'constitutional present' in South Africa. In this paper, I trouble and disrupt the teleological conception and redemption of

---

[8] MR Trouillot *Silencing the Past: Power and the Production of History* (1995) 48.

[9] While this article focuses on the English-speaking tradition of social anthropology at the University of the Witwatersrand, the distinction between the social anthropology tradition and the *volkekunde* tradition, based at historically Afrikaans-speaking universities, has been critiqued and rejected by scholars such as Mafeje and Magubane. I concur with both Mafeje and Magubane in understanding these apparently different traditions as two complementary constituents of the same tradition of settler colonial anthropology.

[10] Trouillot (note 8 above) 82.

[11] Ramose (2002) (note 2 above).

[12] Ibid 464–465.

[13] Ibid 467.

anthropology in South Africa. By unsettling a teleological analytic, the mutability of historical antagonisms and the structured recurrence of historical 'ruptures' become sites for developing a line of critical inquiry into the settler colonial present. It becomes possible to think about conquest *in* constitutionalism, rather than conquest *and* constitutionalism. Tracing the intellectual history of anthropology at the University of the Witwatersrand through apparently shifting historical and political landscapes thus allows for the description of continuities that are obfuscated by triumphant narratives invoked by 'apartheid' and 'post-apartheid' discourse. In the following sections, I discuss four seminal moments in the last century of anthropology at Wits, tracing the silencing of conquest by white anthropologists who took for granted their dubious right to presence in the country.

3. Producing the 'savage slot':[14] Bantu Studies and the 'Native Question'[15]

Anthropology was established as a formal university discipline in Africa some 40 years after the Berlin Conference of 1884–1885. The advent of the discipline at the University of Cape Town (UCT) in 1921 and the University of the Witwatersrand in 1923 was interpolated into the development of 'native administration' after the union of South Africa in 1910.[16] Anthropology's construction of 'primitive'/'savage' and 'advanced'/'civilised' slots[17] was articulated through the nexus of social anthropology, white liberalism and the conceptualisation of the so-called 'Native Question', a 'set of colonialist concerns about how to manage Africans within the changing racial jurisdictions of South African society'.[18] The 'Native Question' was articulated in the context of rapid urbanisation and the attendant migration of Africans to urban areas that installed new crises in white supremacy in South Africa from 1910–1950.

The Department of Bantu Studies at the University of the Witwatersrand included ethnology as one of its main subjects, taught by anthropologist Winifred Hoernlé, along with Bantu linguistics taught by Clement Doke. It was established with financial support from the Rand mining industry through the Native Recruiting Corporation and Witwatersrand Native Labour Association - subdivisions of the Chamber of Mines.[19] The epistemological locus of possibility for the establishment of the department is well represented in articles written by two of its founding staff members in

[14] MR Trouillot *Global Transformations: Anthropology and the Modern World* (2003).

[15] The object of this paper is anthropology at Wits. The discipline's discourse includes problematic terms such as 'Bantu' and 'Native'. I reproduce these terms here as they appear in the textual data, and as anthropologists have historically deployed them. Following P Wolfe's 'Note on terminology' in *Settler Colonialism* (note 5 above), when I intend to refer to the indigenous people of South Africa, rather than anthropologist's representations of them, I use the term 'indigenous'. I use the term Black following the Black Consciousness tradition's disruption of the racist settler colonial categorisation of 'non-white' population groups by including 'Asians' and so-called 'Coloureds' within an historical and political identification contrasted against the conquering white settler minority group.

[16] South African Prime Minister Jan Smuts personally invited British social anthropologist Alfred Radcliffe-Brown to establish the first Chair of Social Anthropology at UCT.

[17] Trouillot (note 14 above).

[18] K Gillespie 'Containing the "wandering Native": racial jurisdiction and the liberal politics of prison reform in 1940s South Africa' (2011) 37 *Journal of Southern African Studies* 499, 499.

[19] WD Hammond-Tooke *Imperfect Interpreters: South Africa's Anthropologists 1920–1990* (1997) 34.

the local newspaper media.[20] The administrative dimension cited in these articles should be read alongside the department's financial links to the mining industry on the Witwatersrand, which was concerned with improving control and governance of the Black labour force. In a 1923 article in the *Rand Daily Mail*, linguist Clement M Doke, in his capacity as senior lecturer in the department, suggests that:

> [I]t is, at present, the aim of the Bantu Studies department of the University to deal with the education of the European in all matters dealing with the natives of South Africa [...] To get "at the back of the black man's mind," [...] the ethnology of his race must be scientifically studied and accurately recorded [...] The administrator in native territories, whether magistrate or native commissioner, the missionary, the public official who deals directly or indirectly with natives, the municipal superintendents of native affairs [...] all of these need training in native history, native traditions and folk-lore, native indigenous law, in the social customs and religion of the native people [...][21]

In another *Rand Daily Mail* article published in 1923, Hoernlé, in her capacity as ethnology lecturer in the department, expands on the topic of 'scientific' study towards better administration over the 'native'. She writes that:

> [Europeans] must start from a sound knowledge of the outlook and beliefs of the natives, if they wish to introduce among them European principles of administration or change their habits of daily life ... This knowledge of the natives is necessary to any successful administration of them ... According as they gain this insight or not, will they be wise and successful in their administration, and rule over contented peoples.[22]

Anthropological discourse on the 'native' was reinforced in the form of the journal *Bantu Studies* (published today as *African Studies*), which had been established by John David Rheinallt Jones in 1921. The journal was considered 'the leading outlet for the publication of social anthropological knowledge about the [southern African] region' at the time.[23] The subtitle description – 'a journal devoted to the scientific study of Bantu, Hottentot and Bushmen' – again designates the link between the emergent social scientific and empiricist project in early twentieth century South Africa, which constructed 'civilised' and 'savage' slots central to the settler colonial projects of governance and trusteeship.

Joseph Reilly contends that rather than constituting a discontinuity with Social Darwinism, the functionalist tradition of anthropology that emerged in South Africa in the early twentieth century realised 'important continuities' both in 'discursive notions, assumptions, logics, as well as in its methodological applications' with it.[24]

[20] In both the quotes below, there is some slippage between 'ethnology' and 'social anthropology'. This is not unusual, as these words have sometimes functioned loosely as synonyms. The first department of *social* anthropology in the world was established in Cape Town in 1921, so the term was only just growing into official and professional usage at the time these newspaper articles were published. The *Encyclopedia of Social and Cultural Anthropology* offers the following definition for ethnology: 'Broadly, a synonym for social or cultural anthropology. In early nineteenth-century Britain, the term often implied a monogenic theory of humankind, whereas "anthropology" implied a polygenic theory. Often in Continental usage, "ethnology" means social anthropology and "anthropology" means physical anthropology. In yet another usage, Radcliffe-Brown distinguished ethnology (the study of culture history and relationships) from social anthropology (the study of society)' A Barnard & J Spencer (eds) *Encyclopedia of Social and Cultural Anthropology* (2002) 903.

[21] CM Doke 'Bantu Studies – getting at the Natives' mind, Rand as field for research' *The Rand Daily Mail* (1 November 1923).

[22] AW Hoernlé 'Must know the Natives – how to gain their goodwill, social anthropology and administration' *The Rand Daily Mail* (2 November 1923).

[23] A Bank *Pioneers of the Field: South Africa's Women Anthropologists* (2016) 35.

[24] JD Reilly *Teaching the "Native": Behind the Architecture of an Unequal Education System* (2016) 10.

Settler concerns with 'contact' and 'race relations' took the form of 'scientific' and positivist investigation. Rich argues that anthropology in the early twentieth century '[r]eformulated many of the ideas of the nineteenth-century "civilising mission" fostered by the missions in newer, more secular terms whilst avoiding a more detailed economic analysis of the role and function of African societies in the workings of the South African political economy'.[25] The secularised ideology of settler liberal anthropology was at the same time anti-historical, focussing on the production of lengthy monographs on African social and political structures conceived within the ethnographic present and through the methodology of participant observation. This is commonly referred to as the 'Golden Age' of South African ethnography.[26] John Fage suggests that the 'non-historical way of investigating and evaluating the cultures and societies of "primitive" peoples' of early anthropology was a 'symptomatic outcome' of processes of conquest, which required the moral justification of Hegelian and Darwinian principles of 'primitive' and 'advanced' societies.[27]

Anthropology's 'Golden Age' depended on and reproduced the line between civilisation and barbarism, and silenced conquest in the historical imagination of the settler. Settlers were united in their persuasion that to properly rule over, or provide trusteeship for – depending on variations in political orientation – the indigenous population of South Africa, a sound 'scientific' knowledge of their customs and organisation was necessary. The establishment of the Bantu Studies department at Wits was predicated on and reproduced the figure of the 'native', who could be scientifically studied through the methodology of ethnology towards the ends of developing better modes of administration. Settler anthropologists did not question the dubious right to conquest that secured their posterity in South Africa. Rather, they worked towards the establishment of a 'civilised' society based on a European model, into which the 'native' could be educated and assimilated. The early history of social anthropology at Wits was thus rooted in a Eurocentric power-knowledge system that accepted and silenced the dubious European right to conquest in much the same way as the Afrikaner nationalist *Volkekunde* tradition would later do.[28]

4. Troubling 'radical rupture': the neo-Marxist turn

> We now come to the group that has longest enjoyed confidence from the black world – the liberal establishment, including radical and leftist groups. The biggest mistake the black world ever made was to assume that whoever opposed apartheid was an ally.[29]

---

[25] PB Rich *White Power and the Liberal Conscience: Racial Segregation and South African Liberalism* (1984) 57.

[26] Hammond-Tooke (note 19 above); Bank (note 23 above).

[27] JD Fage 'The development of African historiography' in J Ki-Zerbo (ed) *General History of Africa* vol 1 (1981) 32.

[28] *Volkekunde* is a form of anthropology that Hammond-Tooke traces to the work of Werner Eiselen and his student PJ Coertze's work at Stellenbosch University in the 1930s, and which 'dominated the discipline at all Afrikaans-language universities for almost half a century'. He offers the following description: 'Afrikaans anthropology never followed the "revolution" in Britain caused by the adoption of the functionalist approach of Malinowski and Radcliffe-Brown, especially the strong Durkheimian preoccupations of the latter. [Werner] Eiselen conceived the discipline in broad terms, and appears to have favoured the American approach of "Cultural Anthropology" – an eclectic approach, thought of as "the study whole study of man", that takes "culture" as its key concept, rather than "society" (as does Social Anthropology).' Hammond-Tooke (note 19 above) 120, 124.

[29] S Biko *I Write What I Like: A Selection of His Writings* (1987) 68.

Anthropology in South Africa until the early 1970s saw the rise of various traditions other than the foundational structural functionalist tradition. These included the ethnological section of the South African Department of Native Affairs, headed by NJ van Warmelo from 1930 to 1969 and the rise of the Afrikaner *Volkekunde* tradition, pioneered by PJ Coertze at Stellenbosch University, the University of South Africa, the Orange Free State and the University of Pretoria.[30] It also included a range of new studies on urbanisation beginning with the work of Ellen Hellman in *Rooiyard: A Sociological Survey of an Urban Native Slum Yard*, published in 1948, work by Philip Mayer on urbanisation and network analysis in East London in the late 50s and 60s, and by Monica Wilson and Archie Mafeje on Langa in Cape Town in the early 1960s.[31] Since the 'Golden Age' in the thirties and forties, during which South African ethnographies held central positions in the British structural functionalist tradition as well as in American cultural anthropology, and the urbanisation tradition, South African anthropology underwent a decrease in publication rates and lost much international recognition.[32]

The next major apparent paradigm shift in anthropology at Wits materialised in the 1970s in the form of the neo-Marxist turn. This followed closely on the heels of the so-called 'radical' turn in South African historiography.

> Social scientists and historians in the major English-speaking universities now developed a neo-Marxist account of South Africa, which included a critique of anthropology as conservative, and overly concerned with cultural difference. Ethnicity was false consciousness, manipulated by the regime. It was world capitalism that in truth shaped South African society. All anthropologists could effectively contribute was a critique of the discourse of cultural identity, and the documentation of the terrible effects of government policy.[33]

The categories of analysis that anthropologists at Wits adopted during this conjuncture shifted to concentrate on the effects of apartheid and state repression. Studies focussed on the processes and effects of territorial apartheid, population movement, and labour migration. Conflict and antagonism in South African society was conceived according to a brief historical timeline, focussed on apartheid policy, and emerging capitalist labour relations in the twentieth century. Research and knowledge production focussed on the immediate effects of apartheid on South African society, rather than understanding the period as another stage within the history of white supremacy in South Africa stretching back to 1652. We also see the advent of 'applied' and 'activist' anthropology, most notably in the figures of David Webster and Jeremy Keenan, both lecturers in the department. As Ernest Wamba dia Wamba suggests, however, 'Voluntaristic alignment to oppressed classes per se does not make one produce revolutionary historical knowledge'[34] – or anthropological knowledge for that matter. Webster and Keenan took up the more 'immediate' concerns of the effects of apartheid through activist work, while remaining within the academy and silent on their own implication in structures of racialised power

[30] Hammond-Tooke (note 19 above) 109, 119–120.
[31] A Kuper 'South African anthropology. An inside job' (1999) 45 *Paideuma: Mitteilungen Zur Kulturkunde* 83, 95–96.
[32] Hammond-Tooke (note 19 above) 182.
[33] Kuper (note 31 above) 96.
[34] E Wamba dia Wamba 'How Is historical knowledge recognized?' (1986) 13 *History in Africa* 331, 342.

dependent on the mutability of conquest and white supremacy. The turn to activist politics was possible only through either a profound ignorance or a wilful silencing of or disengagement from existing Africanist and Black Consciousness critiques of white 'non-racialist' activism in South Africa. The apartheid state assassinated Webster in 1989, and he has since been sentimentalised as a struggle hero in such a way that critique of the neo-Marxist moment in anthropology seems to have become morally treacherous ground.[35]

Bernard Magubane has argued that the so-called radical paradigm was another attempt 'by beneficiaries of colonial usurpation to transcend that legacy'.[36] He groups the liberal and neo-Marxist traditions together as 'exercises in irrelevance,' which exposed a misunderstanding of African realities and struggles.[37] Shireen Ally has argued that the neo-Marxist turn in South Africa, particularly in the sphere of sociology at Wits, 'revolved squarely around the intellectual and political reconfiguration of the race-class debate', and adopted an 'oppositional intellectualism as a critique of liberalism, and as a response to the racial politics inspired by Black Consciousness'.[38] Ally conceives of this moment in the South African academy as primarily a 'reactionary disengagement' from the politics and philosophy of the Black Consciousness movement.[39] Marxism and class analysis offered white intellectuals in South Africa 'not just a powerful theoretical lens to explain apartheid, but a powerful political tool […] to deal more comfortably with questions of race'.[40]

Following Magubane and Ally, I read the neo-Marxist turn in anthropology at Wits as a (re)articulation of settler scholarship in a 'radical' guise. This moment in anthropology depended on the following two forms of colonial unknowing:

1. By understanding the immediacy of apartheid as the fundamental antagonism of South African society, white anthropologists engaged in historically myopic analysis which functioned to occlude conquest, and their own implication in structures of racism and power; and
2. The non-racial praxis of white leftist anthropologists at Wits did not engage with, and thus silenced, a tradition of Africanist thought which had critiqued white non-racialism in South Africa since the mid-century.[41]

---

35 After presenting an earlier version of this paper at the *South African Journal of Human Rights* Colloquium on 'Conquest, Constitutionalism and Democratic Contestations' in Johannesburg in May 2017, I was privately taken aside and accosted by an elder scholar after the public question-and-answer session was closed. The elder scholar chastised me for talking about Webster, because I never knew him personally. He did not substantially engage with any of the arguments I had made. Rather, he chose to intimidate me for engaging in an intellectual critique of a 'struggle hero'.

36 B Magubane 'Whose memory – whose history? The illusion of liberal and radical historical debates in HE Stolten (ed) *History Making and Present Day Politics: The Meaning of Collective Memory in South Africa* (2007) 251, 277.

37 Ibid 274.

38 S Ally 'Oppositional intellectualism as reflection, not rejection, of power: Wits Sociology, 1975– 1989' (2005) 59 *Transformation: Critical Perspectives on Southern Africa* 66, 74.

39 Ibid 82–83.

40 Ibid 73.

41 M Vimalassery, JH Pegues & A Goldstein 'Introduction: on colonial unknowing' (2016) 19 *Theory & Event* <https://muse.jhu.edu/article/633283>. The authors define 'colonial unknowing' as an epistemology which 'render[s] unintelligible the entanglements of racialization and colonization, occluding the mutable historicity of colonial structures and attributing finality to conquest and dispossession'

The mutability of conquest and racism in South Africa was obfuscated through neo-Marxist praxis, which also offered white scholars a supposed 'exit' from a schema that implicated them as settlers and oppressors. The 1970s and '80s are commonly understood as a moment of radical rupture in humanities and social science praxis at historically English-medium universities in South Africa. Hammond-Tooke reads this moment in anthropology as a fundamental rupture of the very foundations of anthropology as a discipline: 'The influence of Marxism cannot be ignored. The fact that for almost twenty years, students at the two largest universities, Wits and UCT, were actively directed away from the traditional concerns of anthropology, tended to create an intellectual hiatus that cut them off from the very roots of the discipline and its current theoretical debates.'[42] This narrative is undermined by the underlying continuity in settler scholarship and colonial unknowing, which functioned to occlude the mutability of conquest[43] in South Africa during the turn.

5. Reproducing the 'savage slot': culture and the myth of the postracial

In the 1990s, Wits anthropology returned from its apparent hiatus during the neo-Marxist turn. While the 'valuable aspects of the materialist approach [were] internalised (such as the questions of conflict, power and 'who benefits?'), there [was] a return to the central idea of culture as an explanatory concept.'[44] This conjuncture was informed by a series of interrelated and shifting landscapes. The first was the democratic transition at the political and national level. The second and related shift was an institutional transition characterised by the implementation of massification programmes designed to increase the admission of Black students at historically white universities.[45] Massification schemes were not concerned with the dismantling and reconceptualisation of the university structure or curricula, but with the inclusion of black students into the colonial institution as a mode of reproducing epistemic power. The university established an academic development centre that aimed to 'assist black South African students to assimilate to Wits' through a 'culturative' academic process.[46] The third was a broader disciplinary transition to cultural studies stimulated by the publication of *Writing Culture: The Poetics and Politics of Ethnography* in 1986.[47] This moment constituted a shift away from the long-standing dominance of British social anthropology paradigms such as structural functionalism and political economy, and was characterised by a return to concerns with culture and ethnicity, influenced by debates within American anthropology.[48] The broader milieu of the 1990s obscured an important epistemological continuity within the apparent shift to

---

[42] Hammond-Tooke (note 19 above) 184.

[43] M Vimalassery, JH Pegues & A Goldstein, 'Introduction: on colonial unknowing' (2016) 19 *Theory & Event* <https://muse.jhu.edu/article/633283>.

[44] Hammond-Tooke (note 19 above) 184.

[45] M Mamdani 'Research and transformation: reflection on a visit to South Africa' (1992) 27 *Economic and Political Weekly* 1055, 1059; GC Moodie 'The state and the liberal universities in South Africa: 1948–1990' (1994) 27 *Higher Education* 1.

[46] CA Taylor personal interview with author (Johannesburg, 2016).

[47] J Clifford & GE Marcus (eds) *Writing Culture: The Poetics and Politics of Ethnography* (1986).

[48] The shift in anthropological praxis can be seen quite clearly in the inclusion of American culture theorists such as Marshall Sahlins and Clifford Geertz in new courses such as 'political economy, culture and aesthetics', as well as in the topics of graduate research theses, for example 'The role of Ndebele beadwork in reinforcing the

culture theory, however – the continuity of anthropology's racialised 'savage slot' in the transition to a 'non-racial' discourse on culture and ethnicity.

The re-development of the ethnological museum and the establishment of a course in material culture and museum curation at Wits was an important feature of the anthropology department's return to culture. The ethnological collection – which Winifred Hoernlé initiated in the 1920s and which was maintained until the 1960s, when interest in the museum and the ethnological collection lapsed – was reimagined as a venue for the 'contemplation of matters of "cultural knowledge"' in the 'non-racial' democratic era.[49] It housed various activities including a workshop on 'public representations of colonial Africa', and a display on 'collecting Zulu material culture' that reflected on three periods of material culture collection. The department also curated the WFP Burton collection, which went on loan to the Centre of African Studies at UCT in 1993, provided items for the CM Doke centenary exhibition, which was displayed during the annual meeting of the Association for Anthropology Southern Africa the Wits department hosted in September 1993 and collaborated with various other institutions, including the Africana Museum, on an exhibition of the Louis Fourie collection of 'Bushman' and Ovambo materials.[50]

The refurbishment of the museum was accompanied by the initiation and development of a 'highly successful full scale' honours course in museum practice – 'Museums and Material Culture'. The course required students to present seminars, produce reviews of exhibitions, write a paper based on a field trip, and curate an exhibition of their own. One of the displays set up in the museum provides a striking signification of the colonial problematic which underwrote the cultural turn in anthropology at Wits. The exhibition, which remained up for two decades, until the early 2010s, was a mirror with the image of Sarah Baartman on it. One staff member said about the exhibition, and the moment more generally:

> There had been some attempts in the 1990s to shift some things around there. And it was interesting how quickly that dated, because they were done at a time when the urgent thing was to get Wits students, who were then white students, thinking about the representation of culture, and the politics around the representation of culture [...] By the time it was taken down, you would look at this stuff, and it was really obvious how explicitly it was addressed to a white audience. So, there was a mirror which had Sarah Baartman's figure on it. And the invitation was to imagine yourself as an Other [...] And that obviously had a very powerful effect in the early 1990s, in a moment when white South Africans were having to confront these questions.

By inviting a white audience to imagine itself as Other, the display functioned to 'deracialise' and trivialise historical power and white supremacy in South Africa, while simultaneously re-inscribing the ethnographic object as an 'ethnicised' alterity. That the display stayed up for two decades is revealing of how fundamental this colonial schema was to the work of anthropology in the 'democratic era'.

---

patriarchal household' and 'Cultural trends and community formation in a South African township: Sharpeville 1943–1980'.

[49] Department of Social Anthropology 'Review for the period August 1988 to August 1993' vol 1 (Johannesburg, 1993) 9.

[50] Ibid 54.

How can we understand this moment? What tricks were deployed so that anthropology's old haunts paraded in plain sight during what was supposedly a decolonising moment? Jemima Pierre has already addressed this question in relation to Africanist anthropology. It is worth quoting her at length here:

> My analysis will [...] explore how race structures the current anthropological project itself, fundamentally shaping the discipline's epistemology and methodology. Consequently, I will show that processes of racialization continue to underpin ethnographic practice and are manifest in two ways: (i) the deployment of an ambiguous notion of 'culture' that continues to have racial underpinnings; and (ii) the often unsuspecting role of Africanist anthropology in naturalizing African cultural difference. In other words, the seeming acceptance of cultural difference as given without the acknowledgement of the subtleties of race implied in this difference, authorise ethnographic practice that reinforces Africa's (global) marking as the site of racial otherness.[51]

In short, the cultural turn in anthropology was not an (epistemic) turn at all, but a turn in terminology. The 90s moment at Wits inaugurated a 'postracial' Savage Slot. 'Culture' became a substitute for 'race' and allowed anthropological discourse to continue in much the same colonial fashion, but in 'postracial' disguise.[52] The 'shift' to culture covered, and continues to cover, what is a 'contemporary commonsense slippage' between 'race' and 'culture', or 'the embeddedness of race in prevailing anthropological "cultural" conceptions'.[53] As Jon Soske has also argued, '[T]he concepts that social scientists frequently use to critique racism, like ethnicity and culture, are embedded within the history of racial thought and often serve as racial euphemisms.'[54] Garth Stevens, Norman Duncan and Brett Bowman have also argued that racism underlies and structures that *making* of culture and ethnicity in political and scientific discourse in South Africa:

> '[N]otions of cultural and ethnic difference in historically racialized societies are not as innocuous as they may appear, as they frequently play a critical role in current re-articulations of the ideology of racism [...] [R]acism is constantly re-inventing itself, and currently we are dealing with a racism "whose dominant theme is not biological heredity but the insurmountability of cultural differences.'[55]

And indeed, anthropology has been a predominant disciplinary mechanism for the production of cultural difference, and the continuity of racism in South Africa. As the authors suggest, '[D]espite the hefty contemporary critiques levelled against the concept of race, it has not only resisted change under varying historical and material conditions, but has also displayed a phenomenal ability to adapt, mutate and function in the service of new forms, processes and prosaic rituals of social marginalisation, exclusion and domination.'[56]

---

[51] J Pierre 'Anthropology and the race of/for Africa' in PT Deleza (ed) *The Study of Africa, Volume I – Disciplinary and Interdisciplinary Encounter* (2006) 40-41.

[52] DT Goldberg *Are We All Postracial Yet?* (2015).

[53] Pierre (note 51 above) 41.

[54] J Soske 'The impossible concept: settler liberalism, pan-Africanism, and the language of non-racialism' (2015) 47 *African Historical Review* 1, 2–3.

[55] G Stevens N Duncan & B Bowman 'Ethnicity: it's about making a difference" in G Stevens, V Franchi & T Swart (eds) *A Race Against Time: Psychology and Challenges to Deracialisation in South Africa* (2006) 68.

[56] Ibid 60.

Despite the shifting landscapes around anthropology at Wits in the early 1990s, there were two things that remained relatively unchanged – anthropology's makers and its objects[57]. According to Mafeje, reflexive anthropology was supposed to dispense with the subject/object dichotomy in ethnographic discourse.[58] The dichotomy remained clear and heavily racialised – anthropology's makers and teachers were largely white, and anthropology's objects were various iterations of Black alterity. This continuity reflects an ignorance of the critiques of anthropology emerging from the continent since at least the 1960s, as well as a reflection of the protraction of the primary historical-political antagonism of conquest in South Africa in the 'post-apartheid' period. The reproduction of a discourse of racialised alterity by South African anthropology is then also a reflection of outstanding historical injustice.

6. Anthropology and the settler colonial present

Since at least the 1950s, Anthropology was systematically critiqued by African nationalist movements for its complicity in colonial rule in Africa. In some instances, this resulted in a complete rejection of the discipline by African independence movements, politicians, scholars and institutions.[59] Many believed anthropology to be incompatible with the epistemological and political project of African independence, and invested in alternative disciplinary spaces, such as sociology and African studies, to develop an endogenous social science praxis.[60] In the Independence era, anthropology on the continent went 'underground' until two African congresses, one in Yaoundé in 1989 and one in Dakar in 1991, were organised to review and assess the status of and possibilities for anthropology in Africa.[61] During these congresses, some African anthropologists 'raised the slogan "post-anthropology", while some went as far as to declare the death of anthropology'.[62] Among the latter were Ifi Amadiume and Archie Mafeje. According to Mafeje, however, the popular concern was with reorganising rather than with deconstructing anthropology.[63] During this moment, African anthropology was tentatively resurrected and underwent a 'resurgence' at African universities in the 2000s, according to Paul Nkwi.[64] This resurrection and resurgence was possible through an uneasy relationship with radical critiques of anthropology's colonial epistemic schema, and the outright rejection of the possibility of African anthropology by scholars such as Amadiume and Mafeje. This broader unresolved tension concerning the possibilities of anthropology on the continent has subsequently authorised the continuity of the discipline in South Africa.

In 'Anthropology and the savage slot', Trouillot traces anthropology's relationship and continuity with the symbolic and discursive construction of the West.[65] His

[57] A Mafeje 'Who are the makers and objects of anthropology? A critical comment on Sally Falk Moore's "Anthropology and Africa"' (1997) 1 *African Sociological Review* 1.
[58] Mafeje (note 1 above) 9.
[59] VY Mudimbe *The Invention of Africa: Gnosis, Philosophy, and the Order of Knowledge* (1988) 78.
[60] Mafeje (note 1 above) 20.
[61] Ibid; H Sharawy *Political and Social Thought in Africa* (2014).
[62] Sharawy (note 61 above) 203.
[63] Mafeje (note 1 above) 21.
[64] PN Nkwi 'Editorial: resurgence of anthropology at African universities' (2007) 14 *The African Anthropologist* v.
[65] Trouillot (note 14 above) 8.

contention is that despite possible variations within praxis across different institutional or historical contexts, anthropology continues to be over-determined by the 'historical weight of the field of significance' that it inherited at birth. Anthropological discourse continues to be premised on a wider symbolic field in which it reproduces the racialised 'savage slot' necessary to the continued hegemony of the West. For Trouillot, a reflexive anthropology requires the reappraisal of the *longue durée* of anthropology and its maintenance of the 'savage slot' in the present.[66] Having roughly mapped out such a history, I briefly consider the contemporary conjuncture of anthropology at Wits in the vignette below.

***

An important event in the Wits anthropology department's recent calendar was the formal re-opening of the newly renovated Anthropology Museum in 2016. The department invited an artist who had done work on the cataloguing of objects and archives in museums in Johannesburg to think through the role of the museum, and to curate its reopening. The main exhibit of the reopening constituted a reflection by the artist, in conversation with staff and students in the department, on the politics of ethnographic objects, representation, and the history of colonial anthropology at Wits. In the foyer of the museum, the old cabinets were filled with toilet paper and bottles of Oros to commemorate the role played by the space as a storage room for the 2015 #FeesMustFall movement at Wits. Across the surface of the glass doors of the foyer cabinets the following was printed:

> In 2013 the Department of Anthropology undertook to refurbish the Anthropology Museum not only revamping the architectural design, but also ushering in a new era for reimaging [sic] the epistemologies of the museum and the Department. The original cabinets of the old Museum still line its walls./The decision to keep these Victorian-style display cabinets, is a pointed one [sic.]. In conceptualising the possibilities for a new Museum, members of the Department did not want to erase the problematic legacy of the collection and the display thereof./During the 2015 #FeesMustFall protests at Wits, the student movement used the foyer of the museum as a storeroom for donated supplies and an informal meeting space. The floor was lined with orange bottles of Oros, and the walls with towers of toilet paper. The immediacy and makeshift nature of the space as an ad hoc storeroom threw the anachronous austerity of the empty cabinets into stark recognition./However, since it's reopening the cabinets have remained empty. Their emptiness contrasts with the lively debate that happens around the large table in the Museum's main room where seminars, tutorials and meetings are held./These tensions attest to an uneasiness within the department regarding the status of the objects in their collection, collected since the department's establishment in 1923. The empty cabinets (previously used to display these objects) embody a yet-to-be-answered question; what is to be done with this inherited collection?

In the seminar room the cabinets were filled, on the one side, with piles of ash, and on the other with cement castes of bowls that were part of the old ethnographic collection housed in the Wits Art Museum. Quotes reflecting on fire as a generative concept were printed on the glass cabinets, including from CLR James' *The Black Jacobins*[67], Kerry Chance's '"Where there is fire, there is politics": ungovernability and

[66] Ibid 9.

[67] CLR James *The Black Jacobins: Touissaint L'Ouverture and the San Domingo Revolution* 2 ed (1989).

material life in urban South Africa'[68] and a memorandum by the Wits Registrar on the fire in the main university building in 1931. The conception of the museum opening leading up to the event was that it would constitute a moment of cleansing. The exhibition would critically display and engage with the past of anthropology at Wits to be able to look forward, and start anew; the colonial past of anthropology was offered up as sacrifice. At the same time the exhibition, through associating the department with the 2015 student movement, constructed an apparently 'decolonised' and radical identity and praxis in the present and moving into the future.

Three #FeesMustFall activists disrupted the event during the formal speeches. Several critical questions were posed to the department. The activists commented on the white curation of the space, and the politics and ethics of representation it reproduced. They contended that the #FeesMustFall movement was rendered as a spectacle through the use of Oros and toilet paper and argued that this spectacle was capitalised upon by the department and the curator, whose academic projects were furthered by the apparent progressive agenda of the project. Ultimately the activists contended that the exhibition constituted a reproduction of the colonial power/knowledge system in that it materialised the trope of the white curator/scholar theorising the data of Black alterity. This disruption echoed Mafeje's 1997 critique of the continuity of anthropology's dependency on and reproduction of a settler colonial schema in the 'post-apartheid' period.[69]

***

The idea that change and long-term continuity are compatible does not necessarily inform the contemporary reflexive project at Wits. Steven Feierman argues that the challenge of historical analysis is 'to create a method and a form of ethnographic description which can capture ... categories as both continuous and in transformation ... actors as both creating new language and speaking inherited words, all at the same time'.[70] In this way, it is possible to trace continuities in discourse 'without tying each moment in the formation of discourse mechanically to the immediate narrow interests' of those speaking.[71] The brief vignette offered above describes a moment in which the anthropology department fashioned a seemingly radical new language which condemned 'classical' anthropological tropes but that spoke an inherited tongue at the same time. This tongue is the manifestation of an underlying structural problem – the continuity of settler colonialism in the present. It follows that while there might be radical classrooms or ruptures of anthropology in South Africa, the discipline continues to be structured and over-determined by the mutability of conquest in South Africa. This structure manifests in the disciplinary sphere through the continued dominance of Euro-American theory and the silencing of African philosophy and theory in curricula, and in a sustained concern with Black alterity as anthropology's subject.

---

[68] KR Chance '"Where there is fire, there is politics": ungovernability and material life in urban South Africa' (2015) 30 *Cultural Anthropology* 394.
[69] Mafeje (note 57) above.
[70] S Feierman *Peasant Intellectuals: Anthropology and History in Tanzania* (1990) 13.
[71] Ibid 21–22.

It is also reflected in the broader national landscape of anthropology, as is evidenced in an emerging literature. A renewed interest in the intellectual history of liberal anthropology in South Africa has surfaced in the form of several new books published in the last five years. The new studies, *Inside African Anthropology: Monica Wilson and Her Interpreters*, edited by Andrew and Leslie J Bank;[72] *The Fires Beneath: The Life of Monica Wilson, South African Anthropologist* by Séan Morrow;[73] and *Pioneers of the Field: South Africa's Women Anthropologists* by Bank,[74] reveal a growing concern with and investment in the intellectual history of white English-speaking anthropologists in South Africa. A review of this recent literature reveals that it is often ideologically sympathetic with the project of colonial liberals and takes what Sharawy terms the 'Apologetic Stand', which 'continues the conservative position by maintaining that the anthropologist was a "colonialist against his will", that many of them enjoyed their work, and were fond of the people they worked with'.[75] For example, Bank's *Pioneers of the Field* sympathetically discusses the work of six white liberal anthropologists, arguing that the figures should be mainstreamed in the South African anthropological canon. While the book offers useful historical data, Bank's partiality to the idea of a 'non-racial' project over-determines the discussion and represents white anthropologists as radical humanists, rather than as settler scholars.[76] The 'reluctance to acknowledge the role of Eurocentrism […] implies that 21st-century anthropologists and historians may be inadvertently justifying its continuity'.[77] This new generation of intellectual histories does the work of constructing a humanist past of social anthropology in South Africa, while at the same time occluding its settler colonial present.

One key trick through which anthropology secures its posterity is to claim singular knowledge through ethnographic fundamentalism. Ethnography not only apparently absolves the anthropologist from the necessity of engaging in meaningful historical inquiry and reflection, but it is also the method through which the researcher exits historical structures of power, entering a fictitious plain of human interaction with their research participants. Take for instance this excerpt from Hammond-Tooke's *Imperfect Interpreters*, which provides an example of this position:

> Anthropologists have been accused of being part of a colonial dominance and arrogance, and this may well have been the case. Yet this is a complete misunderstanding of the ethnographic field situation. Here, at least, anthropologists are totally at the mercy of their hosts, who can withhold information and make life impossible if they so wish. The anthropologist comes among them (if he or she wishes to be successful), not as an authority figure, but as an ignorant stranger, who must sit at their feet and be educated like a child in their ways.[78]

If, as Linda Tuhiwai Smith insists, research is 'an institution of knowledge that is embedded in a global system of imperialism and power'[79] and, as Tuck and Yang

[72] A Bank & LJ Bank (eds) *Inside African Anthropology: Monica Wilson and Her Interpreters* (2013).
[73] S Morrow *The Fires Beneath: The Life of Monica Wilson, South African Anthropologist* (2016).
[74] A Bank (note 23 above).
[75] H Sharawy (note 61 above) 202.
[76] A Webster '*Pioneers of the Field: South Africa's Women Anthropologists*' (2017) 40 *Anthropology Southern Africa* 147.
[77] K Cereso '*Inside African Anthropology: Monica Wilson and Her Interpreters*' (no date) 75 *African Studies Bulletin* 129, 132.
[78] Hammond-Tooke (note 19 above) 190.

insist, social science research is a form of settler colonial knowledge which fulfils the need to know fundamental to conquest and colonial governance,[80] ethnography needs to be deconstructed as an innocuous methodology which strips the anthropologist of power, and through which the anthropologist gains a consummate knowledge of their field/subject. The opposite is just as likely true – ethnography reproduces (knowledge about) racialised alterity, while disguising itself as a methodology free of power.

7. Conclusions

Since I completed my study on the anthropology department at Wits in 2016, some changes have taken place. For the first time in the department's history, the staff component is majority Black and African. In the wake of the Rhodes Must Fall and Fees Must Fall student movements, curricula are also much more mobile than they have been in the last decades, and there is institutional room for debating and reimagining the role of anthropology going forward. This is not the first historical rupture that has provided room for change, however. And if there is one key point to take from this paper, it is that epistemological continuity is possible through apparently radical transformations and shifts.

Teachers and students of anthropology have inherited a complex and difficult past that remains alive in the present and requires rigorous interrogation and study if further reproduction is to be avoided. In Patrick Wolfe's words, it is necessary to 'trace the genealogies of certain classic anthropological narratives whose ideological half-lives continue into the present'. Wolfe's concern in his study of settler colonialism and anthropology in Australia was 'with the present as it selects out of the past'.[81] This kind of work has not yet been done in the South African context. Rather, critique of anthropology in South Africa has been characterised by a sustained historical parochialism. It has been bounded within the discipline's internalities, or what Trouillot terms its 'electoral politics'[82]. Debates have been focussed and assembled around the apparent differences between the Afrikaans and English traditions of anthropology, and are often articulated through a politics of apology and redemption. This parochialism has foreclosed the possibility of opening the discipline up to a *longue durée* critique, thereby reproducing colonial unknowing, which endeavours to 'render unintelligible the entanglements of racialisation and colonisation, occluding the mutable historicity of colonial structures and attributing finality to conquest and dispossession'.[83] If anthropology's epistemological collaboration with settler colonialism is not apologetically revised,[84] it is often understood to be a fact contained in the past. It is commonly accepted that the simple acknowledgement of the historical fact

[79] LT Smith *Decolonizing Methodologies: Research and Indigenous Peoples* 2 ed (2012) ix.

[80] Tuck & Yang (note 5 above).
[81] P Wolfe (note 5 above) 3.
[82] Trouillot (note 14 above) 8, describes 'electoral politics' as: 'the set of institutionalized practices and relations of power that influence the production of knowledge from within academe: academic filiations, the mechanisms of institutionalization, the organization of power within and across departments, the market value of publish-or-perish prestige, and other worldly issues that include, but expand way beyond the maneuvering we usually refer to as "academic politics."'
[83] Vimalassery (note 43 above).
[84] See for example A Bank (note 23 above).

of anthropology's complicity in the colonial 'past' itself separates contemporary anthropological praxis from that past. Historical reflexivity functions to acknowledge the past while simultaneously fastening and securing it in time, separating and distancing it from the supposedly post-(settler)colonial present. The acknowledgement of the past thus functions to obscure its continuity in the present.

Mafeje's critique of anthropology, and the social sciences more broadly, was assembled around the idea that the discipline was unable to escape its foundation in a racialised conceptualisation of alterity. The continuity of the 'objects' of anthropology[85] in the present is consistent with the growing critical contention that there was no substantive rupture between the 'colonial past' and the 'constitutional present' achieved through the CODESA Negotiations in the early 1990s in South Africa. Conquest, 'colonisation and its sequels are the ever present context of survival for the peoples anthropologists study.'[86] Before any kind of constructive work around the future possibilities of the discipline can be done, a thorough historical understanding of the ways in which anthropology and social scientific production more generally have been and *continue to be* central to the reproduction of what Wolfe has theorised as the *structure* of settler colonialism is required.[87]

Acknowledgements

The author is deeply grateful to Kelly Gillespie, Shireen Ally, Hylton White, and Nolwazi Mkhwanazi for their support and intellectual guidance during the research. And is also indebted to the wonderful group of elders and interlocutors present at the *South African Journal on Human Rights* colloquium on 'Conquest, Constitutionalism and Democratic Contestations' in May 2017, including Prof. Mogobe Ramose, Joel Modiri, Ndumiso Dladla, Sanele Sibanda, Charmika Samaradiwakera-Wijesundara and Tumelo Modiselle.

Disclosure statement

No potential conflict of interest was reported by the author.

Funding

This paper was completed with the support of National Research Foundation Freestanding, Innovation and Scarce Skills Masters Scholarship SFH150723130181, and the Patrick and Margaret Flanagan Scholarship.

[85] Mafeje (note 57 above).
[86] Ettienne & Leacock cited in Reilly (note 24 above) 25–26.
[87] P Wolfe (note 5 above).

The liberation of history and the end of South Africa: some notes towards an Azanian historiography in Africa, South[1]

Ndumiso Dladla

ABSTRACT

In this article we will argue that beyond its general status and identity as the supreme law of South Africa, the 1996 constitution[2] (hereinafter the constitution) is also a historiographical paradigm. We shall begin by providing general description and overview of Azanian critical philosophy focussing on its relationship to the constitution. This will be followed by a discussion on the nature of history itself and the relationship between historical knowledge and power. We will then turn to the history of South Africa in particular, which is understood both as a history of conquest as well as the conquest of history. The final parts of the article will argue that the wholesale resumption of the history of liberation is the most crucial possibility condition for the liberation of history itself.

1. Introduction

Our starting point is that 'South Africa' is the ultimate philosophical problem for the indigenous people conquered in the unjust wars of colonisation.[3] It is a problem with ethical, legal, political, epistemological and even metaphysical implications. Although

---

1 In memory of Kenneth Hashi Tafira, our brother in the struggle for reason, who passed away earlier this year while developing his own theoretical examination of South African history from a Black point of view. May his soul rest in peace and his ideas continue to cause restlessness.

2 The convention in terms of which the South African constitution is written with an initial capital letter to signify its status as supreme law is reminiscent of the convention of capitalising the writing of 'god' in the so-called 'world religions'. Following Wole Soyinka *The Burden of Memory, The Muse of Forgiveness* (1999) 32, we question the ethical tenability and soundness of maintaining the convention that capitalises the 'world religions' as well as their gods and adherents until it is applied to all religions. We must bear in mind the fact that the displacement of the living gods of various indigenous peoples conquered in the unjust wars of colonisation, often in the very name of these religions, was no voluntary and peaceful process but part and parcel of the same murderous epistemicide. It is the same too with law; we identify the constitution so described as the conqueror's law – the status of its supremacy is by no means unchallenged. This article may be taken as an elaboration of its ethical untenability and reprehensibility.

3 For an elaboration of this formulation see MB Ramose 'An African perspective on justice and race' (2001) 3 *Polylog* <https://them.polylog.org/3/frm-en.htm> fn 12.

this article will be focussed on the epistemological problem it presents for historical knowledge, our critique is basically an ethical one, even though it shall touch on a variety of the problem's expressions. Understood *in toto*, the article is a critique of the idea South Africa and the reality it has been producing from the perspective of Azanian critical philosophy.

In recent discourse, people who have suggested that the South African constitution is an ethical and political problem have been labelled using a variety of derogatory terms. Those labelled have included parties who are not ethical and intellectual critics but have regarded the constitution as a legal and political inconvenience at various times, and have as such been seen with great suspicion by the liberal establishment in South Africa.[4] There are also those like ourselves who are proponents of a theory that regards the end (that is the conclusion) of South Africa as an ethical and political necessity. It is especially those among us who have rejected the justice and necessity of the constitution who have been described using a variety of terms. Depending on the focus of contention, we have been called fascists, African nationalists (used derogatively), reverse racists (used without irony), constitutional delinquents, nativists, constitutional denigrators[5] and constitutional abolitionists by the defenders of the constitution. We must admit partiality to the last of these descriptions, 'constitutional abolitionists', except to qualify that it is not constitutioness[6] itself that we argue must be abolished but rather the continuous succession of the conqueror's constitutions purporting to be 'our' law. This article is an attempt, among other things, to elaborate our general theory and apply it in particular to the subject of history in South Africa.

The first section of the article will provide a very brief and general discussion of Azanian critical philosophy. We will then turn to a discussion of the nature of history and historical knowledge. Once this has been done, we will focus upon South African history, in particular, appraising its historiography from the point of view of Azanian critical philosophy.

We will conclude with a discussion of the historical and ethical tensions that the constitution presents, even if a detailed discussion of the resolution of these contradictions – that is 'what is to be done' – falls outside of the scope of this article.

2. Azanian critical philosophy

There are many debates concerning the etymology of Azania and its precise meaning.[7] Our discussion here, however, will be limited to its life as a political and philosophical term in South African history. Azania is a name that was introduced to the South

---

[4] We mean here to describe former president Jacob Zuma, who at one point declared, very common-sensically, that the judges of 'the constitutional court were not god', which caused a great number of liberal media houses to become hysterically concerned. <https://www.businesslive.co.za/rdm/politics/2016-04-07-jacob-zuma-vs-the-constitution-its-a-fight-to-the-bitter-end/>

[5] This term was used by Justice Dennis Davis at the colloquium entitled 'Conquest, Constitutionalism and Democratic Contestations' held at the University of the Witwatersrand in Johannesburg, South Africa in May 2017.

[6] See MB Ramose *African Philosophy Through Ubuntu* (1999) and T Madlingozi 'On settler colonialism and post-conquest *constitutionness*: the decolonising constitutional vision of African Nationalists of Azania/South Africa' (forthcoming). <https://www.academia.edu/33747352/On_Settler_Colonialism_and_Post-Conquest_Constitutionness_The_Decolonising_Constitutional_Vision_of_African_Nationalists_of_Azania_South_Africa>

[7] See RG Diaz *Azanism: A Critical Analysis of the Mytho-reality Complexity of the Azanian Nation* (2009).

African political lexicon by the Pan Africanist Congress of Azania (PAC), formed in 1959 by proponents of the Africanist tendency with the African National Congress.[8] In the PAC's postulation, Azania is the true name of the territory that has been called South Africa since the South Africa Act 1909 of British Parliament, which established the Union of South Africa in 1910. This political event concluded the Anglo-Boer or 'South African War' – a war between two European invading communities over the title to territory and sovereignty over a territory they had wrestled from the indigenous people after conquering them. These constitutional origins of South Africa reveal that it has its basis on the loss of title to territory and sovereignty over it by the indigenous people conquered in the unjust wars of colonisation. One clear example of formal continuity between present-day constitutional South Africa and its constitutional 1910 predecessor are the various names of the provinces and cities of present-day South Africa. More often than not – when they aren't simply the retention of the names given to political territory by the conqueror – these are indigenous-language translations or indigenous-name versions of the commodities that are of value within the conqueror's economy, often at the historical expense of the indigenous people. They do not reflect the historical significance of those areas to the indigenous people conquered in the unjust wars of colonisation: names such as the Northern, Eastern and Western Cape (from the division of the Cape Colony of the Union constitution) and cities including George, King William's Town, East London and Queenstown named after various British monarchs. The so-called Free State province (from the old Boer Republic of Oranje Vrijstaat), Emalahleni (where coal is found), Egoli (where gold is found), eMpumalanga ('east' in the Nguni languages from the former Eastern Transvaal) are names that do not reflect the historical, political and cultural significance of these places in the history of their historical inhabitants. In the PAC's understanding, it was necessary if the title to territory and sovereignty over it were sought that South Africa itself be repudiated even epistemologically. Azania was understood as the end to which the repudiation was directed; it was a signifier of the will towards the restoration of full political as well as epistemological sovereignty. It was more than just another name of the country to be employed once the indigenous people had succeeded their conquerors in title to territory.

Azania was to be a wholly African polity rather than the old colonial vision of a little Europe in Africa.[9] It was to be a different idea of nationhood, of law and justice, national culture, values and democracy.[10] Azania may be understood as the ends to which Africanist ideology and liberation philosophy were aimed. It is necessary, therefore, to discuss some basic tenets of the Africanist understanding of and approach to the struggle for liberation.

---

[8] GM Gerhart *Black Power in South Africa* (1978).

[9] LE Neame *White Man's Africa: The Problem of a White Nation in a Black Continent* (1952), JC Smuts *Africa and Some World Problems* (1930) and CJF Muller *500 Years – A History of South Africa* (1969) all conceive of South Africa as a white man's country, an African province of Europe. This is a status South Africa retains to date, both in the minds of the indigenous conquered people and their conquerors. It is not, for example, unheard of in South Africa to refer to visiting another African country as having visited 'Africa' or to refer to Africans from beyond the Limpopo as Africans to differentiate them from South Africans, even of the indigenous variety. Other dimensions of this schizophrenia include the continued use of terms such as 'African restaurants' and 'African attire' (which is no synonym for 'local' in South Africa) to refer to the cuisine and fashion of the indigenous conquered people. The specification is, of course, a marker of alterity, distinguishing whatever is specified from the South African variety.

[10] See T Delport 'Asazi ukuthi iyozala nkomoni: Robert Mangaliso Sobukwe's historical imagination of the future' (2016) 50 *Psychology in Society* 35.

Among the most important features of Azanian thought that are of relevance to the present elaboration are:

1. The insistence by Azanians that the objective of the liberation struggle was the recovery of sovereign title to territory (rather than the mere attainment of civil and political rights).
2. The insistence that the title to territory itself belongs exclusively to the indigenous people conquered in the unjust wars of colonisation.
3. The rejection of multi-racialism. This includes incredulity to the tenability of non-racialism as a means and upholding it only as an end achievable only once the title to territory had been restored to the indigenous conquered people.[11]
4. The recognition of 'South Africa' as a polity and idea inextricably bound to the will of the conqueror and requiring state succession by a liberated polity with a restored relationship and continuity with the rest of the African continent. This is against a political history of South Africa having constructed its identity as distinctly European and bearing no cultural resemblance and relationship with 'the rest of the continent'.

The Azanian approach to thinking and struggle spreads beyond the boundaries of the PAC both in time (that is, beyond the historical period of the PAC's greatest influence) and beyond space (understood as the boundaries and identity of the party or movement itself). The Black Consciousness Movement of Azania (BCMA), which gained ascendancy in the late 1960s, was to adopt both the name Azania to describe the territory as well as the application of the theory of liberation developed by the PAC, except for a few modifications. After the Black Consciousness Movement (BCM), the ideal of Azania was to be adopted by a variety of political organisations, including the Azanian People's Liberation Army (APLA), the Pan-Africanist Student Movement of Azania (PASMA), the Azanian Political Organization (AZAPO), the Socialist Party of Azania (SOPA) and Azanian National Youth Unity. The spread of the movement beyond the confines of the PAC's period of greatest political influence was not restricted to the future but in its interpretive guise extended also to the past. Although this article will conclude with a prolegomenon to an Azanian historiography, it is pertinent to state at this point already that one of the distinctive features of Azanian thought is precisely its historical orientation. At various points, whether among the Africanists of Anton Lembede's Youth League, Mangaliso Sobukwe's PAC or proponents of Bantubonke Biko's Black Consciousness philosophy, the Azanians insisted that the struggle for liberation (understood as the restoration of sovereign title) predated the advent of European-educated African intellectuals and their political parties and movements. Instead, they saw themselves and their movements as merely contemporary iterations in an already thitherto multi-century war of resistance against colonial conquest. They counted the great kings and their warriors, figures such the brother kings Shaka and Dingane ka Senzangakhona, Ikumkani uHinsta ka Khawuta, Kgosi Sekhukhune, Kgosi Mampuru, Khosi Moshoeshoe and the great

---

[11] See N Dladla 'Contested memory: retrieving the Africanist (liberatory) conception of non-racialism' (2017) 64 *Theoria* 101.

warrior Inkosi uBhambatha as forbears[12] in their approach to the struggle for liberation.

By Azanian critical philosophy, however, here we mean to describe contemporary theoretical and pratical activity that has its foundation on the historical activities and thinking of the above political movements and the thinker-actors they produced. It includes a sustained study of the work of intellectuals, most of who were produced by these movements, who continued to write and practise[13] even after 1994, some in the academy, others outside of it.[14] Although these figures are not all academic philosophers, it is the principle underpinnings upon which their work is predicated that is instrumentalised and developed in Azanian critical philosophy, which may be understood as a tendency in the discourse on post-colonial African philosophy.[15] In the discourse of African Philosophy then Azanian thought could be categorised into the group Henry Odera Oruka called nationalistic-ideological[16] philosophy.

This approach to philosophy is one that originates in the experience of the struggle against colonial (and then neo-colonial) domination in Africa. Historically, many of its central theoreticians were gifted African intellectuals, educated in various fields, sometimes in Western academic philosophy itself, for example, Kwame Nkrumah and Lembede. Few of them were, however, simply academics. They were soldiers, activists, organisers, lawyers and freedom fighters, who distilled their thought in the process of the engagement of struggle. With a few exceptions, such as Nkrumah, many of their

---

[12] See A Lembede *Freedom in Our Lifetime: The Collected Writings of Anton Muziwakhe Lembede* (2015); RM Sobukwe *Speeches of Mangaliso Sobukwe, from 1949–1959 and Other Documents of the Pan-Africanist Congress of Azania* (1979); and Gerhart (note 8 above).

[13] The inclusion of practice here is to make the point that ethical and intellectual activity finds expression beyond the facility of writing. These practices include the very choice by some of our elders to leave the cosy conditions of universities in Europe and America and come back home to teach in South Africa, where some have been marginalised for political reasons. The refusals to participate in the activities in which the freedom of Africans was sacrificed for comfort in the 'new' South Africa form part of a historical record from which we are able to study both theoretical and practical ethics as well as social and political theory.

[14] Motsoko Pheko of the PAC has been an active voice during the entire post-1994 period. His work has included making connections between the constitutional compromise and the 'Freedom Cheater', as he calls it, as well as repeatedly insisting that there can be no talk of liberation without land. Other figures include South African Students' Organisation (SASO) member, AZAPO founding member and Black Consciousness labour organiser Mandla Seloane, who works as an independent researcher and publisher; and former SASO activist and exile, philosophy professor Mogobe Ramose. Others include historian and founding member of the South African Youth Revolutionary Council Malesela Steve Lebelo, and mathematician and community teacher Molora Mabeba.

[15] The election of the term postcolonial rather than the oft-used 'decolonial' has an ethical as well as intellectual basis; it is elected on the basis of intellectual sovereignty. In this choice, we follow our esteemed elders, for example EC Eze *Postcolonial African Philosophy: A Critical Reader* (1997) and T Serequeberhan 'Philosophy and post-colonial Africa' in EC Eze *African Philosophy: An Anthology* (1998) 9-22. The point, really, is that Africans are no strangers to colonial conquest or thinking and acting against it. The justification for the use of the term decoloniality by its proponents (see R Grosfoguel 'The epistemic decolonial turn' (2007) 21 *Cultural Studies* 211) is the straw-man claim that postcolonial theory is based on the false assumption that colonialism is totally over, whereas they (the decolonialists) recognise its residue in the forms of the 'coloniality of being, knowledge and power', as well as postcolonial theory's supposed uncritical basis upon Eurocentric thought. That Eurocentricity is a critical problem or that colonialism remained in former colonies in more insidious forms after the formal end of colonial administration was of course not news to us in Africa. Numerous anti-colonial theoreticians dedicated serious study precisely to these residual phenomena. Kwame Nkrumah's *Neo-colonialism: The Last Stage of Imperialism* (1965) is just one example. There is no reason why we should adopt the now in vogue decoloniality/coloniality and ignore our heritage. Whereas we are quite open and willing to learn from the struggles and thinking of other peoples, such as the Latin American intellectuals who have been theorising under the banner of decoloniality theory since the mid-2000s. Our exercise is firmly grounded in the African experience and the theoretical and practical resources it has generated since the advent of colonialism.

[16] See HO Oruka 'Four trends in current African philosophy' in PH Coetzee & APJ Roux (eds) *Philosophy from Africa: A Text with Readings* (2002) 120–124.

works are not written as extended treatises in the fashion of academic philosophy. Instead, they survive as pamphlets, speeches, letters and notes that are nevertheless rich sources of social, legal, economic and political philosophies as well as epistemology, metaphysics and ethics. Sobukwe's writing on Africanism, Léopold Senghor's on Negritude, Julius Nyerere's on Ujamaa and Kenneth Kaunda's on African 'humanism' come to mind as examples in this regard, not forgetting the poetry and writings of physician-presidents Agostinho Neto and Félix Houphouët-Boigny. Henry Oruka, describing the character of nationalistic-ideological philosophy writes that: 'It is clear that this philosophy is claimed to be rooted in the traditional or communal Africa, but it is explicit that it is actually a philosophy of the individual author concerned. Thirdly, this philosophy is practical and has explicit problems to solve, namely those of national and individual freedom.'[17]

Azanian critical philosophy also meets the minimum criteria set by Mogobe Ramose, Tsenay Serequeberhan and Theophilus Okere, among others, for the practice of African philosophy, namely that it has its basis upon 'the culture and experience of African peoples' and the 'African philosopher would at the very minimum be arguing for the liberation of African philosophy from the yoke of dominance and enslavement under the European (Western) epistemological paradigm.'[18]

Sobukwe, the founding president and important theoretician of the first organisation that was founded on an explicitly Africanist basis, did not study academic philosophy formally (he was an academic linguist whose thesis explored the philosophical significance of various African proverbs). He was, however, explicitly engaged in political philosophy derived from African culture and, in part, from his practical involvement in politics. He argued in several instances for the liberation of Africanist philosophy from the dominance of the Western epistemological paradigm.

In the recent past, ideas coming out of the Azanian tradition have gained influence in a variety of ways. The Economic Freedom Fighters (EFF) political party, the Rhodes Must Fall movement (which inspired several other eruptions beyond Azania's borders) as well as the Black First Land First (BLF)[19] political party have been inspired by this tendency. The African National Congress (ANC) government has even recently considered the changing of the country's name to Azania[20] and, of course, 2018 has already seen the beginning of talks to amend the constitution's property clause to make possible land expropriation without compensation.

In the academy too there have been a number of emerging theoreticians who have relied upon and developed this tendency. Besides our own work, see work by Joel

---

[17] Ibid 141.

[18] Ramose (note 6 above) 37.

[19] Although the BLF was formed in late 2015, its leader, Andile Mngxitama, has been a leading and influential proponent of the Azanian critique of the 'new' South Africa both in his journalistic writings in several national newspapers and his foundation and co-editorship of the influential pamphlet series *New Frank Talk* with another Azanian intellectual, art critic Athi Mongezeleli Joja. Mngxitama has also been at the forefront of numerous Black Consciousness organisations such as Blackwash and the September National Imbizo, and was an ideologue of the EFF prior to his expulsion in 2015.

[20] See J Tee 'Nathi Mthethwa: South Africa to change its name to… Azania?' (13 June 2017) <http://www.transafricaradio.net/index.php/2017/06/13/nathi-mthethwa-south-africa-change-name-azania/>

Modiri and Tshepo Madlingozi.[21] Central to this developing body of work is a general incredulity towards the idea of the new South Africa and an insistence on a material and ideological continuity between the period at which the indigenous people were first conquered in the earliest unjust wars of colonisation, beginning in 1652 and the period following the negotiated settlement of the early 1990s. Azania, then, more than simply being a reiteration of the name favoured by Sobukwe's PAC and Biko's BCMA is also the foundation of a theory, that is a particular account of the underpinnings of reality as well as an ethic. This ethic is one that considers the decisive antagonism in South African history to have been the very establishment of 'South Africa' itself. Here, South Africa is considered as an expression of the will and imagination of the conqueror and his successors in title. This colonial project began in 1652, during the first wars of colonisation. Liberation is, as such, understood as the initiation of a period of history Ramose has called 'post-conquest'.[22] Post-conquest South Africa or Azania will require nothing else than the restoration of title to territory to the indigenous people conquered in the unjust wars of colonisation, of the restoration of their encumbered sovereignty over it, as well as reparations for their unnecessary multi-century deprivation, suffering and preventable death.

Azanian critical philosophy, then, may be understood as a discourse of outstanding liberation that understands its task in its contemporary guise as the exposition of this on-going un-freedom and its history and philosophy. Its sources include the very struggle for liberation since 1652 and its various artefacts in the form of oral literature, struggle songs, poetry, speeches and political pamphlets, as well as lengthier treatises and theoretical elaboration by its proponents.

This article, in particular, is an attempt at a sketchy elaboration of the Azanian critical philosophy of history, using the categories of 'conquest', 'apartheid' and 'sovereignty' as they have been developed in the thought and practice of our forebears.

3. On the meaning of history: historiography, the philosophy of history and the law

Narrowly construed, historiography consists in the study of the writing of history. Historiographers typically concern themselves not with a study of historical facts together with their arrangement and interpretation, as do the historians. Instead a historiographer studies the work of the historians, assesses the methods they relied upon as well as a variety of theoretical and ideological underpinnings that make for the differences between varying historical accounts. Some of the theoretical and practical underpinnings of history are of a philosophical nature. These sorts of underpinnings include, for example, what might be described as the metaphysics of history – for example, what is history at all? What are the conditions of possibility to be able to speak of genuine historical

[21] JM Modiri 'The jurisprudence of Steve Biko: a study in race, law and power in the "afterlife" of colonial-apartheid' Unpublished PhD thesis, University of Pretoria (2018), T Madlingozi 'On settler colonialism and post-conquest *constitutionness*: the decolonising constitutional vision of African nationalists of Azania/South Africa' in B de Sousa Santos (forthcoming) and N Dladla 'Towards an African Critical Philosophy of Race: Ubuntu as a Philo-praxis of Liberation' (2017) 6 *Filosofia Theoretica: Journal of African Philosophy, Culture and Religions* 39–68.

[22] Ramose (note 2 above).

activity? Does history have laws that inform its unfolding through time? There are philosophical anthropological questions too, such as what kinds of human beings and societies produce history? Epistemological considerations include questions such as what is historical knowledge at all, and how is it possible to know something that took place when no one alive today was present? The philosophy of history must also consist of ethical and political questions regarding the kind of political activity history itself is employed across time to justify.

In the course of this article, the term 'historiography' will be used in an all-encompassing way to include even the description of theoretical activity and practical considerations that are basically philosophical, even if the actors are not themselves academic philosophers.

Regarding the historiographical status of law itself, it is worthwhile to note, with South Africa not being an exception, that legal histories often ground themselves upon particular political-historical accounts. Some famous histories and general theoretical works on law in South Africa[23] begin by telling the reader that the 'Bantu tribes' arrived in South Africa at approximately the same period as their European conquerors. These historical claims are not at all insignificant trivia but essential ethical and political justifications for the implantation of the European conqueror's law as the supreme law of South Africa. These 'facts' are included to silence the curious mind who might ask, 'Why is this book silent about the law of the indigenous peoples conquered in the unjust wars of colonisation?' They are included precisely to justify the unjust wars of colonisation as taking place between foreign and invading parties with equal claim to title differentiated only by the force of arms, intellect and history at their disposal.

3.1 What is history?

'History' is an ambiguous word, since it covers both '(1) the totality of past human actions and (2) the narrative account we construct of them now'.[24] Historians are not 'content with the simple discovery of past facts: they aspire, at least, not only to say what happened but also to show why it happened'.[25] The Shorter Oxford English Dictionary defines a fact as 'a datum of experience as distinct from conclusions'. The enterprise of historical writing comprises far more than the discovery of facts; it is also the coterminous exercise of their representation and interpretation. Of course, even the historian's consideration of what is 'fact' at all – that is, which 'facts' are worthy of recording and becoming *historical* – is already a procedure of interpretation. In view of these considerations, history may be construed as the historian's subjective selection of 'facts' from the past and an interpretation of those 'facts' according to the conventions of history as a scientific discipline.

---

[23] For instance, HR Hahlo & E Kahn's famous *The South African Legal System and its Background* (1968) and their *The Union of South Africa: The Development of Its Laws and Constitution* (1960).

[24] P Walshe *The Rise of African Nationalism in South Africa: The African National Congress, 1912–52* (1970) 16.

[25] Ibid 18.

3.2 What are historical facts?

Although the term 'historical fact' appears to be clear and straightforward, either describing ordinary facts occurring in the past or, alternatively, facts about the technical discipline of history, this straightforwardness is quite misleading. Historical facts are not just any among the infinite number of ascertainable facts about events that have passed in time.

Rather, they describe that special class of facts about the past that is considered, on the basis of history as a science, to be historically significant. Although under the influence of Leopold von Ranke[26] historians used to claim that 'facts speak for themselves', it is, in fact, rather so that, '[F]acts speak when they are called by the historian who decides which facts to disclose, in what context and order.'[27]

In order to demonstrate by example just how it is that facts become historical facts, Edward Carr uses Julius Caesar's crossing of the Rubicon as an example, he writes: '[I]t is a historian who decided that Caesar's crossing of that petty stream, the Rubicon, is a fact of history whereas the crossing of the Rubicon by millions of other people before or since, interests nobody at all.'[28] He goes on to suggest, and here we will use our own example, that any X that swam in a pond in Pretoria an hour ago is just as much a fact about the past as Caesar's crossing the Rubicon. It will, however, be very likely ignored by historians. Carr writes about the actual process of the graduation of facts about the past into historical facts by suggesting, for example, that a respected scholar of history at some prestigious university[29] merely considering an event, which was not considered as historically significant before, may cause other historians to develop interest in that fact; through studying and recording its status may then be converted from an ordinary fact about the past to a historical fact.[30]

Elaborating on the contingency of historical facts and their force in the enterprise of history, Carr goes on to write:

> Our picture of Greece in the fifth century BC is defective not primarily because so many bits have been accidentally lost, but because it is, by and large, the picture formed by a tiny group of people in the tiny city of Athens. We know a lot about what fifth century Greece looked like to an Athenian citizen but hardly anything about what it looked like to a Spartan, a Corinthian or Theban not to mention a Persian or a slave or other non-citizen resident in Athens. Our picture has been preselected and predetermined for us by people who were consciously or unconsciously imbued with a particular view and thought the facts which supported this view worth preserving.[31]

---

[26] L Ranke *The Theory and Practice of History* (1973).

[27] E Carr *What is History?* (1961) 8.

[28] Ibid 9.

[29] Both conditions, that a scholar be respected or respectable as well as that he or she be based at a prestigious university, are politically interesting. This is because the conference of these statuses is dependent on power relations within the academy and society at large. As feminist and race scholars (see S Sullivan & N Tuana (eds) *Race and the Epistemologies of Ignorance* (2007)) have shown for a long time now, white males who dominate the history of and current state of the academy for example often do not cite or study the work of women and African scholars. Such scholars are also underrepresented in the staff members of these 'prestigious universities'. This leads to the racing, sexing and geo-politicisation of 'respect' and scholarly authority required to convert natural facts into historical ones.

[30] Carr (note 27 above) 9.

[31] Ibid 13.

Greek philosopher Cornelius Castoriadis echoes this insight about the problem of history being produced by historical actors with an identity with attendant interests and the effect this has on the capacity of transparency and universality for such knowledge when he asks:

> When we speak of history who is speaking? It is someone of a given period, class and society – in short someone who is himself a historical being. And this very fact, which founds the possibility of historical knowledge (for only a historical being can have an experience of history and can talk about it) prevents this knowledge from ever acquiring the status of complete and transparent knowledge – since it is itself, in its essence, an historical phenomenon which demands to be apprehended and interpreted as such. The discourse on history is included within history.[32]

Our point here is simply that accounts of the past, histories and the facts of those histories gain their status as a result of several 'unscientific' factors, some of which are purely accidental but many of which involve political and institutional power, identity and politics. This point is of great importance in the consideration of the history of history in South Africa; as such we shall elaborate on this point before directly examining historical trends in South Africa.

3.3 History and interpretation

It is the generally established view among academic historians and historiographers that there was no history produced in South Africa before the 1820s. In order to justify this view, Andrew Bank, for example, has written: 'The travel narratives of the seventeenth, eighteenth and early nineteenth centuries, so extensively mined by latter-day historians, document specific, subjective and personal encounters with the African landscape and people.'[33] While this assumption is useful in establishing a finite scope for our discussion of South African historiography, it cannot be taken for granted. The reason is that there is a long-standing assumption, even with pretensions to scientificity, that Africans did not possess any history at all prior to European colonisation.

The German philosopher Georg Wilhelm Friedrich Hegel, in his *The Philosophy of History*, wrote among other things about the continent that, 'Africa is not a historical continent; it shows neither change nor development.'[34] In another passage, he writes that its Negro populations were 'capable of neither development nor education'.[35] The eminent African historian John Fage, trying to explain why this view was current among Hegel and other European intellectuals during their time, writes, 'European intellectuals persuaded themselves that the purpose, knowledge and power and wealth of their society were so strong that it must prevail over all others; therefore its history was the key to understanding, and the history of all other societies was irrelevant.'[36]

---

[32] C Castoriadis *The Imaginary Institution of Society* (1975) 21.

[33] A Bank 'The great debate and the origins of South African historiography' (1997) 38 *The Journal of African History* 261, 262.

[34] GWF Hegel *The Philosophy of History* quoted in JD Fage 'The development of African historiography' in J Ki-Zerbo (ed) *UNESCO General History of Africa I: Methodology and African Prehistory* (1981) 30.

[35] Ibid 30.

[36] Fage (note 34 above) 30.

While it is true that European arrogance and white supremacy more generally are among the factors that explain these attitudes, these assumptions also had and continue to have deadly consequences for their objects of doubt. The assumption concerning Africa's a-historicality, which is really a small part of a racial epistemology,[37] was one of the pillars in the moral justification of the conquest of the indigenous people in the unjust wars of colonisation and their disseizin of territory. Accompanying this doctrine of 'history-lessness' were the doctrines of *terra nullius* (the so-called empty land thesis) as well as the invention of 'Blackness' (the characteristic of being human-like but 'empty of reason').

Ever since the conquest of the indigenous people in the unjust wars of colonisation, South African history has seen an evolution in terms of which 'Blacks' have correspondingly devolved from those arbitrarily branded as 'without reason and history' to those 'without land', 'without rights (including the right to citizenship or life) (legal objects)' and those 'without freedom'. 'Whites', on the other hand, attained their whiteness from an imaginary ontological exclusivity being a natural endowment with surplus reason and conferring upon them the titles of 'landowners', 'rights bearers (legal subjects)' and exclusive bearers of freedom. As political theorist Cedric Robinson puts it: 'The Negro, that is the colour black, was both a negation of African and an opposition to white. The construct of [black] unlike the terms "African", "moor" or "Ethiope" suggested no situatedness in time, that is history or space, that is ethno- or politico-geography.'[38]

An African philosophical reading of South African history will show that this 'de-situation' and displacement, as well as the de-historicisation of the indigenous peoples conquered in the unjust wars of colonisation, were essential to the invention of its complementary fiction of whiteness. The fiction of whiteness in South Africa required the disfigurement of the history of the indigenous peoples conquered in the unjust wars of colonisation in order to uphold such mythical dogmas as, 'South Africa is a white man's country.'[39] It required this disfigurement also to produce the narrative of the indigenous peoples conquered in the unjust wars of colonisation as savages and beasts of burden. As Robinson reminds us: '[T]he creation of the negro, the fiction of a dumb beast of burden fit only for slavery, was closely associated with the economic, technical and financial requirements of Western development from the sixteenth century onwards.'[40]

We will nevertheless confine our discussion of history in the next section on the basis of Bank's study of history 'beginning' in the 1820s. This is because the purpose of our exercise here is precisely a reading of the white historiography of South Africa. Concerning the existence of African history itself in the South or elsewhere on the continent, the interested reader is invited to visit the eight-volume (and growing) *UNESCO General History of Africa*, the reach of which exceeds one hundred centuries into our past, long before the invention of racism and even Europe itself.

---

[37] See S Sullivan & N Tuana (eds) *Race and the Epistemologies of Ignorance* (2007).
[38] CJ Robinson *Black Marxism: The Makings of the Black Radical Tradition* (1983) 81.
[39] Neame, Smuts & Muller (note 9 above).
[40] Robinson (note 38 above) 81.

4. The conquest and colonisation of South African historiography

The historical sociologist Bernard Magubane, among others, has argued that despite claims to the contrary, what passes, in reality, for African history are the collective experiences of the European conquerors in South Africa.[41] It is our basic contention, in this section, that (despite endless debate on the matter between historians) South African academic history could be uncontroversially characterised, with little exception, as white.

The African proverb 'Until the lion tells the tale, stories of the hunt shall always glorify the hunter' is apposite for the present discussion. In the instance of a conquered and colonised people, the lion is a metaphor for the indigenous, conquered people and the hunter for the conqueror. The problem is, however, greater than the knowledge and telling of the story of the hunt. The unjust wars in which the indigenous people were conquered were wars with colonisation as their end. The colonisation of Africa by Europe, following Valentin-Yves Mudimbe, may be understood as the transformation of territory itself and its cultural and intellectual practices into 'fundamentally European constructs'.[42] This has meant that the very discipline of history, including the determination of what counts as history, reflects the prejudices and interests of the hunter.

Examining precisely this relationship between power and 'official history' in South Africa, Magubane writes: 'Forces that emerged victorious in the struggles between the colonizer and the colonized created South African history, as written by recognized historians. If one looks at the history of higher education in South Africa [the universities of which produced what today passes as history], there is no question that the forces that endowed its institutions were the major beneficiaries of African helotry.'[43]

Not only were the 'political'[44] writings of the indigenous, conquered people banned during crucial periods of South African history, African history in South Africa also was and remains marginalised.

A study of history reveals that the historical enterprise is neither objective nor value free. Instead, history always reflects and is affected by power relations and people's interests. The historian is not exempt. As a result, the history of South African history reveals in itself interpretive trends that correspond closely with the political interests of the communities of historians who were involved in its production. Such historians belong not simply to historical societies and communities but also to so-called 'national' and 'political' groups. This affects various things, including the institutions where they are trained and what they are taught there.[45]

In one of only two book-length surveys of South Africa published in English,[46] historiographer Ken Smith goes to some length to make the point that there are no

---

[41] See BM Magubane 'Whose memory – whose history? The illusion of liberal and radical historical debates' in H Stolten (ed) *History Making and Present Day Politics: The Meaning of Collective Memory in South Africa* (2007) 251–279.

[42] VY Mudimbe *The Invention of Africa: Gnosis, Philosophy, and the Order of Knowledge* (1988) 14.

[43] Magubane (note 41 above) 252.

[44] The term 'political' was sometimes interpreted broadly enough to include any idea or activity that suggested, even moderately, that the indigenous, conquered people were full human beings second to none.

[45] N Dladla 'Racism and the marginality of African philosophy' (2017) 18 *Phronimon* 204 explores the politicisation of higher education in South Africa in relation to the history of philosophy in the country.

[46] The other is FA van Jaarsveld's 1964 *The Afrikaner's Interpretation of South African History*, which focuses particularly on Afrikaner-nationalist historiography.

black historians in South Africa. However, in the same volume, Smith does include numerous works by white so-called amateur historians of the Settler, British, Afrikaner and Marxist schools. More than a handful of works written by Africans from an African point of view give a systematic account of the past. These include but are not limited to Jordan Ngubane's *An African Explains Apartheid* and even historical-sociological texts such as Magubane's *The Political Economy of Race and Class in South Africa* or his *The Making of a Racist State: British Imperialism and the Union of South Africa 1875–1910.*

The exclusion of these texts under a description of African history in South Africa is the result of an ideologically suspicious arbitration that remains undisclosed. Why is it that the travelogues of amateur European travel writers are taken as the early beginnings of history in South Africa, whereas the historical writings of Africans in varying degrees of formality remain outside its bounds?

In the case of Smith, these claims appear to strengthen his dubious point about the disinterest in history of Africans, a point that can only be sustained through silencing the considerable number of voices that call this belief into question. In the course of the pursuit of liberation, the necessity of the study and reinterpretation of the past by Africans according to their own experience is a point that is well recorded by several Azanian thinkers, such as Lembede, Sobukwe and Biko. Thus in what follows, we will read the history of history in South Africa from an African philosophical point of view. That is, we will read it from the point of view of the indigenous people conquered in the unjust wars of colonisation.

4.1 Colonial historiography

The following section will not be a detailed survey of South African historiography, which we do elsewhere.[47] It will consist of only a very brief listing and discussion of historical trends in South Africa, which will be assessed in relation to their standpoint on conquest and settlement, title to territory, race and liberation.

4.1.1 The conservative school

South African historiographers typically speak of distinct historiographical paradigms including the British/Imperialist, Settler and Afrikaner-nationalist schools. Although we think there is merit in this from a political point of view since the historical interests of the communities these historians represented were at some points distinct, we shall nevertheless treat them synthetically in relation to their general and explicit agreement on the questions of conquest, title to territory and race.

According to Smith, the British school emerged around the mid-19th century. It consisted of the writers prior to George McCall Theal who were apologists for the British takeover of the Cape.[48] These authors tended to view the British colonies as part of the empire, rather than as independent entities, and the Cape Colony was no different in this regard. The authors focussed on events after the first British

[47] See N Dladla 'The racism of history in South Africa', chapter 3 in *Here is a Table: A Philosophical Essay on the History of Race in South Africa* (2018) 83–110.

[48] K Smith *The Changing Past: Trends in South African Historical Writing* (1988).

occupation of the Cape. They focussed on important British administrators and politicians and the Settlers and 'their struggle against the Xhosa on the eastern frontier and the fate of the British settlers in Natal'.[49] The British school tended to think of imperialism as a positive force that brought South Africa into world civilisation.

The British writers, Smith writes, 'had an anti-Afrikaner bias in the same way as much historical writing in Dutch and Afrikaans had an anti-English bias [...] [B]oth English and Afrikaans writers shared an anti-black image of the past [...] They saw the frontier from a white point of view and were uncomplimentary about the Xhosa.'[50] The Imperialist school were also defined by their defence of slave owners who faced charges from early liberals, such as the Rev. Dr John Phillip, about mistreating slaves.

The historical work of the Imperialist school ultimately tended to be unified either by actively justifying the Imperial mission in South Africa or taking it for granted. It was the history of civilisers, of men struggling to bring civilisation to a dark and wild terrain, and triumphing against various odds, from the indigenous 'savages' to the unruly Boers. It was 'at its height at the time of the Anglo-Boer War and in the aftermath of the war when all the states in South Africa were British colonies, and it seemed as if South Africa had been won as a permanent part of the British Empire'.[51]

Among the conservative schools, the Settler school is noteworthy for its position that South Africa was to be its own polity rather than a mere dominion of Great Britain. Among the Settler school and all white history thereafter, Theal's name warrants some mention. Various historians are of the opinion that, 'No other historian has stamped his authority on the study of South African history to the same extent as [Theal].'[52] In 1962, Merle Lipton wrote of Theal's continuing importance and influence as 'illustrated by the fact that not only are school textbooks (the only history that most people read) largely based on him, but there are still historians today who consult him'.[53]

Theal is firstly considered a pioneer in South African history because of his archival contribution. He collected volumes of primary documents and historical sources, systematically documented and published them as Basutoland Records, the Records of the Cape Colony and the Records of South-Eastern Africa.[54]

Secondly, Theal is important in the history of South African history because he was also much loved by Afrikaner-nationalist historians, and his work was translated into Dutch and used by educational institutions in the Boer republics. Afrikaners regarded Theal's history as the history of South Africa.[55] He was even by white standards considered to be thoroughly 'pro-white and in particular pro-Boer, anti-missionary and anti-black'[56] in his standpoint. In conservative circles he was reputed

49 Ibid 19.
50 Ibid 9.
51 Ibid 29.
52 Ibid 31.
53 M Lipton (1962) quoted in Smith (note 48 above) 31.
54 Smith (note 48 above) 31.
55 Ibid 36.
56 Ibid 36.

to be 'the first English historian to comprehend the striving and struggles of the republican Afrikaners'[57] Theal identified strongly with the 'colonial nationalist' attitude, according to Smith, and for the first time in historical writing, he also explored and justified the idea of white supremacy in South Africa. He 'extended the idea of the Cape alliance between the English and Afrikaner northwards across the Orange and Vaal Rivers, developing the theme of the formation of a new white South African society ruled whites of both Anglo-Saxon and Dutch heritage'.[58] His historical work typically portrayed black people or 'the coloured races of South Africa' as 'fickle barbarians prone to robbery and unscrupulous in the shedding of blood fit only for the supply of labour'.[59] In Theal's interpretation, '[B]lacks did not play a major role in the history of South Africa […]. [I]t was the history of whites and their efforts to open up South Africa and bring civilisation and Christianity to a wild untamed country.'[60]

It can be argued that he established, in some sense, the most important school of history for whites in South Africa. In some sense, all the white histories that follow from his are variations of Settler history. All of these histories, for example, take for granted the 'right to settle', which arises from the prior and dubious 'right to conquest'. Although Theal is considered the most important figure of Settler-nationalist historiography, George Cory and Frank Cana, who succeeded him in this school, challenged various aspects of his work, yet on largely technical rather than ideological grounds.

Subsequent debates in approaches that followed the Settler school tended to be about a 'more fair' representation of blacks or whites, but all of them took for granted the fact of settlement itself and implicitly the right of conquest, which was its foundation. The Settler school unapologetically took the white Settlers and their interests as its vantage point in the interpretation of events. The white Settler was understood as engaged in a struggle to develop civilisation where there was none, faced with the difficult obstacles of fighting off the indigenous savages as well as liberal do-gooders who, misunderstanding the true place of the savages, were foiling progress.

Theal's work, unlike some that followed, did not even attempt to justify colonial conquest; it was assumed to not only be natural but also ethically necessary.

Theal, for example, writes:

> The settlement of the Europeans in the country was disastrous to the aborigines. Bushmen were still numerous along the interior mountain range, but in other parts of the colony there were hardly any left. One may feel pity for the savages such as these, destroyed in their native wilds, though there is little for regretting their disappearance. They were of no benefit to any other section of the human family, they were incapable of improvement, and it was impossible for civilized men to live on the same soil with them, it was for the world's good that they should make room for a higher race.[61]

Although the traditions that were to follow the Settler and Afrikaner-nationalist schools presented themselves both as ethical and technical improvements of this

[57] Ibid 37.
[58] Ibid 36.
[59] Ibid 36.
[60] Ibid 38.
[61] GM Theal in Smith (note 48 above) 255.

work, an examination of the underlying epistemological paradigms reveals instead that they share considerable philosophical affinity and ideological resemblance. Theal's great ideological significance and its foundational status for subsequent history lies in its essence as a history of conquest, a history of settlement and ownership of South Africa, thereafter represented as a white man's country with black people either to be excluded (in conservative approaches) or included (in the so-called liberal and radical approaches).

Theal would become one of the founding theoretical sources for the world-famous Afrikaner historiography. In its beginnings Afrikaner historiography was at least explicit in its ends; from the onset it would appear that one of the primary goals of history written by Afrikaners was 'to mobilise Afrikaner nationalist sentiment and see this employed in achieving the Afrikaner's political aims'.[62]

The Afrikaner interpreted history as a bitter struggle for survival in the face of various adversities, which included a physically hostile territory populated by 'dangerous savages'.[63] The second British occupation of the Cape in 1806 signalled the beginning of a relationship of antagonism between the British and the Afrikaners that to some degree continues till this day.[64] In the course of their struggle for self-determination, both political and cultural, the Afrikaners developed an Anglophobia that was to be a central interpretive base in their historical writing.[65] The British were understood as oppressors, enemies and sympathisers with the savage blacks. In truly ironic fashion, the Afrikaner's 'historically orientated nationalism' was peppered with a 'virulent anti-colonial and anti-imperial vision of the past'.[66] There are some general features, pillars one might call them, which are shared by the works that fall within the Afrikaner tendency within the conservative school.

The theological underpinnings of the Afrikaner-nationalist school were devised to provide metaphysical as well as moral justification for their conquest of the indigenous people in the unjust wars of colonisation as well the disseizin of their land following these military defeats. There are explicit comparisons to themselves and the Israelites who were enslaved in Egypt. In their case, the Egyptians were the British Imperialists, and the interior of South Africa was their promised land.[67] The Great Trek is generally a founding event in the history of the Afrikaner nation and took place during the 1830s. It was represented as an odyssey for justice, in which god's[68] chosen people, escaping British injustice, went on a great *exodus*, or *trek*. Some historians explain how after the abolition of slavery, the liberal British political administration attempted to create a false equality between blacks and Afrikaners, which was, according to the reasoning of the latter group, unjust. They then set out into the interior to find habitable territory where they could build a 'just' and christian[69] nation where, among other things, 'proper relations between master and servant'[70]

---

[62] Smith (note 48 above) 58.
[63] Ibid.
[64] Ibid.
[65] Ibid 59.
[66] Ibid.
[67] See TD Moodie *The Rise of Afrikanerdom: Power, Apartheid, and the Afrikaner Civil Religion* (1975).
[68] See note 1 above.
[69] Ibid.
[70] Smith (note 48 above) 59.

were restored. In the Afrikaner-nationalist interpretation of history, the indigenous peoples who resisted their aggression became enemies of god's will and indeed god himself, and their eventual defeat was portrayed as a vindication of their belief that the war they waged was, in fact, god's will.

Just as an example, according to this interpretation of history, the Voortrekkers (as these migrants were known) secured Natal after making a 'covenant' with their god, who helped them to defeat King Dingane and his army in 1838. When the British pursued them and conquered Natal in 1843, thereby establishing Natal as a British colony, most Afrikaners moved again towards their promised land. They were for a number of years left to their own devices in the Orange Free State and Transvaal. The discovery of minerals would change this situation, first with diamonds being discovered in the Free State in 1867. This drew the British to the area, and by 1868 they had taken all the Basotho people under their protection. The British annexed the diamond fields in 1871 and the Transvaal in 1877 in an attempt to bring the entire territory of South Africa under the British flag.[71] In 1880, the Afrikaners took up arms against the British in a war of independence that resulted in the eventual restoration of independence by the British (this conflict is in the literature referred to either as the 'war of independence' or 'the first Anglo-Boer war'. This war and the Great Trek became the two poles of Afrikaner historiography.[72] The central symbols of these poles became 'Dingaan's Day', later renamed 'the Day of the Covenant' and then later 'the Day of the Vow' and, more recently, 'the Day of Reconciliation'.

The Afrikaners' search for a promised land away from pharaonic Britain was to continue with the National Party's rise to power in 1948 and the establishment of apartheid and a systemic juridical actualisation of god's now old will. The 1961 decolonisation and declaration of independence in 1961 was to complete their acquisition of their promised land, which, according to some, was once again disrupted by the end of apartheid. It is nevertheless our opinion that Voortrekker leader Piet Retief's covenant with god, in fact, reached its fulfilment in the constitution.

4.1.2 The English liberal-pluralist school

According to Neville Alexander, the disaster of Adolf Hitler's National Socialism and of the Holocaust 'marked a turning point in the history of racism in general and in the historiography of all racist societies'.[73] This is because of the various declarations of the United Nations, in which the theory and practice of racism were condemned and exposed as having no basis in human biology.[74] The other reason, according to Alexander, is because '[T]he social division of labour necessitated by both technological developments and by the exigencies of war had begun to do away with the iron barriers that had kept most "non-white" people out of the modern industrial sector of the South African economy above the level of unskilled labour.'[75] For Alexander, the salience of race as a factor in the development and implementation of

---

[71] Ibid.
[72] Ibid 59.
[73] N Alexander *An Ordinary Country: Issues in Transition from Apartheid to Democracy in South* Africa (2002) 13.
[74] Ibid.
[75] Ibid.

the policy of segregation under the governments of Jan Smuts and JBM Hertzog, who were 'responding to the gradual development of a secondary (manufacturing) industry in South Africa and the concomitant demand for semi-skilled and skilled black labour'[76] led to the development of liberal historiography. It led to professional – specifically liberal – historians reinterpreting South African history in terms of 'race-relations' and later in terms of 'a plural-society paradigm.'[77]

Historiographers seem to agree that the most important among the liberal historians were Eric Walker, WM Macmillan and CW de Kiewiet. Alexander's criticism of both Macmillan and De Kiewiet is that despite the extent to which they introduced class into their analyses, they still perpetuated the view that racism is inimical to capitalist development.

Macmillan and De Kiewiet, on the other hand, held that the 'rational, colour-blind logic of the market would, even if only in the longer term, lead to the disappearance of race as a factor in South Africa'.[78] In their uncritical subscription to these assumptions, Alexander suggests, these liberal historians were followed by a generation of historians as well as other social scientists who 'consolidated this liberal-pluralist orthodoxy of the period between approximately the 1920s and the 1970s';[79] among those he counts Edgar Brookes, Leonard Thomson, Leo Marquard, Monica Wilson and Rodney Davenport. Alexander's observation is that such scholarship could be considered 'a continuation of the Anglo-Boer War by historiographical means'.[80]

One of the central political and ethical implications of their work, even before the beginning of infamous apartheid, was that the Afrikaners were to blame for the racial problems of South Africa. One of the resilient dogmas of the work of these scholars is the theory of the 'frontier tradition', which Alexander suggests was posited as some kind of South African Wild West. In terms of this idea, it was as a result of the Boers leaving the taming and civilising effects of British liberalism in the Cape Colony and venturing across the frontier that led to their brutality and power politics.[81]

Liberal historiography is credited with supposedly 'bringing African people on to the stage of "History"'.[82] Alexander writes that both Macmillan and De Kiewiet mentioned African groups and individuals in their writings; however, '[I]n the final analysis, the indigenous African people were even for them an undifferentiated, relatively passive mass who had not yet become historical actors.'[83]

Alexander writes that it was only with the publication of the first volume of *The Oxford History of South Africa*[84] that it became possible to speak of 'African agency becoming manifest in mainstream South African historiography'.[85] This text, however, did not deviate from one of the central liberal-pluralist historiographical

---

[76] Ibid 13.
[77] Ibid.
[78] Ibid.
[79] Ibid.
[80] Ibid.
[81] Magubane (note 41 above) 251–279.
[82] Smith (note 48 above), Alexander (note 73 above).
[83] Alexander (note 73 above).
[84] M Wilson & L Thompson (eds) *The Oxford History of South Africa* (1969).
[85] Alexander (note 73 above) 17.

dogmas, namely 'what the authors considered to be the deleterious economic and social effects of segregationist and apartheid policies'.[86] Magubane's assessment of the great liberal Oxford history is much more critical. He suggests that the decision to include an anthropologist (Monica Wilson) as one of the editors was precisely in keeping with the racist dogma of ahistorical Africans.[87]

Ultimately, liberal historiography could be considered the expression of the liberal political mission in historiographical terms. The conservative tradition, on the other hand, by and large maintained that not only were black people not full human beings, their incapability of attaining full humanity was also seen as the basis for segregation from them, as well as their subjugation.

The liberals argued (by implication)[88] instead that some black people could, in fact, attain full humanity, since the problem was not biological but civilisational. On the conditions of cultural and religious assimilation to be achieved through submission to Western education, black people were to be allowed to participate in a predetermined political system as citizens. Liberal historiography was also then an 'inclusion' of black people in already pre-determined conditions of historicity on the basis of the morality that accorded them a humanity contingent on the conditions already discussed. Upon close examination, it should be clear that liberal historiography did not mark a departure in interpretive terms from the legitimacy of the 'right of conquest'. The important question – about where liberals derived their standing and authority to grant black people admission into citizenship, history or humanity – was not taken up. Liberal historians themselves derived their very status as citizens and historians on the historical basis of the conquest of the indigenous peoples and the disseizin of their lands. Magubane, describing the hypocrisy of the white historiographies that attempted to distance themselves from the conservative approach, writes, both 'The liberal and radical paradigms were attempts by beneficiaries of colonial usurpation to transcend that legacy. Both the liberal and radical paradigms feed on memories of historical betrayal. Their transcendence does not really involve accepting the reality of a new nation in which Africans, by virtue of the demographic reality, are the majority.'[89]

We now turn to a discussion of the final major tendency in white historiography, which was founded as much on the supposed ethical critique of the liberal paradigm as the latter was set out as a critique of the conservative.

4.1.3 The neo-Marxist/radical school

Smith writes that despite the radical academic historical tradition emerging in the 1970s, the neo-Marxist or radical school owed much of its impetus to the shortcomings of the *Oxford History* discussed above.[90] Smith's idea of the *Oxford History*'s shortcomings, however, differs substantially from that of Magubane. Before discussing these shortcomings, a critique of which basically led to the establishment of the

---

[86] Ibid.

[87] Magubane (note 41 above) 274.

[88] See N Dladla 'Book review: *Friends of the Natives: The Inconvenient Past of South African Liberalism* (Eddy Maloka)' (2015) 11 *New Voices in Psychology* 138.

[89] Magubane (note 41 above) 277.

[90] Smith (note 48 above) 155.

radical/neo-Marxist tradition, it is important to point out that long before the 1970s, the Non-European Unity Movement scholars and activists Dora Taylor and Hosea Jaffe had in 1952 produced early examples of often-unacknowledged Marxist historical analysis. Hosea Jaffe, writing as 'Mnguni', produced a text entitled *Three Hundred Years* that countered the celebratory mood of the early apartheid government's planned tercentenary celebrations of the conquest of the indigenous people in the first wars of colonisation in 1652. Taylor, as Nosipho Majeke, wrote *The Role of the Missionaries In Conquest.* Alexander describes these texts as 'a rebuttal of racist Eurocentric approaches, whether of the settler or liberal varieties'.[91] Interpreting history from the point of view of the indigenous, conquered people (even as they did so to the exclusion and ignorance of African intellectuals themselves), these works were certainly not without value, as they called into question some existing dogmas of South African history, such as the coterminous arrival of the Dutch[92] and Bantu-speaking peoples, and the innocence of Retief when Dingane had him and his party killed.[93]

A great number of the works that make up what has become known as radical historiography were written by what Alexander calls 'white draft-dodgers studying mostly in Great Britain'[94] in the 1970s. They were 'men and women [who] studied in the milieu produced by the 1968 revolts on European campuses and the anti-Vietnam War demonstrations, under the influence of extremely stimulating and creative historiographical works of the left-wing socialist, communist and ex-communist generation of post-war scholars'.[95] He writes that all these scholars developed their original theses in critique of the great liberal *Oxford History.*

Among the most important objects of their critique was that of the widely held assumption that apartheid was anti-capitalist or at least systemically incompatible with capitalism. Their doctrine held that the development of capitalism in South Africa would destroy apartheid in several ways, for example through growth and the demand of skilled labour at a rate that the racist policies of apartheid could not afford. The radicals instead showed that apartheid was thriving precisely as a result of capitalism and that the two systems made up the highly compatible couple of 'racial capitalism'. Other criticisms were levelled against the liberals' attempts to suggest that the Boers, in the famous frontier-thesis tradition, introduced racism; instead, the radicals argued that British imperialism was the bedrock of racism. Some of the work of radical scholarship[96] ironically demonstrated that it was the founders of the liberal paradigm in South Africa who helped Smuts and Hertzog create the systematic institutionalisation of racial discrimination in daily life that came to be called 'segregation' (and was later intensified under apartheid).[97]

---

[91] Alexander (note 73 above) 19.
[92] HJ Mnguni *Three Hundred Years* (1952) 10.
[93] Ibid.
[94] Alexander (note 73 above) 20.
[95] Ibid.
[96] See D O'Meara *Volkskapitalisme: Class, Capital and Ideology in the Development of Afrikaner Nationalism 1934–1948* (1983); CC Saunders *The Making of the South African Past: Major Historians on Race and Class* (1988), and T Keegan *Colonial South Africa and the Origins of the Racial Order* (1997).
[97] Alexander (note 73 above) 21.

Ultimately, the radicals held that apartheid would eventually be overthrown by revolution rather than dissolve as a natural development of capitalism, as the liberals believed. The end of apartheid for the radicals (who were associated in many instances with the ANC) would be the adoption of a socialist society based on the Freedom Charter (which their forebears had drafted in the 1950s).[98] This was the conception of justice underpinning their historical enterprise. Of course the Charter, which famously holds that 'South Africa belongs to all who live in it, black and white',[99] also has its basis in the right of conquest. This is because the declaration must invite any inquisitive mind or property lawyer to ask the historically and ethically pertinent question, 'Just how did it come to belong to whites?' The refusal to take this question seriously was precisely the reason that led the Africanists/Azanian school to break with the Congress movement in the late 1950s.

Our discussion of South African historiography should have established by now that there is good reason to understand the supposed purported variegation of South African historiography as basically superficial. South African historiography is basically white historiography since, despite its claims to either bring 'black people into history' or interpret history from their vantage point, it is based on the avoidance of the right of settlement, which is in turn based on the right of conquest. As such, it is in various ways ultimately an attempt to uphold the right of conquest rather than to repudiate it. In the next section, we try to show that the constitution has its very basis upon this white historiography, and this is the reason why it – unsurprisingly – also upholds the 'right of conquest'.

5. The liberation of history and the constitution

The constitution as the supreme law and purported guarantor of justice in South Africa has some implicit and explicit historical pretensions. It came to be adopted at a moment generally seen as concluding a period of multi-century historical injustice in South Africa.

The explicit historical pretensions are to be found in the constitution's supremacy, which was to form a test of justice against which all laws of the past were to be measured. All those found wanting, or provisions within such laws that were found to be wanting, were to be repealed (this has happened numerous times since the constitution came into being). In the second place, various sections of the constitution make reference to the unjust past; the preamble and so-called property clause, s 25, are good examples of this.

The implicit historical pretensions are to be found in the very architecture of the document itself, which contains purported historical remedies and artefacts. The names and geographical areas of the provinces[100] mentioned earlier originate from the colonial past. The national anthem, although not prescribed as far as lyrical content is concerned, is the constitutional responsibility of the president to proclaim and has since the advent of the new constitution been a historical amalgamation of the

---

[98] Sobukwe (note 12 above).

[99] See M Seloane & B Mokoena *Reflections on the Freedom Charter* 2015.

[100] See Chapter 14, Schedule 125 of the constitution.

anthem of the conqueror and that of the conquered people. The conqueror's anthem, *Die Stem van Suid Afrika/The Call of South Africa*, has been sung since the period of the Union of South Africa, together with *God Save the Queen/King* until 1957, after which it was sung exclusively. It is a song that asserts, at various points, the white political theology of South Africa being a country delivered to white people by god, a country that they are willing to die for to keep.

Like the new anthem, the constitutional 'recognition' of some of the indigenous languages and of indigenous law, as well as the intention to create formal equality before the law, are responses to the historical past in which people were unequal by law, and indigenous languages and law were also unequal by law.

The constitution itself can be considered as a marker of a historical reality, an overarching structure that supposedly over-determines the historical events of its time. As Csaba Varga has argued, '[I]f the law is viewed in its entirety and not in being stripped to instrumentality, it turns out to have its own history as well, and through this, it acts as a shaping factor in the history of mankind.'[101] Where previous historical periods of South African history were described as pre-colonial, colonial and apartheid periods, the present period is called, variously, post-apartheid, constitutional or democratic[102] South Africa (owing to the first supposedly democratic constitution in South African history).

The historical questions and exigencies that inform the present constitutional order are, in fact, derived from white historiography. They are a direct result of the historical exclusion of African philosophy; African history; and historians from the ethical, political and historical discourse that informs the order – something that we have discussed throughout this article. It is precisely because the perspectives of the indigenous, conquered people have been silenced and ignored – as exemplified by the marginalisation of the Azanian tradition – that the constitution's tenets are now beginning to haunt the negotiated settlement with increasing vividity. The object of the negotiated settlement has, on the other hand, never been so fragile as it is now, becoming yet more faint, confronted with a quite indeterminate historical cry, the sound of which is loudened and defined by the suffering of white history's victims.

Ramose has suggested, in the context of the constitutional settlements of Zimbabwe and South Africa, that there remains a 'tension resulting from the inclusion of some "natural facts" and the exclusion of others from the universe of juristic facts'.[103] His examination is interested particularly in the extent to which 'the fact of

---

101 C Varga *Law and Philosophy: Selected Papers in Legal Theory* (1994) 481.

102 This is a view that our reading of South African history must contend with, even when one restricts the period of consideration exclusively to the time since the defeat of the indigenous people conquered in the unjust wars of colonisation. What certainly emerges is an exclusive democracy not unlike that of Ancient Athens. The democratic representation mischievously implies that the apartheid state and the colonial governments that preceded it were the result of the work of a few unpopular tyrants rather than of a political system that the majority of the white populace in South Africa supported. Important to note, also, is that neither the United Nations (UN) nor many Western countries doubted the democratic credentials of pre-1994 South Africa. Pre-1994 South Africa was a member of the UN and had ambassadors representing it in many Western countries (see N Dladla *Here is a Table: A Philosophical Essay on the History of Race in South Africa* (2017) 11). It goes without saying, of course, that South Africa has also had numerous constitutions before the present one.

103 MB Ramose 'I conquer, therefore I am the sovereign: reflections upon sovereignty, constitutionalism and democracy in Zimbabwe and South Africa' in Coetzee & Roux (note 16 above) 543.

conquest, in the history of the voyages of "discovery" and colonisation, has been included or excluded from the universe of juristic facts'.[104]

Our argument in this article heretofore has been that these natural facts have in South African or white historiography not even been graduated into historical facts, and so they cannot make up part of the 'universe of juristic facts' that forms the basis of the South African constitution and its legal system at all. When the South African constitution is examined soberly from the point of view of these excluded historical facts, the seriousness of its status as basis for a historically just legal and political order quickly becomes dubious. Let us examine just a few of its aspects from such a point of view.

5.1 Constitutional supremacy

Despite the territory called South Africa having had several constitutions prior to the present one,[105] none of them have enjoyed the status of supreme law until now. In other words, it was not until the indigenous people conquered in the unjust wars of colonisation were finally able to have a say in the political and legal order of South Africa that parliament was subjected to a superior constitution in order to limit its exercise of popular power.[106] When popular power to make and change law was exclusively in the hands of the white population, there was no supreme constitution, since the citizens (white people themselves) were supreme. With the formal loss of this exclusive political power, their will was transferred to the constitution, which would be able to be used to exercise the will of its drafters[107] regardless of whether or not it had a basis in the populace.

5.2 The status of indigenous law

This same supreme constitution accords the lowest status, in terms of recourse to the law and legal philosophy, to the indigenous people, who are an overwhelming majority in the country. In South African jurisprudence under the constitution, the law of the indigenous people, which is called 'customary law', suffers a status lower than that of their colonial conquerors, the so-called Roman-Dutch and English laws. In terms of the judicial hierarchy of South Africa, decisions made in terms of 'customary law' may be overturned by appeal to even the lowest of the Roman-Dutch courts of law. As a matter of fact, 'customary law' is accorded an even lesser status than the law of other nations.

---

[104] Ibid.

[105] This goes back as far as the time prior to the South Africa Act 1909. The Boer republics and English colonies all had constitutions – none of which were supreme law. See HR Hahlo & E Kahn *The Union of South Africa: The Development of its Laws and Constitution* (1960).

[106] As Ramose has demonstrated, the proposals for constitutional supremacy are, of course, not unheard of but were rejected in the past. See Ramose (note 103 above) 571.

[107] Although it is popular to represent the constitution as having been drafted by multiple parties, especially those from the ranks of the liberation movements, our general charge is that its historical thrust is a reflection of the conqueror's imagination. In this regard, one should consider the 17 March 1992 referendum of white citizens in which then state president FW de Klerk promised to protect property rights of white South Africans if they consented to a transition into a 'new South Africa', see A Strauss 'The 1992 referendum in South Africa' (1993) 31 *The Journal of Modern African Studies* 346–349.

5.3 Natural and historical justice

In addition to the Eurocentrism of South African jurisprudence under the constitution, the spirit of its content violates well-established principles of justice even within Western law and philosophy. The principle expressed in Latin as *jus ex injuria non oritur* (a legal right or entitlement cannot arise from an unlawful act or omission) or its relative principle *commodum ex injuria sua nemo habere debet* (a wrongdoer should not be enabled by law to take any advantage from his actions) are just two examples. The constitution violates these principles precisely through its fundamentalisation of the right to property. The violation is not restricted to the law of property, however, and applies, really, to the entire identity of the state that in its name, and legal and cultural order formally upholds the values of the colonial conqueror.

If one considers that under colonialism and the period of apartheid that followed, together spanning more than 350 years, the European conqueror and his descendants acquired property through the disseizin of the indigenous people's land and property (a racially differentiated crime), the question is, 'Who exactly had property to protect in 1996?' In other words, 'Precisely whose property was being protected by the constitution?' The answer to this question makes the claim that the constitution was founded upon the value of non-racialism and its many proponents' insistence that it is compatible with the philosophy of ubuntu rather dubious. Rather, it is our argument that the constitution, for the reasons set out above is, in fact, a white supremacist document. The right to property in South Africa is a logical and practical extension of the so-called 'right of conquest'.

6. Towards an Azanian critical philosophy of history

Robin Collingwood, in order to explain his understanding of what the philosophy of history consists of, makes the point that, 'The philosophizing mind never simply thinks about an object, it always, while thinking about any object, thinks also about its own thought about that object.'[108] With regards to history, then, its philosophy involves our study of historical thought itself. Whereas historians concern themselves with the pursuit of historical knowledge through the substantiation of accounts of past events by the use of various kinds of sources and evidence, the task of the philosopher of history is the examination of those very activities and the various conditions that surround them, whether in epistemological, ethical or political terms. In his own attempt to devise a method of philosophising about history, Collingwood subjects history as a discipline to Aristotle's four causes of being. When dealing with the final cause, namely what history is for, he answers this question by saying that, '[H]istory is for human self-knowledge.'[109] He goes on to say, '[K]nowing yourself means knowing what you can do; since nobody knows what he can do until he tries, the only clue to what man can do is what man has done. The value of history then is that it teaches us what man has done and thus

[108] RG Collingwood *The Idea of History* (2014) 1.
[109] Ibid 10.

what man is.'[110] William Henry Walsh, still confined largely to an epistemological conception of the philosophy of history, suggests four areas comprising the proper task of the critical philosophy of history: (1) questions about the very nature of historical thinking,[111] (2) truth and fact in history,[112] (3) historical objectivity[113] and (4) explanation in history.[114]

The purpose of the critique throughout this article was to clear ground for the development of a new and critical philosophy of history – and then indeed a new history. We did so by showing the ideological devaluation and ignorance of African history, the unethical process by which historical facts were fabricated and selected, and the political compromising of historical objectivity. The contention we advanced is that white/South African historiography's end has been to provide the moral and intellectual support for the constitution, which emerges as a logical, moral and political necessity out of history itself.

Using some basic categories derived from the Azanian tradition, we have tried to show that history is not an affair free from political and ethical conditions. We have argued that historians are political and un/ethical actors who invent/interpret history on the basis of the historical interests of the political communities they represent. The communities of the conqueror and his descendants are well represented in the various perspectives that populate the history of South African history, to the virtual exclusion of any other perspectives, hence the necessity (both epistemological and ethical) for history and historical thinking to be examined from the point of view of the indigenous people conquered in the unjust wars of colonisation. Critiquing historical knowledge from this point of view is the possibility condition for the necessary generation (or graduation) of liberated historical facts. These natural-historical facts will have to inform the juristic universe if the indigenous, conquered people – and, by extension, all the inhabitants of Africa, South – are to attain a historically just and sustainable constitutional order.

7. The end of South Africa

The African American freedom fighter and thinker Martin Luther King Jr. – echoing a sentiment that underpins the idealist philosophy that holds that history is necessarily progressive, and the future is, in the aggregate, always better than the past – once quoted the following in his writing, '[T]he arc of the moral universe is long, but it bends toward justice.'[115] To some extent, a similar understanding of history has underpinned a great amount of historical activity in which historians have not only tried to explain the past but have also shown the future ideal towards which it is unfolding. The problem appears to be less about whether the arc of history is indeed

---

[110] Ibid.
[111] WH Walsh *An Introduction to the Philosophy of History* (1951) 17.
[112] Ibid 19.
[113] Ibid 21.
[114] Ibid 23.
[115] ML King Jr. 'Out of the long night' *The Gospel Messenger* (8 February 1958) 3, 14 <https://archive.org/details/gospelmessengerv107mors/page/n165>.

bending towards justice or not so much than it is about the meaning justice itself. In South Africa, the end to which history was directed was the conservative: white supremacy in the form of god's promised racial polity, where the 'superior race' would rule over its 'inferiors'. (Until now we have argued that this perspective is the one that is fulfilled by the constitution.) For the liberal, it was a South Africa in which there would be 'equal rights for all civilised men', whereas for the radical, the requirement of civilisation was dropped, and justice was for all those who lived on and worked the land. For the Azanian, history's arc must surely bend away from South Africa. For justice to be done, South Africa itself must come to an end.

Acknowledgements

An acknowledgment is owed to my supervisor, Mogobe Ramose, who commented on early drafts of the paper. It is also due to both the special editor and the blind reviewers whose comments led to considerable improvements in later drafts.

Disclosure statement

No potential conflict of interest was reported by the author.

Funding

Portions of this research were carried out with financial assistance from the National Institute of Humanities and Social Sciences under the South African Humanities Deans' Association grant.

ORCID

Ndumiso Dladla http://orcid.org/0000-0003-1723-261X

Contested substantive equality in the South African Constitution: beyond social inclusion towards systemic justice

Catherine Albertyn

ABSTRACT

This article briefly traces South Africa's contested archive of equality, as it emerged in the twentieth century, and identifies the different liberal egalitarian, social democratic, socialist and radical ideas of equality that are appropriated and reconstructed within different struggles. It then suggests that the equality-centred, democratic Constitution represented an important anti-colonial and anti-patriarchal achievement, but that the plasticity of equality meant that it would always be open to different interpretations by the executive and parliament, as well as by courts tasked with enforcing the Constitution. The conditions of the transition and early years of democracy saw the emergence of a social democratic/liberal egalitarian equality as the dominant political and legal, if not economic, idea, most especially in the jurisprudence of the Constitutional Court. This jurisprudence was often powerfully inclusive, but less likely to be transformative, would prefer process over substance (especially in socio-economic rights) and was better at addressing inequalities of recognition than redistribution. Although it clearly registers a commitment to substantive rather than formal equality, it also reveals the differences within substantive equality between a social democratic/liberal egalitarian model and a more transformative approach. The article identifies these differences and suggests how we might reinterpret constitutional equality within a transformative approach to better address the deep and systemic inequalities in our society. It suggests that we should move through and beyond a dignity-based concern with social inclusion and sufficiency towards an idea of systemic and material justice. It proposes that the *value* of equality can be developed as an idea of 'equality of condition', aligned with an idea of substantive freedom, that would better resonate with the struggles of our past and present, and suggests how the *right* could be subject to more transformative interpretation and application.

1. Introduction

Equality has inspired multiple struggles across the world. In South Africa, it has motivated humanitarian struggles within the colony, and class-based, anti-colonial, anti-racist and feminist struggles that challenged colonial, apartheid and capitalist rule. In part two, this article briefly traces this contested archive of equality, as it emerged in the twentieth century, and identifies equality's various liberal egalitarian, socialist and radical forms as the idea is appropriated, reconstructed and localised within different struggles. I then argue, in part three, that the idea of equality, embedded at the centre of the 1993 and 1996 constitutional texts, was influenced by several historical and contemporary interpretations of equality, but most particularly by social democratic, liberal egalitarian, feminist and socialist views. Particularly important here was a clear choice of substantive over formal equality. The Constitution of the Republic of South Africa, 1996 does not treat everyone as if they were in the same position in society and merely outlaw all race or sex-based differentiation, nor does it merely convert existing interests into rights, thus risking the entrenchment of an unequal status quo. On the contrary, it expressly seeks to address and overcome the structural, social and economic, public and private inequalities of race, gender and so on, inherited from our past. Substantive equality, as defined in politics or law, requires a concern with recognition, redistribution and redress, and an eradication of actual, 'real-life' inequalities. But, it is also a contested concept.

Constitutions emerge from politics, and South Africa's equality-centred Constitution represents an important anti-colonial, anti-racist and anti-patriarchal achievement, even as it is the product of a negotiated settlement. However, the plasticity of equality means that it would always be open to different interpretations by the executive and legislature, and by courts tasked with enforcing the Constitution. The question of how to overcome the past – and the precise interpretation of equality – is thus open to political, economic and legal debate. I suggest that the transition and early years of democracy saw the emergence of a social democratic/liberal egalitarian model of substantive equality, based initially on sufficiency, as the dominant political and legal, if not economic, idea. It shaped redistributive policies that, inter alia, extended welfare benefits, sought to meet basic needs and addressed affirmative action in the workplace. It also found an 'intellectual home' in the jurisprudence of the Constitutional Court, which I discuss in part four. This jurisprudence was often powerfully inclusive, but less likely to be transformative, would prefer process and accountability over substance (eg, in socio-economic rights), and was better at addressing inequalities of recognition than redistribution.

I go on to argue, in part five, that the contestation in South Africa is generally not between formal and substantive equality (although that tension is present) but about different meanings of substantive equality. These, of course, can be found in politics and in law. Focussing on the courts' interpretation of the constitutional value of 'achieving equality' and of the s 9 equality right, I illustrate how social democratic/liberal egalitarian substantive equality can be distinguished from transformative substantive equality – a more inchoate but radically egalitarian idea. I briefly suggest how the value of 'achieving equality' – as a frame for policy, law and constitutional interpretation – can be developed beyond the idea of 'equal concern and respect' and 'meeting basic needs', to an idea of systemic and material justice based on equality of condition, as a deeper idea of the fundamental and systemic change required in our society. Finally, turning to s 9, I describe how the courts might interpret and apply the equality right for more transformative ends.

In this article, I work with equality as a political idea (especially in the history section) and as a constitutional value and right (especially in parts four and five).

Of course, politics and law cannot be neatly separated, and political ideas of equality inevitably shape legal interpretations. Moreover, the constitutional value of equality, as well as an awareness of the prescripts of the right, should frame all state action and always be the subject of public debate. For the purpose of this article, I focus on law and the courts, as one particular site of struggle and deliberation over how best to address the deep and ongoing structural inequalities of race, class, gender and so on, which persist after 25 years after democracy. As such, it forms only part of a much wider conversation about 'achieving equality' and systemic and material justice.

2. A contested history/archive[1]

Ideas of equality in South Africa emerged from the crucible of struggles against the deep political, social and economic inequalities that were inscribed and normalised in colonialism, segregation, apartheid, patriarchy and South Africa's particular brand of racialised accumulation and capitalism. They also emerged within the colony, and have generally been contested and changed over time. In this section, I identify the historical threads that inform our contemporary understandings of equality, and could help understand what might be a more 'indigenous' egalitarian project to address the deep structural race, class and gendered inequalities of today. By 'indigenous', I mean an idea of equality that emerges from local struggles and conditions, and speaks to local needs, even as it draws on global ideas. By reflecting on history, I seek to expose the contexts, continuities, discontinuities, gaps and reconstructions that shape the past, present and future meanings of equality in South Africa.

It is impossible to do justice to a rich and complex history in this short section, so I offer an overview of broadly liberal, social democratic and socialist/critical ideas, as well as the key ideas emerging from gender struggles, and the anti-colonial and anti-apartheid struggles of Pan-Africanism and Black Consciousness.

2.1. The different arcs of liberal equality and social democracy

To start, we can identify the humanitarian, liberal ideas that emerged within the colony as a concept of equal rights (most visibly to vote, land, work) within an overarching idea of white (and male) civilisation. 'Cape liberalism', as it was known, developed in the nineteenth century out of a British liberalism that insisted on the responsible exercise of power, and extended political and property rights on the basis of a stake in the system rather than universal claims.[2] This impetus to equality was founded on a gradualist vision in which rights of citizenship 'would only be recognized if colonized peoples renounced customs and cultural traditions considered anathema to progress and civilisation'[3] and participated in the economic life of the Cape Colony. In this way, a limited common society, based on dominant colonial norms, would develop.

---

[1] The analysis and arguments in this section are based on a chapter from a monograph on equality in preparation by the author.
[2] TRH Davenport & C Saunders *South Africa: A Modern History* (1988) 6.
[3] S Dubow *South Africa's Struggle for Human Rights* (2012) 36.

Contrary to the idea of universal moral equality, this was a conditional and evolutionary concept that enabled rights and citizenship subject to certain (colonial and paternalistic) standards of civilisation. Increasingly central to this was the enhancement of opportunities to participate in the expanding economy. Thus, by the 1940s, as David Everatt writes:

> Liberals based their vision of future equality on the development of an African middle-class through the extension of educational and social welfare services, and gradual incorporation into state structures, which the government was called upon to create, in tandem with equally gradual incorporation into the body politic for 'civilised' and later 'suitably qualified natives'.[4]

In the 1940s and 1950s, this evolutionary idea of equality accompanied an economic liberalism seeking to open the labour market to a settled black urban community. Over time, this developed to adopt legal ideas of formal equality: racial discrimination was irrational where it placed arbitrary barriers on economic development and the individual pursuit of economic opportunities. Liberal parliamentary political parties (the Progressive Party, founded in 1959) supported gradual reform, through constitutional and legal change, to a race-blind meritocracy (widening economic opportunities) but did not advocate for social equality, or full political equality.[5] The Progressive Party only supported an unqualified, universal franchise in the late 1980s.

In extra-parliamentary politics, liberal ideas of equality took on a more robust egalitarian form based on the moral equality and equal worth of all persons, rather than economic rationality and formally equal opportunities.

In white extra-parliamentary politics, the Liberal Party adopted a greater egalitarianism and commitment to a social democracy.[6] It embraced the idea of a democratic, non-racial South Africa, based on a universal franchise, the repeal of racially discriminatory legislation, access to health care and quality education, and equal human rights for South Africans of all races. White 'radicals' (defined by the ruling National Party to include liberals and communists of different ideological hues) formed the South African Congress of Democrats (SACOD) in 1953[7] within the Congress Alliance, giving whites a role in the national liberation struggle as a separate organisation under black stewardship.[8] The SACOD stood for universal suffrage and full race and gender equality. It called for 'equal political rights and economic opportunities for all South Africans, irrespective of race, colour or sex, and [sought to] win for all South Africans their freedom of speech, assembly, movement and

---

[4] D Everatt *The Origins of Non-Racialism in South Africa: White Opposition to Apartheid in the 1950s* (2009) 19.

[5] See, for example, S Uys '"The Progressive Party" interview with Dr Zach de Beer' (Apr–Jun 1960) 4 *Africa South* 17 <http://www.disa.ukzn.ac.za/index.php?option=com_displaydc&recordID=asapr60.4>; M Wilson & L Thompson (eds) *The Oxford History of South Africa* (1969–1971).

[6] D Irvine 'The Liberal Party, 1953–1968' in J Butler, R Elphick & D Welsh (eds) *Democratic Liberalism in South Africa: Its History and Prospect* (1987) 116, 118.

[7] The Congress of Democrats (COD) was formed in January 1953 and joined other organisations to form the SACOD nine months later. Everatt (note 4 above) 103–110.

[8] Under African National Congress (ANC) leadership, the Congress Alliance comprised the racially based organisations of the ANC, SACOD, the South African Coloured People's Organisation (SACPO), the South African Indian Congress (SAIC), as well as the 'non-racial' South African Communist Party (SACP), the South African Council of Trade Unions (SACTU) and the Federation of South African Women.

organisation'.[9] Although disputed, white radicals also called for the nationalisation of banks and land, a national health service and increased industrialisation.[10] In the end, white liberal and social democrats, as well as socialists, supported full political and social equality and human rights for all, but disagreed on the role of the state in the economy and the limits of redistributive policies.

In the 1940s, the African National Congress (ANC) moved from a formal endorsement of equal rights with whites (and a qualified franchise) to a more substantive equality, entailing more fundamental change under black leadership (and universal suffrage). The Atlantic Charter and its promise of social welfare and self-determination for all nations influenced this, in part.[11] By the end of World War II, under the 1943 African Claims, the ANC was campaigning for full equality, endorsing a social democratic programme based on universal suffrage, equal rights, the rule of law, land redistribution, a mixed economy and the provision of social welfare.[12] Although not articulated as rights, the inclusion of free education, health-care, etc., in *African Claims* reveals an egalitarian, welfarist approach to equality. Importantly, and partly under the influence of more assertive Africanists within its ranks, the ANC rejected the idea of inclusion in the white state and the same rights 'as Europeans' to imagine a common South African citizenship and a non-racial democracy, thus articulating an anti-colonial idea of a common humanity.

This vision was spelt out in the 1955 Freedom Charter, which captured the aspirations of the Congress Alliance and mediated its liberal, Africanist and socialist influences.[13] While retaining a strong liberal egalitarian core, it reached out to socialist ideas of equality and redistribution. Simons argues that (liberal) equality was at the centre of the Charter, the idea of a 'united, non-racial and democratic South Africa' that rejected discrimination of the basis of race, colour, sex or creed and advocated for equal rights and freedoms for all.[14] This idea of equality was a rights-based legal concept, requiring freedom from discrimination and equal rights and protection under law. As such, the Charter was consistent with mainstream world opinion, reflected in international rights documents, such as the Universal Declaration on Human Rights, and the idea that racism and apartheid violated the dignity of human beings and required an equal recognition of human rights, and an equal concern with everyone's social welfare.

But if it cohered with global ideas, it was also an indigenous response to apartheid in its particular emphasis on race and apartheid exclusion, including land, education and the economy. The call for non-racialism was a direct response to racial domination. In its call for redistribution, the Charter was influenced by socialist ideas and local conditions in recognising the deeper economic roots of colonialism and apartheid that had produced South Africa's particular brand of racial capitalism. Hence, its

---

[9] *Advance* (27 November 1952) 1 cited in Everatt (note 4 above) 46.

[10] Ibid 23.

[11] The Atlantic Charter (1941) <http://www.un.org/en/sections/history-united-nations-charter/1941-atlantic-charter/index.html>.

[12] *African Claims in South Africa* (14 December 1943) <www.anc.org.za/content/african-claims-south-africa>.

[13] Everatt (note 4 above) 125.

[14] J Simons 'The Freedom Charter – Equal rights and freedoms' (30 June 1985), <http://www.anc.org.za/show.php?id=2624>.

call for everyone to share in the country's wealth; for mineral wealth, banks and monopoly industry to be 'transferred to the ownership of the people as a whole';[15] and for the land to be 'shared amongst those who work it'.[16] In the end, with its commitment to individual rights and a minimum threshold of goods, as Jack Simons argues, the Charter expresses a radical liberal, rather than a socialist egalitarian, approach.[17] It looks to a limited equality of outcomes via an adequate provision of social goods that would be possible through social investment and social welfare expenditure, and some redistribution (a form of social democracy, liberal egalitarianism and distributive justice). A socialist idea of equality, in Simons' words, a substantive 'equality of power and opportunity' achieved by 'transferring the means of production to public ownership and distributing rewards [...] according to [...] needs', was not the immediate goal of the national liberation struggle but was deferred to a democratic government.[18]

2.2. The thread of socialism and a more substantive equality

As discussed above, socialist ideas developed alongside, and intersected with, liberal equality ideals in twentieth century South Africa. Ideas of class, and also race and gender equality, emerged within the Communist Party of South Africa (CPSA) and trade unions. Firmly within the international communist fold, the CPSA's ultimate aim was the overthrow of the capitalist system and the achievement of a substantive social and economic equality (as equality of outcomes according to need). Equal rights were a 'bourgeois idea'. However, a commitment to racial equality in the sense of organising workers 'of all ranks and races' to 'propagate the Communist gospel'[19] was fundamental to the CPSA's belief that 'the problems of the working class can only be solved by a United Front of all workers *irrespective of colour*'.[20] The CPSA also endorsed no discrimination of race or sex, and resolved to struggle for a universal franchise, equality of rights and the abolition of racially discriminatory laws as early as 1928.[21]

Socialist thinking emphasised the structural underpinnings of inequality, most particularly in understanding racialised capitalism and the manner in which colonialism and apartheid systematically subordinated, excluded and oppressed black South Africans. Indeed, the entire economy and polity had been built on the subordination of people by race and class. As discussed above, these ideas are present in the 1955 Freedom Charter but were also deferred, as the South African Communist Party

---

[15] 'The people shall share in the country's wealth' Freedom Charter (1955), <http://www.anc.org.za/content/freedom-charter>.

[16] 'The land shall be shared amongst those who work it' Freedom Charter, ibid.

[17] Simons (note 14 above). See further DM Davis 'The Freedom Charter: A challenge and bequest' in N Steytler (ed) *The Freedom Charter and Beyond: Founding Principles for a Democratic South African Legal Order* (1991) 1; P le Roux 'The social democratic nature of the Charterist economic vision' in N Steytler (ed) *The Freedom Charter and Beyond: Founding Principles for a Democratic South African Legal Order* (1991) 120.

[18] The 'two-stage revolution' theory saw national liberation secure a liberal democracy, after which a black majority government would develop a socialist state.

[19] *Manifesto of the Communist Party of South Africa* (1921) <www.sacp.org.za/docs/history/manifesto21.html>.

[20] A Lerumo 'The turn to the masses' *Fifty Fighting Years. The Communist Party of South Africa 1921–1971* <http://www.sacp.org.za/main.php?ID=3943> (original emphasis retained).

[21] Ibid.

(SACP)[22] accepted the need for political freedom and national democracy before more fundamental social and economic transformation.[23]

2.3. Gender equality

Alongside and within struggles against colonialism and apartheid, women's struggles for equality and rights occurred in different ideological contexts. Within white politics, women argued for inclusion in the white state and equal rights in the family and workplace.[24] Within extra-parliamentary politics and the national liberation struggle, although subservient to those struggles,[25] an important local archive shaped our contemporary understanding of gendered 'substantive equality'. For example, the Women's Charter of 1954 explicitly centred black women (not yet within a discourse of intersectionality) to call for 'equal rights with men in relation to property, marriage and children and for the removal of all laws and customs that deny women equal rights', as well as extensive social welfare and municipal services to sustain women's roles as mothers within the racial burden of poverty.[26] Although reflecting its times by defining women as mothers,[27] the 1954 Charter is an important precursor to a substantive idea of gender equality across the public/private divide.

Gender equality did not develop politically or theoretically until the late 1980s.[28] By 1990, with clear socialist feminist influences, a feminist idea of substantive equality was captured in the ANC's national executive committee's 'Statement on the emancipation of women in South Africa':

> Gender oppression is everywhere rooted in a material base and is expressed in socio-cultural traditions and attitudes [...] which are supported and perpetuated by an ideology which subordinates women. In South Africa it is institutionalised in the laws as well as the customs and practices of all our people. Within our racially and ethnically divided society, all women have a lower status than men of the same group in both law and practice. And as with racism, the disadvantage imposed on them ranges across the political, economic, social, domestic, cultural and civil spheres.[29]

This statement sees gender inequality to be embedded in structural, social and economic inequalities, and inscribed in public and private norms, institutions, rules and practices. It recognises women's burden of domestic labour, their economic

---

[22] The CPSA was banned under the Suppression of Communism Act 44 of 1953 and reconstituted underground as the South African Community Party (SACP) in 1953.

[23] There is insufficient space to discuss the growth of 'democratic socialism' in trade unions and civil society organisations in the 1970s and 1980s. See R Turner *The Eye of the Needle* (1972); D Glaser 'Changing discourses of democracy and socialism in South Africa' in AJ Norval & D Howorth (eds) *South Africa in Transition: New Theoretical Perspectives* (1998) 3.

[24] C Albertyn 'Women and the transition to democracy' 1994 *Acta Juridica* 39, 42–3; C Walker *Women and Resistance in South Africa* (1982) 145–51; J Segar & C White 'Deconstructing gender: Discrimination and the law in South Africa' (1989) 4 *Agenda* 95.

[25] J Beall, S Hassim & A Todes 'A bit on the side? Gender struggle in the politics of transformation in South Africa' (1989) 33 *Feminist Review* 30 (discussing the 1970s and 1980s). Walker (note 24 above) 156–60, 279–82.

[26] The Women's Charter (1954) <http://www.anc.org.za/content/womens-charter>.

[27] Walker (note 24 above) 279–82. See also Albertyn (note 24 above) 43–6; S Hassim 'Texts and tests of equality: The Women's Charters and the demand for equality in South African political history' (2014) 28 *Agenda* 7.

[28] Albertyn (note 24 above) 44–6; Beall et al (note 25 above); Walker (note 24 above).

[29] ANC national executive committee 'Statement on the emancipation of women in South Africa' (1990) <http://www.anc.org.za/show.php?id=7140>.

subordination and the manner in which race deepens inequality. Post-apartheid policies would need to 'address simultaneously the material base, the political and other institutions and the ideological and cultural underpinnings of gender oppression'.[30] Inter alia, this means that, '[L]aws, customs, traditions and practices which discriminate against women shall be held to be unconstitutional. Patriarchal rights, especially but not only with regard to family, land and the economy need serious re-examination so that they are not entrenched or reinforced'.[31]

This statement, and the later Women's Charter for Effective Equality of 1993, rooted in women's struggles, provide some of the most extensive and elaborated ideas of substantive equality in the transition and provide a base for developing transformative ideas of equality.

2.4. The legacy of Africanism and Black Consciousness

If women's struggles foregrounded structural gender inequalities across the public and private spheres, the archives of Africanism and Black Consciousness raise profound questions about racial inequality and its resolution.

A more militant African nationalism in the ANC Youth League in the 1940s emphasised that black South Africans were a single African nation (rather than different tribes),[32] and laid the basis for Africanism in the ANC and the break-away Pan Africanist Congress (PAC) in 1959. Radical Africanists rejected the ethos of non-racism which, they argued, gave disproportionate political weight to whites, coloured and Indians and called for Africans, defined as those who owed allegiance to Africa (not by skin colour), to liberate themselves. African people should be able 'to exercise the most fundamental of human rights, the inalienable right of indigenous people to determine and shape their own destiny'.[33] Democracy would only be possible once white supremacy was destroyed and racialised economic exploitation overcome. Rights would flow from a common African, not South African, identity.[34]

Although not expressed in the language of substantive equality, this identified the need to address the structural underpinnings of racial inequality. This idea of equality directly challenged liberal equality (egalitarian or otherwise) and the idea of social and economic inclusion within the prevailing racial system. It also challenged a non-racial and/or class-based, socialism. It describes racial inequality as deep-rooted and systemic, requiring systemic social and economic change. The emphasis was on equality of outcomes, not opportunities,[35] and a significant redistribution of land, wealth and resources to eradicate white domination. While this has important overlaps with socialist and feminist approaches in recognising the structural determinants of inequality, and the need for systemic change, it is solely race-based.

---

[30] Ibid.
[31] Ibid.
[32] M MacDonald *Why Race Matters in South Africa* (2006) 102–3.
[33] PAC Manifesto (1959) <http://mayihlomenews.co.za/wp-content/uploads/2009/06/panafricanmanifesto.pdf>.
[34] R Sobukwe 'Inaugural address at the founding of the PAC' (1959) <http://www.sahistory.org.za/archive/document-58-robert-mangaliso-sobukwe-opening-address-africanist-inaugural-convention-4-april>.
[35] Ibid.

In the wake of brutal state suppression in the 1960s, the re-emergence of resistance under the banner of Black Consciousness was a critical development in the 1970s. Predominantly captured in the writings of Steve Biko and heavily influenced by Frantz Fanon (and US critical race theory), Black Consciousness directly challenged white domination and privilege. As Biko argued, white economic and political domination was so entrenched and naturalised, that both black and white had come to believe in racial superiority and inferiority. White domination imprisoned blacks in a state of fear and powerlessness, undermined their humanity and robbed them of their ability to define themselves in their own terms.

Liberals, as much as other whites, feared black majority rule and believed that blacks could not develop without white guidance and trusteeship.[36] According to Biko, their version of non-racialism was based on a limited concept of integration:

> [It was] full of unquestioned assumptions that embrace white values […] [A] concept long defined by whites and never examined by blacks. It [was] based on the assumption that all is well with the system apart from a degree of mismanagement by irrational conservatives at the top.[37]

The solution lay in 'the liberating effect of the autonomy of black thinking, and the power of black solidarity'.[38] Blacks should take responsibility for their liberation, to free the human spirit and claim their free humanity. As an ideology, '[B]lack consciousness was meant to lift black people out of despair and instill […] hope about a future that was in their own hands'.[39] Black emancipation was an internal process to embrace a positive racial consciousness and be proudly and openly black.

Barney Pityana writes that Black Consciousness 'never attempted in any systematic sense to formulate a manifesto for a new South Africa. It was […] not about engaging loyalties from different movements, but about seeking ways of transcending such divisions by articulating a meta-narrative of liberation that was unifying rather than particularizing'.[40] Indeed, Black Consciousness fed into a plurality of political ideas. He suggests that Biko's writing produced 'a vision of a common humanity and the affirmation of a society founded on justice, without any privileges or considerations for minorities'.[41] Overcoming white domination and hegemony was central to this: '[B]lack consciousness would be irrelevant in a colourless and non-exploitative egalitarian society'.[42]

Equality in Black Consciousness thought implies the reconstruction of relations of power. It was a critical and relational approach to equality, understanding that hierarchical relations of racial domination, constructed by decades of colonialism and apartheid, were systemic and ever present. However, they could be reconstructed, and equality could be achieved in the absence of 'domineering whites and acquiescing

---

[36] S Biko 'Black Consciousness and the quest for a true humanity' (1978) 8 *Ufahamu: A Journal of African Studies* 10, 11.
[37] Ibid 12.
[38] B Pityana 'Higher education transformation: What is to be done?' Steve Biko Lecture University of the Witwatersrand (2015) 3.
[39] B Pityana 'Reflections on 30 years since the death of Steve Biko: A legacy revisited' The Steve Biko Lecture UNISA (12 September 2007).
[40] Ibid 8.
[41] Ibid.
[42] Biko (note 36 above) 10.

blacks'.[43] Although political freedom would have been an objective, the focus was on undoing psychological oppression and hierarchical social relations. Black Consciousness spoke particularly to the politics of recognition.

2.5. Our contested archive

Although this is a brief sketch of a contested archive, a number of characteristics emerge. First, our ideas of equality developed in changing historical conditions of struggle and resistance, and in conversation with each other. While they draw on global ideas (especially liberalism, socialism and social democracy, but also socialist feminism and critical race theory, etc.), they do not merely reproduce them, but are responsive – in differing ways – to local conditions, struggles and debates. In other words, these ideas – within different threads of liberal, socialist and critical thought – emerge in response to particular conditions of race, but also class and gender, inequalities in South Africa. They do not merely reproduce Western or colonial ideas but seek to appropriate and transform these ideas via local conditions and anti-colonial, anti-racist and anti-patriarchal struggles. As Kenan Malik suggests: 'It was not colonialism but anticolonial movements that truly developed Enlightenment ideals' by demanding that equality and freedom 'applied to them too'.[44] Second, although articulated within different politics, there are important similarities across different archives of thought. For example, an understanding that inequalities are structural and systemic, requiring fundamental change, is common to socialist, feminist, ANC, Africanist and Black Consciousness approaches.

Reading across these archives, I suggest that a substantive, if evolving, political idea of equality, as broadly connoting meaningful changes in the concrete social and economic conditions of people's lives, has long been present in liberal egalitarian, social democratic radical and socialist forms. Within the Congress Alliance and extra-parliamentary politics, a robust non-racial (and, from late 1980s, non-sexist), liberal egalitarian and social democratic idea of substantive equality existed alongside a more socialist, centralised and redistributive approach (that imagines a centralised economy and state). In addition, the more socialist and redistributive approach present in the Congress Alliance has much in common with the Africanist approach of the PAC in their understandings of the structural underpinnings of inequality and the need for substantial redistributive strategies. Of course, the political divides around race and class are significant, especially concerning non-racialism and Africanism, but there are no clear silos of thought.

Further, the idea of non-racialism is, itself, contested. In the 1950s, it was almost a politically convenient way of uniting against apartheid. Like equality, it can be embraced by liberals, egalitarian liberals, social democrats and socialists and can be tied to different political and economic outcomes. However, in the core document of the Congress Alliance, the Freedom Charter, the idea of non-racialism is one way of re-imagining the nation with a black majority in power who engages in significant

---

43 Donald (note 32 above) 116.

44 See K Malik 'The great British Empire debate' *The New York Review of Books* (26 January 2108) <http://www.nybooks.com/daily/2018/01/26/the-great-british-empire-debate/?printpage=true>.

economic and social restructuring to rid South Africa of colonialism and apartheid, transform our society and secure freedom and equality.

Finally, alongside these ideas of substantive equality, feminist struggles have emphasised the importance of the private sphere, thus opening up radical spaces to disrupt liberal ideas of the public/private divide, patriarchal tendencies across all forms of struggles and cultural and religious ideas of the family, society and women's place.

This varied and contested archive of ideas was present as South Africa entered the transition in the early 1990s. While the meaning of equality in the new South Africa remains contested, it was the ideas of the Freedom Charter, with all its nationalist, social democratic and socialist tensions, forms of liberal egalitarian equality and women's struggles for gender equality that came to define an idea of substantive equality in the constitutional text.

3. Constitutional settlement: entrenching a constitutional framework of 'substantive equality'

By any account South Africa's transition to democratic rule was fraught with uncertainty, conflict and violence. Nevertheless, consensus was reached on the Interim Constitution[45] that established majority rule in 'a united, democratic, non-racial and non-sexist' South Africa. In 1990, the government and ruling National Party (NP) and the ANC, the lead organisation in the national liberation movement, were far apart. The government and NP wanted a consociational democracy, based on power-sharing by 'ethnic minorities', minority group vetoes and a rotating presidency.[46] With little sense of historic irony, the NP opposed the 'domination of minorities' and called for cultural and language difference to be respected.[47] It further called for all reasonable people to rally around 'civilised values', including a 'sound economy based on proven economic principles and free enterprise', 'the elimination of all discriminatory measures and practices', and 'equality before an independent judiciary'.[48] The thin, formal idea of equality underlying these proposals sought to retain the political, social and economic status quo; to limit if not prevent the racial redistribution of power, wealth and property; and to ensure the continuation of dominant white norms.

In contrast, the ANC reiterated its call for majority rule and a universal franchise in a unitary, non-racial and non-sexist South Africa committed to equal human rights and a democratic society based on the Freedom Charter. The 'centuries-old legacy of colonial conquest and white domination' would be swept away, and the 'structure and institutions of apartheid [...] dismantled and replaced by democratic ones'.[49] This envisaged the redistribution of power and resources, including land, through

---

[45] The Constitution of the Republic of South Africa, Act 200 of 1993 (Interim Constitution). The Interim Constitution has been repealed.

[46] R Spitz & M Chaskalson *The Politics of Transition: A Hidden History of South Africa's Negotiated Settlement* (2000) 16. See SA Government 'Views on a constitution-making body' submission tabled at Congress for a Democratic South Africa Working Group 2 (1991).

[47] RP Meyer (Deputy Minister of Constitutional Development) 'Speech to SAASSPER' (27 June 1990) in South African History Archive (1990) 1:4 *History in the Making* 58–60.

[48] Ibid.

[49] ANC 'Constitutional guidelines for a democratic South Africa 1989' (1989) <http://www.anc.org.za/content/constitutional-guidelines-democratic-south-africa>.

state intervention within a 'mixed economy'.[50] ANC policy also supported the emancipation of women in political, cultural and economic life. Although these proposals revealed ubiquitous tensions within the ANC over nationalist, social democratic and socialist ends,[51] they contained a common aspiration to a substantive and redistributive notion of equality and to substantial political and socio-economic transformation under a democratic government.

It is the latter vision for a democratic South Africa that endured, as the conditions of political negotiation and peace seeking saw ideas of substantive equality and an inclusive, non-racial and non-sexist democracy become dominant.[52] This drew all parties into the Multi-Party Negotiations Process (MPNP) in 1993, including the PAC (who had opted out of negotiations that did take place in an elected constituent assembly and guaranteed a more immediate and radical redistribution of land and power[53]) and the ethnically based Inkatha Freedom Party, homeland governments and far-right white political parties (all of whom sought group-based or regional power).[54]

It is trite to say that equality was central in the constitutional settlement of the 1990s. At the cusp of post-apartheid democracy, it was an idea on which everyone could agree. Underlying this broad agreement of principle, however, equality remained contested between the formal, liberal equality of white political parties and government, and the substantive ideas of the ANC and its allies. The formal equality of classic or neo-liberalism was now embraced in one form or another by almost all white parties, mostly without its more overt racist deference to 'civilised standards' as a measure of rights. Instead, it manifested itself as a libertarian call for individual liberty and restraints on state intervention. The dominant concerns were individual freedoms and equal political and civil rights, with equality seen as non-discrimination and formal protection against race and other forms of differentiation. This limited the ambit of positive measures to redistribute wealth and resources, and constrained state intervention in society and the economy. For these parties, the Constitution was a bulwark against change and protection for white privilege.

The ANC and its allies, as well as a mobilised constituency of women, advocated for a redistributive and interventionist value of substantive equality and a powerful equality right to address discrimination across the public and private spheres. Here, the democratic Constitution would enable the equalisation of power and wealth. Substantive equality was at the centre of this. Indeed, early ANC versions of the proposed equality clause included the redistribution of property, as well as jobs and

---

[50] Ibid. See also the ANC 'Discussion document on economic policy' (1990) <http://www.sahistory.org.za/archive/discussion-document-on-economic-policy>.

[51] See the debates on the Freedom Charter in Steytler (note 17 above).

[52] This was confirmed in principle in the 'Record of understanding' (September 1992), which opened the way for the Multi-Party Negotiations Process and the development of the Interim Constitution. See Spitz & Chaskalson (note 46 above) chapter 2.

[53] Up to then, the PAC did not shift from this position articulated in 1990. PAC 'Discussion paper: On a negotiated political settlement' in South African History Archive (1990) 1:1 *History in the Making* 30–3; PAC 'Guiding position on negotiation' produced at the PAC Consultative Conference, Harare (21–23 September 1990) in South African History Archive (1991) 1:4 *History in the Making* 51–3. All parties in the national liberation movement adopted a similar position until the ANC and government agreed to the two-stage process in the 'Record of understanding' (note 52 above).

[54] See Spitz & Chaskalson (note 46 above) chapter 12.

education, within the meaning of equality.[55] Although the ANC did not advance a socialist economic policy or state, deemed largely impossible in the local and global conditions of a post-1989 world,[56] it did foresee a key role for the state in enabling 'socio-economic transformation'.[57] At the very least, it anticipated that everyone's basic needs would be met by a democratic government and supported the inclusion of social and economic rights to this end. Although the Constitution was not written to prescribe an economic system, the inclusion of socio-economic rights certainly envisaged – at minimum – a welfarist/social democratic regime based on sufficiency.

These competing ideas of equality went to the heart of political conflicts between the parties and how best to protect the interests of their constituencies. In the end, the 1993 text[58] articulates an idea of substantive and redistributive equality, which is further strengthened in the final text, the Constitution. Several characteristics across these texts bear testimony to this. First, equality is a central value of the new democracy, opening space for substantive, redistributive and transformative interpretations of that democracy. Second, there is a clear intention to draft an equality right to enable it to be interpreted as 'substantive' rather than 'formal' equality.[59] Third, after some dispute between women and traditional leaders, the 1993 text partly allowed the application of equality to the private sphere of culture.[60] This concern with private inequalities was made explicit in the 1996 text, which enables horizontal application generally, including the equality right, as well as a commitment to reproductive autonomy, protection against 'public and private forms of violence' and greater clarity on the place of culture and religion in the Constitution.[61] Fourth, specific provision is made for positive and redistributive measures (not limited to a narrow idea of affirmative action).[62] Finally, the commitment to equality of rights as a substantive concern is significantly expanded by the addition of social and economic rights, and the requirement of positive measures to achieve these, in the 1996 text.[63]

While these all point to the possibilities of substantive and redistributive equality, nevertheless, there are markers of contestation in the 1993 text. In relation to equality, these are seen in the compromise on equality in the private sphere in this text and greater court oversight over positive measures.[64] However, these compromises were diluted in the 1996 text, rendering the private sphere much more open to scrutiny and softening court oversight of positive measures, together with the insertion of positive socio-economic rights and powerful gender rights. The final 1996 Constitution was by no means a traditional, liberal-democratic text. As pointed out by Karl Klare and others, its principled commitment to substantive equality, positive and redistributive measures, socio-economic rights, cultural diversity, legal pluralism,

---

55 Ibid 302.

56 See generally H Klug *Constituting Democracy: Law, Globalism and South Africa's Political Reconstruction* (2000).

57 See 'Ready to govern: ANC policy guidelines for a democratic South Africa' (1992) para A.3 <http://www.anc.org.za/docs/pol/1992/readyto.html RDP>.

58 Note 45 above.

59 See C Albertyn 'Gender and constitution making in South Africa' in H Irving (ed) *Gender and Constitutions* (2017).

60 In s 8(2) and 33(4) of the interim text. See Albertyn ibid; Albertyn (note 24 above);

61 Sections 9(4), 12, 15, 30, 31. See Albertyn (note 59 above).

62 Sections 9(2), 25–9.

63 Sections 25–9.

64 There is no space to discuss the textual compromises further, but issues of property and economic rights would also be examples. See generally Spitz & Chaskalson (note 46 above).

horizontality and participatory democracy created a framework for more substantial change.[65] It was thus a constitution that could serve as the basis for transformation, rather than a bulwark against change. As such, the strategies of the ANC and its allies generally prevailed over the defensive politics of the white government and minority parties. With the equality-centred Constitution as an enabling framework, the expectation was that the new majority government would develop policies, laws and programmes to address the deep structural legacies of colonialism, apartheid and patriarchy.[66]

As stated previously, law and courts are but one part of 'achieving equality' under the Constitution. Indeed, government and politics, not law and courts, are primary drivers of change.[67] Even in a context of judicial review, the burden of transformation falls predominantly on government and parliament, and their ability to implement constitutional commitments through policies, budgets, laws and programmes. Nevertheless, the role of the courts in interpreting and enforcing the Constitution is a powerful one. When equality is implicated, the courts provide a forum for citizens to make claims for inclusion in social and economic life, and for the state to defend its positive and redistributive measures. As such, courts can ultimately determine the lines of social recognition, inclusion and exclusion, political participation, the obligations of government and the ambit of positive measures and redistribution. In this sense, the courts' approach to equality is one measure of the nature of change and the principles that govern our society, and how it interprets the Constitution matters very much. Courts mediate competing ideas of equality, consciously or unconsciously advancing different conceptions. And these ideas of equality potentially frame all government action.

It is uncontroversial to claim that the Constitution is a contested document, enabling different interpretations of equality. If the constitutional negotiations saw conflict between formal and substantive ideas of equality, this is less true of the equality jurisprudence that later emerged in the courts. The courts, with some early exceptions, rejected more formal and defensive equality claims and focused on what 'substantive equality' means. Thus, the more important debate is between different forms of substantive equality: a dominant liberal egalitarian/social democratic form adopted by the Constitutional Court and a more inchoate, but transformative idea. These ideas, expressed in law, demonstrate some continuities with the liberal egalitarian/social democratic and critical/socialist and radical ideas of our past struggles.

4. (Neo)liberal economics and a liberal egalitarian/social democratic jurisprudence

The Constitution does not prescribe a particular economic system, and economic policy choices fall squarely in the realm of government. Here, early promises of social and economic transformation captured in the Reconstruction and Development

[65] KE Klare 'Legal culture and transformative constitution' (1998) 14 *South African Journal on Human Rights* 168.

[66] See the commitments in these ANC policy documents: 'Ready to govern' (note 57 above); 'RDP White Paper discussion document' (September 1994) <http://www.anc.org.za/content/rdp-white-paper-discussion-document>.

[67] An oft-overlooked point made by Klare in his seminal article (note 65 above) 147.

Programme (RDP) soon encountered deep structural problems in the economy and the need to generate more resources for growth and redistribution. In the global economic conditions of the 1990s, and the dominance of the 'Washington Consensus', it is perhaps unsurprising that the ANC government 'sought recourse in neo-liberal economic policy'.[68] The 1996 Growth, Employment & Redistribution (GEAR) policy package committed the state to greater fiscal discipline and liberal economic policies in the hope of stimulating the economic growth necessary to meet social-redistribution needs. Within these limits, Jeremy Seekings and Nicoli Nattrass have pointed to a significant redistributive effort under the Mbeki administration to broaden the black middle class, at the top, and alleviate poverty at the bottom.[69] Thus affirmative action, especially in the public sector, saw the massive expansion of jobs to those previously excluded, while black economic empowerment redistributed wealth to a small politically connected black elite. On the other end, a mass roll-out of social grants, RDP houses, and water and electricity connections lifted the floor of absolute poverty.[70] However, this was ultimately a concern with sufficiency rather than a more fundamental redistribution, and, as Seekings and Nattrass admit, economic policies have both mitigated and reproduced poverty, and deepened inequalities.[71] Moreover, Jeremy Cronin and others have noted that these were not always sustained and were never structurally transformative. Thus, the GEAR policy package and those that followed have continued to lock South Africa into 'a jobless growth path that [has] reproduced racialised and gendered inequality and poverty'.[72] More fundamentally, it is suggested that these policy choices confirm an 'elite pact' between established monopoly capital and elements of the new ANC political elite that has enriched a few, protected white economic interests and left racialised inequalities largely intact.[73] Nevertheless, the redistribution that has occurred - via positive measures, affirmative action, broad-based black economic empowerment, charters, mineral rights, land, etc. - has generally been permitted and enabled by the constitutional text.[74] More radical measures are yet to be tested.

The impact of the Constitution in areas of social equality is perhaps more visible with significant legislative and judicial efforts to secure equal rights and recognition for disadvantaged groups, although questions remain as to the nature, extent and resilience of these changes, and how much they overturn the entrenched social norms, structures and privileges of race, gender, sexuality and so on.

[68] DM Davis 'From the Freedom Charter to the Washington Consensus' in D Everatt & V Maphai (eds) *The Real State of the Nation after 1990* (2003) 31, 47.

[69] J Seekings & N Nattrass *Poverty, Politics and Policy in South Africa: Why Has Poverty Persisted After Apartheid* (2015).

[70] Ibid.

[71] Ibid.

[72] J Cronin 'Jeremy Cronin: The Mbeki camp needs to own up to its role in state capture' *Business Live* (19 June 2017) <https://www.businesslive.co.za/rdm/politics/2017-06-19-jeremy-cronin-the-mbeki-camp-needs-to-own-up-to-its-role-in-state-capture/>.

[73] H Marais *South Africa: Limits to Change* (2001); S Terreblanche *A History of Inequality in South Africa 1652–2002* (2002).

[74] See those supporting affirmative action (*Minister of Finance v Van Heerden* 2004 (6) SA 121 (CC); *South African Police Service v Solidarity obo Barnard* 2014 (6) SA 123 (CC); *Solidarity v Department of Correctional Services* 2016 (5) SA 594 (CC)) and mining rights (*Agri South Africa v Minister for Minerals and Energy* 2013 (4) SA 1 (CC)).

In turning to interrogate the equality jurisprudence of the courts, and especially the Constitutional Court, I identify the ideas of equality that are articulated by the courts, and the possibilities of moving beyond what I identify as a dominant liberal egalitarian legal form. Here, I am interested in which ideas of equality the Constitution enables and excludes. In particular, I enter the debate on the relationship between the Constitution and transformative change, and the extent to which we might be able to rely on constitutional equality to frame, enable and/or defend transformative anti-colonial, anti-racist and anti-sexist equality projects.

4.1. Equality interpretation

South Africa has a deeply impoverished legal history of equality. Anti-segregation cases in the twentieth century were largely fought, and occasionally won, on administrative law principles: did the authorising statute permit classification on the basis of race?[75] Only in rare judgments do we glimpse the liberal idea that racial differentiation was, in itself, irrational and immoral.[76] In South Africa's racialised society and formal legal culture, even formal equality was a step too far.[77] As the new Constitutional Court began to give content to equality, its sources were often external, especially literature and emerging case law on 'substantive equality' developed in response to the limitations of formal equality in other jurisdictions. However, it also resonated with local ideas.

From the start, the South African Constitutional Court distinguished itself from the narrow equal protection jurisprudence of the US Supreme Court.[78] The formal equality of classic or neo-liberalism – as equal treatment, subject to tests of rationality – is neither captured in our constitutional text nor, generally, in judicial interpretation. If it continues to be articulated by parties seeking to defend particular interests,[79] and in the occasional judgment,[80] the Constitutional Court's overall approach has been to craft a jurisprudence of substantive equality that can best be characterised as liberal egalitarian. In doing so, it has drawn on several resources, including the idea of 'substantive equality' espoused by the ANC alliance and women's groups in the early 1990s, feminist and liberal egalitarian legal scholarship and emerging Canadian jurisprudence.

Broadly, substantive equality *in law* is the recognition that equality is not a formal requirement of equal treatment that equates differential treatment to irrational discrimination. Rather it is a concern with the actual impact or results of social and legal classifications: the problem is not differentiation, per se, but the (systemic) harm that might flow from it. To evaluate the harm, the matter must be examined contextually,

---

75 See S Kovalsky 'The validity of municipal by-laws' (1937) 54 *South African Law Journal* 170.

76 See Gardiner J (minority judgment) *Minister of Posts and Telegraphs v Rassool* 1934 AD 167, 185–91.

77 M Chanock *The Making of the South African Legal Culture 1902–1936* chapter 2, especially 31.

78 See *Brink v Kitshoff NO* 1996 (4) SA 197 (CC) per O'Regan para 44 (calling for interpretation in our context); *Van Heerden* (note 74 above) paras 147–148 (distinguishing SA from US Supreme Court on affirmative action).

79 See arguments on affirmative action by Solidarity in *Barnard* (note 74 above) and *Correctional Services* (note 74 above). In sexual orientation cases, see arguments by government in *National Coalition for Gay and Lesbian Equality v Minister of Home Affairs* 2000 (2) SA 1 (CC) paras 33–34 and the amicus, Marriage Alliance of South Africa, in *Minister of Home Affairs v Fourie* 2006 (1) SA 524 (CC).

80 One could argue the majority judgments in *S v Jordan* 2002 (6) SA 642 (CC) and *Volks NO v Robinson* 2005 (5) BCLR 446 (CC) constitute formal equality approaches to the extent that they fail to take account of context and substantive effects of law.

with a clear understanding of the conditions of people's lives and the actual effects of the impugned action. Importantly, it is constitutional values that give content to the right and guide us in determining whether a differentiation is 'constitutionally' harmful. While formal equality assessments are guided – often in an abstract manner – by the value of consistency or same treatment; a substantive equality evaluation may be guided by values of equal dignity, equal capabilities, the eradication of disadvantage and subordination, or equal substantive opportunities. Thus, substantive equality can vary considerably according to how context is defined, the values pursued and the remedies identified to bridge the gap between the identified inequality and desired result. Below, I briefly describe the dominant egalitarian approach to substantive equality and then suggest how a more transformative approach, that seeks a more systemic justice, might be developed.[81]

4.1.1 The liberal egalitarian approach

There is strong evidence of a liberal egalitarian, social democratic approach to equality in the Constitutional Court's judgments and extra-curial statements. This approach draws on a Western archive in general, and Canadian jurisprudence in particular[82] but is also influenced by local ideas, struggles and conditions, and most immediately by the nature of the claims brought by equality groups in South Africa (especially those fighting sexual orientation discrimination).

In general, this approach gives a foundational role to dignity by defining equality as the idea that everyone has intrinsic moral worth (or dignity) and is entitled to *equal concern and respect*. This echoes the Court's primary characterisation of apartheid as a denial of inherent dignity.[83] Although the Court often recognises the systematic subordination, oppression and impoverishment on the basis of race over centuries,[84] it prioritises the restoration of human dignity, promised by the Constitution, as a marker for achieving equality. And, while it acknowledges equality's role in remedying disadvantage (drawing on feminist thinking and accepting the asymmetrical nature of substantive equality), overall it defines equality as the right to be treated with equal concern and respect, or equal dignity.

This idea echoes the core liberal idea of basic equality, that all members of society are morally equal. It aligns with Ronald Dworkin's depiction of substantive equality not as a right to equal treatment (the principle of non-differentiation), but as a right to be treated as an equal, and with equal concern and respect (thus permitting principled differentiation).[85] It has proved to be an authoritative basis for securing equality rights for multiple outsider groups defined by sex, gender, race, sexual orientation

---

[81] This work again forms part of a larger monograph on equality by the author, where it is developed in more detail.

[82] There were strong influences from Canadian jurisprudence. See A Sachs 'Equality jurisprudence: The origin of doctrine in the South African Constitutional Court' (1999–2000) 5 *Review of Constitutional Studies* 76.

[83] See O'Regan J in *S v Makwanyane* (1995) 3 SA 391 (CC) para 329 and Ackerman J in *Prinsloo v Van der Linde* 1997 (3) SA 1012 (CC) para 31.

[84] See *City Council of Pretoria v Walker* 1998 (2) SA 363 (CC) paras 46–47 (historic impoverishment of black residential area) and *Zondi v Member of the Executive Council for Traditional and Local Government Affairs* 2005 SA 589 (CC) paras 39–42 (landlessness and race).

[85] On Ronald Dworkin, see A Chaskalson 'From wickedness to equality: The moral transformation of South African law' (2003) 1 *International Journal of Constitutional Law* 590, 600, 607.

and nationality.[86] The jurisprudence was often powerfully inclusive and extended rights and even material benefits to disadvantaged and excluded groups,[87] but usually on terms that did not fundamentally dismantle dominant norms and the socio-economic status quo.[88]

Extending the principle of equal concern and respect to socio-economic rights means that the legitimate needs of every member of society must be treated with equal concern. In liberal egalitarian or social democratic terms, this aims at sufficiency or to meet people's basic needs through a minimum threshold or adequate provision of social goods. This idea is picked up in South African socio-economic rights jurisprudence. As (then) Chief Justice Arthur Chaskalson noted in a 2000 public lecture, as socio-economic rights jurisprudence began developing, the Constitution does not contemplate 'equality of goods or wealth', but it does recognise the need for threshold of 'basic needs, such as housing, health-care, food, water and social security'.[89] In *Government of the RSA v Grootboom*, dealing with access to emergency housing under s 26 of the Constitution, the Court stated that equality, together with dignity and freedom, required that the 'basic necessities of life [be] provided to all'.[90] Thus, it is targeted at securing a minimum threshold necessary to affirm the dignity of the poor. However, in socio-economic rights jurisprudence, the idea of equal concern and respect does not speak to the provision of actual goods or substantive conditions but rather to fair or reasonable process, and to accountability by government and participation by citizens, in achieving these.[91]

Theoretically, this liberal egalitarian approach echoes the ideas of liberal egalitarians, such as Dworkin, in its concern with 'equal concern and respect', as well as Amartya Sen and Martha Nussbaum's concern with capabilities and a minimum threshold to secure dignity.[92] The idea of a basic minimum thus coheres with the liberal-egalitarian and social-democratic idea of sufficiency within a welfare state.[93]

By identifying the Court's jurisprudence with liberal egalitarian forms of substantive equality, I do not suggest this is merely the reproduction of ideas produced elsewhere (although these are important reference points). On the contrary, the Court was constructing a jurisprudence that sought to respond to local conditions and struggles – of the past and present – by drawing on strands of liberal egalitarian,

86 See, for example, the cases discussed in C Albertyn & B Goldblatt 'Equality' (chapter 34) in S Woolman & M Bishop (eds) *Constitutional Law of South Africa* 2 ed (2007) 53.

87 Despite problems of inclusivity and implementation, litigation on LGBTI rights extended important relationship rights, while cases on gender discrimination in customary law secured important marriage and property rights for women.

88 See, for example, C Albertyn 'Substantive equality and transformation in South Africa' (2007) 23 *South African Journal on Human Rights* 253.

89 A Chaskalson 'The third Bram Fischer Lecture: Human dignity as a foundational value of our constitutional order' (2000) 16 *South African Journal on Human Rights* 193, 202

90 2001 (1) SA 46 (CC) para 44.

91 See, for example, R Dworkin *Sovereign Virtue* (2000) 1–2 on the theoretical point. On the procedural/accountability aspects of socio-economic rights, see *Mazibuko v City of Johannesburg* 2010 (4) SA 1 (CC) paras 46–68, 71, 159–165; KG Young 'A typology of economic and social rights adjudication: Exploring the catalytic function of judicial review' (2010) 8 *International Journal of Constitutional Law* 385; D Bilchitz 'Are socio-economic rights a form of political rights?' (2015) 31 *South African Journal on Human Rights* 86.

92 M Nussbaum 'Constitutions and capabilities: "Perceptions" against lofty formalism' (2007) 121 *Harvard Law Review* 1.

93 See S Moyn *Not Enough: Human Rights in an Unequal World* (2017) 2–3.

social democratic and critical thought from our own history (aligning with interpretations of the Freedom Charter), as well as global ideas.[94] Moreover, together with Canada, South Africa was recognised to be innovative and at the global cutting edge of substantive equality jurisprudence. South Africa's socio-economic rights jurisprudence has been similarly lauded. What emerged was an idea of equality that foreshadowed a more redistributive, respectful and inclusive society, thus establishing new norms for an egalitarian non-racial, non-sexist South Africa, in direct opposition to the apartheid, if not colonial, past.[95] As noted above, this jurisprudence was powerfully inclusive, but not always transformative.[96] While we should push through and beyond this liberal egalitarian jurisprudence, if we seek more transformative ends, we should not make the mistake of conflating the real conceptual and practical advances, secured by this jurisprudence, with the narrow forms of 'colour-blind' equality and liberalism that have hindered progress and caused disillusionment with 'equal protection' jurisprudence in the USA.[97]

Insofar as this dominant idea of dignity-based equality is more likely to include groups into the social and economic status quo than fundamentally disrupt or transform that status quo, it is contested by those who seek to centre ideas of disadvantage, structural inequalities, unequal power relations and more radical ideas of difference and systemic justice. As deep structural social and economic inequalities persist, there is some urgency to find new and transformative ways of addressing inequalities. For some, this might mean making liberal egalitarianism work in practice,[98] for others it means drawing on different ideas of substantive equality to develop beyond inclusion and sufficiency. In the next section I sketch out what that might mean.

5. Transformation and 'indigenous' possibilities: equality as systemic justice

In advancing a more transformative idea of equality, I do not seek to overemphasise the role of the Constitution and of law achieving change. As Joel Modiri says, '[A]partheid is not a simple legal mistake that can be rectified through new laws and policies'.[99] The possibilities of change are primarily found in politics. While courts do generate change, this is likely to be incremental, often procedural and only sometimes substantive. Nevertheless, cases and constitutional interpretations matter, especially if we understand law and rights as sites of struggle that can 'advance the social project of human liberation and emancipation'[100] and where ideas, such as equality and

---

94 Sachs (note 82 above).

95 See generally *Makwanyane* (note 83 above) e.g. per Mohamed J para 262.

96 See Albertyn (note 88 above).

97 See Derrick Bell's disillusionment with US equal protection jurisprudence in D Bell 'Racial realism' in K Crenshaw, N Gotanda, G Peller & K Thomas (eds) *Critical Race Theory* (1995) 302.

98 See D Bilchitz & D Glaser 'Egalitarian liberalism: What are its possible futures in South Africa?' (2014) 61 *Theoria* 1; D Bilchitz 'Egalitarian liberalism, distributive justice and the new constitutionalism' (2014) 61 *Theoria* 47.

99 JM Modiri 'The colour of law, power and knowledge: Introducing critical race theory in (post-)apartheid South Africa' (2012) 28 *South African Journal on Human Rights* 405, 409.

100 IG Shivji 'Law's empire and empire's lawlessness: Beyond Anglo-American law' 2003 (1) *Law Social Justice and Global Development Journal* <http://www2.warwick.ac.uk/fac/soc/law/elj/lgd/2003_1/shivji2/>.

freedom, can be appropriated and reconstructed in different contexts. If the Constitution can provide a bridgehead for more transformative change, then our interpretation of equality should enable that. In other words, it should provide a normative roadmap, a conceptual frame and a legal resource to fight inequality and to nurture and defend transformative change. In defining equality, we should consider 'bottom-up' constitutionalism[101] and draw more on our own archives of struggle (including feminist and critical race thinking, and redistributive ideas of equality) in the context of actual inequalities in our society. We should also interrogate the jurisprudence to extract elements of a nascent, critical egalitarian approach that is occasionally present. What follows is a brief description of a larger project to develop further our idea of equality – both as a constitutional value and as a right – to enable more remedial, redistributive and transformative ends, and a more deeply systemic and material justice.[102]

5.1. The constitutional value of equality

The Constitution identifies equality, dignity and freedom to be core values of the South African democracy. Unlike dignity, the values of equality and freedom have not been substantially and explicitly developed by the Constitutional Court, despite their importance in interpreting the Constitution generally, and the rights in the Bill of Rights in particular. In this section, I argue for an understanding of the value of equality that goes beyond a concern with social inclusion, and with 'sufficiency' or a minimum threshold of goods, to advance a more transformative vision of substantive change and systemic justice.

There is little dispute that inequality in South Africa is structural and systemic, created and reproduced over centuries of colonialism, apartheid, capitalism and patriarchy, as well as heteronormativity, ableism and a host of other intersecting power relations. During constitutional negotiations, this understanding elicited strong support for the entrenchment of 'substantive equality' in the 'socialist' sense, as an idea of real equality, 'not just equality as a right or a theory but equality as a fact and as a result'.[103] Although theoretically undeveloped at the time, such a constitutional commitment to 'achieving equality' was not merely to moral equality – to equal concern and respect or equal dignity – but to a deeper social and economic justice, to redistribution and to dismantling and restructuring social and economic relations that maintained multiple forms of domination and subordination. This understanding of equality recognises the manner in which different groups (in all their complexity) are subject to relational and intersecting political, social/cultural, economic and legal inequalities, and affected by different configurations of misrecognition and maldistribution in public and private spheres.

Beth Goldblatt and I sought to capture the idea of transformative, substantive equality as follows:

---

101 See M Chanock 'Constitutionalism, democracy and Africa: Constitutionalism upside down' (2010) 28 *Law In Context* 126.

102 As noted above, this is drawn from a larger project on equality by the author.

103 P Jordan *Sunday Times* (26 August 2001) cited in Terreblanche (note 73 above) 35.

> We understand transformation to require a complete reconstruction of the state and society, including a redistribution of power and resources along egalitarian lines. The challenge of achieving equality within this transformation project involves the eradication of systemic forms of domination and material disadvantage based on race, gender, class and other grounds of inequality. It also entails the development of opportunities [that] allow people to realise their full human potential within positive social relationships.[104]

Although the idea of equality expressed in that article has sometimes been reduced to an idea of economic, rather than intersecting, forms of equality, and to group-based disadvantage that elides the individual,[105] it was an attempt to offer a comprehensive and nuanced understanding that took account of both social and economic inequalities (of recognition and redistribution); of structural disadvantage and individual well-being; of the complicated and intersectional nature of inequalities; a relational idea of difference and the recognition that people are at the heart of relations of (in)equality.[106] We argued that the Constitution aspired to substantive equality as the need to address material, or actual, social and economic inequalities experienced by people in their day-to-day lives, not merely to accord individuals what we saw, at the time, to be an abstract notion of individual concern and respect.

At the time, we did not theorise it completely, and there has been little further development of this idea in courts or legal academia, with most critical scholarship engaged in critique, rather than reconstruction. As a result, the constitutional value of substantive equality – beyond the more limited idea of equal concern and respect that underpins the right – has remained elusive, as has a normative frame for more radical change. I suggest that we might further develop the value of equality towards an idea of more systemic justice by developing the idea of 'equality of condition' articulated by John Baker, Kathleen Lynch, Sara Cantillon and Judy Walsh. 'Equality of condition' focuses attention on transforming the systemic conditions of inequality, namely, the 'changing and changeable social structures and particularly structures of domination and oppression',[107] including:

> Capitalism (a predominantly market-based economy in which the means of productions are privately owned and controlled), patriarchy (systems of gender relationships that privilege men over women), racism (social systems that divide people into 'races' and privilege some 'races' and privilege some 'races' over others) and other systems of oppression.[108]

Equality of condition goes beyond inclusion, sufficiency and a minimum threshold of goods to aspire to the massive reduction and even elimination of major inequalities.[109] It aspires to change social structures, and their taken-for-granted norms and conventions, that create and reproduce inequality, whether these be around class, race supremacy, gender (such as women's care responsibilities and gender roles), heteronormativity, the concept of work, etc. It seeks greater equality of outcome by putting in place the conditions necessary to provide people with a broad range of choices among real and

[104] C Albertyn & B Goldblatt 'Facing the challenge of transformation: Difficulties in the development of an indigenous jurisprudence of equality' (1998) 14 *South African Journal on Human Rights* 248, 249.

[105] H Botha 'Equality, plurality and structural power' (2009) 29 *South African Journal on Human Rights* 1, 4; K van Marle 'Haunting (in)equalities' in R Hunter (ed) *Rethinking Equality Projects in Law: Feminist Challenges* (2008) 125.

[106] Albertyn & Goldblatt (note 104 above) 251–254.

[107] J Baker, K Lynch, S Cantillon & J Walsh *Equality: From Theory to Action* 2 ed (2009) 33. See generally Chapter 1.

[108] Ibid.

[109] Ibid.

equivalent options.[110] Everyone should be afforded real, substantive opportunities to work, to secure a quality education, to access good healthcare or to form relationships or – in Fraser's terms – to just and transformative recognition and distribution.

This approach differs from a liberal egalitarian idea of capabilities in two important ways: first, it focuses less on individuals and more attention on changing the conditions of inequality. Second, it envisages far more fundamental change beyond enabling social inclusion or meeting a minimum threshold of basic needs or sufficiency within the existing system. While this might be immediately important to lift people out of absolute poverty, it cannot be enough. 'Equality of condition' exhorts us to address the political, social and economic conditions, structures, processes and institutions that create and reproduce relations of inequality; that prevent substantive participation and active, meaningful choice between alternatives of similar worth; and that impede substantive freedom and self-determination. The goal of equality and egalitarian projects is to remove systemic barriers to substantive freedom and actively to create conditions of equality, including attention to restructuring relations of equality at individual, institutional and societal inequalities. It is also to take account of the intersectional nature of inequalities in comprehending the problem and identifying its solutions.

In other words, there is no simple answer to the 'equality of what' question. Even if we agree on the general idea of 'equality of condition', what that means in any setting is a question for deliberation and debate. As such, this approach recognises the multi-dimensional nature of (in)equality and shares Sen's idea of equality as an evaluative space.[111] The constitutional commitment is to 'achieving equality'. This presumes that debate, hard work and imagination are necessary to identify the conditions of inequality and to work towards transforming them into the conditions necessary to secure equality, freedom dignity and systemic justice. Deliberation is required over the precise content of the value (what does equality mean in this instance?), as well as the means of achieving it (can legal change help, and if so, what kind of remedy is required?). This might sometimes require remedies that are alternative, tentative, even experimental, as they seek to dismantle relations of inequality and enable substantive equality of condition. Further, in undoing or transforming unequal social structures, we should think about how to ensure that people have a wide variety of choices in outcomes, and to act on these choices, thus to have 'real choices amongst real options'.[112]

This understanding of 'achieving equality' should guide not only courts in interpreting the Constitution but, more importantly, other branches of the state. The value of substantive equality as equality of condition goes beyond law and legal strategies to provide a frame for political and economic policies, laws and programmes.

Developing this further is beyond the scope of this article. In the remaining section, I consider how we might rethink the equality right, even as we know that substantive equality is not solely attainable through legal strategies, and certainly not through the equality right alone. However, this right can play a role in addressing

[110] Ibid 33–4.
[111] A Sen *The Idea of Justice* (2009) 232–3, 295–8.
[112] Baker et al (note 107 above) 34.

vulnerability, exclusion, disadvantage and oppression arising out of group-based disadvantage.

5.2. The right to equality

I have suggested there are two ideas of substantive equality in South African equality law: liberal substantive equality and transformative substantive equality. Both speak to different local and global strands of equality, some of which are highlighted above. In interpreting the equality right, both approaches share characteristics that are generally said to distinguish substantive from formal equality. They are: attention to difference and intersectionality, a concern with context and impact, and value-based adjudication (the principles that guide findings of discrimination and inequality). However, there are key differences in how these are understood and applied within each approach. In the following section I outline a possible transformative mode and highlight how it would differ from the (dominant) liberal egalitarian mode.

5.2.1. Difference and intersectionality

Attention to difference is a defining feature of substantive equality across all jurisdictions, and shifts focus from equality as 'same treatment' to the disadvantageous effects of direct and indirect forms of differential conduct. As noted by Sachs J in the first sexual-orientation case: 'Equality means equal concern and respect across difference. It does not presuppose the elimination or suppression of difference'.[113] In liberal substantive equality, this led to a concern with impact (indirect discrimination), the limits of affirmative action, and the principles that might distinguish permissible from impermissible differentiation. This is also true for the model of transformative substantive equality. However, whereas the liberal egalitarian model works with binary and inclusive forms of difference, transformative substantive equality poses a more complex and intersectional idea of difference. And, while the former tends to reproduce dominant structures, norms and processes, the latter seeks to make them visible, and then find ways of disrupting and dismantling them.

In focusing on the manner in which difference is tied to complex hierarchies, exclusion and disadvantage, transformative substantive equality pays attention to understanding non-binary difference and intersectionality. This accepts that categories such as race, gender or sexual orientation may contain multiple differences. For example, not just a simple binary of male/female but multiple forms and combinations of sexuality, desire and identity; not a solely black/white dualism, but diverse configurations and hierarchies of race, ethnicity and colour. It further recognises that plural forms of difference are intersectional, and the position of individuals and groups may be defined by several intersecting mechanisms of inequality.

By failing to recognise the complexity of hierarchical difference, the Constitutional Court's dominant liberal substantive equality approach has tended to reproduce some existing inequalities, even as it extends the scope of rights protection. A well-known

[113] *National Coalition for Gay and Lesbian Equality v Minister of Justice* 1999 (1) SA 6 (CC) para 132.

example of this is its use of heterosexual civil marriage as a privileged norm in gender and sexual-orientation cases.[114]

Both liberal and transformative substantive equality law prohibit difference linked to harm (differently defined) and affirm positive forms of difference, diversity and pluralism. Here again, boundaries differ. Positive measures within a liberal substantive equality approach broaden the base of inclusion, while a transformative approach seeks more redistributive and disruptive approaches. Overall, the transformative approach aims to facilitate and establish new, non-hierarchical normative frameworks of pluralism, participation and inclusion. The challenge is to identify the dominant norms, institutions and processes at play in any particular case, to avoid the use of dominant norms as comparators for assessing equality needs, and to identify remedies that aim to disrupt and dismantle these.

5.2.2. Context and impact

Central to substantive equality is attention to the impact of inequality on the individual and group, with due understanding of the concrete conditions of that individual and group's life. This contextual analysis separates substantive from formal equality, but liberal and transformative approaches to substantive equality differ on how to approach context.

Colleen Sheppard argues that the transformative potential of Canadian equality jurisprudence was lost, as a theoretical acceptance of context was rarely translated into 'actual, concrete application'.[115] Similarly, in South Africa, contextual analyses often eschew complexities and can even amount to a formal approach. In a liberal substantive approach, the courts are likely to start with a law or policy, look at its particular history or context, what it sought to achieve and how it operates in practice. But, this legal analysis can reduce the complexity of reality and social relationships.[116]

Transformative substantive equality requires judges and lawyers to understand that the context in which inequality occurs is one of complex, structural and systemic social and economic conditions. The interrogation of the social, political and legal context in which an alleged rights violation occurs requires an examination of the substantive arrangements that determine a group's social or economic position, including the relationship between disadvantaged and more powerful groups. In arguing for equality claims to be viewed through a 'substantive, procedural and relational lens', Sheppard notes that substantive equality should not only focus on substantive outcomes and concrete effects (impact) but also on the 'structures, processes, relationships and norms' that reproduce hierarchy, marginalisation, exclusion and inequality in everyday life (context).[117] This 'prompts an inquiry into both the actual realities and conditions of inequality, and the social, political and institutional processes that account for its reproduction'.[118]

---

[114] P de Vos 'From heteronormativity to full sexual citizenship? Equality and sexual freedom in Laurie Ackermann's constitutional jurisprudence' (2008) *Acta Juridica* 254; E Bonthuys 'Race and gender in the Civil Union Act' (2007) 3 *South African Journal on Human Rights* 526; Albertyn (note 88 above) 253.

[115] C Sheppard *Inclusive Equality: The Relational Dimensions of Systemic Discrimination in Canada* (2010) 33.

[116] A good example of this approach is the minority judgment of O'Regan & Mokgoro JJ in *Volks* (note 80 above).

[117] Sheppard (note 115 above) 4.

[118] Ibid 8–9.

Thus, transformative substantive equality seeks to grasp complex, structural, intersectional and relational inequalities. At a broad level, these relate to structures of capitalism, patriarchy, racism, hetero-normativity, etc., that create and reproduce inequality, but in any particular instance one would map the multiple, intersecting and cascading inequalities that affect particular groups and individuals. Here Sheppard's work is particularly useful in specifying multiple layers of context: a micro-level that focuses on the 'experiential harm' of discrimination from the individual/group perspective; an intermediate level that considers the manner in which inequality is reproduced in social, political and economic institutions (family, workplace, educational institution, community, etc.); and a macro-context that examines the larger political, social and economic context of structural inequalities and unequal power relations.[119]

In seeking this, it is important to 'embrace the voices and stories of exclusion and discrimination, information about institutional policies, practices and the systemic dynamics of exclusion, and knowledge of the larger social and structural realities of inequality'.[120] As Hester Lessard notes:

> [Attention to context can] transform the way we define legal issues. It does not simply correct the imbalance by adding some more voices to the debate over whose context would count the most in a particular legal dispute. Rather it changes the context of the debate and the nature of the debate's resolution.[121]

5.2.3. Values

The values and principles that underlie equality are critical signposts in equality enquiries. As Baker et al note: '[B]ecause principles of equality are always about other values, we must assert them at the same time as we assert the claims of equality'.[122] Here, again are important differences between liberal and transformative substantive equality. Liberal substantive equality has identified dignity, as equal concern and respect, as the marker of substantive equality. This seeks moral equality in the legal treatment of individuals, consistent application of standards and full inclusion of rights. As previously argued, this enables significant inclusion but limited transformation.

A transformative approach seeks to enable the restructuring of complex and intersectional relations, structures and processes of inequality toward systemic justice. It seeks not 'equal concern and respect', but a multi-faceted and multi-layered equality of condition. This requires attention to several principles to orient policy makers and courts, and to enable them better to interrogate the complexity of inequality and the changing conditions of disadvantage within and across different groups. Legal scholars have long pointed to the need for multiple values in equality adjudication.[123] Much of this work has drawn on critical feminism (arguing for the inclusion of

---

119 Ibid chapter 3. A judgment that gets closest to this is Sachs' minority judgment in *Volks* (note 80 above).

120 Sheppard (note 115 above) 66.

121 H Lessard 'Equality and access to justice in the work of Bertha Wilson' (1992) 15 *Dalhousie Law Journal* 55, 60–61.

122 Baker et al (note 107 above) 49.

123 For different iterations of the need to recognise different principles underlying the equality right, see Albertyn & Goldblatt (note 104 above); S Fredman 'Redistribution and recognition: Reconciling inequalities' (2007) 23 *South African Journal on Human Rights* 214; Botha (note 105 above); Albertyn 'Constitutional equality in South Africa' in O Dupper & C Garbers (eds) *Equality in the Workplace: Reflections from South Africa and Beyond* (2009).

anti-disadvantage or anti-subordination principles) and on Nancy Fraser's frame of recognition, redistribution and participation, which effectively describes the intersecting paradigms of economic, social and political inequalities across different groups.[124] Sandra Fredman, for example, has proposed a framework of four 'dimensions' of substantive equality that aim to address stigma, stereotypes, prejudice and violence (recognition); redress socio-economic disadvantage (including redistribution); facilitate participation; and value and accommodate difference through structural change.[125]

This debate originated in South Africa and Canada, where the developing jurisprudence elicited questions as to whether the principles of dignity and/or disadvantage captured the essence of equality.[126] Some argue that the idea of dignity or disadvantage alone should determine equality. Both Sheppard[127] (Canada) and Chris McConnachie[128] (South Africa) make this argument about disadvantage but define disadvantage with reference to a range of principles. Denise Réaume[129] (Canada) and Rosaan Krüger[130] (South Africa) do the same with dignity. Whether it is dignity or disadvantage, one value cannot effectively stand for everything. I agree with Fredman that working with multiple competing and complementary principles is an effective and transparent approach that provides flexibility across different dimensions of inequality and different claims for equality. However, I do not believe that disadvantage should be reduced to one of four competing principles. Rather I suggest that the idea of anti-disadvantage (as the imperative of anti-subordination) should be recognised as a cross-cutting principle to ensure just outcomes. In other words, in working across all principles described below, one is always concerned to understand and remedy particular, and often complex, forms of systemic disadvantage. One should always ask the 'disadvantage question' as a principle of asymmetry, a guide to contextual enquiries and a marker of the hierarchical nature of structural inequalities: what is the nature and impact of disadvantage, within any particular dimension, and across multiple dimensions, suffered by those who are bringing the claim?

Further, achieving a transformative equality of condition, within the setting of the South African Constitution, requires us to develop and work with principles that capture different facets of our constitutional values: *dignity* (recognition and social/cultural *equality*), redistribution (economic *equality*), participation (*democracy* and political *equality*) and *freedom* (substantive choice and self-determination).[131] I briefly highlight the meaning of these values below, leaving the detail of an 'indigenous' content to another time.

Recognition captures some of the idea of dignity in liberal egalitarian thinking, namely the idea that we are all of equal moral value and should not suffer stigmatisation, prejudice and stereotype. However, the idea of dignity as recognition under the

[124] N Fraser *Justice Interruptus* (1997). Proponents of multiple values follow similar, but not identical, approaches in identifying these values.
[125] S Fredman *Discrimination Law* 2 ed (2011) 8–33.
[126] Albertyn & Goldblatt (note 104 above); D Davies 'Equality: The majesty of Legoland jurisprudence' (1999) 116 *South African Law Journal* 398; S Cowen 'Can dignity guide our equality jurisprudence?' (2001) 17 *South African Journal on Human Rights* 34.
[127] Sheppard (note 115 above).
[128] C McConnachie 'Human dignity, unfair discrimination and guidance' (2014) 34 *Oxford Journal of Legal Studies* 609.
[129] DG Réaume 'Discrimination and dignity' (2003) 63 *Louisiana Law Review* 645.
[130] R Krüger 'Equality and unfair discrimination: Refining the Harksen Test' (2011) 128 *South African Law Journal* 479.
[131] I am aware of the potential role of values such as of solidarity, ubuntu and caring but leave their development for another time.

Constitution must go beyond a liberal concern with the individual effects of social prejudice to a relational concern with how groups are systematically stigmatised, denigrated, exploited, and subject to violence and abuse,[132] and take account of the insights of critical race and feminist theory in South Africa, in our past and present, to advance systemic change.

The principle of *redistribution* relates to equality in an economic sense and is concerned with whether people's overall resources are more equally distributed, so that they have 'roughly similar' prospects for pursuing their lives in ways that matter to them and for interacting with each other as peers.[133] Its inclusion addresses the effects of policies, laws and conduct on economic inequalities, and interrogates a more equal distribution of resources and benefits, not only as a threshold but also as a ceiling. It also highlights several consequences for equality law. First, equality law cannot confine its enquiry to social equality, recognition or dignity as the measure of equality, constitutional or otherwise. Second, ideas of social equality and recognition should not displace important considerations of material disadvantage, including economic deprivation, exploitation and subordination. Finally, a coherent value of material equality and redistribution is necessary to adjudicate positive measures. This speaks particularly to social democratic and socialist ideas of equality – Marxist and feminist – in the South African archive.

Participation (which, as Henk Botha usefully argues, is linked to the constitutional value of (participative) democracy at all levels of life)[134] asks whether conditions are such that people are able to participate fully in social, economic and political life, across the public/private divide? Does everyone have a roughly equal say in political, social and economic institutions, regardless of wealth, property, class, power and privilege (whether based on race, gender, class etc.)?[135] This resonates generally with historic claims, including feminist claims that highlight participation in the private sphere.

Finally, it seems that many accounts overlook the role of *freedom* in the equality enquiry. Of course, freedom is contested across different philosophical approaches. Here I understand freedom not in an abstract liberal sense, nor in the Constitutional Court's current emphasis on freedom, which is still largely in negative terms (as an intimate space of autonomy where the state must not interfere);[136] but rather as a substantive understanding of agency and self-determination, which requires both negative and positive actions and which might manifest differently for different groups within and across different domains (e.g. the workplace, health care, education). Freedom and equality are intertwined in a substantive sense. The ability to make real choices depends upon the conditions that exist to enable this. In interrogating inequality, we must understand how the structures, institutions, relationships and norms of inequality impede this freedom. And in seeking solutions to inequality, we need to ask how we reconstruct conditions and relationships to secure substantive freedom? What does it mean to be free in a particular context?

By including substantive freedom in evaluating equality claims, I seek a more transformative set of solutions that places structural disadvantage at the centre of

---

[132] See Fraser (note 124 above); IM Young *Justice and the Politics of Difference* (1990).
[133] Baker et al (note 107 above). See Fraser's idea of participatory parity in redistribution, ibid.
[134] Note 105 above 10–16.
[135] Sheppard (note 115 above) chapter 6.
[136] See most recently the judgment of *AB v Minister of Social Development* 2017 (3) SA 570 (CC).

equality claims but does not define subordinate groups solely by their disadvantaged status and position. Part of the enquiry is whether and how people exercise agency, however constrained, while simultaneously aiming to deepen and enhance their substantive freedom. The task of remedying inequality requires a commitment to overcoming structural disadvantage in ways that enhance freedom and do not lock people into systems of protection, patronage and dependence.

6. Conclusion

Equality is a contested idea in South African history, but, together with freedom, it has constituted a central demand of political struggles for centuries. It was enshrined at the heart of the democratic Constitution, itself a product of those struggles. Although contested, I have argued that the constitutional idea of equality has liberal egalitarian, social democratic and radical, critical roots that reach back into our history and have been redefined in the present. While the Constitutional Court has placed a particular liberal egalitarian stamp on equality, the idea of substantive equality enables more transformative interpretations and applications towards the kind of systemic justice that our society requires if it is to flourish. Here the Constitution provides a frame for working through and beyond liberal egalitarian substantive equality to further develop it as a normative roadmap, conceptual frame and legal resource to fight inequality and influence and defend transformative change. I have suggested how this might be done in advancing systemic change through an idea of 'equality of condition' and a more transformative approach to interpreting and enforcing the right. Although space did not allow a detailed exposition, the idea of 'equality of condition' can be developed in political and legal terms: both as a reference point for policy and legislation, and as a value that guides the interpretation of the Constitution towards systemic justice. In doing so, we should continue to draw on local ideas, contexts and struggles, so that equality (and freedom) are always responsive to the deep social and economic inequalities of contemporary South Africa.

Disclosure statement

No potential conflict of interest was reported by the author.

Funding

This article is based on research supported in part by the National Research Foundation of South Africa (Grant Numbers 113265 & 115567).

ORCID

Catherine Albertyn http://orcid.org/0000-0003-4182-5079

Decolonisation, compensation and constitutionalism: land, wealth and the sustainability of constitutionalism in post-apartheid South Africa

Heinz Klug

ABSTRACT

This paper explores the relationship between the protection of property rights and the effort to embed constitutionalism in South Africa since 1994. While the question of land will be central to the paper, property must be understood more broadly to include government's distributive efforts in the democratic era beginning with the Reconstruction and Development Programme through the provision of various social-grant programmes to the adoption of affirmative action, black economic empowerment and preferential government procurement rules. Finally, the paper will focus on the re-emergence of the demand for land. While I acknowledge that a number of factors might hinder or promote post-colonial constitutionalism – including legal education, the need for constitutional ideas to be articulated in indigenous languages and the extent of participation in the political process – the paper focuses on the underlying political economy of colonial and post-colonial society, including the legacies of continued inequality and exclusion, to explore whether a sustainable constitutionalism is possible.

1. Introduction

While there are many good reasons to be critical of the South African government and the ruling African National Congress (ANC), particularly when it comes to the failure to address the extraordinary inequalities created by apartheid and colonialism, it is not possible to understand these failures without taking cognisance of both the historical legacies and the conditions of the country's democratic transition. This approach to understanding the process of decolonisation in South Africa is especially important at a time when some political leaders, commentators and academics find it easier to lay the blame for present conditions on the choice to pursue a negotiated solution in the early 1990s rather than acknowledging the limits of that transition and seeking ways to address the continuing legacies of colonialism and apartheid today. The 'miracle' of South Africa's transition, in avoiding a predicted and completely destructive civil war,[1] was premised on leaders from all sides eventually recognising that they could negotiate beyond the military and political stalemate of that era. Today it is vitally important that the promise of the Constitution of the Republic of South Africa, 1996, adopted as the crowning achievement of that historic moment, is fulfilled, as it provides the space and opportunity for social transformation through legally mediated processes. By confronting the vast inequalities that reflect the country's historic legacies and using the political authority contained in the Constitution to do so, there is an opportunity to challenge the present failures to address these legacies and to build a common project of decolonisation that might, in time, fulfil the 1955 Freedom Charter's promise that 'South Africa belongs to all who live in it.'[2]

Given the military and strategic stalemate that heralded South Africa's democratic transition, the ANC recognised in the early 1990s that a negotiated transition would preclude simply dispossessing the *ancien regime*. Even an early proposal to adopt a wealth tax, premised on the post-war equalisation tax in what was then West Germany, was quickly abandoned when the proposal came under intense media and political attack.[3] Instead, the ANC sought less direct means to address the economic legacies of apartheid. Apart from developmental plans, such as the Reconstruction and Development Programme (RDP), which aimed to redistribute opportunities by addressing the unequal distribution of infrastructural and social resources – including housing, health, education, pensions and other government entitlements or programmes – the ANC adopted the ideas of restitution and affirmative action as means to benefit those who had been historically excluded. It is these two latter concepts, restitution through the land claims process[4] and affirmative action in the form of the Preferential Procurement Policy and black economic empowerment (BEE),[5] that became the chief foci of redistribution. Unlike BEE and procurement, which have become a means of wealth creation for a relatively small class of beneficiaries,[6] the land claims process promised to redress the legacy of the Natives Land Act, 1913, one of the central grievances of colonial dispossession and apartheid.

Stark economic inequalities, marked by unemployment and rural underdevelopment, continue to be a hallmark of South Africa's social structure.[7] While these inequalities may be recognised as a clear legacy of apartheid, especially resulting from the disparate impact that apartheid policies had on land ownership, job opportunities and education, it is important to also understand how these different legacies have been exacerbated in the post-apartheid era. The ANC first adopted the RDP with the goal of 'mobilizing all our people and our country's resources towards the final

[1] As Mahmood Mamdani notes, '[I]f Rwanda was the genocide that happened, then South Africa was the genocide that didn't.' in M Mamdani (ed) *When Victims Become Killers: Colonialism, Nativism, and the Genocide in Rwanda* (2001) 185.

[2] Preamble to the Freedom Charter, adopted at Kliptown (26 June 1955) <http://www.historicalpapers.wits.ac.za/inventories/inv_pdfo/AD1137/AD1137-Ea6-1-001-jpeg.pdf>

[3] See B Krige 'ANC plan for wealth levy: 'reparation' bid would force individuals to pay third of their assets' *Sunday Times* (13 October 1991) 1; editorial 'Looney tunes' *Sunday Times* (13 October 1991) 22; H Sauer 'It's not just the north in a tizz about that tax' *The Star* (18 October 1991) 14.

[4] C Walker *Land-marked: Land Claims & Land Restitution in South Africa* (2008).

[5] X Mangcu, G Marcus, K Shubane & A Hadland *Visions of Black Economic Empowerment* (2007).

[6] S Bridge, S Clow-Wilson, T Mackay, J Serrao & C-C Wu (eds) *Trailblazers: South Africa's Champions of Change* (2007).

[7] See J Seekings & N Nattrass *Class, Race, and Inequality in South Africa* (2005).

eradication of apartheid and the building of a democratic, non-racial and non-sexist future'.[8] This policy framework was replaced within two years by the Growth, Employment and Redistribution (GEAR) strategy, which sought to stimulate economic growth by reducing inflation, fiscal deficits and barriers to trade.[9] While achieving these macroeconomic goals, GEAR failed to produce greater employment opportunities or reduce inequality and was ultimately replaced first by the Accelerated and Shared Growth Initiative for South Africa (ASGISA) in 2005, the New Growth Path in 2010 and, finally, by the National Development Plan 2030 (NDP) in 2013. Despite these plans, various factors, which include the global economic crisis and the escalation of corruption and undermining of state-owned enterprises under President Zuma's watch, created a precarious economic situation in which even the modest gains made in reducing poverty through the distribution of social grants are now threatened.

It is in this context that this article seeks to explore the relationship between the distribution of wealth and the effort to embed constitutionalism in South Africa in the post-apartheid era. More specifically, the focus will be on debates over the constitution's protection of property[10] and an argument that, despite specific provisions designed to ensure land reform - through restitution, redistribution and tenure reform - the Constitution precludes effective government action to achieve redistribution. However, before addressing the property debate, I will first consider the broader claim that the Constitution was an unnecessary compromise that is today an impediment to addressing the country's economic and social inequalities, which had originally motivated the struggle against apartheid and colonialism. From this perspective, true decolonisation requires a fundamental recasting of our constitutional order and, for some, the rejection of constitutionalism more broadly. In considering the failure to achieve even modest levels of land redistribution promised by the ANC in 1994, the article focuses only on the constitutional history and debates without considering the vast array of bureaucratic, policy and implementation failures that have contributed to the slow pace of change. Finally, the article concludes by emphasising the relationship between these efforts to address existing levels of inequality and by proffering the hope of building a sustainable constitutional democracy.

2. Imagining what might have been?

Given the demographic structure of South Africa, it is difficult for many 'born frees' - those young South Africans who had never experienced formal apartheid - to imagine why the struggle against apartheid ended in a compromise in which the fundamental distribution of wealth was left unchallenged, and those working for the apartheid

8 African National Congress 'The Reconstruction and Development Programme: A Policy Framework' (1994) 1 para 1.1.1.

9 Department of Finance, Republic of South Africa 'Growth, Employment and Redistribution: A Macroeconomic Strategy' <http://www.treasury.gov.za/publications/other/gear/chapters.pdf>.

10 I should disclose here that I served as a member of the ANC Land Commission secretariat from 1990–1992 and as a researcher for Zola Skweyiya, chairperson of the ANC Constitutional Committee from 1989–1993. From this vantage point I both witnessed and engaged in these debates. I have based this article on documentary evidence to the greatest extent possible, but it is also informed by my own experiences.

bureaucracy were guaranteed continued employment for the first five years of the democratic era. Some view this outcome as both a moral and political failure.[11] But few offer either a plausible alternative scenario for what might have been or even a clear analysis of the conditions prevailing at that time. Instead, it is either suggested that the struggle could have continued until victory was obtained by insurrection or revolutionary violence,[12] or it is argued that the ANC, once elected into power, quickly succumbed to either the power of neoliberal globalisation or the class interests of the emerging elite.[13] While these perspectives and critiques of post-apartheid policies and governance failures provide important insights, they often imagine alternatives that seem far removed from the conditions that prevailed in South Africa and internationally in the late 1980s and early 1990s.

For those who imagine that insurrection or armed struggle remained a viable means of taking power from the apartheid regime at the end of the 1980s, the conditions that prevailed at that time need to be recalled. Not only had the country been subjected to states of emergency and repression from 1985, but military raids and apartheid support for counter-revolutionary forces, both in South Africa and across the Southern African region, had severely constrained the ability of the liberation movements to provide armed defence or support for revolution in South Africa. Often forgotten is the fact that the United Nations (UN) brokered process for the independence of Namibia in 1990 included an internationally endorsed agreement that Umkhonto we Sizwe (MK) personnel and equipment be withdrawn from the Republic of Angola, its last remaining Southern African base.[14] Furthermore, the ANC had been informed, as early as November 1986, that the process of 'perestroika' and the winding down of the Cold War[15] would mean that the Soviet Union and its allies may not be able to provide the military support that MK relied upon. The transportation of the bulk of MK personnel from Angola to new camps in Uganda or to civilian ANC facilities in Tanzania and elsewhere in 1989 not only extended MK's extraordinarily long-distance lines of communication and logistics, but also effectively precluded the degree of logistical supply and rear-base protection needed for the waging of a successful guerrilla war.[16]

At the same time, the apartheid regime was facing its own crisis, brought on by the combined strategies of mass mobilisation and international isolation that marked the culmination of decades of anti-apartheid resistance.[17] Even if the regime was able to militarily dominate the country, it was unable to legitimate its rule. The 1983

---

[11] Speaking to the Oxford Union in late November 2015, Julius Malema, former president of the ANC Youth League and now leader of the opposition EFF in parliament, criticised the legacy of Nelson Mandela by stating that: '[T]he Nelson we celebrate now is a stage-managed Mandela who compromised the principles of the revolution, which are captured in the Freedom Charter [. . .] The deviation from the Freedom Charter was the beginning of selling out of the revolution.' Furthermore, Malema stated that the EFF is 'not going to compromise like Madiba did'. See M Meintjies 'EFF's Malema takes aim at "sellout black billionaires" in Oxford address' *Business Day* (26 November 2015).

[12] T Reddy *South Africa, Settler Colonialism and the Failures of Liberal Democracy* (2015) 143–150.

[13] P Bond *Elite Transition: From Apartheid to Neoliberalism in South Africa* (2014).

[14] S Thomas *The Diplomacy of Liberation: The Foreign Relations of the ANC Since 1960* (1996) 199–203.

[15] A Brown 'Perestroika: reform that changed the world' *BBC News* (10 March 2015) <https://www.bbc.com/news/world-europe-31733045>.

[16] See T Simpson *Umkhonto We Sizwe: The ANC's Armed Struggle* (2016).

[17] See L Brock, V Gosse & A Lichtenstein (eds) 'The global antiapartheid movement 1946–1994' (2014) 119 *Radical History Review*.

'tricameral' Constitution was designed to provide a level of legitimacy that proved impossible to attain.[18] Instead, the call to make the country ungovernable was taken up by the mass movements. While attempts to stimulate forms of popular government were uneven and often crushed by the regime, the ideological space created by the resistance of the anti-apartheid movement undermined the regime's attempts to preclude the banned and exiled organisations from a future order acceptable to the international community. It was in this context that both sides began to prepare for negotiations. And yet elements on both sides still expected to gain the upper hand by either getting the international community to endorse their vision of the future, or by overwhelming their enemies through co-optation, repression or insurrection. On the one hand, it could be regarded as remarkable that constitutionalism emerged in these circumstances as a solution to the conflict, while on the other hand, the international moment that emerged from the end of the Cold War both enabled this process and for a brief time made constitutional change the preferred solution in processes of state reconstruction that swept the world in the last decade of the twentieth century.

Decolonisation in this context meant that South Africa committed itself to a constitutionalist path that was unimaginable in the early 1980s. It is the perceived failure of this path to achieve a degree of economic and social decolonisation that is essential to its own sustainability; this perceived failure has, in turn, produced numerous challenges to constitutionalism that are being vented in social and political struggles across South Africa, several of which are discussed in this special issue of the *South African Journal on Human Rights*. The burning question is whether constitutionalism in the post-apartheid context is as transformative as is claimed by the Constitutional Court and those who believe in its promise, or if adherence to constitutionalism in the form of constitutional supremacy embraced by South Africa's constitution-makers has not, in fact, precluded the degree of change necessary to build a sustainable society. It is this question that underlies the debate over whether land reform, a necessary ingredient for addressing a history of dispossession and legal exclusion, requires an amendment to the property clause of the Constitution to be effective. While the Constitution specifically provides for processes of land restitution and redistribution, the failure of government to ensure an effective change in the racial distribution of property ownership in the democratic era has led to demands that the property clause either be removed from the Constitution or that an amendment be made to the clause allowing expropriation without compensation.

3. Land and demands for redistribution

In December 2017 the ANC National Conference once again raised the question of land distribution. The conference declaration noted that the delegates had resolved that: '[T]he ANC should, as a matter of policy, pursue expropriation of land without compensation.'[19] Five years earlier, as the ANC moved towards its National Conference in 2012, there were repeated calls for greater government intervention in the distribution of

[18] Republic of South Africa Constitution Act 110 of 1983.

[19] 'Declaration of the 54th National Conference of the ANC' (20 December 2017) <http://www.anc.org.za/content/declaration-54th-national-conference-african-national-congress>.

property, particularly land. In the lead-up to the organisation's mid-year policy conference that year, there were calls from various ANC constituencies, the youth league and trade unions in particular, for a constitutional amendment to remove what they understood to be a constitutional requirement of 'willing-buyer, willing-seller' that they blamed for the slow pace of economic transformation and land reform.[20] In response to these calls, the official opposition, the Democratic Alliance, issued a press statement warning that the ANC government was 'contemplating dramatic changes to the Constitution […] which threatens the very foundation of our constitutional state'.[21] While at that time the Minister of Rural Development and Land Reform Gugile Nkwinti argued that the debate about changing the Constitution might be irrelevant, as '[T]he ANC had come up with four proposals to transform land ownership in South Africa without changing the Constitution,'[22] the ANC Youth League still called for a 'changing of the Constitution to do away with land expropriation with compensation'.[23]

Demands for constitutional amendments and threats that such amendments will undermine South Africa's constitutional democracy are at one level easily understood as the product of continuing contestation over the distribution of economic resources in post-apartheid South Africa. Less understandable is the focus on 'willing buyer, willing seller' as the target of vilification by those who feel that land reform has been hampered by the constitutional protection of property rights, and as a marker of constitutional rights by those who claim that the protection of property fundamentally underpins the country's constitutional democracy. The fact that the Constitution makes no reference to the 'willing buyer, willing seller' standard is reflected in the argument by former Land Minister Nkwinti, who has acknowledged that a lot more can be done by the government within the confines of the Constitution to advance the goals of land redistribution. However, the government's own claims about the limits of land reform are questionable, since the process of land restitution and redistribution has until now been largely carried out within the confines of a market-based 'willing buyer, willing seller' policy approach. The puzzle, then, is to understand the persistence of this policy approach and the strength of the rhetoric that has until now undermined attempts to shift towards a more aggressive use of state power, including the power of eminent domain, to achieve the government's stated goals of agrarian reform.

Once the focus shifts to the question of expropriation, however, the focus on 'willing buyer, willing seller' becomes more understandable. Although the Constitution may not include a 'willing buyer, willing seller' standard, the apartheid-era Expropriation Act 63 of 1975 did include this standard as a basis for determining the compensation to be paid in the event of expropriation. While the Constitution is supreme in South Africa and explicitly provides a set of criteria for determining compensation in the event of expropriation, in application the state may only exercise its power of eminent domain within the terms granted by the legislature in the expropriation statute. This explains, in part, why the 'willing buyer, willing seller' standard

---

[20] M Letsoalo 'Numsa targets land reform, the Constitution – and Pravin' *Mail & Guardian* (4 June 2012) <https://mg.co.za/article/2012-06-04-no-compensation-numsa-targets-land-reform-the-constitution-and-pravin-gordhan>.
[21] D Smuts 'Property a basic right, not a sunset clause' Democratic Alliance press release, Cape Town (4 March 2012) <http://www.politicsweb.co.za/party/property-a-basic-right-not-a-sunset-clause–dene-s>
[22] South African Press Association 'Changing Constitution not a solution to land problem: minister' (12 June 2012).
[23] Ibid.

has some resonance in the South African debate over expropriation. However, a broader view of the debate, which includes an understanding of the conflict over land in the Southern African region more generally, provides a much clearer perspective on why this standard has such resonance in the political debates over land and the possibility of constitutional change most specifically. More specifically, once the history of struggle over land in Zimbabwe, as well as the pattern of constitutional amendment and crisis in Zimbabwe, is taken into account, it becomes clear why the 'willing buyer, willing seller' language has such power and relevance. In this context, constitutional change and land reform is linked in domestic law and politics to broader international and regional conditions that shape the ways in which constitutional options and land policy might be understood and contested.

The Constitution protects the rights of property holders. Section 25(1) provides that, 'No one may be deprived of property except in terms of law of general application, and no law may permit arbitrary deprivation of property.' The Constitution's property clause also explicitly recognises the state's power to expropriate property for 'a public purpose or in the public interest [...] subject to compensation' and includes provisions that attempt to both protect land reform from constitutional challenge and to ensure that the payment of compensation is tied to a recognition of the history and use of the relevant property.[24] In the first major case challenging the failure of government to protect the rights of a landowner who had obtained an eviction order against thousands of settlers on his land, the Constitutional Court held that the state was under an obligation to either enforce the court-ordered eviction or otherwise to expropriate the land and grant compensation to the landowner.[25] In a second case, the Constitutional Court was asked to decide whether the enforcement of a tax lien against a company through the seizing of two vehicles amounted to a taking of the property of the bank that had financed the purchase of the vehicles.[26] In this context, the Constitutional Court laid out an elaborate scheme for deciding whether there had been an expropriation of property.

Despite this elaborate constitutional schema for determining the constitutionality of any deprivation of property, the practice of expropriation has continued to be governed by the pre-democratic statutory law of expropriation.[27] Although no expropriation may be carried out in violation of the Constitution, the question is not whether the government is providing too little protection but rather if the statutory framework created by the Expropriation Act did not, in fact, place higher burdens upon the state than required by the Constitution. Under the 1975 statute an expropriation must be 'for a public purpose',[28] and compensation is determined by the 'amount which the

---

[24] Section 25(3) of the Constitution provides that: 'The amount of the compensation and the time and manner of payment must be just and equitable reflecting an equitable balance between the public interest and the interests of those affected, having regard to the relevant circumstances, including: (a) the current use of the property; (b) the history of the acquisition and use of the property; (c) the market value of the property; (d) the extent of direct state investment and subsidy in the acquisition and beneficial capital improvement of the property; and, (e) the purpose of the expropriation.'

[25] *President of RSA v Modderklip Boerdery (Pty) Ltd* 2005 (5) SA 3 (CC).

[26] See *First National Bank of SA Ltd t/a Wesbank v Commissioner, South African Revenue Services; First National Bank of SA Ltd t/a Wesbank v Minister of Finance* 2002 (4) SA 768 (CC).

[27] Expropriation Act.

[28] Ibid s 2(1).

property would have realized if sold on the date of notice in the open market by a willing seller to a willing buyer' plus an 'amount to make good any actual financial loss or inconvenience caused by the expropriation'.[29] Public purpose, however, is defined quite broadly in the Act as 'including any purposes connected with the administration of the provisions of any law by an organ of state'.[30] The net effect, however, is that in the case of both the reason for the expropriation, as well as the standard of compensation that should be awarded, the statute privileges the existing holders of freehold title as against both the state and the Constitution's imperative to address past dispossession by providing the state with greater latitude and taking into consideration the benefits the previous owner may have accrued in a market, access to which was racially restricted and in which the state often provided subsidies and other benefits to white landowners. The most important impact this continuance of past law has had on post-apartheid land law and policy is the continued embrace, in practice, of willing-seller, willing-buyer, which is neither required by the Constitution nor has it been helpful in furthering the process of restitution. Instead, this 1975 law has either strengthened the bargaining power of existing title-deed holders or created a perception of its significance among those who feel that the process of restitution and land reform has been unacceptably glacial.

Attempting to address this inconsistency between the statutory law and what is arguably a more permissive constitutional requirement, the government introduced a bill to reform the law of expropriation in April 2008. In its explanation for the bill, the government argued that the new law would create a 'framework to give effect to the Constitution' and in particular the state's 'constitutional obligation to take reasonable legislative and other measures, within its available resources, to foster conditions which enable citizens to gain access to land on an equitable basis'.[31] The new statute would also have required the recognition of unregistered rights[32] as well as provided new institutional mechanisms to regulate expropriations.[33] Significantly, the draft law also revised the standards for compensation including, for the first time, the range of factors that had been negotiated during the democratic transition. Reaction to the bill was vociferous, particularly from those who had fought so hard to protect their property interests during the transition from apartheid.[34]

Many of the objections to the proposed legal reforms mirrored those that had been rejected by the Constitutional Assembly, yet the government withdrew the bill, and political tensions continued to rise around criticisms of the slow pace of land reform as well as demands to reject the policy and practice of 'willing-seller, willing buyer', which was rhetorically blamed for the failures of the state and market to

---

[29] Ibid s 12(1)(a)(i) and (ii).

[30] Ibid s 1, definitions: 'public purposes.'

[31] South Africa, Department of Public Works 'Explanatory summary of the Expropriation Bill' General Notice 440 of 2008 s 2 *Government Gazette* No. 30963 (11 April 2008) 3.

[32] Ibid chapter 4 s 10.

[33] See ibid chapter 3 s 6.

[34] See 'FW de Klerk warns against Expropriation Bill' *Mail & Guardian* (25 June 2008) <http://mg.co.za/article/2008-06-25-fw-de-klerk-warns-against-expropriation-bill>. SF Booysen 'Submission BYSF Steve Booysen: ABSA: Concerns regarding the Expropriation Bill' (9 June 2008) <http://webcache.googleusercontent.com/search?q=cache:vNmqC8xetBoJ:pmg-assets.s3-website-eu-west-1.amazonaws.com/docs/080618booysen>.

address continuing racial inequalities in land ownership. With parliament having failed to pursue the bill, the issue was taken up again at the June 2012 policy conference of the ANC, which responded to popular concerns by making a number of land-related policy proposals – including replacing 'willing buyer, willing seller' with the 'just and equitable' principle in the Constitution, where the state is acquiring land for land-reform purposes; expropriating without compensation land acquired through unlawful means or used for illegal purposes – and maintaining that nationalisation was still an option.[35] At the same time, however, there continued to be more strident demands that there be a constitutional amendment to remove the 'willing buyer, willing seller' principle or even abolish the requirement that the government pay compensation for land taken in the name of redistribution. Responding to these internal pressures, the government reintroduced the Expropriation Bill in 2013, but again it failed to progress through the legislature.

In response to continuing claims for a more effective and speedy process of land reform, the government reintroduced the Expropriation Bill in early 2015. Even in its revised form, the new bill recognised that there is broad scope for a more aggressive land reform policy within the present constitutional framework for property and land reform. In this instance, the bill was finally put to the vote and passed by the National Assembly on 23 January 2016. After the bill cleared parliament, it was sent to then President Jacob Zuma for his assent. In July 2016 the president sent the bill back to parliament, requesting information about the process that was followed in passing the bill, since the presidency had received numerous petitions arguing that parliament and various provincial legislatures had failed to follow certain required procedures, including submitting the bill to the National House of Traditional Leaders, as well as the National Council of Provinces failing to 'facilitate sufficient consultation with the public prior to the adoption of the Bill'.[36] As a result, the bill has yet to become law, and the apartheid-era Expropriation Act continues to be the law. While some have argued that instead of seeing the Constitution as an impediment, we should view the problem as being a failure to implement the Constitution, parliament's failure to pass a new expropriation statute presents a clear political failure rather than simply a problem of implementation, and it is, therefore, important to go back further in the debate over land reform to understand this lack of political will.

3.1. The ANC debate on land reform before 1994

Despite the many principled references to land distribution in the 1995 Freedom Charter, an organised debate over land was only revived in the ANC in late 1989. This coincided with then President FW de Klerk's public announcement in February 1990 of a political opening that set the stage for South Africa's democratic transition. At that moment, the ANC in Lusaka, Zambia, organised a workshop on the land question, which focused on analysing the state of rural South Africa. All the participants, ANC members who ranged from scholars and traditional leaders to peasant activists, assumed that nationalisation of

[35] 'ANC Recommendations from the 4th National Policy Conference' (June 2012) 37.

[36] 'Expropriation Bill process' The Presidency (25 July 2016) <http://www.thepresidency.gov.za/content/expropriation-bill-process>.

existing land holdings would be high on the agenda of a future ANC government. This shared assumption was based in no small part on a commitment to the 1955 Freedom Charter – recognised by the ANC as expressing the will of the South African people – which declares, in part, that the 'national wealth of our country […] shall be restored to the people [and] all the land re-divided amongst those who work it, to banish famine and land hunger'.[37] Despite these assumptions and the liberation movement's general rhetoric on the land question, participants at the workshop had a realistic view of the low priority that rural issues had on the mainly urban-based ANC's political agenda in the late 1980s. They were, however, encouraged by the 'economy and land' sections of the ANC's Constitutional Guidelines, which had been issued in 1988 as part of the ANC's preparations for negotiations.[38] Here, the ANC signalled its future intentions to both the international community and the apartheid regime, by announcing its intention to constitutionally protect property. While this promise went further than what might have been expected, given the rhetoric of socialisation, nationalisation and redistribution so dominant in the ANC at the time,[39] the limited focus on property for 'personal use and consumption' allowed these conflicting visions of redistribution and property rights to coexist. This coexistence was aided by a stated commitment to 'devise and implement a land reform programme […] in conformity with the principle of affirmative action, taking into account the status of victims of forced removals'.[40] With the exact modes of implementation were still open to debate, the Lusaka workshop opted to institutionalise the issue within the ANC by calling for the formation of the ANC Land Commission to address the lack of specific policies within the organisation.

On its return to South Africa in 1990, the ANC Land Commission's secretariat members began working with the already well-established community of lawyers, non-governmental organisations and activists who had long struggled against forced removals in the courts and on the land.[41] This informal coalition provided the organisational basis, knowledge and experience that sustained the struggle for the recognition of dispossessed land rights during the political transition and constitution-making process. While the ANC Land Commission had access to the ANC's internal policy-making processes and could evoke strong public reaction as a voice of the ANC, it was the return to land campaigns of land claimants, and their lawyers' continued engagement with the De Klerk government, that frustrated the apartheid regime's attempts to pre-empt future claims. This the apartheid government attempted to do by repealing the Land Act in 1991 and establishing an advisory commission on land allocation with the purpose of settling all claims before the political transition to democratic rule could be completed.[42]

---

[37] Freedom Charter (note 2 above).

[38] 'African National Congress constitutional guidelines for a democratic South Africa' reprinted in (1989) 12 *Hastings International and Comparative Law Review* 323–324.

[39] See African National Congress 'An analysis of the Freedom Charter, the revolutionary programme of the African National Congress, as presented at the Morogoro Conference, Tanzania, May 1969' reprinted in A La Guma (ed) *Apartheid: A Collection of Writings on South African Racism by South Africans* (1971), pp. 179–204.

[40] 'African National Congress constitutional guidelines' (note 38 above).

[41] For an excellent account of these activities, see R Abel *Politics by Other Means: Law in the Struggle Against Apartheid, 1980–1994* (1995) 385–433.

[42] See Abolition of Racially Based Land Measures Act 108 of 1991.

The debate over land reform and property rights centred first on the ANC's draft bill of rights published in 1990, which contained a single article addressing the 'economy, land and property'.[43] Within the ANC, the Land Commission began hearing from its constituency and opening debates on land reform, nationalisation and restitution. This process began with newly formed branches and communities locked in land conflicts around the country but increasingly focused on a series of internal discussions, joined at times by activists and lawyers of the land movement and members of the ANC Constitutional Committee[44] as well as in engagements with other activists and sectors in a series of conferences initiated by the Constitutional Committee, at which special sessions or subgroups focused on the issue of land and property. Outside the ANC, the Land Commission built links and worked closely with lawyers and activists of the return to land movement and became engaged in wider public debates over land claims and land redistribution. Central to these debates was the status that property rights would have in a future constitution.

Although the ANC's draft bill of rights only protected limited rights to personal property, it became clear at the May 1991 conference convened by the ANC Constitutional Committee that the ANC was under a great deal of pressure to grant greater recognition to property rights. In fact, attempts at that conference to question whether there should be any constitutionally protected property rights at all elicited a highly charged response from one member of the Constitutional Committee, who warned that the rejection of property rights would directly endanger the democratic transition. In response, the participants at the conference called for a reworking of the draft in which land would be recognised as a specific form of property and treated separately from property in general. As such, concern was expressed about the recognition of property rights before the implementation of the necessary process of redistribution. Furthermore, participants made a commitment to include positive rights to land for the landless.[45]

While this internal debate sought simultaneously to limit the reach of existing property rights and to secure a more equitable distribution of property in the future, the response of the regime and the existing economic interests were expressed most clearly by the South African Law Commission. In its August 1991 'Interim report on group and human rights', the Law Commission launched a sustained attack against the ANC draft, charging that the 'ANC's bill […] provides, in a manner which hardly disguises the aim, for nationalization of private property without objectively testable norms for compensation', and that what the ANC intended was 'in fact nothing but nationalization under the cloak of expropriation […] designed to secure state control over property'.[46] Instead, the Law Commission called for the protection of private property and for the payment of just compensation in the event of

---

[43] ANC Constitutional Committee 'A bill of rights for a new South Africa: a working document of the ANC Constitutional Committee' (1990) art 11.

[44] The Constitutional Committee was chaired by Zola Skweyiya, head of the ANC's legal department, under whose authority the land commission initially fell. Skweyiya's interest in and commitment to these issues are reflected in: Z Skweyiya 'Towards a solution to the land question in post-apartheid South Africa: problems and models' (1990) 6 *South African Journal on Human Rights* 195.

[45] ANC Constitutional Committee 'A bill of rights for a democratic South Africa: papers and report of a conference convened by the ANC Constitutional Committee' (1991) 129–132.

[46] South African Law Commission 'Interim report on group and human rights' (August 1991) 359–365.

expropriation in the public interest. Likewise, the Democratic Party proposed a comprehensive right to property that could only be derogated by lawful expropriation in the public interest, and only then, when subject to the 'proper payment of equitable compensation, which in the event of dispute, shall be determined by an ordinary court of law'.[47] Neither of these proposals provided for the restitution of property taken under apartheid and as such failed to comprehend the threat to property rights, and even the very notion of constitutional rights, that the legal entrenchment of apartheid's spoils entails.

While attention was focused on the question of property rights, the ANC Land Commission continued to hold meetings around the country to discuss land issues, both to increase awareness within the ANC, as well as to begin formulating a land policy for adoption by the movement. The first target of this campaign was to commit the organisation to a set of principles upon which a policy could be built. With this as its goal, the ANC Land Commission held a national conference in June 1991 that produced a set of guidelines for the development of land policy. These guidelines were then presented and adopted at the ANC's National Conference in July 1991. The most important features of the Land Manifesto were: its simultaneous commitment to both land restitution and land redistribution, its recognition of a diversity of land tenure forms, and the advancement of a policy of affirmative action as the main device to achieve specific policy goals.[48] With these guidelines the ANC effectively endorsed a strategy against the simple constitutional recognition of private property as recognised by the apartheid state. First, by demanding both restitution and land reform, it questioned and threatened the legitimacy of existing property rights. Second, the recognition of different forms of tenure de-centred private land ownership and provided a basis for the recognition of communal and other forms of land tenure. Finally, the manifesto recognised that affirmative action-type policies would provide a structure in which the multitude of specific policy goals and claims of different constituencies within the ANC could be accommodated and targeted to address land issues and the interests of the rural poor.

At the October 1991 National Conference on Affirmative Action, convened by the ANC Constitutional Committee, a report back to the plenary session from the subgroup on land concluded that a 'wealth tax' would be necessary to fund land redistribution. Given the demand that any expropriation be compensated, the group concluded that the only way to achieve the redistribution of land necessary to overcome the legacy of the Land Act was to create a specific compensation fund. In order to achieve the equitable redistribution required, this dedicated account would need to be funded by those who benefitted from the limited land market created by the Land Act, which had reserved 87 per cent of land for white ownership and control. This could be achieved, it was argued, by the imposition of a 'wealth tax' modelled on the equalisation tax adopted in the Federal Republic of Germany in the aftermath of World War II. The reaction was immediate, the major white-controlled newspapers went ballistic, and within hours ANC members involved were receiving death

[47] See Democratic Party 'Freedom under the rule of law: advancing liberty in the new South Africa' Draft Bill of Rights (May 1993) art 9.

[48] ANC Land Commission 'Land Manifesto for ANC National Conference' (July 1991).

threats.[49] Although senior ANC leaders supported the holding of a debate on a wealth tax, it also became clear that any attempt to conduct an effective redistribution of land rights would meet extremely stiff opposition from the *ancien regime* as well as conflict with alternative demands for resources among the ANC's own constituencies.

Despite the fierce reaction that followed the proposal of a wealth tax, when formal negotiations began at the Congress for a Democratic South Africa (Codesa) in December 1991, it seemed as if the land issue would, once again, be pushed into the background as the parties clashed over the very nature of the political transition. As far as property issues were concerned, they were subsumed in the larger debate over whether the purpose of Codesa was to produce a detailed interim constitution or broad constitutional principles that would guide but not frustrate the work of a democratically elected future constitution-making body. Despite this marginalisation of substantive issues in the negotiations, for land claimants and those active in support of their demands, the struggle over land and property rights continued simultaneously on two planes. First, there were attempts to return to land, from which communities had been forcibly removed, whether by occupation or legal and administrative negotiations with the Advisory Commission for Land Allocation (ACLA) and the De Klerk government. The inability of the ACLA to respond to the demands of communities soon undermined its credibility.[50] Second, there was the level of ideas, including debates over different policy options, continuing at a series of conferences and meetings, either organised by the ANC Constitutional Committee together with various university-based institutes or directly by the academy. One of the most important of these debates was organised by long-time land activist Aninka Claassens, through the Centre for Applied Legal Studies (CALS), to discuss 'the effect that a constitutionally entrenched right to property might have on future land reform legislation and programmes'.[51]

The opening of a discussion on particular options for the recognition of land rights and the consequences a property clause might have on land claims was, at this stage, a vital intervention, making it clear that the issue of land rights could not be divorced from the wider question of property. Furthermore, when this conference is placed in the context of a series of conferences, meetings and workshops held in this period, its significance, as one in a series of intellectual loci of the South African transition, should be recognised.[52] At these events, new substantive ideas were introduced into the public debate while simultaneously being framed through their presentation in the context of different international histories and examples. Among the important substantive interventions

---

[49] Krige (note 3 above).

[50] See Association for Rural Advancement (AFRA) 'ACLA's last chance' AFRA newsletter 19 (November/December 1992) <http://www.sahistory.org.za/archive/acla%60s-last-chance>.

[51] See A Claassens 'Editorial' (1992) 8 *South African Journal on Human Rights* 5.

[52] These included the following conferences: 'Towards a non-racial, non-sexist judiciary in South Africa' ANC Constitutional Committee & the Community Law Centre (CLC), University of the Western Cape (UWC), Cape Town (26–28 March 1993); 'Structures of government for a united democratic South Africa' CLC, UWC, ANC Constitutional Committee & Center for Development Studies, UWC, Cape Town (26–28 March 1992); 'National conference on affirmative action' UWC, ANC Constitutional Committee & CLC, UWC, Port Elizabeth (10–12 October 1991); 'Conference on a bill of rights for a democratic South Africa' Constitutional Committee of the ANC & the Centre for Socio-Legal Studies, University of Natal, Durban, Salt Rock, (10–12 May 1991); 'Constitutional court for a future South Africa' ANC, CALS & Lawyers for Human Rights, Magaliesberg (1–3 February 1991); and 'Seminar on electoral systems' Centre for Development Studies & ANC constitutional department, Stellenbosch 2–4 November 1990).

made at the CALS conference was the public floating of the suggestion for a land claims court, in the form of a report to the conference from a group of lawyers and activists from the 'land claims movement' who were working on this option at the behest of the ANC Land Commission.[53] Other important substantive interventions at this conference included the proposed construction of a legal right to land for the landless.[54] Another intervention demonstrated the continued vitality and existence of an alternative understanding of land rights in opposition to the prevailing legal notions of individual private property rights.[55] There was also a paper on the Canadian decision not to recognise property rights in their 1982 Charter of Rights[56] and discussion of the history of constitutional conflict over land reform in India in the post-independence years.[57] The conference thus introduced both substantive examples of alternative approaches and provided grist for the debate over the dangers of enshrining property rights in a constitution.

It was these interventions that forced the ANC to re-evaluate its own proposed Draft Bill of Rights. After several meetings with land activists and members of the Land Commission, Albie Sachs proposed new sections on land and the environment as well as a separate property clause for the revised text of the ANC Draft Bill of Rights.[58] These new sections essentially expanded the ANC's proposals, making it clear that land rights would remain a central claim of the anti-apartheid movement and that the protection of property would remain subject to these claims. While property rights were given separate recognition for the first time in the new text, the text also suggested that these references to property, along with all other 'principles governing economic life' might be better placed outside the bill of rights in a non-justiciable section of the constitution defined as 'directive principles of state policy', which was the case with similar sections of the Irish and Indian constitutions.[59]

By the time this revised text was first published in May 1992, negotiations with the De Klerk government had formally broken down. At the same time, the government's land claims forum was being rejected by communities[60] who were threatening to physically reoccupy their lands,[61] and the ANC Land Commission was being thrust into an

---

53 E Swanson 'A land claims court for South Africa: report on work in progress' (1992) 8 *South African Journal on Human Rights* 332.

54 G Budlender 'The right to equitable access to land' (1992) 8 *South African Journal on Human Rights* 295.

55 C Cross 'An alternative legality: the property rights question in relation to South African land reform' (1992) 8 *South African Journal on Human Rights* 305.

56 RW Bauman 'Property rights in the Canadian constitutional context' (1992) 8 *South African Journal on Human Rights* 344.

57 J Murphy 'Insulating land reform from constitutional impugnment: an Indian case study' (1992) 8 *South African Journal on Human Rights* 362.

58 A Sachs 'Protecting human rights in a new South Africa' in A Sachs (ed) *Rights to the Land: A Fresh Look at the Property Question* (1990) 9; and A Sachs 'Advancing human rights in South Africa' in A Sachs (ed) *Property as a Human Right* (1992) 68.

59 See 'ANC draft bill of rights: a preliminary revised text (May 1992)' in A Sachs (ed) *Advancing Human Rights in South Africa: Contemporary South African Debates* (1992) appendix 1, 226.

60 See 'Statement from 19 communities on the government's Advisory Commission on Land Allocation' (15 September 1991); see also G Budlender 'Lessons learnt from the land mistake' *Review/Law: Special Supplement to Weekly Mail* (11 December 1992) 2.

61 See letter dated 31 July 1991 from J de Villiers, Minister of Public Works and Land Affairs, responding to a letter from lawyers representing a claimant community and stating in part, 'I do appeal to you to advise your clients not to take the law into their own hands because that would unnecessarily complicate consideration of possible claims. It would only serve to increase the temperature of the debate rather than to arrive at a solution,' cited in Y Dezalay & BG Garth (eds) *Global Prescriptions: The Production, Exportation, and Importation of a New Legal Orthodoxy* (2002) 300.

engagement with new actors – both national and international – who had recognised the centrality of land to the struggle over property rights. The first engagement, which culminated in a meeting in December 1992, was with the Urban Foundation (UF), which asked for a meeting with the ANC Land Commission to discuss land claims and the question of creating a land claims court. At this meeting the ANC delegation, which included members of the Constitutional Committee as well as the Land Commission and its allies in the land movement, were presented with the argument that while some form of limited land claims process might be necessary to legitimise future property relations, both the demand for land among the African majority and the reality of resource needs and allocations for future development required that this process be tightly circumscribed. While the ANC-aligned participants recognised the problem of competition over resources under a future democratic government, they argued that a merely symbolic process of restitution would fail to build the legitimacy the UF and its corporate constituency seemed to recognise was needed to secure property relations in the new South Africa.

The second of these new engagements began in mid-1992 when the World Bank launched its own initiatives in South Africa. The ANC Land Commission's immediate response was to ask who had invited them to South Africa, and to reject the notion of engagement with this institution. The Bank – which had already been rebuffed by other sectors of the anti-apartheid movement, particularly the urban-sector activists – responded to these hesitations by organising an initial seminar outside South Africa, in Mbabane, Swaziland, in November 1992. They invited representatives from different South African political groupings, government and non-governmental bodies to discuss a set of papers prepared by the World Bank and its consultants.[62] These two engagements presented radically alternative possibilities and opportunities. While the UF was convinced that the demand for land reform among Africans was being grossly exaggerated, Hans Binswanger, the senior World Bank advisor who dominated the Swaziland seminar, presented a vision of world development dependent upon the carrying out of a successful land reform. Unlike the UF, which suggested a limited process of restitution to legitimise property rights, Binswanger argued that land claims and even land invasions would drive a process of land reform and suggested that by facilitating land reform, the government would be providing an essential catalyst for sustained economic development. Although the ANC Land Commission remained extremely sceptical of the equities of the World Bank's proposals for a market-driven reform focused on small-scale producers, it realised that the Bank's argument could be deployed to maintain the issue of land reform on the political agenda. With this aim, the ANC Land Commission encouraged Binswanger to persuade the De Klerk government that land reform was an essential part of South Africa's political transition.

3.2. Negotiating the property clause

Prior to the beginning of substantive constitutional negotiations in early 1993, the ANC and the government of the time still held dramatically different notions of how property should be constitutionally protected. On the one hand, the ANC was willing

[62] World Bank 'Experience with agricultural policy: lessons for South Africa' (1992).

to protect the undisturbed enjoyment of personal possessions, so long as property entitlements were to be determined by legislation and provision was to be made for the restoration of land to people dispossessed under apartheid.[63] The government's proposals, on the other hand, were aimed at protecting all property rights and would only allow expropriation for public purposes and subject to cash compensation determined by a court of law according to the market value of the property.[64] In response, the ANC suggested that no property clause was necessary.[65] As negotiations gained momentum in 1993, conflict over the property clause began to focus on specific issues.

Although the ANC had initially insisted that an interim constitution contain only those guarantees necessary to ensure a level political playing field, the momentum for entrenching rights could not be slowed, and before long it became clear that the Interim Constitution[66] would contain a bill of rights. It was in this context that the apartheid government insisted that property rights be included in the Interim Constitution and that the measure of compensation include specific reference to the market value of the property. In response, the ANC insisted that the property clause not frustrate efforts to address land claims and that the state must have the power to regulate property without being obliged to pay compensation unless there was a clear expropriation of the property. Although the government agreed that explicit provisions guaranteeing and providing for land restitution should be included, its negotiators insisted that such provisions should not be located within the property clause.[67]

Mass action played an important part in the ANC alliance's campaign to shape the transition, and groups on all sides employed various public displays of claims, outrage and strength to ensure that their concerns or demands were placed on the agenda at the multi-party talks. These were marked by protests, demonstrations, campaigns and even an invasion by members of the far-right Afrikaner Resistance Movement (AWB) of the World Trade Centre in Kempton Park, the site of the multi-party negotiations. Mass participation in the constitution-making process exhibited both a diversity of claims and a degree of popular frustration with an undemocratic negotiating process. Among these were representatives of communities who were forcibly removed under apartheid, who marched on the World Trade Centre demanding constitutional recognition of their right to return to their land and protesting the proposed constitutional protection of property, which they saw as an entrenchment of the apartheid distribution of property.[68]

---

[63] See 'ANC Draft Bill of Rights: Preliminary Revised Version' (February 1993) art 13.

[64] See Republic of South Africa 'Government's proposals on a charter of fundamental rights' (2 February 1993).

[65] As I noted in H Klug *Constituting Democracy: Law, Globalism and South Africa's Political Reconstruction* (2000) 216, 'As late as October 1995, the Draft Bill of Rights being considered by the Constitutional Assembly's Theme Committee 4, included as Option 2, "No property clause at all".'

[66] The Constitution of the Republic of South Africa, Act 200 of 1993 (Interim Constitution). The Interim Constitution has been repealed.

[67] See R Spitz & M Chaskalson *The Politics of Transition: A Hidden History of South Africa's Negotiated Settlement* (2000) 313–329.

[68] As explained in Klug (note 65 above) 133, 'A march on the World Trade Centre in June 1993, in which a land rights memorandum was delivered to the negotiators, was followed by a march in central Pretoria in September 1993, in which about 600 people from 25 rural communities threatened to reoccupy land from which they had been removed by the apartheid government as a way of highlighting their demands for the unconditional restitution of land, the establishment of a land claims court and guaranteed security of tenure for farm workers and labour tenants. The Transvaal Rural Action Committee, which organized the march, also called for the rejection of the proposed property clause in the Constitution.' In

Answering these demands, the Interim Constitution provided a separate institutional basis for land restitution, which was guaranteed in the corrective action provisions of the equality clause.[69] A compromise on the question of compensation led to the inclusion of a range of factors the courts would have to consider in determining just and equitable compensation.[70] As Matthew Chaskalson argues, the final outcome in terms of the specific wording adopted was as much a result of serendipity, legal ignorance and the particular quirks and concerns of the individual negotiators as the logical product of an informed or even interest-based political debate and compromise.[71] This, he argues, is demonstrated most aptly in the choice of the terminology of public purpose over public interest in the expropriation clause, despite agreement among the parties to give the state as much leeway as possible in this regard.

Even then, the substance of the outcome reflects both the general contours of the political conflict over the property clause and the bounded alternatives available to the parties, from the recognition of existing property rights on the one hand to the recognition of land claims on the other. Significantly, the factors to be considered in the determination of just compensation reflect this outcome. On the one hand, they were directed at the problem of land claims and included: 'the use to which the property is being put, the history of its acquisition, the value of the investments in it by those affected and the interest of those affected',[72] while on the other hand, at the insistence of the *ancien regime* and making possible the inclusion of other factors, it enshrined market value. This compromise marked both the success and limitations of those committed to securing land for the dispossessed, and it was under this constitutional regime that Mandela's government and the first democratic parliament began to address land claims. Acting in terms of the specific clauses of the Interim Constitution, which provided for the establishment of a land claims process, parliament passed the Restitution of Land Rights Act 22 of 1994, setting up regional land claims commissions and the new Land Claims Court.[73]

Despite predictions that there would be very little change in the Interim Constitution during the second phase of the constitution-making process, particularly on such sensitive issues as the property clause and the Bill of Rights, the property issue once again became one of the unresolvable lightning rods in the Constitutional Assembly. Although the committee charged with reviewing the Bill of Rights was at first reluctant to change the formulation of the 1993 compromise, challenges centred on the question of land restitution and reform once again forced open the process. In this case, the impetus came from a workshop on land rights and the constitution organised by a Constitutional Assembly sub-committee, Theme Committee

---

the same book (note 65 above) 243, I also refer to A Hadland 'Demonstrators hand govt land ultimatum' *Business Day* (2 September 1993).

69 Interim Constitution s 8(3)(b).

70 See ibid s 28(3).

71 M Chaskalson 'Stumbling towards Section 28: negotiations over property rights at the multiparty talks' (1995) 11 *South African Journal on Human Rights* 222.

72 Section 28(3) of the Interim Constitution.

73 H Klug 'Historical claims and the right to restitution' in J van Zyl, J Kirsten & HP Binswanger (eds) *Agricultural Land Reform in South Africa: Policies, Markets and Mechanisms* (1996) 391.

6.3, whose task it was to resolve issues related to specialised structures of government such as the Land Claims Commission and Court provided for in the Interim Constitution.[74] Focusing on the land issue, this meeting once again brought together those committed to the cause of land redistribution and raised the problem of protecting property rights in the Constitution. While some participants again raised questions about the very inclusion of a clause protecting property, in a change from the period in which the Interim Constitution was negotiated, participants in this workshop, even those representing long-established interests such as the National Party and the South African Agricultural Union, agreed on the need 'to rectify past wrongs' and to undertake land reform.[75] Disagreement here was over the means. The South African Agricultural Union, for example, continued to assert that, '[I]t should be done in a way without jeopardising the protection of private ownership,'[76] while the National Party now embraced the World Bank's proposals, arguing that land reform should 'be accomplished within the parameters of the market and should be demand-driven'.[77]

The outcome of this workshop and the submissions made to Theme Committee 6.3 was a report to the Constitutional Assembly that both challenged the formulation of property rights in the Interim Constitution and called for a specific land clause to provide a 'constitutional framework and protection for all land reform measures'. While Theme Committee 4, which was responsible for the Bill of Rights, had until that point simply adopted a property clause that merely incorporated the Interim Constitution's restitution provisions into the property clause itself, the report on land rights threw the proverbial cat among the pigeons. Some objected to Theme Committee 6.3's very discussion of property rights, while others sensed an opportunity to reopen the debate on property rights and to once again question their very inclusion in the Bill of Rights. As a result, the Draft Bill of Rights published by the Constitutional Assembly on 9 October 1995 included an option that there be 'no property clause at all'.[78]

It was in this context that an alternative option, a property clause including specific land rights as well as a sub-clause insulating land reform from constitutional attack began to gain momentum. While a strategy to insulate land restitution and land reform from constitutional attack had been implicit from early on in the debate, it was now suggested in a submission to Theme Committee 6.3 that the property clause include a specific sub-clause insulating state action aimed at redressing past discrimination in the ownership and distribution of land rights. The negotiators were able to rely on this formulation as a compromise between those demanding the

---

74 See Constitutional Assembly, Constitutional Committee Sub-Committee: Documentation: Land Rights (9 October 1995); Theme Committee 6.3: Specialised Structures of Government: Land Rights, Documentation (11 September 1995); and Constitutional Assembly, Theme Committee 6.3: Specialised Structures of Government: Documentation Vol 2A: Land Rights (15 September 1995).

75 Constitutional Assembly, Theme Committee 6.3: Specialised Structures of Government: Land Rights, Documentation (11 September 1995) para 1.2 footnote 2.

76 Ibid.

77 Constitutional Assembly, Theme Committee 6.3 Specialised Structures of Government, Report on Blocks 9-10: Land Rights (11 September 1995) para 2 footnote 3.

78 Draft Bill of Rights s 24 option 1 *Constitutional Talk Official Newsletter of the Constitutional Assembly* Working Draft Edition (October 1995) 7.

removal of the property clause and those, like the Democratic Party, who remained opposed to even a social democratic formulation modelled on the German Constitution.[79] Still, the debate raged on, and the draft formulations of the property clause continued to evolve. Political agreement on the property clause was finally reached at midnight on 18 April 1996, when sub-section 28(8), the 'affirmative action' or insulation sub-clause of the property clause was modified to make it subject to s 36(1), the general limitations clause of the Constitution.[80]

The final property clause thus reflects both the democratic origins of the Constitutional Assembly as well as the continuing influence of land-claiming communities and activists. It guarantees not only the restitution of land taken after 1913[81] and a right to legally secure tenure for those whose tenure is insecure as a result of racially discriminatory laws or practices,[82] but also includes an obligation on the state to enable citizens to gain access to land on an equitable basis.[83] Furthermore, the state is granted a limited exemption from the protective provisions of the property clause to empower it to take 'legislative and other measures to achieve land, water and related reform, in order to redress the results of past racial discrimination.'[84]

Despite agreement in the Constitutional Assembly, the property clause was challenged in the certification case before the Constitutional Court.[85] Opponents of the clause claimed it violated the constitutional principles and therefore was a ground for denying certification of the Constitution. Two major objections were raised: first, that unlike the Interim Constitution the new clause did not expressly protect the right to acquire, hold and dispose of property; second, the provisions governing expropriation and the payment of compensation were inadequate. The Constitutional Court rejected both of these arguments. First, the Court noted that the test to be applied was whether the formulation of the right met the standard of a 'universally accepted fundamental right' as required by Constitutional Principle II. Second the Court surveyed international and foreign sources and observed that, 'If one looks to international conventions and foreign constitutions, one is immediately struck by the wide variety of formulations adopted to protect the right to property, as well as by the fact that significant conventions and constitutions contain no protection of property at all.'[86] In conclusion, the Court argued that it could not 'uphold the argument that, because the formulation adopted is expressed in a negative and not a positive form and because it does not contain an express recognition of the right to acquire and dispose of property, it fails to meet the prescription of [Constitutional Principle II]'.[87] The second objection met the same fate, with the Court concluding that an 'examination of international conventions and foreign constitutions suggests that a wide range of

[79] See Constitutional Assembly, Constitutional Committee, Documentation: Volume 2A Land Rights (15 September 1995) 13–41.

[80] See P Bell (ed) *The Making of the Constitution: The Story of South Africa's Constitutional Assembly, May 1994 to December 1996* (1997).

[81] Section 25(7) of the Constitution.

[82] Section 25(6) of the Constitution.

[83] Section 25(5) of the Constitution.

[84] Section 25(8) of the Constitution.

[85] *Ex Parte Chairperson of the Constitutional Assembly: In Re Certification of the Constitution of the Republic of South Africa, 1996* 1996 (4) SA 744 (CC).

[86] Ibid para 71.

[87] Ibid para 72.

criteria for expropriation and the payment of compensation exists',[88] and thus the 'approach taken in NT 25 cannot be said to flout any universally accepted approach to the question'.[89]

4. In the shadow of Zimbabwe

While it is hardly surprising that land was at the centre of anti-colonial struggles in the settler colonies of Southern Africa,[90] there has been little consideration of the impact that these struggles, and the ways they have been addressed in the post-colonial era, is having on debates over constitutionalism in the region. It is often recognised that political events in one country have direct impacts on neighbouring countries, yet discussions over constitutional change treats the processes and issues as essentially legal and therefore located within the confines of each country's legislative and political system. Even when it is recognised that constitution-makers and those engaged in amending their constitutions might be influenced by foreign examples, it is rarely acknowledged that the terms of a constitutional debate often take place within the shadow of neighbouring experiences. There is even less of an understanding of how particular phrasing may, given historical events and global perceptions, serve to trigger reactions and meanings out of proportion to any legal or constitutional meaning that might be normally associated with a particular wording. In the case of land, the impact of the issue of compensation and the 'willing buyer, willing seller' formula, once articulated as a definition of a market-based compensation standard in South Africa's Expropriation Act became a core element of the strategy to protect colonial property holdings in the 1979 Lancaster House Agreement that in 1980 ended the war and led to democratic elections in Zimbabwe.[91]

The Lancaster House Agreement included the text of Zimbabwe's first post-independence Constitution, providing that there could be no amendment to specific clauses for the first ten years of independence. Together with the guarantee of twenty white seats in the new parliament, it included the protection of existing property rights and specified that land could only be obtained by the new government for the purposes of land reform based on the 'willing seller, willing buyer' principle. While retaining its reference to the market, the phrase now included a limitation on the sovereignty of the new government in exercising its power of eminent domain, and not merely by defining the measure of compensation. This constraint lasted ten years, since the new 1980 Constitution continued the tradition of parliamentary sovereignty that Zimbabwe had inherited from Britain. Unlike the post Cold War constitution-makers, who would adopt judicial review, the Zimbabwean Constitution was easily amended by parliament, and the limited power of the judiciary to interpret the rights provisions in the document could easily be undermined by this amending power.

---

[88] Ibid para 73.
[89] Ibid.
[90] See S Moyo 'The land question in Southern Africa: a comparative review' in L Ntsebeza & R Hall (eds) *The Land Question in South Africa: The Challenge of Transformation and Redistribution* (2007) 60.
[91] 'Report: Southern Rhodesia Constitutional Conference held at Lancaster House, London September-December 1979' <https://peacemaker.un.org/sites/peacemaker.un.org/files/ZW_791221_LancasterHouseAgreement.pdf>.

When it came to land, the outcome was unexpected. While the Zimbabwean legislature moved quickly, in 1990, to remove the 'willing buyer, willing seller' limitations in its Constitution,[92] in practice the government continued, in the name of economic stability and foreign investment, to refrain from using eminent domain; instead it purchased land from white farmers for its resettlement and related land-reform efforts. It was only when the ruling Zimbabwe African National Union Patriotic Front (ZANU-PF) began to face a serious electoral challenge in the late 1990s that the slow pace of land redistribution became a focus of government rhetoric. It was in this context that Zimbabwe adopted more aggressive policies of land acquisition, which, after 2000, led to a wave of farm invasions and a subsequent collapse of the economy.[93] While the conditions that led to economic collapse are multiple and complex, it was the adoption of constitutional changes that revoked the duty to pay compensation altogether by tying it to the willingness of the former colonial power to offer financial aid to cover the costs of compensation that has been the focus of attention. Significantly, these provisions of the Zimbabwean Constitution remain a core element of contestation in the country, even after Robert Mugabe's removal from power. No discussion of land reform in South Africa can be regarded as free from this history, or the continuing failures of land-reform projects in South Africa itself.

5. Conclusion: Land, wealth and the decolonisation of constitutionalism in post-apartheid South Africa

The argument that the property clause of the Constitution limits the South African government's ability to address inequality in land holdings to policies based on market mechanisms fails to take into account the history of the debates over the property clause during the constitution-making process and ignores the legacy of dispossession and forced removals that were central to the apartheid project. These processes of dispossession were not only the basic means of colonisation, but continued late into the twentieth century, as the darkest face of apartheid policy.[94] Indeed, land dispossession was one of the key policies that triggered and justified the international community's designation of apartheid as a crime against humanity.[95] It is this legacy – in which millions were forced from their homes and declared pariahs in the land of their birth,[96] in which communities were dismantled brick by brick and their members scattered across the most barren wastelands of the country,[97] in which people clung to the land and refused to give up their claims[98] – that set the stage for the

---

[92] See Constitution of Zimbabwe, 1980 as amended by Amendment Act 16, 2000, s 16A, inserted by s 3 of Act 5 of 2000.

[93] J Hanlon, J Manjengwa & T Smart *Zimbabwe Takes Back Its Land* (2013). See also P Bond & M Manyanya *Zimbabwe's Plunge: Exhausted Nationalism, Neoliberalism and the Search for Social Justice* (2002).

[94] C Desmond *The Discarded People: An Account of African Resettlement in South Africa* (1971).

[95] UN General Assembly Resolution 3068 'Resolution: International Convention on the Suppression and Punishment of the Crime of Apartheid' (30 November 1973) A/RES/3068.

[96] ST Plaatje *Native Life in South Africa* (1916) (ed B Willan, 1987) 6.

[97] L Platzky & C Walker *The Surplus People: Forced Removals in South Africa* (1985). See also Surplus People Project 'Forced Removals in South Africa: The Surplus People Project Reports' vol 1–5 (1983) <https://www.datafirst.uct.ac.za/dataportal/index.php/catalog/581>.

[98] Transvaal Rural Action Committee 'A toehold on the land: labour tenancy in the South Eastern Transvaal' (May 1988).

recognition and shaping of property rights in post-apartheid South Africa. Yet, twenty years after the formal adoption of a post-apartheid constitution, resistance to change by opposition parties and economic interests continues, particularly to the economic structuring and distribution of resources, which is the basic premise of agrarian reform.

It is in this context that demands are being made to remove the property clause from the Constitution. Yet, as this article has argued, there is no need to change the Constitution to do land reform. Land reform is, in fact, required by the Constitution. Moreover, the Constitution allows for the expropriation of land for land reform, even without compensation. This is due to the fact that land reform is specifically protected from the rest of the property clause, including the requirement to pay compensation, by s 25(8) of the Constitution, which states:

> No provision of this section may impede the state from taking legislative and other measures to achieve land, water and related reform, in order to redress the results of past discrimination, provided that any departure from the provisions of this section is in accordance with the provisions of section 36(1).

Because this last phrase of s 25(8) was added as a last-minute compromise, some conclude that the section is meaningless. This can be contested on three main grounds. First, this cannot be the case as a matter of principle, since it is standard constitutional jurisprudence that all sections of the Constitution must have meaning. Second, this section has, to date, never been relied upon politically, by the legislature or the executive, nor has it been subject to judicial interpretation by the courts; it is time that it is applied. Third, the requirement that land reform be carried out in accordance with s 36(1) is no legal barrier to expropriation without compensation for land reform because s 36(1) only requires that the rights in the Bill of Rights may be limited only in terms of law of general application to the extent that the limitation is reasonable and justifiable in an open and democratic society based on human dignity, equality and freedom, taking into account all relevant factors, including:

1. the nature of the right,
2. the importance of the purpose of the limitation,
3. the nature and extent of the limitation,
4. the relation between the limitation and its purpose, and
5. less restrictive means to achieve the purpose.

In other words, a general land reform law that either sets limits on land holdings, expropriates underutilised land or expropriates land for the explicit purpose of addressing past discrimination is consistent with these criteria.

Furthermore, past discrimination, like the fact that the Land Act excluded Africans from the land market, and the Group Areas Act prohibiting Africans, coloureds and Indians from accessing land outside designated urban areas, is quite separate from the restitution claims of those who had property taken from them. Expropriation of land to address both these criteria would clearly be justifiable in an open and democratic society based on human dignity, equality and freedom, taking into account all the relevant factors of s 36(1).

In fact, land reform has been undertaken in many democratic countries, and the issue of compensation, and especially how much, has often been legislated and limited to specific criteria, such as the value of 30 per cent of the harvest over five years in the case of agricultural land.[99] Finally, the question of an uncompensated expropriation is in so many ways a red herring since the amount of compensation could be minimal and be set by legislation that would pass constitutional muster. Nowhere in the Constitution is the policy of 'willing-buyer, willing seller' a requirement; that was a policy decision by the ANC government, and expropriating property for the purposes of land and water reform, even without compensation, is clearly protected by s 25(8) of the Constitution. To this degree, therefore, there is no need to decolonise the Constitution, but rather to decolonise the debate over expropriation.

Disclosure statement

No potential conflict of interest was reported by the author.

[99] J Putzel 'Land reforms in Asia: lessons from the past for the 21st century' (2000) LSE Development Studies Institute Working Paper 00-04 6. See also AJ Ledesma 'Land reform programs in East and Southeast Asia: a comparative approach' (1980) 28 *Philippine Studies* 305–343.

A decolonial critique of private law and human rights

Emile Zitzke

ABSTRACT

Two approaches to private-law scholarship are critiqued in this article. The first problematic approach identified is that of 'private-law purism' that aims to segregate so-called 'proper' dominant private law from everything else. In its classical form, private-law purism involved purifying South African private law (which is largely built on Roman-Dutch foundations) from English influences. In its contemporary form, private-law purism involves shielding dominant South African private law from human rights. The key issue with classical and contemporary purism illustrated in this article is that purism is built on a racist ideology that promotes epistemicide, originally brought about by conquest. The second potentially problematic approach identified is 'transformative private law' that aims to push private law in a more egalitarian direction through infiltrating the discipline with human rights. Although transformative private law is a significant rebellion against purism, the epistemic roots of human rights are perhaps as Western as dominant private law. Transformative private law thus has a neo-colonial flair. For that reason, a fusion of human rights with dominant private law will not necessarily result in a decolonial system of private law. Instead of the purist and transformative approaches to the study of private law, it is argued that Africanisation through conceptual decolonisation – a critical study of private law through African philosophy, not limited to the invocation of ideas with legal authority – could be one way of ensuring a more forceful response to the colonial problems of dominant private law and human rights.

1. Introduction

The private-law stalwart paging through the *Corpus Juris Civilis* of the Roman Emperor Justinian, the writings of the Roman-Dutch author Hugo de Groot, or the *Law Reports* of the South African Appellate Division will find no substantive encounters with the terms 'transformation', 'Africanisation' or 'decolonisation'. Since these authorities do not grapple with these terms, some private-law scholars might reason that these concepts are unimportant for our discipline because the traditional version of the legal-historical method does not require us to philosophise SA private law.[1] This article is an attempt to prove those private-law scholars wrong. I do this by comparing and contrasting different modes for the study of private law, namely (what I will call) the 'purist', 'transformative' and 'decolonial' approaches to private law.

In Part 2, I will delve into the approach of private-law purism. Though I argue that purism has had different manifestations in SA law over time, those are unified by a commitment to insulating the dominant rules and principles of private law (hereafter shortened as 'dominant private law'), sourced from the common law, from those influences that are regarded as not being private-law rules properly so called.[2] I will show that purism, as it has been conceptualised in SA private-law scholarship to date, is a normatively indefensible approach for the study of SA private law. Ultimately, I contend that purism is problematic because it has lent itself to the creation and maintenance of the spirit of conquest and apartheid in SA private-law scholarship, which is closed to the possibility of a continuous reimagination of what private law is and should be.

Secondly, in Part 3, I will consider the capability of a transformative approach for private law to protest the problems associated with purism. Transformation can have many different meanings and implications for different disciplines but, in the context of private law, the term has become associated with the core concern of allowing human rights and private law to collide in spectacular pragmatic splendour.[3] Even though transformative private law is a clear and imperative response to purism, I will argue that transformative private law is not and should not be the only oppositional stance to purism. I will reflect on and pose a challenge to the romanticised idea that human rights hold virtually unlimited potential for the reimagination of SA private law. The belief that I call to question here is that human rights are so alive with possibility that we need no other intellectual machinery to deconstruct and reconstruct private legal relationships.[4] Of course it is possible that some private-law scholars who take human rights seriously are fully cognisant of the limits of those rights and constitutionalism in general, but have, up to this point, not been forthright enough about this awareness. I would count myself to some extent guilty in this class of private lawyers.[5] So here is my overdue, transparent acknowledgement: I am opposed to

---

[1] See the critique levelled against insipid legal historical research by DP Visser 'The legal historian as subversive or: killing the Capitoline geese' in DP Visser (ed) *Essays on the History of Law* (1989) 19.

[2] For a broad overview of purism in SA law, see eg DH van Zyl *Geskiedenis van die Romeins-Hollandse Reg* (1979) 478–494.

[3] This is the general tenor of the major work of DM Davis & KE Klare 'Transformative constitutionalism and the common and customary law' (2010) 26 *South African Journal on Human Rights* 403.

[4] Davis & Klare's appraisal (ibid) is one of the most comprehensive SA essays on the interplay between human rights and private law, canvassing a great body of case law and academic scholarship in this regard. In their review of the literature, Davis & Klare critique (and evaluate the similar critiques levelled by many others against) the current models for human rights infiltration into private law for not doing enough to realise the constitutional promise of egalitarian social transformation. No mention is made of the potentially insurmountable limits of constitutionalism for true egalitarian change. In other words, the constitutionalisation of private law is the fundamental goal, nothing more, nothing less.

[5] See eg E Zitzke 'Stop the illusory nonsense! Teaching transformative delict' (2014) 46 *Acta Academica* 52. In this piece, I attempt to merge classical critical legal studies with the tenets of 'transformative constitutionalism' by using

the uncritical acceptance of the transformative conjugation of human rights and private law as the solution to all of private law's problems. In other words, transformation is by no means a perfect approach to the study of private law. If we want to approach private law radically differently and more critically than we have been doing, we would need to think beyond transformation.

One way of doing this, I argue in Part 4, is to work towards decolonising private law. The term decolonisation, as I use it here, refers to a commitment to 'Africanisation' through 'conceptual decolonisation'.[6] At the risk of oversimplification, I would briefly explain this project as the critical study of private-law concepts through African philosophy, not limited to the narrow study of the constitutionally recognised sources of private law. I by no means intend to suggest that I hold the monopoly over what decolonisation means or should mean. As an exploratory exercise, I am simply interested in thinking about how Africanisation through conceptual decolonisation targets the colonial problem of private law in a more disruptive manner than transformation. The approach that I propose here is a transitory preface to a much bigger task that lies ahead for those of us who are committed to levelling a decolonial critique against private law and human rights.

2. Private-law purism

2.1. The ideology of purism

As already noted, private-law purism is concerned with isolating dominant private law from everything that private-law scholars do not regard as proper private law. Dominant private law, as we know it in South Africa today, is said to be predominantly found in the source of law known as 'common law'. Common law, as first-year students are taught, is the uncodified source of SA law that has its roots in the writings of the prominent seventeenth-century Roman-Dutch authors, sometimes adapted by English law, ultimately developed by SA courts over time.[7] It is crucial to understand that when we speak about purism in private law, we are zooming in on dominant private law and not, for example, African customary private law.

In an earlier historical and political exploration on this issue, I argued that purism has taken on two forms in SA legal history.[8] In its classical form, purism involved cleansing the common law from English influences.[9] The idea was to keep common

---

examples from the law of delict. I surely created the impression here that I swore blind allegiance to the constitutional enthusiasm reflected in KE Klare 'Legal culture and transformative constitutionalism' (1998) 14 *South African Journal on Human Rights* 146. Later work built on that foundational piece include E Zitzke '*RH v DE* 2014 6 SA 436 (SCA): a case of anti-constitutional common-law development' (2015) 48 *De Jure* 467, E Zitzke 'Realist evolutionary functionalism and extra-constitutional grounds for developing the common law of delict: a critical analysis of *Heroldt v Wills* 2013 2 SA 530 (GSJ)' (2016) 79 *Journal for Contemporary Roman-Dutch Law* 103, and E Zitzke 'A brief note on the primacy of the Constitution in the common law's development: *DE v RH* [2015] ZACC 18 / 2015 (5) SA 83 (CC) / 2015 (9) BCLR 1003 (CC)' (2016) 31 *South African Public Law* 232. More recently in E Zitzke 'Constitutional heedlessness and over-excitement in the common law of delict's development' (2015) 7 *Constitutional Court Review* 259, I make a more explicit acknowledgement of the limits of human rights for the development of private-law rules, but nothing quite like I am about to endeavour in this piece.

[6] See eg K Wiredu 'Towards decolonizing African philosophy and religion' (1998) 1 *African Studies Quarterly* 17.

[7] See eg DG Kleyn & F Viljoen *Beginner's Guide for Law Students* 4 ed (2010) 82ff.

[8] E Zitzke 'The history and politics of contemporary common-law purism' (2017) 23 *Fundamina* 185.

law as Roman-Dutch as possible. The classical purist project rose to power during the same time that the National Party and Afrikaner supremacy did. The dual rise of power was no accident, and that classical purism (with its pro-Dutchness/ anti-Englishness) ideologically largely coincided with the Afrikaner supremacy plan of anti-Englishness that followed the South African War that pitted Afrikaners (mostly the descendants of the Dutch) against the English-speaking population in South Africa. Indeed, there is historical evidence to support the strong link between Afrikaner supremacy and classical purism (although, as with most things in law, there were exceptions to this general rule).[10] Purism in its classical form hardly excites the discerning private lawyer in South Africa today. Even by the 1970s classical purism was on its deathbed, in part because the movement was so successful, but also in part because of the rise of comparative law and the belief that Roman-Dutch law was largely in harmony with the European *ius commune* and could not be isolated in an airtight manner from the rest of European law.[11]

However, as classical purism was on its deathbed, a miracle happened in the 1980s, and purism was revived and given new verve.[12] It took on a contemporary form in terms of which the evil to be fought off would no longer be English law but human rights.[13] Pick up the journals of the guardians of Roman-Dutch law during the period in which democratisation in South Africa was imminent, and you will find various black-letter-law private lawyers turning into legal philosophers presenting arguments about why human rights had to be resisted in South Africa.[14] Preferably, for these scholars, human rights should not have been introduced in South Africa as a whole but, at the very least, it had to be repelled from the upright private common law. This was so because they argued, human rights would result in the flourishing of 'sodomy, Satanism, sex shops, suicide, scandalous textual interpretation, and an array of other "evils" not necessarily starting with the letter "s"'.[15] Comments about the 'backwardness' and 'savagery' of Africans also appear in this scholarship.[16] Peculiarly, no private-law scholar to wit responded to the reactionary politically conservative views expressed by their colleagues in the law journals during this time. Silence can, of course, constitute complicity. As Karin van Marle writes:

> [A]ll participants in legal scholarship, law and legal culture could be regarded as complicit to the past (apartheid and legal scholarship, law and legal culture under apartheid), present and future, and how this could be reflected on in legal education. Unless there is substantive, or even radical or revolutionary change or transformation this "this" will continue. "This" designates the way in which legal scholarship and legal education, law and legal culture affirm, confirm and re-affirm the *status quo*, keep things in their place, continue "business as usual". [17]

[9] Ibid 190.

---

[10] See eg M Chanock *The Making of South African Legal Culture, 1902-1936: Fear, Favour, and Prejudice* (2006) 159.
[11] Zitzke (note 8 above) 202.
[12] Ibid.
[13] Ibid 207.
[14] Ibid 208ff.
[15] Ibid 212.
[16] Ibid 213.
[17] K van Marle 'Reflections on legacy, complicity and legal education' (2014) 46 *Acta Academica* 196, 197 (footnotes omitted).

The alarming fact is that more than 20 years after the promulgation of the Constitution of the Republic of South Africa, 1996 the minority of big private-law works expressly commit themselves to breaking free from classical and contemporary purism. Substantively, most of the big private-law works are not devoted to heeding, from start to finish, the spiritual message of human rights and their role in the democratisation of all law in South Africa. Dennis Davis has recently written that the unthinking avoidance of human rights in SA private-law oeuvres has resulted in the cementing of a 'preservative' approach to private law.[18] Preservation, it would seem, is tantamount to purism. In the SA case of private law, preservation historically has gone hand in hand with conservative politics. Or as Lourens du Plessis so eloquently phrases it, 'right-wing reactionary *status quo* theology'.[19]

Given the fact that we have a history of Afrikaner supremacy and blatant racism in SA private-law scholarship, both express and complicit, there is an inference to be drawn about current private-law scholars who are silently abiding by contemporary purism without telling us the normative reasons for their concern. In other words, because there is a religious right-wing tradition in SA private law that rejects human rights, private-law scholars who intend to avoid being labelled as such should probably be explicit about why their (either unambiguous or wordless) denunciation of human rights in private law is different to that of the bigots. The failure to do so could be regarded as an unthinking complicity in the old-order tradition of private law.[20]

2.2. The deeper implications of purism

Our discussion about the roots of purism up to this point sketches the first reason why purism should be treated with some scepticism for the study of private law in South Africa today, and it relates to the ideology implicit in the movement. However, there is another, even deeper reason why purism should be rebuffed. That reason is somewhat less conspiratorial and strikes at the historical, political and epistemological significance of the source of law that purists venerate, namely common law. To recap, in the introduction to this discussion on purism, I indicated that dominant private law is derived from common law, which is based on European law. I will show in what follows that this European law – European private law in particular – has a synergetic relationship with conquest, and why this possesses dominant private law in South Africa today with a racist spirit (a claim that I will conclude to have proven at the end of this part of the article).

The main claim made here is that colonisation caused dominant private-law rules to flourish by annihilating, or in less severe cases, deforming African versions of law. We could call this the 'epistemicidal dimension' of private law in colonisation because the 'epistemology' (in other words, the knowledge systems, shown by 'epistemi-') of African people was 'killed' (shown by '-cide').

---

[18] See eg the recent critique of this stance by DM Davis 'Legal transformation and legal education: congruence of conflict?' (2015) *Acta Juridica* 172, 181ff.

[19] L du Plessis 'Enkele opmerkings oor die Christelike fundering (en verwerping) van menseregte' (1990) 53 *Journal for Contemporary Roman-Dutch Law* 403, 411–412.

[20] Zitzke (note 8 above) 219.

After taking physical, political, economic and social control over the territory today known as South Africa, the epistemicidal dimension of private law could start flourishing. In this regard, Mogobe Ramose says:

> By virtue of this questionable right [of conquest] the conqueror imposed unilaterally upon the conquered the meaning of experience, knowledge and truth. This was the inauguration of epistemicide in South Africa: the killing of the epistemology of the indigenous peoples. The latter's experience and the manner in which it was constructed into knowledge and truth was replaced by the epistemological paradigm of the conqueror. [21]

Dan Kuwali argues that at least one of the reasons for the destruction of African law during the colonial periods on the continent is that African law was seen as pagan nonsense that was incompatible with the religion of the colonisers.[22] It would not be unfair to highlight that missionaries did not only come with a belief in a new religion, but also a belief in their own cultural and intellectual superiority, which was a manifestation of racism. Colonisation is thus a 'veritable intellectual and spiritual holocaust from which the indigenous conquered peoples are yet to recover'.[23] A more detailed discussion of epistemicide in the context of law should be provided, and so in the remainder of this part I will explain how Dutch and English colonisation resulted in African (private) law being exterminated in some parts and modified in others, by European private law. A situation that we see persisting today.

Legal historians teach us that the Dutch afforded no respect to African law and completely ignored its existence while Roman-Dutch law was imposed on African people during the period of Dutch colonisation in the mid to late-1600s.[24] During the period of English colonisation of the Cape Colony (first in 1795 followed by intermittent Dutch control that was finally vanquished in 1806), limited recognition was afforded to African law, but it was subject to testing against English standards of justice, equity and fairness.[25] An English repugnancy clause applied to African law was bound to advance the project of European cultural and intellectual supremacy.[26] Under English rule, Dutch private law mostly remained unscathed with some English garnishing.[27] At no point was it accepted that, being in Africa, African law should predominate the legal system.[28] Conquest thus fuelled the flourishing of European private law on the African continent.

What is more, it was not only African *rules and principles* of private law that were destroyed and replaced by European versions in the process of colonisation. With the imposition of a legal system comes new ways of *reasoning* and different conceptions

---

[21] MB Ramose 'Transforming education in South Africa: paradigm shift or change?' (2003) 17 *South African Journal of Higher Education* 137, 138.

[22] D Kuwali 'Decoding Afrocentrism: decolonizing legal theory' in O Onazi (ed) *African Legal Theory and Contemporary Problems: Critical Essays* (2014) 71, 72.

[23] MR Ramose 'In memoriam: sovereignty and the "New" South Africa' (2007) 16 *Griffith Law Review* 310, 313.

[24] PHJ Thomas, CG van der Merwe & BC Stoop *Historical Foundations of South African Private Law* 2 ed (2000) 9; JC Bekker & C Rautenbach 'Nature and sphere of application of African customary law in South Africa' in C Rautenbach, JC Bekker & NMI Goolam (eds) *Introduction to Legal Pluralism* 3 ed (2010) 32–33.

[25] Thomas et al. (note 24 above) 9; Bekker & Rautenbach (note 24 above) 33.

[26] C Himonga & T Nhlapo (eds) *African Customary Law in South Africa: Post-Apartheid and Living Law Perspectives* (2014) 8.

[27] HR Hahlo & E Kahn *The South African Legal System and its Background* (1968) 575.

[28] Chanock (note 10 above) 243ff.

of *justice*. With English law came the positivist practice that law and justice should be kept separate in legal reasoning by practising lawyers and judges.[29] Dutch law came with abstract notions of 'patriarchal' justice built into rules and principles.[30] For example, the Dutch component of the law imposed on South Africa has ample references to the reasonable man, objectivity, rationality, an emphasis on rights and a general abhorrence towards the imposition of non-contractual duties on individuals to act positively. Some private lawyers would become bilious at the thought of subjectivity, emotion, a strong sense of duty, and the notion of care.[31] While I am mindful of the fact that there is no single voice speaking from the African continent, there are interesting gaps between central themes in African legal theory (broadly understood), the English legal method of positivism, and the Dutch notions of natural justice. For example, justice and law are inseparable concepts in leading accounts of African legal theory, unlike in some strands of English positivism.[32] Furthermore, African strands of normative jurisprudence often place a high value on relational justice and subjective duties or responsibility, while Roman-Dutch jurisprudence emphasises abstract and entitlement-based justice.[33] The abstract, entitlement-based theory of built-in corrective justice, coupled with the positivist legal analysis and discussion, still feature in various forms of private-law scholarship today.[34]

Later, the English colonial model was followed when the kingdom of the Zulu people was invaded in the 1800s,[35] while a Dutch purist model was followed in the Boer Republics (the settlements established by the descendants of Dutch settlers outside of the Cape Colony) around the same period.[36] Conflict between the Boers and the English ultimately caused the trek from the Cape, and conflict between them persisted thereafter, resulting in the South African War (1899–1902).[37] By the time that the English and the Boers made ostensible peace, to the exclusion of Africans of course, South Africa became a union in 1910. We can say with confidence that there was very little unity in the Union because tensions between the Boers and the English were still high, and black people were still excluded from meaningful political participation with their laws still being disrespected.[38] An amalgamated private law, made up of Dutch and English law, would become known as common law.[39] Common law constituted the dominant, uncodified rules of private law. The term common law is problematic because there is really nothing common about it – it is, for all intents

---

[29] A van Blerk *Jurisprudence: An Introduction* (1998) 27.

[30] I use the expression 'masculine' justice in the critical spirit of feminist practical reasoning. See eg H Barnett *Introduction to Feminist Jurisprudence* (1998) 23ff

[31] See especially J Neethling & JM Potgieter *Neethling-Potgieter-Visser Law of Delict* (2015) 142, 158.

[32] FU Okafor 'Legal positivism and the African legal tradition' (1984) 24 *International Philosophical Quarterly* 157, 162; O Taiwo 'Legal positivism and the African legal tradition: a reply' (1985) 25 *International Philosophical Quarterly* 197, 199; W Idowu "Positivists' separability thesis reconsidered: perspectives from African legal theory' (2008) 33 *Journal for Juridical Sciences* 163.

[33] M Edet & S Segun 'The natural law theory in traditional African jurisprudential thought' (2014) 26 *Journal of Law, Policy, and Globalization* 44, 52.

[34] See eg the overview provided by Davis (note 18 above) 181ff.

[35] Thomas et al. (note 24 above) 99.

[36] Ibid 102–104.

[37] See eg L Thompson *A History of South Africa: From the Earliest Known Human Inhabitation to the Present* (2014) 132ff.

[38] Bekker & Rautenbach (note 24 above) 33–34; Himonga & Nhlapo (note 26 above) 9ff.

[39] Hahlo & Kahn (note 27 above) 578.

and purposes, European customary law.[40] For the sake of convention, clarity and coherence in this article, I will continue to refer to it as common law, unless if the context of the argument requires otherwise.

As explained above, some Afrikaner private lawyers were adamant that private common law had to be purified of English influences.[41] However, there were English scholars who fought for a supportive relationship between the Roman-Dutch and English law, and later English liberals fought to rename 'common law' as 'South African law'.[42] The English liberal argument was that the old Roman-Dutch-English rules had been developed by SA courts for South Africans, and the result was a new body of law that deserved a new label. Even though we can agree that the content of the rules had changed since the time of the old Dutch writers and the laws of England, those changes were not out of step with European legal developments at large. Comparative legal studies flourished, and so all that actually happened was that European customary law in South Africa was updated to meet the needs of a European colony, mimicking the laws of Europe where a *ius commune* was said to exist. Indeed, private common law might not have carried the label 'Roman-Dutch-English law' in the strict sense, but it was European customary law nonetheless. It was European law applied and developed by Europeans, for Europeans in a European society.[43] As André van der Walt has argued, the common law related to property was eventually strategically used by the apartheid government in implementing its policies, and sometimes common law was further polluted by apartheid legislation.[44] Apartheid was categorically made possible with the generous cooperation of a series of constitutions that contained no bills of rights or conferrals of testing rights onto the courts.[45] As we might expect, African customary law was once again left in the dark during this phase in SA history.[46] Every time that African law was overlooked, it was disrespected, and so the epistemicidal project of colonisation continued.

We must acknowledge that there were some scholars in apartheid South Africa who attempted to use seemingly subversive provisions of common law in strategic ways to fight the apartheid system.[47] Far from committed to purism, these scholars endeavoured to use whatever source of law was available to undermine apartheid. However, their attempts were largely unsuccessful in the face of a tyrannical government that owned large segments of the courts filled with nationalist confederates.[48] It

---

40 That 'common law' is actually 'customary law' is a point made by A Cromartie 'The idea of common law as custom' in A Perreau-Saussine & JB Murphy (eds) *The Nature of Customary Law: Legal, Historical and Philosophical Perspectives* (2007) 203.

41 Zitzke (note 8 above) 193.

42 Ibid.

43 Chanock (note 10 above) 33.

44 See eg AJ van der Walt 'Reflections on teaching property law in future' (1993) 4 *Stellenbosch Law Review* 88, 92–96.

45 The injustice of this state of affairs is powerfully portrayed in the cases of *Harris v Minister of the Interior* 1952 (2) SA 428 (A); *Minister of the Interior v Harris* 1952 (4) SA 769 (A) and *Collins v Minister of the Interior* 1957 (1) SA 552 (A).

46 GJ van Niekerk 'Legal pluralism' in C Rautenbach, JC Bekker & NMI Goolam (eds) *Introduction to Legal Pluralism* 3 ed (2010) 4–6; Himonga & Nhlapo (note 26 above) 13ff.

47 See eg J Dugard 'The judicial process, positivism and civil liberty' (1971) 88 *South African Law Journal* 181, 197; to some extent also E Mureinik 'Dworkin and apartheid' in H Corder (ed) *Essays on Law and Social Practice in South Africa* (1988) 181.

48 Zitzke (note 8 above) 195–198.

should also be noted that the concern of these near-seditious lawyers was not to undo the effects of colonisation per se but to undo the immediate rights infringements of apartheid. Due to the unsuccessful attempts at using common law in anti-apartheid ways, some scholars in due course turned to the invocation of human rights as a new and independent tool for destabilising apartheid laws.[49] This does not, however, cure the common law of its colonial problem.

Throughout this discussion I have alluded to the fact that dominant private law has been allowed to thrive in the way that it has because of certain beliefs in European intellectual and cultural superiority. This exercise has thus been aimed at identifying the supremacy of dominant private law over African private law as racist. Joel Modiri teaches us that racism, as understood in critical race theory, does not simply relate to patent expressions of hatred based on race.[50] We can also identify systems as being racist in that they uphold white power.[51] As I have attempted to show, dominant private law in a material sense is guilty of the latter type of racism in that it upholds a white system of epistemic power and serves to deny black conceptualisations of the world as legitimate.[52] Modiri overtly identifies the prominence of dominant private law as part of structurally embedded racism in SA law.[53]

Against this backdrop, the question now becomes what we as private-law scholars should do to respond to the racism that lies beneath the surface of private law.

3. Transformative private law

3.1. What is transformative private law?

As indicated in the preceding part, many SA private-law scholars were not quite bubbling with excitement about the possible implications of human rights for the disruption of their discipline. Despite the initial forceful resistance against the infiltration of human rights into private law, as this section will show, the Constitution and its justiciable human rights did bring about significant changes to dominant private law through the courts. The impact that human rights could have on dominant private law is transformative in nature and does, in large part, pose a challenge to the purist approach to private law explained above. This discussion on transformative private law will focus on addressing what transformative private law is, why transformative private law can be regarded as a significant step away from purism, and finally why we could argue that the principal shortcoming of transformative private law relates to its failure to radically disrupt the problems attached to purism.

In my view, transformative private law relates to the study of private law through Karl Klare's understanding of transformative constitutionalism. For Klare, transformative constitutionalism is a long-term project of working with the Constitution in

[49] See eg J Dugard *Human Rights and the South African Legal Order* (1978).
[50] J M Modiri 'The colour of law, power and knowledge: introducing critical race theory in (post-)apartheid South Africa' (2012) 48 *South African Journal on Human Rights* 405, 406.
[51] Ibid 407.
[52] Ibid 408.
[53] Ibid 419.

various ways to bring about a more equal and participatorily democratic society by breaking free from apartheid politics and other power relations.[54] Klare is quite clear about the fact that transformation does more than preservation (applied to our context, purism) and reform (what I would regard as slow legislative changes to law), but nevertheless falls short of being a revolutionary (I will argue, decolonial) understanding of law.[55] It therefore fills a liminal space on the political spectrum. In the thought of Klare, we can only realise constitutional transformation if we, firstly, understand that the substantive provisions of the Constitution are 'postliberal' (or as other have suggested, 'egalitarian liberal') in nature,[56] and secondly, understand that the substantive postliberal provisions can best be brought to fruition through a postliberal reading strategy or method of constitutional interpretation that would aim to infiltrate the substantive constitutional provisions into all other areas of law.[57] This led Davis (pairing up with Klare) to conclude that a transformative legal methodology is:

> an approach to legal problems informed by the values and aspirations of the Bill of Rights and specifically by the constitutional aspiration to lay the legal foundations of a just, democratic, and egalitarian social order. Transformative legal methodology brings these values to bear on a context-sensitive view of the case seen in the light of all pertinent ethical and socio-economic considerations, as best these can be determined. Transformative methodology is attentive to the values of stability, predictability, and administrability. At the same time, the solutions it generates are not eternal; its results are always understood to be 'provisional', that is, as always being open to reconsideration and contestation as experience progresses, understanding deepens, and/or circumstances change.[58]

Davis and Klare argue that s 39(2) of the Constitution, mandating courts to promote the 'spirit, purport and objects of the Bill of Rights' when interpreting legislation or developing the common (and customary) law, is relevant to every private-law dispute because law is always being interpreted or developed. Others, like Stu Woolman, working in the same tradition of transformative private law, have called for a greater reliance on s 8 of the Constitution to ensure the development of a robust constitutional-rights infiltration into private law and not simply the invocation of the indeterminate and manipulable notion of the spirit of SA human rights.[59] In more recent times, Deeksha Bhana has called for an integrated reading of s 39(2) and s 8 where the two provisions operate symbiotically instead of co-destructively.[60] Their technical interpretative differences aside, transformative private lawyers ultimately share a commitment to the constitutionalisation of private law as a legitimate and desirable goal.

---

[54] Klare (note 5 above) 150.
[55] Ibid.
[56] Ibid 151ff.
[57] Ibid 156ff.
[58] Davis & Klare (note 3 above) 412.
[59] S Woolman 'The amazing, vanishing Bill of Rights' (2007) 124 *South African Law Journal* 762.
[60] D Bhana 'The horizontal application of the Bill of Rights: a reconciliation of sections 8 and 39 of the Constitution' (2013) 29 *South African Journal on Human Rights* 351.

3.2. Why is transformative private law a significant response to purism?

The core belief of transformative private lawyers in the infiltration of human rights enshrined in the Constitution into private law stands in clear opposition to the contemporary purist tradition, which is rooted in human-rights avoidance in private-law matters. Human-rights avoidance in private law is undesirable because it ultimately gives the green light to private-law purism in its contemporary form and fails to acknowledge the ideological and epistemic problems underlying dominant private law.

Human-rights avoidance in dominant private law furthermore fails to respect the fact that the African human-rights system created by the African Charter on Human and Peoples Rights (1981, hereafter 'the African Charter') places human-rights obligations on non-state actors.[61] In other words, human rights are meant to invade what we have traditionally understood as the 'private' sphere, and we should embrace this if we are to take the African version of human rights seriously.[62] Furthermore, human-rights avoidance in dominant private law would fail to give effect to the single-system-of-law principle laid down by the Constitutional Court in *Pharmaceutical Manufacturers*,[63] which provides that all law in South Africa derives its force from the Constitution and must be compliant with the human-rights ethos brought about by the democratic order.[64] Finally, human-rights avoidance in dominant private law would stifle the critical project of deconstructing private law and reconstructing it along more egalitarian lines.[65] If the Constitution and its human rights are supposed to bring about a more equal social order, one of the key places where this must happen is in the realm of interactions between non-state actors, traditionally thought of as being regulated by the kingdom of private law.[66] Private lawyers could certainly do deconstruction and reconstruction without the Constitution, but invoking a legal document adds some legal weight to the exercise, and so it comes as no surprise that critical legal scholars in South Africa have sometimes opted for doing trashing through human rights.

Against this backdrop, private-law scholars who have taken human rights seriously in their writings have often done some disruptive work, challenging the politically conservative and legally preservative *status quo*, being mocked in unadventurous faculty corridors for being unintelligent lefties and children of the devil. I by no means want to be understood as belittling the transformative project in private law. With that said, it is not my view that we should teach transformative private law uncritically as the beginning and end. If it is true that transformative constitutionalism is

---

[61] See Zitzke 2017 (note 8 above) 265ff.

[62] J Cobbah 'African values and the human rights debate: an African perspective' (1987) 9 *Human Rights Quarterly* 309; M Mutua 'The Banjul Charter and the African cultural fingerprint: an evaluation of the language of duties' (1995) 35 *Virginia Journal of International Law* 339; D Chirwa 'In search of philosophical justifications and suitable models for the horizontal application of human rights' (2008) 8 *African Human Rights Law Journal* 294.

[63] *Pharmaceutical Manufacturers Association of South Africa: In re Ex Parte President of the Republic of South Africa* 2000 (2) SA 674 (CC) para 44.

[64] See Zitzke 2017 (note 8 above) 267ff.

[65] Ibid 266ff.

[66] On the collapse of the public/private divide in this regard, see eg A Cockrell 'Private law and the Bill of Rights: a threshold issue of "horizontality"' in *Bill of Rights Compendium* (1996) 32A.

based, at least in part, on a method of critique from the left,[67] we must be open to being critical of this paradigm itself. This is so because, even though transformative private-law work has been somewhat disruptive, human-rights proponents in private law cannot claim to have the monopoly over private-law critique. By this, I mean that there are other possibilities beyond human rights that could be explored. As indicated above, Klare's project is openly non-revolutionary. It is because of Klare's pragmatism that I have argued that transformative private law would not support the wholesale relegation of established private law in favour of a pure application of human rights – 'constitutional over-excitement' of this kind is as untransformative as human-rights avoidance in private law because it aims to throw everything out and replace it with a new hegemonic discourse.[68] Even though human rights hold some deconstructive potential for private law, it requires us to use the deconstructed rubble of private law to build something new, using new, constitutionally inspired, cement.

Therefore, the way that I would describe transformative private law is as an ideological model of egalitarian liberal (sometimes social democratic) midway pragmatism that nevertheless holds onto some aspects of the academic-rockstar tradition of 1970s critical legal studies (for example a false-consciousness inspired rejection of the 'normality' of everything we have been taught about private law as unchangeable or immutable).[69] For this reason, I would suggest that transformative private law is fully cognisant of its own limits. To be clear, one of its main limits is the fact that it is not a radical method for the critique of private law, in the sense that transformative private law requires us to evaluate one set of legal rules against another. A truly radical approach to critique, in my view, would involve breaking free from the shackles of using formally recognised law to evaluate the same. Indeed, a radical approach to private law might involve drawing on intellectual resources beyond formal law.

3.3. *Why is transformative private law not a decolonial option?*

Van Marle, writing from a position of leftist scepticism about the possibilities of law in (post-)apartheid South Africa, observes that:

> [T]here is a danger that law, monumental constitutionalism and human rights embody another spectacle, one that could yet again take over the South African imagination to the detriment of the ordinary, the way people actually live and, more pertinently, the complexities of life.[70]

> Law and legal projects as a form of social engineering, whether in civil law, human rights and constitutional law, including possibly also Klare's project of transformative constitutionalism, holds the danger of ignoring or evading the disturbance or discomfort and accepting too quickly or too easily legal "solutions" that bring false comfort and complacency.[71]

---

67 K van Marle 'Transformative constitutionalism as/and critique' (2009) 20 *Stellenbosch Law Review* 286.
68 See Zitzke 2017 (note 8 above) 279ff.
69 See eg J van Doren 'Critical legal studies and South Africa' (1989) 106 *South African Law Journal* 648, 658 & 660ff; A van Blerk 'Critical legal studies in South Africa' (1996) 113 *South African Law Journal* 86, 103ff.
70 K van Marle 'The spectacle of post-apartheid constitutionalism' (2007) 16 *Griffith Law Review* 411.
71 Van Marle (note 17 above) 208.

In short, human rights in (post-)apartheid South Africa could quite easily displace and step into the hegemonic role of common law in the study of private law. Thus, the credulous acceptance of human rights as a game-changer in private law ought to be rejected. In support of Van Marle, the argument that I will present here is that human rights, as embodied in the Constitution, could have certain neo-colonial effects that do not radically disturb or disrupt dominant private law. Neo-colonialism features when independence is achieved on paper while certain 'superpowers' still exercise control over the 'independent' state, and so the colonial order is maintained.[72] When we merge colonial law (in other words common law) with neo-colonial law (here, taking on the form of human rights), we will be left with creole-colonial law and not a decolonial option.

Human rights could be regarded as an example of a legal mechanism through which neo-colonialism takes place. Balakrishnan Rajagopal, a prominent proponent of 'third world approaches to international law' (TWAIL), is ultimately optimistic about the potential of human rights but explains that human rights have formed a part of hegemonic international law that has been used to justify unjust wars.[73] For example, the United States has targeted the Middle East by wearing the faux moral garb of the civiliser who will save the 'natives' from themselves by protecting their human rights and giving them democracy.[74] The US presence and control over the Middle East, and the invocation of human rights as justification for it, has neo-colonial verve. What I am interested in doing here is drawing on this identification of human rights as potentially neo-colonial and deliberating on its implications for the private-law/human-rights interface. My argument is that human rights can be said to have neo-colonial flair, specifically as it features in dominant private-law jurisprudence today, for at least three reasons.

Firstly, we must identify the shared roots of human rights and dominant private law in South Africa. The dominant private law is said to be firmly rooted in the natural-law tradition.[75] Much of the dominant private-law discourse revolves around talk about subjective rights. Wessel le Roux teaches that the centrality of rights in private law stems from the thought of Roman-Dutch natural lawyer Hugo de Groot, who conceptualised ownership as a 'subjective power' and 'absolute right' that a person exercises over property.[76] Effectively De Groot laid the foundations for private law to become fixated on 'subjective rights' that we define today as those rights that legal subjects have over legal objects of various kinds that can be enforced against other legal subjects: there are real rights to property, immaterial property rights to intellectual property, personality rights to aspects of human personality (including dignity, bodily and psychological integrity, privacy, spiritual-moral feelings, and reputation), personal rights to performance, and personal immaterial property rights to unique

---

[72] L le Grange 'Decolonising the University Curriculum' (2016) 30 *South African Journal of Higher Education* 1, 4.

[73] B Rajagopal 'Counter-Hegemonic International Law: Rethinking Human Rights and Development as Third World Strategy' (2006) 27 *Third World Quarterly* 767.

[74] Ibid 773.

[75] See eg D Kleyn & G van Niekerk 'Ulpian's praecepta iuris and their role in South African law part 1: historical context' (2014) 20 *Fundamina* 437, 443–445; D Kleyn & G van Niekerk 'Ulpian's praecepta iuris and their role in South African law part 2: modern-day South African practice' (2014) 20 *Fundamina* 446.

[76] WB le Roux 'Natural law theories' in C Roederer & D Moellendorf (eds) *Jurisprudence* (2004) 40.

abilities and characteristics (for example earning capacity and credit worthiness).[77] These rights are not completely different to human rights as we know them today. Le Roux draws our attention to the fact that John Locke's theory of inalienable natural rights, which many accept as the foundation of human rights, stemmed from a combination of natural law and subjective rights.[78] Infusing human rights into private law (bursting with subjective rights) is thus an updating exercise of a potentially outdated understanding of individualistic natural law. The two parts of law are thus theoretically compatible.[79] In this sense, human rights can be said to form a theoretical continuance of traditional private law and the colonial order, even though human rights may sometimes be capable of transforming the tradition.[80]

The ardent supporter of the African human-rights system could object to this first reason proffered as to why human rights could have neo-colonial effects. They would be quick to emphasise that the African human rights system 'demonstrates a concern for the values of "cooperation, interdependence and collective responsibility" as opposed to the individualistic ring to dominant Western notions of human dignity' and upholds 'a spirit of solidarity, generosity, unity and cohesion'.[81] Thus, the argument would go, African human rights have broken free from the clutches of the West. Of course, these values that are said to pervade the African human-rights system are important indices that the drafters of the African Charter considered African values in executing their task. We could even argue that the African understanding of human rights is compatible with African philosophy in various ways.[82] Be that as it may, it would not be ill-judged to say that the SA Bill of Rights and the African Charter effectively embrace egalitarian liberalism with the sparkle of African values. Undeniably, it is a step closer to incorporating African thought into law that is predominantly European in substance and form but it is by no means a blanket codification of African jurisprudence into positive law. It is not trivial that we have 'bills of rights' and not 'bills of duties' throughout Africa. Thus, the African human-rights paradigm uses the notion of human rights (a specific term developed in Europe as a universal, hegemonic, and dominant discourse) and spruces it up with tiny bits of homegrown flavour to create an ambience conducive to acceptability to the masses.

The second reason why human rights can be said to have neo-colonial effects is because our prime instrument of human rights in South Africa still subordinates African customary law to common law and the supreme Constitution itself. In the discussion of purism above, we have shown how African law has been subordinated to Western laws through structural racism since conquest. This position has clearly not deeply been unsettled. The Constitution does enjoin us to take African customary law more seriously than before, but the Constitution itself fails to give African law the necessary prominence that it deserves. Following the Constitution's s 8, the automatically applicable source of law in South Africa, in the absence of legislation, is

---

[77] An excellent account of the doctrine of subjective rights is found in Neethling & Potgieter (note 31 above) 51ff.
[78] Le Roux (note 76 above) 43.
[79] Zitzke 2017 (note 8 above) 261.
[80] Van Marle (note 17 above) 211.
[81] Zitzke 2017 (note 8 above) 266 (footnotes omitted).
[82] T Metz 'African values, human rights and group rights: a philosophical foundation for the Banjul Charter' in O Onazi (ed) *African Legal Theory and Contemporary Problems: Critical Essays* (2014) 131.

common law. African customary law is conspicuously missing from this section. It is as if African law is regarded as being incapable of giving effect to constitutional rights. While some might regard this as an unfortunate oversight, I would regard this as a microaggression that is in harmony with how private-law modules are sometimes taught at SA law faculties where there is *one* separate module for African private law and *multiple* private-law modules based on common law and legislation to the exclusion of African law. We are told, in a different chapter in the Constitution, in s 211(3) that a court must apply African customary law if it is applicable, subject to the Constitution and legislated African customary law. The separation of African customary law from common law and Western-style legislation in the constitutional design is not insignificant. Conquest and apartheid had the core concern of keeping black and white categorically separated in every sense.[83] This attitude persists in our approach to legal sources in South Africa today. It is not only how we teach private law that subordinates African law – it is also the law reflected in the constitutional design that is problematic. The legal position is that people must opt into the African customary law regime if they want it to apply, and even if it is applied, it is subject to constitutional scrutiny and review.[84]

Some may argue that the fact that African customary law does not constitute the default rules of SA private law is quite acceptable. African customary law as recorded on paper, they would argue, is not a true reflection of African rules and principles due to the fact that some white anthropologists have molested African law to conform to a European taxonomy, and so 'official' versions of customary law are often outdated compared to 'living customary law'[85] that is actually practised in African communities. I simultaneously recognise that African law itself might need some delinking from the thought of the coloniser missionaries that instilled commitments to patriarchy, homophobia and heteronormativity in African communities.[86] For this reason, we will see in the next part that the delinking of dominant private law from conquest will probably not happen through teaching formally recorded African law parallel to Western law. At a minimum, the spirit of justice present in African law and legal theory could and should play an important role in how SA law is continuously reconceptualised. For this to be done successfully we might have to rely on African philosophy more than we do on African law as recorded in the textbooks on customary law. Yet, the Constitution does not make provision for African law to take its rightful place, nor does it mandate a study of law through African philosophy. Instead, the Constitution maintains that Western law is the automatically applicable law of the land.

Thirdly, human rights have neo-colonial flair because of their coinciding legal reasoning. A promising aspect of the constitutional order is that human rights have

---

83 See eg H Botha 'Metaphoric reasoning and transformative constitutionalism (part 1)' (2002) *Journal of South African Law* 612.

84 Bekker & Rautenbach (note 24 above) 34ff.

85 Ibid 28. Also see C Himonga 'The Future of Living Customary Law in African Legal Systems in the Twenty-First Century and Beyond, with Special Reference to South Africa' in J Fenrich, P Galizzi & TE Higgins (ed.) *The Future of African Customary Law* (2011) 31.

86 See eg S Tamale 'Exploring the Contours of African Sexualities: Religion, Law and Power' (2014) 14 *African Human Rights Law Journal* 150, 155ff.

created a space where a complete rejection of the natural-law tradition can no longer be at the order of the day. A specific brand of natural law, the intermingling of law and liberal justice, has become prominent in the Constitutional Court's jurisprudence.[87] However, the interpretation of human rights in private law is often subject to how the West has understood the relationship between private-law rules and constitutional rights. For example, we read early delict cases in the Constitutional Court of *Carmichele v Minister of Safety and Security*[88] and *K v Minister of Safety and Security*[89], and we are delighted to see how state-sanctioned violence against women is decisively reproached. But, in the Court's reasoning we do not find reference to African theories of good governance or African understandings of and responses to the operation of patriarchy and sexual violence. Instead, we find deep engagements with how English, German, Canadian, and United States courts have blended human rights and private law. Although family lawyers had many gripes with *Minister of Home Affairs v Fourie,*[90] we tend to agree that it is great that same-sex couples can now get married. In that judgment, and succession cases such as *Gory v Kolver NO*[91] and *Laubscher NO v Du Plan*[92] (that also relate to the progressively expanding notion of a 'family'), we might find references to legal philosophers and court decisions that are epistemically Western relating to the right to equality and how it should play out in private law, but in all those cases no mention is made to African episteme or court decisions. To be clear, this is more a critique of the Constitution itself rather than of the Constitutional Court - there is nothing in the Constitution that demands that human rights be interpreted through African philosophy or with a commitment to comparative African law.[93] If we turn to more recent private-law cases in the Constitutional Court, the same trend of Western simulation appears (although I am cognisant that reference is now sometimes made to comparative African law, but those references are hardly ever authoritatively adopted into SA law).[94] A lack of cooperation on promoting accessibility of legal information on the African continent is a major challenge to the realisation of stronger Africanist comparative law.[95] However, even comparative constitutional law on the continent does not necessarily aid the process of breaking free from Western mimicry in legal thought. Many other African jurisdictions also rely on Western conceptions of rights and constitutional interpretation, and so our comparison with other African courts might lead to indirect Westernisation. Furthermore, sometimes other African countries are still struggling with the colonial hangover to the extent that conservative religious morality (imposed by the conquerors on the First Nation peoples) still influences judicial interpretation of human rights.[96] In those cases, African law must still be delinked from

---

[87] Zitzke 2017 (note 8 above) 264.

[88] *Carmichele v Minister of Safety and Security (Centre for Applied Legal Studies Intervening)* 2001 (4) SA 938 (CC).

[89] *K v Minister of Safety and Security* 2005 (6) SA 419 (CC).

[90] *Minister of Home Affairs v Fourie (Doctors for Life International and Others, Amici Curiae); Lesbian and Gay Equality Project v Minister of Home Affairs* 2006 (1) SA 524 (CC).

[91] *Gory v Kolver NO (Starke and Others Intervening)* 2007 (4) SA 97 (CC).

[92] *Laubscher NO v Du Plan* 2017 (2) SA 264 (CC).

[93] The Constitutional Court's approach to constitutional interpretation is excellently explained by L du Plessis 'Interpretation' in S Woolman & M Bishop (eds) *Constitutional Law of South Africa* 2 ed (2008) 32–1, 32–159.

[94] See eg *H v Fetal Assessment Centre* 2015 (2) SA 193 (CC); *DE v RH* 2015 (5) SA 83 (CC).

[95] Zitzke 2016 (note 5 above).

[96] See eg Tamale (note 86 above).

the epistemic injustice of conquest. To address the long-lasting effects of conquest on law on the continent and the need for a rediscovery of African epistemology, the next part will demonstrate that African philosophy could be a useful tool in this regard.

Before we get there, it is at this point that many rainbow-nation lawyers will jump up and ask, 'What about Ubuntu?' Legal Ubuntu featured as a feel-good afterthought in the epilogue of the 1993 Constitution to ensure that there would be blanket for-give-and-forgetfulness regarding the injustices of colonisation and apartheid. Reference to legal Ubuntu is evidently missing from the text of the 1996 Constitution even though, as a legal principle, it theoretically still forms part of our law. For the most part, legal Ubuntu has been used in our courts as a tool of public law, for example, to promote the aims of the Truth and Reconciliation Commission, abolish capital punishment, and infuse illusions of hope in socioeconomic-rights jurisprudence.[97] In the context of the dominant rules of private law, legal Ubuntu has had less substantial effects. Those with the urge to remind me about Mokgoro J's judgment in *Dikoko v Mokhatla*,[98] in which she held that the quantum of damages claimed in defamation cases should be moderate in light of a spirit of reconciliation facilitated by legal Ubuntu, will do well to remember that the relevant paragraphs relating to legal Ubuntu constitutes a dissenting judgment. In other words, it is 'soft law'; puzzlingly, 'not binding but persuasive authority'.[99]

With the best intentions, Davis and Klare encourage us to take legal Ubuntu more seriously in the development of private law to push private law in a more egalitarian and altruistic direction.[100] However, hark the warning of Ramose: legal Ubuntu through the Constitution is not the same as the African philosophical concept of Ubuntu.[101] Ramose has repeatedly said that there can be no Ubuntu while African sovereignty still hangs in the balance. For example, Africans are not the supreme democratic authority, but an inanimate document is.[102] True restitution of land has not taken place, making reconciliation impossible – which is why any enthusiasm about the role of legal Ubuntu in *PE Municipality v Various Occupiers*[103] is largely tenuous. Furthermore, the onto-triadic conception of be-ing (the notion that there are three interrelated dimensions of be-ing, namely the unborn, the living and the living-dead) is not properly respected in SA law.[104] A version of Ubuntu that does not recognise these dimensions to the concept gives an inaccurate portrayal of what Ubuntu has meant and does mean, and so mocks and distorts African epistemology by saying that African ideas are acceptable only insofar as they can be reconciled with the Western conception of law. What we end up with when we merge legal Ubuntu with dominant private law is

[97] For an overview of the cases see D Cornell & N Muvangua (eds) *Ubuntu and the Law: African Ideals and Post-Apartheid Jurisprudence* (2012) 31ff.

[98] *Dikoko v Mokhatla* 2006 (6) SA 235 (CC).

[99] J Barnard-Naudé 'Adjudication, interpretation and dispute resolution' in T Humby, L Kotzé & A du Plessis (eds) *Introduction to Law and Legal Skills in South Africa* (2012) 202.

[100] Davis & Klare (note 3 above) 411.

[101] A great synopsis of these arguments is made in MB Ramose 'An African perspective on justice and race' (2001) *polylog* <https://them.polylog.org/3/frm-en.htm>

[102] Ramose (note 21 above).

[103] *Port Elizabeth Municipality v Various Occupiers* 2005 (1) SA 217 (CC).

[104] MB Ramose 'Ubuntu: affirming a right and seeking remedies in South Africa' in L Praeg & S Magadla (eds) *Ubuntu: Curating the Archive* (2014) 121.

a 'functional convergence' of two legal traditions.[105] It creates creole-colonial law – a transformation and not a true mutiny against Eurocentrism. Ramose goes as far as to declare that the way in which Ubuntu is used (and not used) in SA law perpetuates epistemicide.[106]

To conclude the discussion on transformative private law, I make the following synoptic remarks. Transformative private law has played a significant role in rethinking some aspects of the conservative and preservative private-law tradition. However, transformative constitutionalism's roots in liberalism have not been all that effective in dealing with structural inequality.[107] The specific type of structural inequality that we are talking about here is epistemic inequality, built on racist assumptions that have not been materially dismantled in democratic SA. This is why critical race theory would distrust a transformative approach to private law.[108] Transformative private law has neo-colonial flair because it simply requires a marriage of two conceptions of law rooted in the West, does not restore African law to its deserved homegrown eminence and requires us to be internationally fashionable in our understanding of law. The Constitution's text and practice quite simply does not mandate a true political and epistemological decolonisation of dominant SA law. At most, what it gives us is creole-colonial law. My suggestions for the decolonisation of dominant SA private law follow in the next part.

4. Towards 'decolonial' private law?

The purist and transformative approaches to private-law scholarship have a one-up on the decolonial approach that I am about to investigate. That is, the purist and transformative approaches carry some legal authority. Just like the *Corpus Juris* and De Groot do not mention transformation, Africanisation or decolonisation, the Constitution also does not in any way commit itself to Africanisation or decolonisation. In the introduction of this article, I indicated that the decolonisation of private law, as I understand the idea, could involve Africanisation through conceptual decolonisation. In what follows, I will explore what this might mean by firstly explaining what Africanisation entails and then why Africanisation is possibly most defensibly achieved through conceptual decolonisation.

In simple terms, for the purposes of academic enquiry, Africanisation means placing African thought central to a study of a particular discipline in order for that discipline to be contextually sensitive to Africa and the 'characteristics, experiences, practices, beliefs, values and ways of life' of its 'autochthonous black peoples to the south of the Sahara desert', usually with reference to knowledge produced by African people.[109] This description is easier written than practised. Firstly, one could object

[105] GJ van Niekerk '*Amende honorable* and *ubuntu*: an intersection of *ars boni et aequi* in African and Roman-Dutch jurisprudence?' (2013) 9 *Fundamina* 397, 412.

[106] Ramose (note 21 above) 139.

[107] A point made in the context of poverty by S Sibanda 'Not purpose made! Transformative constitutionalism, post-independence constitutionalism and the struggle to eradicate poverty' (2011) 22 *Stellenbosch Law Review* 482.

[108] Modiri (note 50 above) 415.

[109] See eg E Etieyibo 'Why ought the philosophy curriculum in universities in Africa be Africanised? (2016) 35 *South African Journal of Philosophy* 404, 405; M Chemhuru 'Pursuing the agenda of Africanising philosophy in Africa: some possibilities' (2016) 35 *South African Journal of Philosophy* 418, 419; J Mweshi 'On Africanising the

and say that the name 'Africa' is a European construct and therefore 'Africanisation' should not be the term that we use to think about rediscovering homegrown knowledge.[110] Perhaps I can say, like Ramose, that I use the words Africa and Africanisation for the sake of convention without pledging allegiance to the word and its ideological commitments.[111] Secondly, African knowledge has in many cases been obliterated, supplemented or otherwise entangled with the knowledge systems of the conquerors through the process of colonisation, and thus it is difficult to rediscover a true or pure form of African knowledge.[112] Thirdly, we cannot pretend as if Africa speaks with a unified voice.[113] There is not one African reality. There are many African realities. Therefore, within one African region, we may find great disagreement on the identification of and approach to a single problem. If something like SA philosophy exists, it can look very different to Nigerian or Kenyan philosophy. Within South Africa, Zulu philosophy does not necessarily equate to Sotho philosophy. Among Zulu philosophers, different perspectives on similar issues are inevitable. The same is, of course, true about the plurality of ideas coming from the West and the East.[114]

One way of coping with some of the challenges of Africanisation that I have just outlined could be to resort to Kwasi Wiredu's notion of conceptual decolonisation.[115] For Wiredu, one of the prime problems of colonisation is the imperial imposition of foreign systems of knowledge on African people, which has resulted in a break in the free development of African thought.[116] Rediscovering the content and characteristics of African philosophical thought, free from colonial influence, must be central to the exercise of (post-)independence intellectual life in Africa.[117] Ramose complementarily proposes that Africanisation is an ethical necessity in the wake of the African history of colonisation to respect 'human dignity in pursuit of justice and peace in global human relations'.[118] Thus, even though Africanisation through conceptual decolonisation is not legally imperative according to the current constitutional dispensation, there is an ethical obligation on us as private lawyers to actively think about what it could mean for our discipline. Human dignity and justice are promoted in the process of taking African

---

philosophy curricula: challenges and prospects' (2016) 35 *South African Journal of Philosophy* 460, 461; JO Chimakonam 'Can the philosophy curriculum be Africanised? An examination of the prospects and challenges of some models of Africanisation' (2016) 35 *South African Journal of Philosophy* 513, 514.

[110] See eg MB Ramose 'I doubt, therefore, African philosophy exists' (2003) 22 *South African Journal of Philosophy* 113, 114–115.

[111] MB Ramose 'Teacher and student with a critical pan-epistemic orientation: an ethical necessity for Africanising the educational curriculum in Africa' (2016) 35 *South African Journal of Philosophy* 546.

[112] CM Silungwe 'On "African" legal theory: a possibility, an impossibility or mere conundrum?' in O Onazi (ed) *African Legal Theory and Contemporary Problems: Critical Essays* (2014) 17, 20.

[113] Ibid 21.

[114] See eg L Allais 'Problematising Western philosophy as one part of Africanising the curriculum' (2016) 35 *South African Journal of Philosophy* 537.

[115] K Wiredu 'Conceptual decolonization as an imperative in contemporary African philosophy: some personal reflections' (2002) 36 *Rue Descartes* 53, which employs the specific term 'conceptual decolonisation'. In an earlier work Wiredu (note 6 above) speaks about 'decolonization', which I read as forming the preparatory basis for the more detailed explanation provided in the 2002 article.

[116] Wiredu 2002 (note 115 above) 54.

[117] Ibid.

[118] Ramose (note 111 above) 547.

philosophy seriously because it can be seen as an act of resistance against colonial policies, programmes and psychological and sociological oppression.[119] Wiredu suggests that it is possible to rediscover African philosophy free from Western entanglements. His advice is that we start acknowledging the hegemonic effect of Western language as the medium through which Western sources, assumptions and worldviews are taught to the African (something that I have attempted to show in parts 2 and 3 above),[120] followed by the African philosopher theorising in her own vernacular.[121] 'Self-knowledge' is crucial to this endeavour,[122] and we might imagine that different languages and even dialects of the same language can generate different perspectives. We are not in search of African universalism, and so a space is created in which multifarious views are given voices without essentialising a single version of African philosophy. In other words, African language can be used self-reflexively to re-imagine the meaning of certain concepts in order to contest the dominant (in our context, usually a specific version of the Western) understanding of those concepts.[123] Concepts that Wiredu suggests delving into, which are equally relevant to the study of law, include for example 'being', 'object', 'property', 'truth', 'fact', 'opinion', 'responsibility', 'punishment', 'democracy', 'justice', 'life', 'death', 'afterlife'· and 'morality'.[124]

However, the idea is not necessarily to find an African purist way of thinking and to promote that at all costs. To the contrary, the method proposed by Wiredu is critically reconstructive. He says:

> there is no assumption that what comes from Africa is necessarily true, sound, profound et cetera. Much less of course, should there be an over-valuation of what comes from the West. In fact, however, exactly such an over-valuation, at an apparently semi-conscious level, is the hallmark of that infelicity of the mind called the colonial mentality that still afflicts us in African philosophy and other areas of African intellectual life. The cure for that mental condition, however, does not require the disavowal of all foreign sources of possible edification. It seems to me likely that any African synthesis for modern living will include indigenous and Western elements, as well, perhaps, as some from the East.[125]

This cosmopolitan approach is advanced by Wiredu because wisdom and stupidity are spread in equal amounts to all nations around the world.[126] Furthermore, we should not believe that African philosophy is *only* valuable for Africa – it could be a beneficial tool for other parts of the world too.[127] Africanisation, in this sense, means taking African concepts seriously, conscious of the unique experiences and histories on the continent, without believing that Africa is detached from and irrelevant to the rest of the world. Considering this assumption, Wiredu defines conceptual decolonisation as 'the elimination from our thought of modes of conceptualization

[119] Mweshi (note 109 above) 461.
[120] Wiredu 2002 (note 115 above) 55–56.
[121] Ibid 56.
[122] Ibid 64.
[123] Ibid 57.
[124] Ibid 58.
[125] Ibid 54–55.
[126] Ibid 55.
[127] Ibid 64.

that came to us through colonization and remain in our thinking owing to inertia rather than to our own reflective choices'.[128]

Conceptual decolonisation, therefore, means that there should be no uncritical acceptance of any understanding of a particular concept, regardless of its point of origination. On the one hand, we may argue, as Kuwali does, that we too often blindly have accepted colonial knowledge as supreme, in the spirit of Eurocentrism, without asking what would be most appropriate for understanding (and perhaps, if we accept that it is possible, working towards solutions for) the current problems faced by African people in Africa.[129] Thus, we cannot accept Western knowledge complacently. On the other hand, there should also be a recognition that we have a choice in what knowledge we regard as being most appropriate for a given context and issue and, in some circumstances, we might learn from the West and/or the East without needing to enter a relationship of bondage to either parts of the world.

Some may argue that this critically reconstructive method is not radical enough because they want a complete rejection of everything that does not come from Africa. Especially so for ideas that can be labelled as 'Western'. I suspect that some of us will rather uncontroversially agree that it is necessary to problematise Western ideas as normal and superior. However, we should be cautious of Western reductionism. Lucy Allais makes two convincing arguments in this regard. To start with, Allais echoes the point made earlier in this discussion that Western thought encapsulates many voices, including voices that have been critical of, among other problems, white supremacy. Critiques of white supremacy originating in the West written by thinkers who live in the West and make use of Western tools are not unimportant for grappling with the African condition. Critical voices on this issue have been marginalised in dominant Western scholarship, and so throwing out Western thought in totality would result in a further marginalisation of these important dissidents.[130] Moreover, Allais contends that Western ideas are not as pure and autonomous as many would like to think. The history of philosophy teaches us that Western philosophy has been robustly influenced by prominent scholarship from the East and Africa. This means that a wholesale denunciation of Western thought implicitly also involves a rejection of the African and Eastern influences embedded in that thought.[131] Clearly this goes against the project of Africanisation through conceptual decolonisation.

What does this mean for the study of private law? Contrary to reactionary views, the decolonisation of private law does not have to mean pretending that private law as we know it has never existed and plucking brand-new rules and principles from the air. If we accept that Africanisation through conceptual decolonisation is indispensable to and possible for the study of private law, I think it could involve the following. As a point of departure, we should be frank about the Western European colonial roots and superiority complex of the dominant rules of private law that were imposed on African people. Relying on the work of Wiredu and Ramose explained above, this point of departure forces us to problematise knowledge that has been

[128] Ibid 56.
[129] Kuwali (note 22 above) 74.
[130] Allais (note 114 above) 541.
[131] Ibid 542.

colonially imposed on Africa that remains here due to inaction and not because of critical thought. From here, we would pick a concept embedded in the dominant rules of private law and explain what the dominant understanding of the concept is. Describing the prevailing dominant understanding of a particular concept in dominant SA private law will thus involve considering what the (Western-bias) common law says and what the concept might look like after the human-rights chisel has met the common law. Once we have identified what the Western component of SA law involves, Africanisation through decolonisation requires us to critically weigh up the philosophical underpinnings of concepts central to the dominant rules of private law (sometimes already influenced by human rights in the case law) against various versions of particularistic African concepts. I reiterate that the aim of this exercise is not to blindly endorse African versions of particular concepts (whether we derive them from African customary law sources or African philosophy) as the greatest or the best simply because of their point of origin. The aim is to endorse African versions of particular concepts as worthy of central attention and consideration. From here, cultural superiority aside, it might be possible to evaluate which version of a particular concept is most defensible for a particular context and issue.

For white private-law scholars who grew up in a Western world (albeit in South Africa) with resort to only English, Afrikaans and small bits of some additional European language, applying this methodology is bound to be challenging. Scholars such as myself, who are committed to the conceptually decolonial study of private law, will have to rise to this challenge. For the moment, in this piece and for the foreseeable future, I will have to study the scholarly works of those who are eloquent in African languages to find particularistic expressions of African concepts. Hopefully, in due course, we will have students who will be in much better positions than ourselves to do studies of this nature and teach us through their research. May this be the signal of the start of the long-term study of African languages with academic earnestness, which is a small part of the imperative for all white South Africans who intend to stay here and be part of the SA people.

At this point, it would be useful to provide an example of a concept that could be subject to Africanisation through conceptual decolonisation. Space does not allow a thorough, deep or meaningful investigation into any concept. The goal here is simply to provide cursory and tentative thoughts on how we might go about such an endeavour. The concept that I will briefly tackle is that of the 'legal subject' – a concept foundational to the entire discipline of private law. My recent interest in this concept is largely inspired by the work of Charmika Samaradiwakera-Wijesundara related to the implications of affording legal personhood to corporations in light of the coloniality of business and human rights.[132]

The dominant version of the SA law of persons says that, since classical Roman times, there are two entities that are regarded as morally so worthy of protection that they are given subjective rights. Those two entities are natural persons (individual

[132] Two of Samaradiwakera–Wijesundara's papers have had a particular influence on my thinking: 'The fiction of the juristic person: reassessing the personhood of the juristic person in relation to "other" people' (a forthcoming piece in a collection of essays entitled *Doing Human*); 'Played by the rules: the coloniality of business – and human rights' (forthcoming).

human beings) and juristic person (corporations).[133] This common-law understanding of personhood has effectively not changed through the Constitution. Section 8 provides that natural and juristic persons are bound by the rights in the Bill of Rights if and to the extent that those rights are applicable, and a holistic reading of the Bill of Rights makes it clear that natural and juristic persons are entitled to the rights in the Bill of Rights. The Supreme Court of Appeal recently proclaimed that corporations even possess the human right to dignity.[134]

As far as we can tell from the African customary law works, natural persons are regarded as legal subjects, but no mention is made of juristic persons. The notion of personhood in African customary law is usually discussed around issues of status within family units. However, a radically different understanding of personhood is given by Ramose who reads personhood through Ubuntu. Linguistically, Ramose explains that Ubuntu comprises *ubu-* (relating to the general, continuous idea of being) and *-ntu* (relating to the 'nodal point at which be-ing assumes concrete form or a mode of being in the process of continual unfoldment').[135] This means that there is a holism in how African metaphysics understands the universe.[136] Accordingly, being has different manifestations. One manifestation of be-ing is *umuntu* (the natural person in Western thought). But *umuntu* cannot achieve Ubuntu without the assistance of the living-dead and owe certain obligations to the yet-to-be-born.[137] These manifestations of be-ing do not exist separately from one another, because there is cosmic harmony between these be-ings and *u-nkulu-nkulu* (the great ineffable, unknowable).[138] It is quite clear that corporations (as separate legal personalities) do not form part of this onto-triadic understanding of be-ing. Ramose contends that the difference between the Ubuntu conception of personhood and the dominant SA legal conception of personhood and our acceptance of the latter as normal relates to the structural supremacy of European 'facts' and 'truths'.[139]

After identifying this divide between the particular Western and African concepts of legal subjectivity, the next step would be to evaluate which of these best enhances our understanding of the world. Granting legal subjectivity to the yet-to-be-born might come with various problems for the autonomy of women.[140] However, the African concept of personhood could be constructive in the process of rethinking the normality of the legal protectionism afforded to corporations (effectively entitling individuals to skirt personal responsibility in the air of capitalism), and perhaps even reconsidering how we think about the transmissibility of delictual claims of victims who have died before they could have instituted legal proceedings.[141]

Certainly, an influential account of conceptually decolonising legal subjectivity will have to be a much more thorough exercise than what I have cautiously illustrated

---

133 A statement of common law repeated since the time of CA Beck & OH Hoexter (eds) *Maasdorp's The Institutes of South African Law: Book 1 Law of Persons* 5 ed (1929) 1 till today in T Boezaart *Law of Persons* 6 ed (2016) 3–5.
134 *Media 24 v SA Taxi Securitisation* 2011 (5) SA 329 (SCA).
135 MB Ramose *African Philosophy through Ubuntu* (2005) 36.
136 Ibid 41.
137 Ibid 45–46.
138 Ibid 46.
139 Ibid 78.
140 See eg the argument developed in C Pickles *Pregnancy Law in South Africa* (2017).
141 The injustice I have in mind is reflected in *Nkala v Harmony Gold Mining Company* 2016 (5) SA 240 (GJ).

here. At least, what should be apparent is that the decolonial critique of private law will not necessarily look the same as a transformative critique of private law.

5. Conclusions

In this piece, we have seen how private-law purism is too often suffused with problematic right-wing politics and indiscreetly authorises the racism that underlies dominant private law. The racism that possesses dominant private law stems from intuitive cultural and racial superiority that allowed conquest to take place and its accompanying epistemicide to occur and be sustained.

We have also seen that the fusion of human rights with dominant private law, through an approach called transformative private law, is a weighty response to private-law purism but nevertheless proves to be an inadequate tool for a robust exorcism of racism that holds power over dominant private law. This is true because human rights do not have completely dissimilar epistemic roots to dominant private law. Also, human rights are not understood in the SA context as an imperative to restore African sovereignty by affording African law the standing that it deserves. In the interpretation of human rights in South Africa, we habitually resort to comparative practices that are aimed at making SA law internationally fashionable and palatable to the West. These problems of human rights – specifically as they interact with dominant private law – make them neo-colonial. When we try to dispose of the problems of purism through transformation and its commitment to human rights, we end up with a creolised version of private law that is not the same as a radically critical model.

If we intend to rise to the ethical necessity to decolonise private law, this could be done through regarding particularistic African conceptions of law and justice as pivotal to our discipline, without trying to find a unified, condensed version of African legal theory. This is why the decolonial approach to private law that I propose here can be described as committed to Africanisation. This does not mean that we gullibly accept African thought as untouchable without further ado. It also does not mean that white people must leave or that libraries must be burnt down. Conceptual decolonisation, as Wiredu explains it, requires us to critically and normatively embark on an exercise of justifying why we choose to tolerate a specific mode of conceptualisation above others. The approach advanced here is thus best described as Africanisation through conceptual decolonisation.

In conclusion, even though I once again call to attention that I am not giving the only or even most defensible rendition of how private law ought to be decolonised, one thing that I hope has become clear in this discussion is that it is something that ought to be worked towards. This exercise will probably require us to think beyond dominant private law and human rights. It is here in the 'beyond' where epistemic justice might be pursued.

Acknowledgements

This paper was written while I was a postdoctoral research fellow at the South African Institute for Advanced Constitutional, Public, Human Rights & International Law (a centre of the University of Johannesburg, Faculty of Law). Earlier versions of this paper were presented at the Wits Law School and *South African Journal on Human Rights* colloquium on 'Conquest, Constitutionalism and Democratic Contestations' on 19 May 2017, and the NWU Law Faculty workshop on decolonisation held on 4 August 2017. I benefitted from the questions and comments of many participants at both these events. I am indebted to Mogobe Ramose, Karin van Marle, Terblanche Delport, Ndumiso Dladla, Tshepo Madlingozi, Joel Modiri and Charmika Samaradiwakera-Wijesundara, from whom I have learnt so much. Errors nevertheless belong to me.

Disclosure statement

No potential conflict of interest was reported by the author.

South Africa's first black lawyers, *amaRespectables* and the birth of evolutionary constitution*

Tembeka Ngcukaitobi's *The Land is Ours: South Africa's First Black Lawyers and the Birth of Constitutionalism* is a timely and valuable contribution to current debates about the origins, cultural bases and ideological influences of the Constitution of the Republic of South Africa, 1996, as well as to discussions about the role of law in the 'radical transformation' or 'decolonisation' of society. This multi-genre and interdisciplinary book can also be read as an intervention into perennial contestations about 'the soul' of the African National Congress (ANC). This lucidly written book is about the lives, politics and careers of some of South Africa's first black lawyers. Ngcukaitobi tells the story of these lawyers with great care and (sometimes perhaps too much) detail to advance his main thesis. Ngcukaitobi's two-fold thesis is that legal tactics and strategies were at the heart of the struggle against colonialism and that the Constitution is a product of that struggle. Ngcukaitobi reaches into the archives in his attempt to achieve two implicit goals. He employs history to first mount a passionate defence of the Constitution and constitutionalism; and, second, to remind the ruling party that constitutionalism was and ought to be at the core of its essence. Ngcukaitobi narrates the trials and tribulations of these cause lawyers with the intention of showing that these internationally trained lawyers combined indigenous notions of justice, classroom instructions on constitutionalism and social and political exchanges on Pan-Africanism to help draft a series of constitutional and human-rights documents that were anti-colonial in nature.

It is not novel to posit that the normative principles and/or the spirit of these ANC and ANC co-sponsored documents (The African Bill of Rights, 1923; The African Claims, 1943; and the Freedom Charter, 1955) found their way into and influenced the Constitution. The most contentious aspects of *The Land is Ours* are Ngcukaitobi's suggestions, first, that these ANC-aligned elites pursued an anti-colonial agenda; second, that colonial laws were sometimes effective weapons against white supremacy and colonisation; and third, that the Constitution is a decolonising instrument because it is a product of an anti-colonial struggle. Ngcukaitobi's project, then, is not so much a reassessment of the role of lawyers and legal strategies in the struggle against colonialism. Rather, this project is a revisionist history of the impacts of Western modernity and colonisation, the early ANC and the genesis of 'transformative constitutionalism'. This review adopts a decolonisation approach to question two central motifs of this book: (1) that the first group of black lawyers were, albeit with some ambivalence, engaged in an anti-colonial project; and (2) that the roots of the current constitutionalism are autochthonous.

In addition to the historical imperative of granting these lawyers their due place in legal and political history, the immediate impulse behind *The Land is Ours* is to respond to what Ngcukaitobi characterises as 'current suspicions' about the Constitution. Flowing from the

* This chapter has not been peer reviewed.

aforementioned two-fold thesis, Ngcukaitobi submits that the contemporary struggle to overcome the intractable legacies of colonialism and apartheid and, indeed, '[T]he unfinished struggle for land can only take place through a framework of law.'[1] Ngcukaitobi grounds his defence of the Constitution and constitutionalism on three interrelated arguments. First, he rejects charges that the Constitution is an expression of the legal and epistemological paradigm of historical oppressors. As the sub-title of the book intimates, the animating idea behind Ngcukaitobi's project is the notion that the Constitution and the constitutional dispensation it inaugurates are not Eurocentric phenomena. Ngcukaitobi suggests that the constitution is home grown and autochthonous, both in the sense that the Constitution finds its true origins in the constitutional visions of the ANC and ANC-aligned lawyers and that the Bill of Rights is a culmination and an expression of black struggle. Second, flowing from this premise Ngcukaitobi implies that the Constitution is an anti-colonial instrument. In this regard, Ngcukaitobi seeks to demonstrate that the roots of the 'final' Constitution are revolutionary because Pan-Africanist and anti-colonial lawyers planted and shaped them. This claim explains the intriguing, if ultimately puzzling, combination of the title and sub-title of this book. Therefore third, Ngcukaitobi aligns himself with scholars, non-governmental and state officials who propagate the idea that the Constitution is unimpeachable – the 'best in the world' or 'a model for the world'.[2]

Therefore, at one level, *The Land is Ours* aims to demonstrate that black lawyers and intellectuals are the true originators of constitutionalism in South Africa. This book follows the political and intellectual ideas, as well as the legal tactic and strategies of six black lawyers to demonstrate that these activist lawyers stretched the limits of the colonial legal system to promote and uphold principles of legality, fair administrative action and equality. Ngcukaitobi's contention that black lawyers were the midwives of constitutionalism is directed at two camps. The first Ngcukaitobi speaks to is that camp of white legal historians who erase the role played by the first cohort of black lawyers and the early ANC when telling the history of South Africa's constitutionalism. Thus Ngcukaitobi writes that the book aims 'to restore the historical record' by examining the 'forgotten origins of constitutionalism'.[3] By showing how Henry Sylvester Williams, Alfred Mangena, Richard Msimang, Pixley ka Isaka Seme, Ngcubu Poswayo and George Montsioa deployed a mixture of politics and law to launch test cases, Ngcukaitobi also seeks to disrupt the dominant narrative about the evolution of strategic litigation in South Africa. Second, and perhaps most pertinent, Ngcukaitobi's project is a retort aimed at black radical and African nationalist charges that post-1994 constitutionalism is overwhelmingly aimed at guaranteeing the affective, cultural and material belongingness of historical oppressors, and that the Constitution is a 'white thing' in the sense of being a Eurocentric and an alien deity. If the originators of South Africa's constitutionalism are anti-colonialists, and if the Constitution emerged out of black radical thought, then these charges are not only misguided and fallacious, they are counter-revolutionary. This is to say that, at a more profound level, *The Land is Ours* could be apprehended as a counter-argument against calls for the decolonisation of the South African legal system, the Constitution, and indeed the extant polity. Understood in this way, Ngcukaitobi's book is the first book-length engagement with the decolonisation/decolonial turn in constitutional theory.

---

[1] T Ngcukaitobi *The Land is Ours: South Africa's First Black Lawyers and the Birth of Constitutionalism* (2018) 1.
[2] Ibid.
[3] Ibid 38, 273.

1. A critical interlocutor and exemplar for decolonisation-theory scholars

Decolonisation approaches to constitutionalism and the Constitution gained momentum and mainstream visibility in South Africa after the student protests of 2015 and 2016. Decolonisation approaches endeavour to go beyond both liberal analyses and traditional schools of critical thought. Liberal critiques of the Constitution and constitutionalism tend to adopt either institutional or immanent perspectives. Institutional analyses fault courts for adopting legalistic and formalistic adjudicative practices that perpetuate a conservative legal culture. This set of liberal analyses asserts that the full realisation of the promises of 'transformative constitutionalism' is impeded by a conservative legal culture. Some institutional critics also call for a more horizontal application of the Constitution. Another set of liberal critics puts a spotlight on lackadaisical state conduct, poor implementation of court decisions and the governing elite's supposed betrayal of otherwise flawless constitutional ideals. Immanent critiques suggest that some of the wording of the Constitution hampers 'transformative interpretation' such as a core-content reading or an immediate application interpretation of certain socio-economic-rights clauses. These liberal critics, however, resist calls for wide-scale amendments of the Constitution. Rather, these scholars hold that the Constitution is a 'living document' and, as such, judicial and social actors should and will shape the Constitution to enable it to respond to pressing social needs. Immanent and institutional critics are united in their deification of the Constitution. Critical scholars neither deify the Constitution nor subscribe to the myth of judicial neutrality or the fallacy of the separation of law and politics - a fallacy well explored in *The Land is Ours*. These critics point out that the Constitution has not dismantled or is incapable of dismantling power relations that cause and sustain racism, patriarchy, homophobia and economic subjugation. However, most critical analysts do not argue for a post-conquest constitution, or what could loosely be called constitutional abolishment.[4] Wittingly or unwittingly, most scholars of traditional schools of critical thought seek to rescue the post-1994 constitutional project by demanding more gendered, queered, 'pro-poor' and raced readings and applications of the Constitution. The argument here is that such readings and applications would lead to the achievement of social justice/justice in society for historically marginalised groups.[5] Therefore, rather than demanding radical *constitution/constitutional transformation*, most critical scholars call for better and greater 'transformative constitutionalism'.

The decolonisation approach to the Constitution and constitutionalism is a disparate movement united by two broad pillars. The first is the contention that 1994 did not herald the era of decolonisation. The argument here is that white domination transmuted into white hegemony while the majority of black people continue to be pariahs of South Africa. In contrast to liberal and mainstream critical scholars, decolonisation scholars do not regard truncated democracy, structural segregation, institutionalised discrimination as well as the various manifestation of social injustice as crises threatening the post-colonial order. Rather, decolonisation scholars apprehend these crises as symptoms of a dispensation that some regard as on-going conquest while others designate it as neo-colonialism or neo-apartheid. The second fundamental pillar of the decolonisation movement is the

[4] On the fundamental differences between constitution/constitutional amendment and the quest for a post-conquest constitution, see in general T Madlingozi 'The proposed amendment to the South African Constitution: finishing the unfinished business of decolonisation?' (2018) <http://criticallegalthinking.com/2018/04/06/the-proposed-amendment-to-the-south-african-constitution>.

[5] On how the discourse and praxis of social justice in an un-decolonised context perpetuate colonisation, see T Madlingozi 'Social justice in a time of neo-apartheid constitutionalism: critiquing the anti-black economy of recognition, incorporation and distribution' (2017) 28 *Stellenbosch Law Review* 123.

thesis that on-going conquest or neo-colonialism is constituted by, and constitutes, post-1994 constitutionalism. Flowing from these two pivotal pillars, decolonisation scholars call for a post-conquest constitution. The argument here is that only a post-conquest constitution will deal decisively with what, from a constitutional perspective, I regard as the three main legacies of settler colonialism and colonisation, namely: (1) the colonial state form and, conversely, the eternal subjugation of indigenous sovereignties; (2) the entrenchment of a world of apartness and the deliberate failure to resolve the National Question; and (3) the continuing subordination of African lifeworlds and their epistemologies and jurisprudences.[6]

My contribution to the decolonisation turn to constitutional history has been to adopt a critical historical analysis to show that on-going conquest or neo-apartheid is an outcome of a colonist-preservation strategy known as 'evolutionary constitution'. In the context where conquest and settler invasion did not lead to the extermination of 'natives', the ultimate *telos* of this strategy is to transmute settler domination into settler hegemony and in that way secure the Gramscian consent of historically conquered people. An evolutionary scheme of re-constituting the settler-created polity lays a framework for the gradual integration (at least in theory) of some of the historically conquered peoples into the extant polity. It is this integration, and thus transformation, that legitimises and masks conquest and colonisation. The first task in putting the settler minority's long-term strategy into motion is the creation of an elite stratum of conquered people. The colonised elites imbibe the civilising ideology and its teleological notions of progress, improvement, respectability and eventual assimilation into 'civilised society'. Colonial states' inevitable betrayal of these promises radicalises these elites and prompts them to demand accelerated and greater evolutionary (not revolutionary) (re)constitution. An evolutionary scheme of constitutional rearrangement maintains the main edifice of the settler-created polity such that the majority of the historically colonised remain pariahs of the transformed polity.[7] In sum, evolutionary constitutionalists use symbols, procedures and discourses of the system that created them to demand the transformation (not decolonisation) of the settler-created system. An important tool that discontented 'native elites' appropriate is constitutionalism.

The decolonisation scholarship is an inchoate one that is still working through gaps, contradictions and lack of methodological exactitude. Three main issues are relevant for the purposes of this review. First, some decolonisation-theory scholars tend to over-rely on theories and concepts that emerged in contexts vastly different from South Africa. These contexts include Latin America, the United States of America and African countries that did not go through settler colonialism. Besides, not indicating why and how theories and concepts conceived elsewhere can travel to this context, these scholars fail to show how this strategy of conceptual borrowing complements or hinders the twin decolonisation imperative of conceptual decolonisation and excavation and valorisation of own subjugated concepts, theories and proverbs. Second, the failure by some decolonisation scholars to undertake critical-historical research leads to many ahistorical analyses and conclusions. For example, some scholars take analysis from other parts of the historically colonised world and end up making inaccurate analyses and conclusions about the pivotal

[6] On the *essentialia* or the three pillars of a post-conquest constitution, see T Madlingozi (2016) 'Settler colonialism and post-conquest *constitutionness*: the decolonising constitution vision of African nationalists of Azania/South Africa' <https://www.academia.edu/33747352/On_Settler_Colonialism_and_Post-Conquest_Constitutionness_The_Decolonising_Constitutional_Vision_of_African_Nationalists_of_Azania_South_Africa>.

[7] See T Madlingozi *'Mayibuye iAfrika*? Disjunctive inclusions and black strivings for constitution and belonging in "South Africa"' (2018) (unpublished doctoral dissertation) Birkbeck, University of London.

relationships between, and the roles played by, colonists, missionaries and anthropologists in the colonisation of 'South Africa'. Ahistorical analyses can also be seen in the pervasive tendency to conflate colonialism and apartheid. Third, a sizeable percentage of decolonisation scholars focus on compromises made by ANC leaders during the negotiations leading to the 'new South Africa'. In this regard, some of these critics over-emphasise structural factors, thus denying the agency of ANC actors, or they exaggerate the agency of these actors to propagate the 'sell-out' narrative. I would like to propose that decolonisation scholars ought to ground their foundationalist critiques in a method of critical historical revisionism. This approach will enable them to make meaningful contributions to legal scholarship, law and society. Towards this objective, decolonisation scholars would do well to approach *The Land is Ours* as both a critical interlocutor and an exemplar.

Ngcukaitobi undertakes an impressive amount of archival research to trace and unpack the genealogy of conquest and colonisation, the ebbs and flows of resistance strategies, the impact of black transnational thought on nascent African nationalism, the role of law and the judiciary in the consolidation of conquest, and key moments leading up to the current dispensation. However, in his quest to confer anti-colonial credentials on early ANC leaders and clothe the Constitution in revolutionary garb, he omits and deemphasises several important historical facts, overstates the significance of certain pronouncements and statements, and fails to resolve some contradictions in his narrative. Due to strictures of space, this review will only focus on two motifs that run throughout the text. The first motif that threads Ngcukaitobi's thesis is that his five protagonists (I exclude the pioneering Trinidad-born Williams) appropriated Western religion, Eurocentric education and colonial laws to forge an anti-colonial and decolonising political and constitutional vision. The second pillar is the contention that South Africa's constitutionalism and the idea of the Bill of Rights 'germinate from South African soil'.[8]

2. The ambivalence of the New Africans: the land is (some of) ours (*some-time*)

The first motif (the narrative of revolutionary appropriation and upending) is the lifeblood of ANC historiography and myth-making. The story here is that late nineteenth century and early twentieth-century 'Westernised' elites refused their station as mimic persons who were to be a buffer between colonists and the horde of 'savages'. Rather, these converts inverted the colonialist project with the view of imploding the very thing that created them. Therefore, instead of becoming meek lackeys of colonialism, they, 'disrupted the consensus of the colonial state'.[9] The claim here is that education became a vehicle of resistance in the context where military resistance was unavailable.

Ngcukaitobi begins this narrative of Western education and the law of colonisers as weapons of resistance with the Eighth War of Dispossession (1850–1853). This war has the distinction of being the longest of the nine wars of dispossession and the longest sustained military resistance against colonialism in Africa. The inspiration behind the amaXhosa uprising was Mlanjeni, a 'prophet' who vowed to empower amaXhosa to repel European encroachment and subjugation. Mlanjeni's war medicines and charms failed to halt a devastating defeat. It is appropriate to begin the narrative here because the defeat of amaXhosa and allied groups in the 'War of Mlanjeni' further consolidated embryonic beliefs in European invincibility. Before this defeat, most indigenous people regarded

[8] Ngcukaitobi (note 1 above) 1–2.
[9] Ibid 27.

European incursion to be formidable but not indomitable – they had faith that their God, ancestors and indigenous tactics would help them resist conquest and total colonisation. The turning point in the irruption of Western modernity, and perhaps the 'birth of constitutionalism', was the well-known cataclysmic events that occurred between 1856 and 1857. During this period, various amaXhosa groups ceased cultivating their crops, destroyed their corn and killed an estimated 400,000 of their own cattle. This 'cattle-killing mania' is often blamed on Nongqawuse, a young seer who claimed to have received a message from the ancestors that amaXhosa must purify their land. The purification of the land was to prepare for the day of the return of ancestors. The prophecy was that ancestors will bring with them new cattle, and on that day, a whirlwind would come and sweep settler invaders back to the sea. This prophesy did not materialise, and in just over eighteen months, approximately 40,000 amaXhosa died from starvation, famished men and women handed themselves to the Cape Colony as labourers, and their remaining lands were given to white settlers and African clients. As Ngcukaitobi shows, this event was a pivotal moment in the acceleration of Christian proselytisation and the proletarianisation of frontier people.

I submit that the most important ramification of this tragic devastation was that it strengthened the notion that indigenous weapons and ancestors were powerless to resist material, social and spiritual colonisation. Even more importantly, this 'national suicide' swayed the balance in favour of African leaders and other elites who, because of intra-Xhosa rivalry and strategic reasons, had chosen the route of aligning themselves with colonisers and had encouraged their sons and subjects to convert to Christianity and receive Western education.[10] Chief Ngqika and 'prophet' Ntsikana pioneered this response in the early nineteenth century. Chief Ndlambe and 'prophet' Makana (also known as Makhanda) represented a more militant response. These opponents of Ngqika and Ntsikana rejected colonisation, preached a form of black liberation theology and elaborated what could be regarded as black or African nationalism. Makana led amaXhosa and allied groups during the Fifth Frontier War (1818–1819). Makana's medicine did not turn the 'white man's bullets' into water, and colonisers imprisoned him on Robben Island. The point here is that we can detect two African responses to conquest and colonisation from the early nineteenth century: collaboration and submission to promises of trusteeship and assimilation versus appropriating some tools of Western modernity while still fighting for independence and sovereignty.

It is perhaps more important to start the narrative in the early nineteenth century, because this antinomy of African responses helps us trace the genealogies of contemporary responses (liberal, critical and decolonisation) to post-1994 constitutionalism. More immediately, this historical antimony (never compartmentalised and often evolving in reaction to European encroachment and control) speaks directly to the first leg upon which Ngcukaitobi's thesis rests. As we have seen, one of his two pivotal claims is that African elites appropriated the tools of empire to forge an anti-colonial discourse and praxis. Ngcukaitobi writes that his protagonists 'resorted to law *because* a military option was not available to them'.[11] The subtext here is that these elites would have prosecuted an anti-colonial military struggle had it been available to them. However, the fact of the matter is that these converts were not interested in a military struggle and/or any other

[10] Early converts were often members of scorned minorities who considered themselves oppressed by their own kingdoms and clans. These pariahs sought refuge in mission stations and converted to Christianity. For our purposes, it is important to note that some indigenous people derisively referred to these converts as *amambuka* ('traitors') or *amakhafula* ('those spat out').

[11] Ngcukaitobi (note 1 above) 5 (original emphasis retained).

form of struggle that could result in the dissolution of the white system. The lineage of the group of African elites at the centre of *The Land is Ours* is the lineage of indigenous people who 'chose' the strategy of conversion and integration into the settler-created system. In this regard, Leon de Kock notes that even though Ntsikana had a small following during his lifetime, he planted a seed that produced 'New African' figures: 'Christians trained by missionaries and fully "Westernised"'.[12]

The New African Movement found philosophical basis in the writings of Tiyo Soga (1829–1871). Soga's father was Ntsikana's disciple, and Ntsikana took young Soga into a mission station and subsequently sent him to be educated at Lovedale Missionary Institution, the citadel of missionary education. Soga later studied in Scotland and returned to the Eastern Cape as the first black missionary in the territory that later became South Africa. Soga, the most educated Xhosa of his time, returned in 1857, the year of the 'cattle-killing mania'. Soga's education and vocation put him at a strategic position to point the way for his people. Soga proposed that Africans will only survive in this 'new world' if they embraced Western civilisation and Christianity. Soga, however, was aware that amaXhosa were proud of their traditions and customs. He, therefore, proposed that amaXhosa ought to embrace Western modernity and Christianity without totally renouncing themselves. Soga's story is germane to this review because his ambivalence towards Western modernity and the colonial state laid down a template for Ngcukaitobi's protagonists.

Ngcukaitobi notes that 'Westernised' elites had an ambivalent relationship with the colonial state and Western modernity.[13] The most felicitous line in *The Land is Ours* is arguably the following: 'Perhaps this is the lesson of this book: the lesson of ambiguity.'[14] This intriguing line closes off the introductory chapter. Ngcukaitobi writes this line almost in ellipsis; without further commentary. It feels as if the author added this sentence *ex post facto*. It seems what Ngcukaitobi means by this is that these lawyers appropriated and slyly deployed the language of colonialism – 'the language of rights, freedoms and equality' (it is not clear how and why this is 'the language of colonialism') – to subvert colonialism. Ngcukaitobi should have done much about this idea if, indeed, it is the most important lesson of the book. Celebration and affirmation of ambivalence and ambiguity form the bedrock of post-modernism-inflected postcolonial (contra-decolonial) theory scholarship most notably associated with Homi Bhabha. The most important, and less sanguine, text in the South African context is Shula Marks' *The Ambiguities of Dependence in South Africa: Class, Nationalism, and the State in Twentieth-Century Natal* (1986).

3. Radical rhetoric, assimilationist desires and elite nationalism

Crucially, Ngcukaitobi concludes that these converts were able to cultivate an anti-colonial consciousness because, '[T]hey retained a certain distance from their colonisers even as they adopted elements of their culture.'[15] Ngcukaitobi's contention here is that this posture of voluntary and determined estrangement is what enabled these elites to 'stand up to the system'. As mentioned earlier, this argument is central to ANC historiography. Propagators of what we could call a theory of insurgent hybridity often put forward two

[12] L de Kock 'Sitting for the civilizational test: the making(s) of a civil imaginary in colonial South Africa' in L de Kock, L Bethlehem & S Laden (eds) *South Africa in the Global Imaginary* (1996) 117, 57.
[13] Ngcukaitobi (note 1 above) 34.
[14] Ibid 7.
[15] Ibid 272.

pieces of evidence to substantiate this line of argument: (1) statements and pronouncements made by colonised elites showing support of certain aspects of indigenous culture, and (2) the alliance between some of these intellectuals and certain kings and chiefs.

It is true that some 'New African' figures made statements that could be read as evidence of the fact that they remained loyal to or respectful of African ways of being in the world. This is part of the reason why Ngcukaitobi maintains that these educated elites were never de-cultured.[16] Rather, they fused elements of the indigenous world and the colonisers' world to become, 'African and Christian'.[17] Therefore, contrary to the wishes and intentions of 'civilisers', educated elites did not become mimic persons. Their resolute distance-taking enabled them to become a menace to missionaries and colonists. This claim is, however, highly debatable. In the first place, the separation between the elite stratum of conquered people and colonisers was a result of the simple fact that assimilation and co-existence are impossible in the colonial context. This is the big lie at the heart of missionary and Enlightenment promises: conversion and becoming 'civilised' never results in integration into the polity of 'civilised people'. In other words, distance from colonisers was mainly the outcome of the fact that Western modernity simultaneously summons and rejects the colonised subject. More to the point, Ngcukaitobi is unable to see that it is this ambivalence at the heart of colonialist praxis that induces the ambivalence of converts towards the colonial system. In other words, colonised elites do not set out to adopt a posture of radical ambivalence, let alone distance-taking. It is the ambivalence of the project that creates them that leads to psycho-social destabilisation, feelings of rejection and abandonment and the subsequent posture of enfeebling ambivalence on the part of colonised elites.

Furthermore, ambivalence did not lead to an anti-colonial consciousness. From the beginning, 'Ntsikana's children' wished to survive conquest through a framework of acculturation, recognition and integration. However, inter-subjective recognition and pluralist integration are made impossible in the colonial context. Rather than achieving the next best prize of being hybrid persons who belong to both worlds, these elites become liminal figures trapped in a no-man's land. It is this liminal positionality that caused some 'traditionalists' to distrust converts and to derogatorily refer to them as *amalulwane* (bats) – two-sided creatures who claimed to be loyal to ancestors and 'African ways' when they were among non-converts but professed total loyalty to the British Empire and to Christianity when they were among colonists.[18]

It would have been preferable for Ngcukaitobi to further theorise his claim that these elites were 'African and Christian'. It seems what he means by this proposition is that these educated elites remained loyal to the 'old world' and in solidarity with 'uneducated' Africans, even as they became 'Westernised'. To be sure, many (certainly not all) of these New Africans sometimes made pro-African pronouncements. However, this did not mean that these elites became anti-colonialists who aspired to see the fall of imperialism and colonialism and the concomitant restoration of the material, spiritual and social worlds of conquered peoples. Most of the colonised elites wished to be granted all rights due to British subjects. In addition to this integrationist posture, most of these Western-educated elites believed that 'uneducated' people suffered from a deficiency of cultural, moral and political maturity. At best, educated elites' solidarity and responsibility towards the rest of

---

[16] Ibid.

[17] Ibid.

[18] S Masondo 'Indigenous conceptions of conversion among African Christians in South Africa' (2015) 28 *Journal for the Study of Religion* 87, 95.

Africans extended to the conviction that as 'civilised natives' they would eventually bring enlightenment to their fellow 'backward' black people.[19] As Seme often suggested, 'civilised' elites hoped that they could uplift 'raw natives' using European standards to enable the latter to eventually evolve into a standard befitting of responsible citizenship of a 'civilised society'.[20] This is the most pertinent point related to evolutionary constitution (contra revolutionary reconstitution) and the current dispensation where the majority of Africans still suffer from material and affective non-belongingness to the 'new South Africa'. Today, the majority of impoverished black people are still not deemed deserving of rights available to all citizens. That the majority of black people are still interned on the underside of this settler-created polity should be understood as an outcome of early ANC leaders' elite nationalism and belief in evolutionary constitution. The majority of early black intellectuals could talk a radical game while harbouring assimilationist desires.

In this regard, the *amaRespectables* (men and women who were enamoured with Victorian notions of respectability, progress and upliftment; what Msimang designated as 'more respectable natives') were following in Soga's footsteps. Soga is sometimes thought of as the father of African nationalism and Black Consciousness in South Africa. As already mentioned, Soga returned to the Eastern Cape as the first African missionary. Even before he was sent to study in Scotland, Soga had always been on the side of colonists when conflict broke out between them and the indigenous peoples. However, starting from the 1860s, Soga began making explicitly race-conscious statements. For instance in 1865, Soga responded to a social Darwinist's newspaper letter by articulating what is clearly a Black Consciousness and Pan-African position. Soga argued that the amaXhosa are part of a distinctive and robust African race, he recounted African civilisational achievements, and he expressed faith in the future renascence of African nations. However, this did not mean that Soga had developed an anti-colonial consciousness. As one biographer of Soga has shown,[21] Soga remained loyal to the British Empire and continued to espouse the benefits of conquest, even as he gestured towards Black Consciousness and African nationalism. Furthermore, writing in 1864, Soga reflected on the successes he achieved in the aftermath of the 'cattle-killing mania' in the following terms: 'The people who sat in darkness saw great light; and to them which sat in the region and shadow of death, *light is sprung up*!'[22] The crucial point here is that similar to today's neo-colonial elites, colonised elites could articulate African nationalist, and even nativist statements, while (1) still wishing to be part of the settler-created system, (2) looking down upon 'raw natives', and (3) arguing that 'raw natives' are not ready to exercise all rights due to 'civilised men'.

To be sure, this was the case with Seme. Similar to other biographers of Seme, Ngcukaitobi looks to Seme's enduring 1906 'Regeneration of Africa' speech to make sense of his radicalism and what Ngcukaitobi regards as his 'anti-colonial consciousness'.[23]

---

[19] One of the interesting aspects of *The Land is Ours* is the transmission lines that Ngcukaitobi draws between leaders of the *amakholwa*, such as John Dube and Seme, and black leaders in the USA, such as Booker T Washington and WEB du Bois. However, it is often forgotten that although Washington and Du Bois were bitter political rivals, they both looked down upon 'unuplifted' black people and, crucially, that both Washington and Du Bois had assimilationist desires in the early twentieth century. Du Bois carried this influence to the Pan-African congresses he co-organised. Thus the Second Manifesto of the Pan African Congress moved from the premise that black elites needed to uplift 'backward and suppressed groups'. Seme, Du Bois and Alain Locke's elitist Pan-Africanism should be contrasted with Marcus Garvey's populist and mass-based Pan-Africanism.

[20] Ngcukaitobi (note 1 above) 1.

[21] D Williams *The Journal and Selected Writings of the Reverend Tiyo Soga* (1983) 2.

[22] Cited in G Duncan 'Tiyo Soga (1829–1871) at the intersection of "universes in collision"'(2018) 74 *HTS Theological Studies* 1, 8 (original emphasis retained).

[23] Ngcukaitobi (note 1 above) 158.

However, Seme's award-winning speech reprised Soga's salvationist and elite-nationalism sentiments. Indeed, Seme concluded his decidedly Pan-African and undoubtedly radical speech with a conviction that internationally trained Africans would return to Africa to 'drive darkness from the land'. Ngcukaitobi is, therefore, correct to assert that these 'Westernised elites' saw themselves as the Du Boisian Talented Tenth.[24] In Ngcukaitobi's telling, the Talented Tenth saw it as their duty to use their intellectual abilities and professions to achieve social and political emancipation for both themselves and for 'uneducated' elites.[25] This optimist view is, however, contradicted by these elites' unequivocally elitist and self-serving political agenda. These elites' radicalism was not for the liberation of everyone. Theirs was a struggle for the extension of political and civil rights to 'civilised men'. This was the guiding philosophy of the men who formed political organisations that were the precursors of the ANC.

African elites who came of age after the final War of Dispossession of 1879 followed Soga's example of making radical statements but not wishing to elaborate an anti-colonial vision in the sense of the restoration of subjugated sovereignties, return of land and valorisation of indigenous cultures. Following Soga, they also adopted colonial discourse to represent themselves in Western modernity and to claim rights due to them as 'civilised people'. These elites took advantage of the assimilationist promises of colonial governments to apply to be exempted from being subjected to 'customary law'. 'Exempted natives' wished to belong to colonial civil society, to be governed by the British legal order and to acquire rights flowing from that legal system. However, successive colonial governments frustrated this longing. These rejections shaped the political consciousness of converts. Colonised elites used newspapers to articulate the need for 'progress', to raise grievances related to difficulties surrounding the 'exemption' system, and to forge a trans-ethnic nationalism.

Towards the late nineteenth century, these property owners and middle-class professionals formed various vigilance and political associations to defend their 'national rights'. These vigilance associations are the progenitors of constitutionalism *only* in the sense that they were formed to guard against the erosion of the rights African elites had under the limited franchise system and the rights to purchase land that they had under the quite dissimilar dispensations prevailing in the Natal and Cape colonies. Therefore, defence of 'national rights' here meant the defence of rights that they believed were due to them in colonial societies: right to purchase land, freehold land tenure, right to vote and other civil rights. 'Westernised' elites' unyielding demand was for 'rights equal to those of all civilised men'. Being a product of the 'civilising mission' and Cape liberalism, these colonised elites' constitutionalism did not extend to universal suffrage and equality to all. Thus, in their testimonies to various native affairs commissions, these elites regularly insisted that a distinction be drawn between themselves ('civilised men') and the rest of the native masses ('raw natives'). These *badumedi/amakholwa* ('believers' in the Word of God and in the potency of the written word) believed that their identity and their recognition as such should result in bestowal of citizenship rights as British subjects. At the very least, the expectation and the main demand of *amaRespectables* were that they ought to be treated differently vis-à-vis the rest of the ('uncivilised') African masses. However, the 'discovery' of minerals towards the end of the nineteenth century and concomitant demands for cheap African labour led to more restrictions on the rights of African farmers, peasants and property owners. The ability of chiefs and kings to buy land for

[24] Ibid 37.
[25] Ibid 37, 272.

communal settlement was also threatened by this latest round of land dispossession. This partly explains the alliance that formed between New Africans and chiefs and kings at the turn of the century. This explains why monarchs were invited to the inaugural meeting of the first truly national political movement of Africans in 1912.

Seme was the 'moving spirit' behind the formation of the South African Native National Congress (SANNC).[26] Seme moved for the formation of a national movement after previous organisations, and the deputation tactic failed to halt the establishment of the Union of South Africa as a 'white man's country'. The unification of South Africa posed further threat to the rights of African landowners, African middle-class professionals and 'traditional' leaders. The SANNC, which later became the ANC, was formed in 1912. Ngcukaitobi seems not to be sure what to make of the early ANC. On the one hand, he concedes that Seme's conception of equality was restricted to a 'civilised few'.[27] On the other hand, he reads Seme's letter of motivation for the establishment of a national movement for Africans as a humanist declaration rooted in non-discrimination and inclusiveness.[28] Moreover, Ngcukaitobi argues that the organising principle of the SANNC was anti-colonial.[29] However, can it really be said that a political organisation is anti-colonial and humanistic, and a genuine propagator of constitutionalism, when it reserves equality only for a 'civilised few'; when it pledges loyalty to the Empire; and when its clarion call was not so much 'the land is ours' than a demand for the right to live anywhere in the country, to purchase land or to acquire 'sufficient land'?

As previously mentioned, Ngcukaitobi argues that the SANNC's was originally conceived as an anti-colonial movement. However, he notes the constitution of the SANNC outlined one of its aims as being to educate 'Bantu people on their rights, duties and obligations to the state'.[30] Msimang, the third protagonist of *The Land is Ours*, drafted this constitution. Reverend John Dube, an 'exempted native' who grew up on a mission station and studied in the United States, was elected president-general. In his inaugural conference address, Dube laid down a manifesto of evolutionary constitution. He urged Africans to use this new platform in order to proceed 'into the higher places of civilisation and Christianity – not backward into the slump of darkness nor backwards not the abyss of the antiquated tribal system'.[31] Dube also proposed that the SANNC should retain a 'deep and dutiful respect for the rulers whom God has placed over us'.[32] In light of the afore-going, it is difficult to understand Ngcukaitobi's claims that colonised elites such as Seme had an 'anti-colonial consciousness' and that the organising principle of the SANNC was 'anti-colonial'.

4. Constitutionalism from whom, for whom, for what?

I now turn to the second motif of *The Land is Ours*, namely, that these elites formulated anti-colonial constitutional documents, the spirit of which was eventually carried into the Constitution. This theme is important to Ngcukaitobi's thesis that the idea of a bill of rights and, by implication, post-1994 constitutionalism originate in the writings, cases and

---

[26] B Ngqulunga *The Man Who Founded the ANC: A Biography of Pixley ka Isaka Seme* (2017) 46.
[27] Ngcukaitobi (note 1 above) 190.
[28] Ngcukaitobi (note 1 above) 175.
[29] Ngcukaitobi (note 1 above) 155
[30] Ngcukaitobi (note 1 above) 144.
[31] Cited in S Marks *The Ambiguities of Dependence: Class, Nationalism, and the State in Twentieth-Century South Africa* (1986) 53.
[32] Cited in Ngqulunga (note 31 above) 60.

political campaigns of African intellectuals and lawyers. In this regard, Ngcukaitobi writes that, '[I]t is not possible to draw a straight line between the writings of early African intellectuals and the present Constitution.'[33] This is a sensible statement for two reasons. First, as I have already argued, early African intellectuals did not put forward a capacious, inclusive and universal idea of human rights. Second, the genealogy of the Constitution is a highly contested subject. Perspectives here range from scholars who trace the Constitution to the 1854 Orange Free State constitution and those who locate it in the three ANC and ANC co-sponsored documents, to those who refer to the apartheid government's 1989 Law Commission report on a bill of rights, those who refer to the ANC's constitutional guidelines of 1989 and those who demonstrate that the Interim Constitution[34] was influenced by the constitutional visions of the Democratic Party and the National Party and 'constitutional borrowing' from mainly the German, US and Canadian models.

An altogether different question is whether constitutionalism originates from South African soil and specifically from the ideas of African intellectuals in the late nineteenth century and early twentieth century. Ngcukaitobi conveys his position in the sub-title of the book. The answer to this question is, however, also complex. First, mid-nineteenth century African intellectuals' ideas about constitutionalism can be traced to 1853, when the Cape Colony's government became representative. A crucial part of this new constitutional arrangement was the system of qualified but non-racial franchise. As can be gleaned from African-focused newspapers in the second half of the eighteenth century, *amakholwa* began making constitutional arguments and claims based on this spirit of Cape liberalism. Secondly, colonised elites' ideas about liberalism and constitutionalism were augmented and sharpened by constitutional ideas that came with Africans who studied in the United States and in Britain towards the turn of the century. African law students who studied internationally returned to South Africa empowered by constitutional theories formulated by European jurists such as Montesquieu and AV Dicey.[35] Ngcukaitobi's narrative shows that these returning students, most notable Seme and Mangena, influenced the early ANC's language of rights, unbiased judiciary and legality. Given all these influences, is it correct to suggest that South Africa's constitutionalism emanates from ideas formulated by African intellectuals and lawyers?

A final question is whether the ANC's three human-rights documents were anti-colonial. On Empire Day 1923, the ANC adopted a 'declaration or statement or Bill of Rights'. The bill called for equality, property rights, right to unrestricted ownership of land, right to vote and the universal application of Cecil Rhodes' framework of 'equal rights to all civilised men south of the Zambesi'. Ngcukaitobi mentions this bill to answer charges that the current Bill of Rights is animated by a 'Eurocentric mindset'. His answer is that the 'idea of a Bill of Rights had its origins in South Africa'.[36] This answer does not discharge the allegation that the Bill of Rights is animated by a European mind-set. I have spent a long of time charting the intellectual history of early colonised elites precisely to dispute the notion that these intellectuals did not have a 'Eurocentric mind-set'. Furthermore, the nature of the rights outlined in that 1923 Bill of Rights could be said to have a European pedigree. A missing piece of the puzzle in ANC historiography is a discussion of what influenced the ANC's thinking in coming up with a bill of rights in 1923. Ngcukaitobi's submission that, '[T]he idea of a Bill of Rights had its origins in South

[33] Ngcukaitobi (note 1 above) 5.
[34] Constitution of South Africa, Act 200 of 1993 (Interim Constitution). The Interim Constitution has been repealed.
[35] Ngcukaitobi (note 1 above) 156–158.
[36] Ibid 1.

Africa [emanating] from a group of black intellectuals and legal practitioners at the beginning of the twentieth century'[37] is only sustainable if these internationally trained lawyers did not have any outside influences. Perhaps Ngcukaitobi's claim is narrower: that the current Bill of Rights was not an imposition by foreign powers. Decolonisation scholars are, however, not making that charge.

Ngcukaitobi points to the ANC's 1943 African Claims as, 'South Africa's first Bill of Rights'.[38] However, as he notes, this document arose directly from the Atlantic Charter. Finally, Ngcukaitobi asserts that this document is an 'anti-colonial statement' and that, '[T]he idea of the Bill of Rights was a negation of colonial violence.'[39] This assertion has merit. Although this document did not call for the return of land and the restoration of subjugated indigenous sovereignties, it contained an extensive list of claims and rights that, if accepted by the Smuts government and implemented, would have led to liberal order. Liberal order and not postcolonial order, because the drafters of African Claims explained that, given the fact that white settler minorities were 'politically entrenched', they were not asking for self-determination. Rather, they were asking for full citizenship rights and *participation* within the structures of the settler-created state.

5. Conclusion

The lives of the men that Ngcukaitobi writes about were remarkable, almost epic. Most of them left South Africa at a young age, lived and studied in other countries, contributed to the birth of early Pan-Africanist thought and came back to fight for rights that they believed were due to them. Their fight involved rewriting Western modernity to ensure that they have a place in it and setting up trans-ethnic political organisations, newspapers and business organisations; and they sought to combine law and politics to launch test cases. As I have tried to show in this review, these elites were not passive recipients of the colonial order. Early black lawyers' political ideas and legal strategies contributed to the (re)constitution of Western modernity and the colonial order. Most importantly, these ambiguous men played a decisive role in the spread of principles of Western constitutionalism as originally formulated by European theorists. Scholars and students of settler colonialism, legal history and legal philosophy, the liberation struggle and Pan-Africanism should consider *The Land is Ours* essential reading.

Tshepo Madlingozi

[37] Ibid 1–2.
[38] Ibid 267.
[39] Ibid 7, 2.

Index